THE DYNAMICS OF RIGHT-WING PROTEST

MICHAEL B. STEIN

The Dynamics of Right-Wing Protest: a political analysis of Social Credit in Quebec

UNIVERSITY OF TORONTO PRESS

©University of Toronto Press 1973
Toronto and Buffalo
Printed in Canada
ISBN 0-8020-1721-5
Microfiche ISBN 0-8020-0290-0
LC 79-185740

To the memory of
Clarence R. Gross,
devoted friend and father-in-law

Contents

Contents viii

Tables

Preface

There have been many studies of political protest movements of both the right and left in recent years. Few, however, have attempted to encompass the entire lifespan of a movement over several decades. Even fewer studies have combined in a single volume a description of the political evolution of a movement with a systematic social and political analysis of its leading members. And none, so far as I know, offers an explanation of the internal dynamics of right-wing protest movements.

This study attempts to do all these things. It is first of all a description of the evolution of the Social Credit movement in Quebec from its founding in 1936 until 1970, emphasizing its patterns of coalition and conflict. It provides at the same time a partial view of Quebec social and political history during a period of social and economic transformation and revolutionary turmoil. It attempts to explain how rural and small-urban lower middle class leaders in Quebec were induced to join a right-wing protest movement in response to these economic and social pressures. It highlights in their own words the fears, outrage, and reformist zeal which prompted many of them to join a movement committed to economic and political change at a time when all such movements were considered taboo by Quebec elite groups and government officials. It lays bare the right-wing protest ideology which appealed to these discontented individuals and shows its relevance for French Canadians. The study records their quarrels, intrigues, and schisms; it describes their alliances and political campaigns; it documents their successes and their failures.

The study is secondly a social, attitudinal, and behavioural profile of the lower middle class leaders. It describes the elements in their family backgrounds, their economic and social positions, and their political and partisan formations which contributed to their choosing to belong to the Social Credit movement in Quebec. It illuminates some of the political attitudes and underlying political orientations which shaped their initial decision to engage in political action and their later patterns of behaviour. It details their patterns of participation in the movement. It describes the subgroups which are the major catalysts of splits and traces their patterns of alliance in the movement.

It is thirdly, and most important, a case study which is directly concerned with the formulation of a theory of right-wing protest movements. Out of general categories of comparative political analysis, the study develops a framework which ought to have relevance for other manifestations of right-wing protest, and perhaps also for other protest and revolutionary movements. It tries to relate protest and factionalism, two characteristics found to be so prevalent in this movement, to the social background, attitudes, and behaviour of different subgroups of leaders of the movement. And it tries to explain why these two characteristics are also important in other types of political movements.

Such a multipurpose study cannot rely upon a single methodology or analytical approach. A number of different modes of inquiry were used: analysis of unpublished newspaper, pamphlet, and leaflet material, informal and unrecorded interviews, mailed questionnaires, recorded depth interviews, and structured surveys. They were tried in succession with varying degrees of success over a period of five years.

I owe a great deal to many people for their assistance during the course of the study. First of all, the leaders and members of the Quebec Social Credit movement deserve mention. With rare exception, they were most kind and generous in their hospitality and their time. Special thanks must be accorded to Laurent Legault, the former president of the Ralliement Créditiste, for providing me with valuable material and information from his personal files. My three research assistants for the 1965 and 1967 interviews and the data analysis which followed, Howard Aster, Neil Caplan, and Mark Krasnick, gave me the benefit of their considerable intelligence and imagination and their organizational skills.

The Canada Council, McGill University, and Carleton University supported parts of the revised study and provided much-needed financial assistance. A special thanks is owed the Center of International Studies of Princeton University, which gave me generous financial assistance for the structured interviews conducted in 1967 and also provided the facilities, secretarial assistance, and intellectual atmosphere which were conducive to beginning the revision of my dissertation in the summer of 1967.

Several colleagues have also read the revised manuscript in whole or in part. In particular, Professors Henry Ehrmann, Maurice Pinard, and Harold Waller of McGill University and Vincent Lemieux of Laval University offered valuable suggestions for revision, and Professor Hugh Thorburn of Queen's University kindly selected and edited an extract from this book which appeared in the revised third edition of his *Party Politics in Canada*. My thesis supervisor, Professor Harry Eckstein of Princeton University, provided the original stimulus for the study. His considerable intellectual powers and practical acumen were generously offered throughout the initial period of thesis research and writing. He also helped to initiate the extensive revisions in the dissertation which were required for the publication of the study.

I am indebted to several typists who typed the various drafts of the manuscript and in particular to Margaret Blevins, who painstakingly produced the final draft. Diane Nelles and R. I. K. Davidson of the editorial staff of the University of Toronto Press offered most valuable advice.

This book has been published with the aid of a grant from the Social Science Research Council of Canada, using funds made available by the Canada Council.

Finally, a special word of thanks goes to my wife, Janice. She is able to offer that rare combination of intellectual and emotional support which is found only among wives who share their husband's training and concerns. I alone know how unlikely it is that the book could have been written without her.

MICHAEL B. STEIN
Montreal, December 1971

PART I

SOCIAL CREDIT IN QUEBEC: ITS NATURE

1

The Nature of the Créditiste Phenomenon: A Right-Wing Protest Movement

It has been a decade since Réal Caouette first led the Ralliement des Créditistes, the Quebec wing of the Social Credit party, to a stunning success in the 1962 Canadian federal election. In that election, the first it contested, the party confounded all predictions by winning twenty-six seats in the province of Quebec and capturing 26 per cent of the popular vote. The Ralliement was then united with the western Social Crediters, headed by Robert Thompson, who had managed to elect only four members. Together the two wings commanded thirty votes in the House of Commons and exercised the balance of power in a minority government situation. Despite a later split with the western members and a decline in the Ralliement Créditiste's legislative representation, it continued to hold this strategic position over the next six years of minority government rule.[1] And in 1968 it withstood the strong challenge of 'Trudeaumania' in Quebec and elected fourteen members.

At the time of its rise, most political observers were inclined to dismiss the party as an ephemeral, unimportant, and even somewhat comical phenomenon, although a few expressed their fear that it posed a threat to democracy in Canada.[2] No one then thought that the party would endure for very long, or that it would have much impact on the policy-making process. Yet by the early 1970s the Ralliement Créditiste had not only survived a period in which its older and more mature western counterpart declined and almost disappeared, it had even expanded on the national and provincial levels. On the national level it moved gradually to fill the void left by the moribund organization of the western-based Social Credit national movement.

1 The name was changed from Ralliement des Créditistes to Ralliement Créditiste in 1963. Henceforth these names will be used interchangeably.
2 For example, the *Montreal Star*, in an editorial which appeared two days after the 1962 election, wrote: 'These [Quebec Social Credit] people have been preaching their own crackpot variations on the old Aberhart crackpot theme ... These characters, to whom Fate has given the power to make and unmake governments, believe that the Bank of Canada is an inexhaustible source of credit to be used as they see fit to make us all happy ... They remind us of the new recruits sent to reinforce Wellington's army. "I don't know what the enemy will think of them," said the Iron Duke, "But by God, Sir, they frighten me." ' *Montreal Star*, 20 June 1962.

Réal Caouette became the national leader not only for Quebec Social Crediters, but also for the dwindling handful of English-speaking Canadians who clung to their earlier faith in the movement of William Aberhart and E.C. Manning. On the provincial level the Ralliement, after eight years of hesitation and soul searching, finally decided to enter the Quebec election of 1970. Under the forceful leadership of Camil Samson, a Caouette protégé whose political style closely resembles that of the federal Ralliement 'chef,' the provincial wing captured eleven seats and won 12 per cent of the Quebec vote. It immediately assumed an important role as the only Quebec party offering a clear federalist alternative to the Liberals and as the most genuine spokesman for rural and small-urban Quebec interests in the National Assembly.[3] As a result, the party has earned a grudging recognition, if not respect, from most Canadian political observers.

Yet despite its durability, visibility, and importance in Canadian politics, the Ralliement Créditiste has received comparatively little scholarly attention. As a result, the party remains largely an unknown quantity both in English and in French Canada. It is generally understood simply as an economic protest party which is particularly strong in rural areas of Quebec and which is directed against the modern urban-oriented and bureaucratic state. But there is one important exception to this rule. The electoral base of the Ralliement Créditiste has received much detailed and careful scholarly attention. Two Quebec social scientists, Vincent Lemieux and Maurice Pinard, have presented a thorough analysis of the Créditiste voter both by extrapolating from existing census data and voting results and by generating new survey data.[4] Their findings, along with those of William Irvine,[5] can be summarized under four broad headings: socioeconomic characteristics, partisan characteristics, group characteristics and psychological characteristics.[6]

Among the principal socioeconomic characteristics which define a voter are his

3 The terms 'rural' and 'urban' are drawn from the classification of polls in each riding by the Chief Electoral Officer in federal elections. Since 1962, the Ralliement des Créditistes has drawn its support not only from constituencies made up primarily of rural polls, but also from those comprised largely of urban polls in population centres outside metropolitan Montreal and Quebec City. These are referred to as 'small-urban' constituencies. For a more detailed definition, see chapter 3.

4 Lemieux's analyses of the Créditiste voter are based primarily on aggregate data, in the tradition of electoral sociology. See, for example, Vincent Lemieux, 'Les dimensions sociologiques du vote créditiste au Québec,' *Recherches Sociographiques*, VI, 2 (1965), 181–95, and 'The Election in the Constituency of Lévis,' in J. Meisel (ed), *Papers on the 1962 Election* (Toronto: University of Toronto Press, 1964), 33–52. Pinard's writings on the Quebec Social Credit vote are based on a survey of the Quebec electorate which he conducted in 1962 as a member of Le Groupe de Recherches Sociales. See Maurice Pinard, *The Rise of a Third Party: A Study in Crisis Politics* (Englewood Cliffs, NJ: Prentice-Hall, 1971), and 'One Party Dominance and Third Parties,' *Canadian Journal of Economics and Political Science*, 33 (1967), 358–73. Although all of their writings are based on data collected in the early 1960s, their findings are still authoritative for the current supporters, since the electoral base of the Ralliement Créditiste in 1970, while smaller, has not shifted dramatically.

5 W.P. Irvine, 'An Analysis of Voting Shifts in Quebec,' in Meisel, *Papers on the 1962 Election*, 129–44.

6 Similar headings are used by Pinard in *The Rise of a Third Party* and by Lemieux in 'Les dimensions sociologiques.'

age, sex, ethnic group, income, occupation, education, and place of residence. Of all age groups, Créditiste voting support is strongest among the youngest group of voters, presumably because that age group is more rebellious and alienated than any other.[7] There is a greater likelihood that the Créditiste voter will be male than female.[8] He is not only most certainly of French-Canadian ethnic origin; he is also probably from an area in which French Canadians are most highly concentrated and where very few anglophones reside. He has a low median income, although it is not as low for those who live in those more highly urbanized and industrialized constituencies which have consistently elected Créditiste members, such as Chicoutimi and Lac Saint-Jean.[9] The Créditiste voter is clearly not from among the poorest strata in Quebec society. Yet although he has an income placing him above the poverty line, he still finds himself in an economic condition which in recent years has been deteriorating rapidly.[10] On an occupational status scale, he can be considered to have a low status occupation. There is some disagreement, however, as to which occupations are most characteristic of Créditiste voters. Lemieux argues that the Créditiste voters are most likely to be manual labourers, transportation and communication workers, and artisans.[11] Pinard contends that the strongest vote for Social Credit comes from the middle segments of the working class (the semi-skilled workers) rather than from the unskilled and service workers, and from farmers with medium-sized farms rather than those with very small farms.[12] The Créditiste voter has less formal education than the average Quebecker.[13] He lives outside the metropolitan area of Montreal, most likely in a satellite city tributary to a major urban centre[14] or in a rural village with a population of between 1,000 and 5,000.[15] Among those who live in satellite cities or larger towns, Social Credit support increases with the size of the community, particularly among the middle-income group. However, in the rural villages this support decreases with an increase in residential population, a phenomenon which may be explained by the pattern of group and community relationships discussed below.[16] According to this socioeconomic profile, the Créditiste voter may be described as part of the lower stratum of Quebec society, but he is certainly not from the poorest or most downtrodden groups. In social class terms he is not easily

7 Pinard, *The Rise of a Third Party*, 164.
8 Lemieux, 'The Election in the Constituency of Lévis,' 42.
9 One might assume that areas of high francophone concentration are also areas in which ethnic conflict is less intense; hence, possibly, the lukewarm support accorded to nationalist appeals in many of the Créditiste strongholds. Irvine, 131, 132.
10 Pinard, *The Rise of a Third Party*, 138, and Lemieux, 'Les dimensions sociologiques,' 183.
11 Lemieux, 'Les dimensions sociologiques,' 183.
12 Pinard, *The Rise of a Third Party*, 138, 141. Pinard seems to have modified his position somewhat, for on page 92 he argues that 'the support of the party was concentrated among small businessmen, farmers and workers.' He therefore allows for significant support from some elements of the lower middle class.
13 Irvine, 133, and Lemieux, 'Les dimensions sociologiques,' 183.
14 Irvine, 134. According to Irvine, there are at least twenty-seven major urban centres in Quebec outside the metropolitan area of Montreal and fifty-five satellite cities tributary to them.
15 Lemieux, 'Les dimensions sociologiques,' 183.
16 Pinard, *The Rise of a Third Party*, 156.

pigeon-holed into any single, well-defined, and widely accepted sociological category such as working class, agrarian class, or lower middle class.

In partisan terms the Créditiste voter had supported either the Liberals or the Conservatives prior to 1962, unless because of his age he was ineligible to vote before that election. He was not one of those voters who through apathy or alienation had failed to vote in federal elections prior to 1960.[17] If, as has been alleged, he is twice as likely to have been a former Conservative voter as a former Liberal,[18] his previous allegiance to the Conservatives was a weak and temporary one.[19] He may very likely have been among those who were subjected to the propaganda of the Créditiste bimonthly newspaper, Vers Demain, in the 1940s and early 1950s. He may also have voted for the Union des Electeurs, the Ralliement Créditiste's predecessor, in several federal and provincial elections during the 1940s if he was then of eligible age. At any rate he is likely to reside in an area of former Créditiste strength where, as in many areas of the province, there has been reactivation of an earlier Créditiste tradition.[20]

Another partisan factor producing the shift to Créditisme in the early 1960s was a widespread desire among many Quebec voters to find an outlet for their dissatisfaction with the longlived federal Liberal party. The Créditiste voter wished to give political expression to his social and economic grievances arising from his declining economic fortunes. The main target for these grievances was the federal Liberal party, which had not only dominated the province (apart from brief periods of Conservative success) since the beginning of the century, but had also governed at the federal level for most of the period since the depression. In 1958 many Quebec voters temporarily supported the Progressive Conservatives under John Diefenbaker, who won an overwhelming national victory, but their hopes for economic improvement and a better deal for Quebec were not fulfilled. When this traditional outlet for the expression of dissent closed, and the Quebec Conservative organization in the early 1960s presented an image of weakness and decay, the discontented voter turned naturally to the only other available alternative to the Liberals, Réal Caouette's Ralliement des Créditistes.[21]

A third factor contributing to the partisan shift among Créditiste voters was the general unrest and social criticism which had begun to develop in Quebec following the death in 1959 of Premier Maurice Duplessis, the conservative strongman and Union Nationale leader. Social and economic changes were first initiated under his

---

17 Irvine, 130.
18 Lemieux, 'The Election in the Constituency of Lévis,' 47.
19 Pinard, The Rise of a Third Party, 24.
20 Lemieux, 'Les dimensions sociologiques,' 182–3.
21 Pinard, The Rise of a Third Party, chapter 2. See also Pinard, 'One Party Dominance and Third Parties.' Pinard's explanation of the rise of the Social Credit party in Quebec is intended to be part of a more general explanation of the rise of third parties in different societies. The structure of the single-party dominant system provides the element of 'structural conduciveness' which, along with 'strain,' are the two necessary conditions for the rise of third-party movements. The explanation is an application of a framework for the study of social movements offered by Neil Smelser in The Theory of Collective Behavior (New York: Free Press, 1963).

successor Paul Sauvé and were considerably accelerated by Liberal leader Jean Lesage after his 1960 Quebec provincial election victory. These changes in the province affected Quebec's reaction to federal politics, and traditional partisan attachments were questioned by some Quebec voters who were attacking established attitudes and modes of political action. It is not surprising, therefore, that former supporters of the Liberals and Conservatives, particularly the young, discontented, and weakly partisan, were ready to test a party which at least offered new ideas, programs, and personalities.[22] Out of these forces acting on the traditional two-party system in Quebec there emerged a new type of partisan voter, the Créditiste. Most of these converts or reconverts to Créditisme of the early 1960s have retained their third-party attachments ever since. Moreover, their Créditiste allegiances have been buttressed by the continued presence of most of the political, social, and economic conditions which were so conducive to their original partisan shifts.[23]

The group characteristics of the Créditiste voter also have a role, although a less important one, in influencing him to support Social Credit. They may be subdivided into three aspects: primary group influences (including the immediate family, relatives, and friends), secondary group attachments (including membership and participation in occupational organizations and social and religious groups), and community associational ties. The strongest group influence on the Créditiste voter is his immediate family. Créditiste voters tend to come from large families of five or more children in which Social Credit ideas are actively debated and disseminated.[24] Moreover, close social contact between friends particularly during the period just before an election is another important factor in diffusing Social Credit ideas and attracting a voter to the Créditiste party. This is especially true where one's close friends are of the same occupational background and are therefore likely to share the same outlook on the ideas and attractions of the movement.[25]

With respect to secondary group attachments, the Créditiste voter is generally a relatively active member of occupational, social, and religious associations, rather than a socially isolated individual. His occupational association may initially have acted as a restraining factor in his decision to support the party. However, at some point in time the occupational group as a whole had probably been won over to the criticisms of the Créditiste militants against the political establishment and had identified itself as an alienated economic sector. The occupational association of the Créditiste voter therefore is likely to diffuse Créditiste ideas and encourage support

22 Lemieux, 'Les dimensions sociologiques,' 185–7. Pinard makes a similar argument in *The Rise of a Third Party*, 81.
23 The two principal conditions for the emergence of third parties presented by Pinard, single-party dominance and strain, are both still present. The federal Liberals are facing little opposition in Quebec from either the Progressive Conservatives or the New Democratic party, despite the fact that they are in power and their policies are being subjected to severe criticism by many Québécois. The presence of high unemployment amid continuing inflation, and recurring ethnic tensions between francophones and anglophones in the province over reforms in education and language, are adding a strong element of strain to the structural conduciveness of the single-party dominant system at this time.
24 Pinard, *The Rise of a Third Party*, 111–12.
25 *Ibid.*, 198–9. See also Lemieux, 'The Election in the Constituency of Lévis,' 37.

for the party. The same pattern is true for his social and religious club memberships. This is especially the case if opinion among the primary groups to which the voter belongs is also favourable to Créditisme.[26] Finally, whether or not community associational ties play an important role in encouraging a voter to support Social Credit depends largely on the size and degree of integration of the community in which he lives. If it is small and highly integrated, it is likely that the community network initially acted as a restraining force on his decision to vote for the Créditistes. Later, however, if strains within the community intensified and the message of Social Credit won greater favour from community leaders, the network probably served to mobilize support for the party.

Thus many Créditiste voters come from small, highly integrated communities which vote for the party almost en masse. In the case of larger, less integrated areas, the loose community network initially worked to liberate those individuals who because of their social background, partisan outlook, or psychological predisposition, wished to support Social Credit in spite of the prevailing negative sentiment in the community at large. However, in later stages of the development of the party's electoral support, the large size and weak integration of the community acted as a dampening force on the expansion of the movement.[27]

A final dimension of the Créditiste voter which has been partially probed is his psychological outlook, although Pinard tends to regard this aspect as the least important in influencing voters to support Social Credit. He argues that Créditiste voters are not more authoritarian or intolerant than other Quebec voters; nor are they more conservative either in economic or non-economic terms.[28] They are, however, more alienated, partly because of social and economic factors such as their low socioeconomic status or their susceptibility to economic strains. And among Créditistes with wide group attachments this alienation is even stronger than among those who are weakly integrated. Pinard identifies their alienation as a form of 'rebelliousness' rather than 'retreatism' and suggests that it is more likely to occur among voters in times of political crisis.[29]

It is obvious that this cumulative profile of the Créditiste voter supports the crude assumptions of contemporary observers that the Ralliement Créditiste is a lower-class protest phenomenon. However, this total concentration on the voter at the expense of other members of the party has left us with an incomplete understanding of the precise nature of this phenomenon. What was it that gave the initial impetus to these voters to identify with an idea like social credit? What produced the Quebec brand of social credit popularly known as Créditisme? We know almost nothing about the movement's origin, development, ideology, or pattern of organization and

26 Pinard, *The Rise of a Third Party*, 217–18. See also Lemieux, 'The Election in the Constituency of Lévis,' 37.
27 Pinard, *The Rise of a Third Party*, 203. Here he argues that at a still later stage 'large communities regain their greater conduciveness.' Thus Créditiste support in larger, more unintegrated communities should be as strong as in the small, highly integrated communities. This hypothesis requires further exploration.
28 *Ibid.*, 227–8, 232–3.
29 *Ibid.*, 241. The concepts, as Pinard acknowledges, are taken from William Erbe, 'Social Involvement and Political Activity: A Replication and Elaboration,' *American Sociological Review*, 29 (1964), 206.

leadership.[30] We are not really able to explain how the party has managed to endure over a decade and even increase its legislative support at times against heavy odds. In short, we know a great deal about the Créditiste voter and virtually nothing about Créditisme itself. It is this lacuna in Canadian scholarship that this study attempts to fill.

The first task in explaining Créditisme is that of defining precisely what kind of social or political phenomenon it is. In this respect other studies of Créditisme are of very little help. They fail entirely to deal with the question whether Créditisme is a political party, a political movement (of the right, centre, or left), a pressure group, or a hybrid of all three.[31] This question is more than academic, since it is by defining the phenomenon that we shall be able to acquire at least an initial understanding of its emergence, pattern of development, and strength.

The Ralliement Créditiste was founded in 1957 as a political party. It declared itself as such in its original constitution. Like any other political party, it has concentrated its activity and efforts almost entirely on electoral action. Its often-stated objectives are similar to those of any other political party in Canada: namely, to win enough seats in the legislature to form a government and thereby implement its program.[32] The party has an elected leader, a constitution, well-defined structures including national, regional, and local executives, an electoral fund, a party news-paper, and even an official membership card.[33] It operates at both the federal and the provincial levels, although its major activity until recently has been concentrated almost entirely in the province of Quebec.[34]

But the Ralliement Créditiste is not the entire Créditiste phenomenon. Nor do

30 Except for the study of the Créditiste success in Lévis by Lemieux, in which some aspects of party organization and campaigning are discussed. Lemieux, 'The Election in the Constituency of Lévis.'
31 Pinard does state at one point that he considers Social Credit in Quebec to be a protest movement, or one of a type of 'political movements arising as a response to economic crises and whose main overt goals are the redress of economic grievances ... They include class movements and mainly, but not exclusively, those of the reform type (as opposed to the extremist type); socialist movements in general, but also conservative ones, such as Social Credit and the Poujadists, would also fall in this group; even fascist movements arising in periods of economic crises would fall in this category.' *The Rise of a Third Party*, 224–5. But this is the only instance in which Pinard offers a definition of his concept of political movement.
32 For an attempt to define a political party as distinct from a social movement, see Rudolf Heberle, *Social Movements: An Introduction to Political Sociology* (New York: Appleton Century-Croft, 1951), 10. See also Walter Young, *The Anatomy of a Party: The National CCF, 1932–61* (Toronto: University of Toronto Press, 1969), chapter I.
33 For a more detailed discussion of these aspects of the party organization, see chapter 3 and Michael B. Stein, 'The Structure and Function of the Finances of the Ralliement des Créditistes,' in Committee on Election Expenses, *Studies in Canadian Party Finance* (Ottawa: Queen's Printer, 1966), 405–58.
34 Some unsuccessful efforts at organizing voters in New Brunswick and northwest Ontario (primarily in constituencies with large French-Canadian populations) were made by the Ralliement Créditiste in the election campaigns of 1965 and 1968. After 1968, when all federal Social Credit candidates from the west were defeated, the federal Ralliement party decided to expand its efforts into other regions of Canada in an attempt to revive the national Social Credit party. For a more detailed discussion of these national efforts, see chapter 3 below.

most of its most active members see themselves only as political party members. The Ralliement Créditiste was initially founded and is still viewed by a majority of its leaders as the political and electoral arm of a larger political and social movement which preceded the establishment of the party in 1957 by almost twenty-five years. The Ralliement Créditiste is a political party which has absorbed the political energies of a determined group of active supporters of social credit in Quebec in the last decade. But the Créditiste phenomenon is a political movement which has enveloped the lifestyles, shaped the political and social goals, and embodied the utopian aspirations of a smaller but even more dedicated group of social credit militants for over thirty-five years. This smaller but more devoted group first founded and continues to form the nucleus of the leadership of the Ralliement party. It is this group and its motivations, activities, conflicts, and co-operative efforts which have shaped much of the party's strategy and development over the past decade. If one is really to understand the Ralliement Créditiste, one must place it within the context of the larger Créditiste movement and interpret the behaviour of its leaders and followers in terms of the origin, development, ideology, goals, and behaviour of the members of a firmly rooted and long-standing political-social movement.

A DEFINITION OF A RIGHT-WING PROTEST MOVEMENT

The concept of a political-social movement has not been well-defined in the social science literature, because most writers fail to make a distinction between a political and a social movement. A social movement has been broadly defined as any form of collective action which involves the mobilization of groups of people who aim to bring about fundamental changes in the social order.[35] Central to most definitions of social movement is the shared feeling of dissatisfaction by its members and the general desire for change.[36] A political movement is one form of a social movement, namely one directed at change in the political order. It shares a number of characteristics with other political structures, such as political parties and pressure groups which also compete for influence within the political sphere, in that it involves the organization of individuals around common ideas and interests which they seek to promote by political means.[37]

However, the ways in which political movements differ from the more conventional political structures are more important. In the first place political move-

35 Heberle, 6. For a similar definition, see Joseph R. Gusfield, *Protest, Reform and Revolt: A Reader in Social Movements* (New York: Wiley, 1970), 2.
36 See, for example, Eric Hoffer, *The True Believer* (New York: Harper, 1951), part I, chapters 1–2; William Bruce Cameron, *Modern Social Movements* (New York: Random House, 1966), 7; K. Lang and G.E. Lang, *Collective Dynamics* (New York: Thomas Y. Crowell, 1961), 490; M. Zald and R. Ash, 'Social Movement Organizations: Growth, Decay and Change,' in Barry McLaughlin (ed), *Studies in Social Movements: A Social Psychological Perspective* (New York: Free Press, 1969), 461–85. Heberle points out that the concept 'movement' has the connotation in all languages of 'a stirring among people, an unrest, a collective attempt to reach a visualized goal, especially a change in certain social institutions; that is, the intention to change the patterns of human relations and social institutions is the essential characteristic of a social movement' (6). Etymologically, the term 'movement' signifies action directed towards change.
37 See Heberle, 9.

ments generally have broader goals than most other structures of political competition.[38] They do not seek merely to win power or to obtain concessions for their members from government authorities. Their goals generally involve education on a broad scale, mass mobilization, and a variety of other modes of action designed to promote political change. Second, political movements are generally organized around a set of utopian beliefs or goals which are embodied in a political ideology. This ideology is intended to act as a solidifying force and a means of propelling the members of the movement towards the attainment of their goals. It also serves to interpret the social and political environment against which its members are reacting.[39] Third, political movements involve a structuring or ordering of political roles and a distribution of power, influence, and authority among its members which differ from that of other political structures. The organizational structure tends to be tighter in its core or leadership group and looser among its followers. The leadership group is generally made up of those most committed to the movement's ideology and its goals, who are likely to concentrate power and authority in themselves and to maintain tight control over decisions involving the strategy and tactics of the movement.[40] The followers, on the other hand, are often loosely affiliated to the movement and less concerned about decision-making structures and details of program; rather, they focus their attention and their energy towards achieving the broad goals of the movement. They are therefore inclined to follow the directives of the leaders in matters of strategy and tactics.[41]

There are two broad types of political movements – protest or revolutionary – which differ from each other in the scope and limits of their objectives.[42] All political movements are opposed to the ways in which political decisions are made in the society in which its members operate. All are committed to some form of transformation or change in the political sphere. Those movements which pursue the more far-reaching objective of overthrowing the system and capturing political power in order to restructure the social order may be labelled 'revolutionary'; those with the more limited objectives of changing the manner in which decisions are made or the norms which guide and delimit this process of decision-making without destroying the system itself may be called 'protest movements.'[43]

Protest movements are organizations (institutionalized groups) of individuals who seek to educate or convert the populace to their ideology and goals by resorting

38 The concept 'structures of political competition' is borrowed from Professor Harry Eckstein, Department of Politics, Princeton University.
39 Heberle, 12, 434.
40 Lang and Lang, 495.
41 Heberle, 284. Cameron also points out that the simultaneous desire to maintain tight control over the core group of active devotees and to expand the movement to include less dedicated sympathizers often creates a conflict for the founders of a movement (15).
42 See Robert J. Jackson and Michael B. Stein, *Issues in Comparative Politics: A Text with Readings* (New York: St Martin's Press [Toronto: Macmillan], 1971), 266–8. A similar distinction is implicit in Gusfield, 8. There are, of course, other ways of categorizing and distinguishing between different types of movements. For example, Neil Smelser distinguishes between norm-oriented and value-oriented movements (chapters IX, X). Lang and Lang differentiate between reform and revolutionary movements (503).
43 Jackson and Stein, 266.

to a series of rebellious or dissenting actions against the political regime or its rulers in order to draw public attention to their grievances. Their aims are to convince the regime or its rulers to change or modify decision-making procedures in order to alleviate or diminish the plight of the discontented. They may attempt to achieve these objectives in one of two ways: either by converting the existing rulers or ruling groups to their cause or by capturing power, displacing these rulers, and themselves carrying out the decisions necessary to remove the existing disabilities. But these activities do not include a wholesale transformation of the prevailing political order and its decision-making process or a complete restructuring of the social structure and value system.

Protest movements may be characterized as right-wing or left-wing depending on the nature and direction of the reforms which the movement advocates.[44] A right-wing protest movement advocates policies or reforms which involve a return to or a reinforcement of the values identified with the past. Generally right-wing ideas appeal to those segments of the population of a society which are experiencing long-run social and economic decline, such as the peasantry in industrial society or the unskilled blue-collar worker in post-industrial society. A left-wing protest movement, on the other hand, tends to articulate the norms of and advocate a more rapid transformation to a proposed future society. Left-wing ideas are generally popular among segments of the population which are in a disadvantaged position but are gradually increasing in size and influence as time progresses. The blue-collar worker in industrial society and the skilled white-collar salaried employee in post-industrial society are examples of such groups. Sometimes, however, the goals and ideology of the movement are framed in sufficiently general terms to attract followers from both the left and the right.[45] This is because both left-wing and right-wing movements express their dissent and articulate their proposed reforms in general and highly emotive and moral tones designed to appeal to the utopian aspirations of all discontented or dispossessed groups in society.

It is a major contention of this study that the Social Credit movement in Quebec – Créditisme – is a prototype of a right-wing political protest movement.[46] More-

44 *Ibid.*, 277–8.
45 This point is emphasized by Pinard: 'As far as the unincorporated masses are concerned, the support of a new movement does not entail much congruence between that movement's and its followers' ideology or belief system – if by chance the latter have any – but simply requires the development of a *generalized belief* which identifies the sources of strains in the system and envisages an overall cure.' This lack of congruence between the ideology of the movement and the class composition and outlook of its adherents is more likely to occur among voting supporters than among the leaders. Pinard, *The Rise of a Third Party*, 95–6. (Italics in original.)
46 A right-wing protest movement, as defined above, must be distinguished from a populist movement. Populism has both a broader and a more specialized connotation. There are many different types of populist movements which may exhibit either left- or right-wing, fascist or egalitarian, forward-looking and progressive or backward-looking and nostalgic characteristics. They may be reformist or revolutionary in their goals. See Kenneth Minogue, 'Populism as a Political Movement,' in G. Ionescu and E. Gellner (eds), *Populism: Its National Characteristics* (London: Weidenfeld and Nicolson, 1969), 200. Hofstadter has isolated five major characteristics in American populist ideology: 1/ the idea of a golden age,

over, an understanding of the substantial electoral support for the Ralliement Créditiste in Quebec in the last decade and a clear grasp of the party as a political phenomenon can only be attained by analysing the party as the most recent electoral manifestation of this much older and more deeply rooted right-wing protest movement.

Créditisme fits the definition of a right-wing protest movement in every sense in which that term has been defined above. The Créditiste movement first arose in the mid-1930s in Quebec in a time of great economic and social stress. From its inception the founders of Créditisme envisaged their organization as a movement, and they carefully nurtured their creation to conform with this image, so that Créditisme exhibits the three characteristics of a political movement. First, through the formation of a vast organizational network, through the distribution of pamphlets, leaflets, and a bimonthly newspaper, *Vers Demain*, and through skilful use of radio and television, the Créditiste message was spread across the vast expanse of Quebec's hinterland. The founders thereby succeeded in converting an elite group or activist element to the monetary reform ideas of Major Douglas. These were cleverly interspersed with those social and political doctrines of the Roman Catholic church which were compatible with them. In this manner they succeeded to a considerable degree in achieving their broader objectives of political education and mobilization, although only among a small segment of the population. Second, they created among the rural and small-urban elites in Quebec an ideology and a set of utopian beliefs which have served as a kind of Weltanschauung for this same small group of militants for over thirty-five years. This is the core group which has served as the backbone for the later electoral success of the Créditistes.[47] Third, they evolved an organizational structure called the Union des Electeurs which served both to consolidate (and later to undermine) their own control of the movement and to attract to the fold large numbers of loosely affiliated sympathizers and supporters. This organizational structure, including its constituency network, its study groups, its method of collecting funds, and its communications links between leaders and led, served as the foundation for a much more formally structured and loosely controlled organization which was established under the Ralliement Créditiste. But the Union des Electeurs differed from the Ralliement in its essential conformity with the structures typical of a movement, involving tight control at the top, and loose, poorly defined structures at the local level.[48]

2/ a concept of natural harmonies (once exploiters are removed), 3/ a dualist version of the social struggle, 4/ a conspiracy theory of history, 5/ the primacy of money. See Richard Hofstadter, *The Age of Reform* (New York: Alfred A. Knopf, 1955), chapter 2. At least the first four characteristics can be generalized to other national and cultural contexts. In short, 'populism is a type of movement found among those aware of belonging to the poor periphery of an industrial system, and is therefore a reaction to industrialism' (Minogue, 209). If populism is defined in these general terms, all Social Credit movements, including that in Quebec, are populist movements. But they are a particular kind of populism, namely, right-wing non-revolutionary populism, such as is typically found in North America.

47 See chapter 2.

48 See chapter 2 and Stein, 'The Structure and Function of the Finances of the Ralliement des Créditistes.'

Créditisme is, moreover, a protest rather than a revolutionary movement. In its early days the movement seemed for a time to take on a more radical cast, calling for transformation of the system of parties, of the relationship between the representative and his electors, and of the relationship between the cabinet and administration. The founders were pessimistic about the chances of achieving the desired monetary reform without substantial changes in the political sphere. However, at no time did they call for destruction of the constitutional system created by the British North America Act or for abandonment of the liberal-democratic ideal.[49] In later phases of the movement's development, its major wing came to accept all aspects of the existing framework of government and began to operate as a conventional political party within the established electoral and political processes.[50] Nevertheless, each major wing in each successive phase of the movement maintained the essential protest appeal embodied in the doctrine of social credit. Each Créditiste group challenged the manner in which the distribution system worked within the economic sector and, in particular, the way in which the banking and monetary systems were operated. Each offered criticisms of the existing government and party systems. But they did not reject the legitimacy of the constitutional order or advocate dismantling the capitalist economic system itself.[51]

Finally, Créditisme is a right-wing protest movement because its appeal is essentially conservative and oriented towards preservation of a social and economic order in Quebec which is rapidly crumbling. Créditistes believe that traditional values such as obedience, duty, and morality, which they claim pervaded the Quebec social system in earlier times, will be re-established once the corrupting influence of monopoly capitalism and the avaricious inclinations of bankers are curbed through the system of social credit. They foresee the regeneration and ultimate prosperity of the farmer, the small-town merchant, and the artisan once they have sufficient credit to rebuild their shattered finances. They believe that the church and religious institutions will be resuscitated and the confessional school system saved. They call for insulation of the small-town communications system from the corroding effects of the media in the large-urban environment.[52]

But it is not sufficient merely to establish that Créditisme fits the description of a right-wing protest movement. It is also important to show how in its development and behaviour it also conforms to this model. Thus one may explain the development

---

49 The latter argument (adherence of the Créditistes to the constitutional framework of the British North America Act and the liberal-democratic ideal at all times) must be qualified. For a brief period between 1944 and 1948 the directors of the Union des Electeurs advocated establishing a separate parliament of electors' representatives which would act as a parallel legislature to the House of Commons. For a more detailed discussion of these ideas, see chapter 2.

50 See chapter 3.

51 See chapters 2 and 3.

52 From formal and informal interviews with various Créditiste leaders from 1963 to 1971. This statement is also based on my careful reading of Créditiste newspapers such as *Cahiers du Crédit Social, Vers Demains, Regards, La Nation*, and *L'Ordre Nouveau*, organs of successive wings of the Créditiste movement. Finally, it is based on a study of policy resolutions of various federal and provincial congresses from 1963 to 1971.

and pattern of evolution of Créditisme in terms of certain inherent tendencies which operate in political movements in general and in right-wing protest movements in particular.

B DEVELOPMENT OF A RIGHT-WING PROTEST MOVEMENT

In this respect the general literature on political movements, although sparse, is helpful. Considerable attention has been given to the role of leadership in these movements and to the definition of the types of leaders which tend to emerge at different phases of the movement's development. Zald and Ash have explained that the need to focus on the leaders of political movements is due to the leadership being 'an even more crucial aspect of a movement than of any other large-scale organization, since the situation of a movement is unstable, its organization has few material incentives, and its tasks are less routinized.'[53]

Three broad types of leaders are generally associated with a political movement, corresponding roughly to three broad phases in a movement's development. There are first of all the prophets or men of words. These people assume positions of leadership because of their capacity to articulate the main ideas of the movement and to convert new members to its cause. Their authority rests either on their recognized superiority as interpreters of the faith or on their qualities as agitators and diffusers of the movement's message or both. Their role is likely to be predominant at the early phases of the movement's development – the mobilization phase – when support is rallied and there is a rapid expansion in membership. Second, there are the administrators or agitators who acquire their pre-eminence through their capacity to organize the membership into units which are effective in different forms of dissenting political action, such as election campaigning, mass demonstrations, and pressure group appeals, or through their ability to promote and proselytize on behalf of the movement. Their authority rests on their ability to translate the ideas of the movement into practical forms of action and their capacity for maintaining unity of purpose and co-ordination, financial support, and enthusiastic devotion and service to the movement. Their role is most important in the middle phases of a movement's development – the confirmation or consolidation phase – when energies are directed away from recruitment and towards the achievement of concrete results. Finally, there are the statesmen or pragmatic politicians who direct the movement on its political course after it has acquired a certain stability and legitimacy. Their authority rests on their success in maintaining power or political support for the movement through negotiation, refined strategies and tactics, and pragmatic compromises. Their role is most important in the latter or mature phase of a movement's development when it either transforms itself into a conventional political structure such as a party or pressure group or becomes an educational and ideological adjunct to the political power holders in society. This phase has been described as that of stabilization or institutionalization.[54]

53 Zald and Ash, 479–80.
54 Lang and Lang, 359, 518–20. The ideas presented here about the pattern of leadership and organization during the mobilization phase are drawn from Hoffer, chapter xv; C.W. King, *Social Movements in the United States* (New York: Random House, 1956), 72; Smelser, 361;

The course of development of the movement is largely engineered by the leaders and core group of activists within the movement. They draw their support from a much larger group of alienated individuals in the society in a typical pattern which has been described as 'the natural history of development of mass phenomena.'[55] Broadly speaking, the pattern is as follows. In the mobilization phase a core group emerges consisting of individuals who are attracted to a set of dissenting ideas for a variety of motivations, including economic, political, and social grievances and collective and individual needs and interests.[56] They may be recruited from a number of different sectors of society, including both marginal elements and respectable groups.[57] What primarily distinguishes the leaders from the movement's rank and file is their deeper commitment to the cause of the movement and their willingness to devote greater time and effort to define and realize the movement's goals.[58] This core group, therefore, serves to mobilize and channel the emotions and grievances of the alienated masses. A spark goes out from the leadership to other groups in the society, touching their deep-rooted feelings of unease and directing them along a specific path dictated by the movement. The leadership group supplies these recruits with its directing cadres and also consolidates its position of authority by claiming to be the sole or principal ideological spokesman for the movement.[59] In the consolidation and institutionalization phases of the movement's development, the pattern of leadership is modified to reflect the changing needs of and external constraints on the movement. Several important transformations will occur: first, the movement will create more tightly knit and clearly defined structures; second, it will alter and redefine its strategy and tactics; and third, it will engage in much internal quarrelling and struggle.[60]

The high degree of factionalism which exists in political movements has been widely observed by social scientists, and several have attempted to explain it. One contributing factor which has been mentioned is intergenerational conflict which may manifest itself in terms of a struggle between types of leaders and leadership styles.[61] A second factor which leads to factionalism is the development of new

John P. Roche and Stephen Sachs, 'The Bureaucrat and the Enthusiast: An Exploration of the Leadership of Social Movements,' in Barry McLaughlin (ed), 208; and Lewis N. Killian, 'Social Movements,' in Robert E.L. Faris (ed), *Handbook of Modern Sociology* (Chicago: Rand McNally, 1964), 441–3. The ideas concerning the pattern of leadership and organization during the consolidation phase are drawn from Hoffer, chapter XVII; King, 72–4; Lang and Lang, 520; Killian, 441–2, and Smelser, 361.

55 Lang and Lang, 359. On page 342 the authors refer to the larger group of alienated individuals as the 'alienated mass.'
56 The motivations for joining a political movement have been thoroughly analysed by Hadley Cantril, *The Psychology of Social Movements* (New York: Wiley, 1944), chapters 2–3; Hoffer, chapters I–III; Heberle, chapter 5; and Gabriel Almond, *Appeals of Communism* (Princeton: Princeton University Press, 1954), chapters 4–6, 9.
57 Heberle, chapter 8, and Hoffer, chapters IV–XI.
58 Heberle, 279.
59 Lang and Lang, 495.
60 Heberle, chapter 16; Lang and Lang, 520, 533.
61 Heberle, chapter 6, and Smelser, 361. Heberle defines a political generation as 'contemporaries of approximately the same age who, on account of their age, have more in common

bases of power outside the original leadership group, which is sometimes the result of the growing heterogeneity of the movement as it develops.[62] Factionalism has also been explained by the weakness of the central control apparatus of most political movements, particularly of the non-revolutionary or protest type.[63] A fourth factor intended to account for this tendency to factionalism is the constant reorientation of the movement's strategy and tactics, particularly in its later phases. The changes in strategy and tactics may appear in the form of an ideological struggle between those who desire to maintain the movement's doctrinal purity and those who seek more pragmatic solutions. Depending on which group is in power, a challenge will arise from its opponents calling for either greater militancy or greater moderation.[64] What may begin as an ideological struggle or a disagreement over strategy and tactics may eventually result in a schism between the top leaders and those who challenge the entire basis of their authority and control.[65]

These tendencies to division, which emerge in most political movements, are likely to be particularly acute in right-wing protest movements. Although very little in the way of systematic inquiry in this direction has been undertaken thus far, the following

with each other than with older or younger people.' The binding force in a political generation is the shared political and social experiences during the formative period of the generation. Also, 'younger people tend to differ from older people in their outlook on life and consequently in their political views' (Heberle, 118–19). These insights are clearly applicable to the Créditiste movement, where generational differences existed between the first generation of Créditistes headed by Louis Even and Gilberte Côté-Mercier and the second generation of Créditistes led by Réal Caouette, Laurent Legault, and Gilles Grégoire, leading to a schism in 1957, and then again between the second generation and the third generation of Créditistes led by Camil Samson, Phil Cossette, René Matte, and André Fortin, which produced tensions in the 1970–1 period. The manifestation of intergenerational struggle between types of leaders and leadership styles is of course illustrated by the Créditiste movement. The first generation was led by prophets like Even and Côté-Mercier, the second generation by propagandists and administrators like Caouette, Grégoire, and Legault, and the third generation by more pragmatic politicians like Samson, Cossette, Matte, and Fortin.

62 Lang and Lang, 533, Smelser, 361, and Zald and Ash, 478. This factor was less obvious in the Créditiste movement, since most conflicts occurred between generations within essentially the same core group and social base, although each succeeding generation attempted to broaden that original base somewhat. Attempts were made by new Créditistes such as Dr Marcoux to develop a new base of support from outside and capture the leadership from the more devoted and ideologically committed Créditistes, but they failed. Attempts were also made to broaden the base of the movement to include new regions (such as Montreal), classes (such as middle-class professionals), and ethnic groups (such as anglophones within and outside Quebec) by Caouette in 1960–2 and again in 1967–71, but they also achieved little success. For further details, see part II below.

63 Lang and Lang, 533. A similar explanation has been offered for factionalism in right-wing revolutionary movements such as Nazism. Here, however, charisma is used to reinforce institutional controls. See Joseph Nyomarky, *Charisma and Factionalism in the Nazi Party* (Minneapolis: University of Minnesota Press, 1961).

64 Smelser, 361. This factor was extremely important in producing splits in the Créditiste movement. See part III.

65 Zald and Ash, 477–9. This is precisely what occurred in the split between first and second generation Créditistes and led to the founding of the Ralliement Créditiste party by Caouette in 1957.

trends seem likely to occur in such movements.[66] First, because the ideology of the movement is right wing, its appeal is usually limited to a sector of the population which is in gradual decline. Its opportunities for eventual success or the achievement of political power through democratic means are therefore likely to be limited. In times of severe strain, such as a general depression or internal civil strife, the appeal of such a movement may extend well beyond its original class base.[67] When such strain is less intense or is absent altogether the limited scope of the appeal will gradually lead to frustration in the attempt to achieve the movement's goals. At the same time, if the movement is reformist rather than revolutionary, as protest movements by definition are, then the set of ideas around which the leaders rally is likely to be loosely defined and subject to a considerable range of different interpretations. These two factors will contribute simultaneously to the emergence within the core group of activists of opposition groups which will challenge the prevailing leaders. They will force them to adopt new lines of strategy and action which are either more moderate (thereby producing a trend towards transformation of the movement into a conventional structure) or more militant (thereby setting the movement off on a more revolutionary course). If the leaders refuse to acquiesce to their demands, then they are likely to reject the legitimacy of the leaders and break away from the movement entirely.[68]

It is my contention that these insights provided in the literature of social and political movements in general and right-wing protest movements in particular help to explain much about the pattern of development of the Créditiste movement in Quebec over its thirty-five year history. The founders and early directors of the movement, in particular Louis Even and Gilberte Côté-Mercier, were prophets or people of words rather than people of action. They were brilliant popularizers and interpreters of the Douglas doctrine who could make it relevant for rural and small-urban Québécois. They were therefore ideally suited for their positions of leadership in the early phase of the movement's mobilization and expansion. They succeeded in igniting a spark which spread rapidly in the 1940s among the alienated French-Canadian masses who were caught within the vice of rural poverty and were threatened by further decline in status and income but at the same time wished to preserve their religion, language, culture, and traditional economic way of life. They maintained their top leadership positions and their unchallenged control over the movement for a period of almost twenty years (from 1939 to 1957) on the basis of what

66 Among important book-length monographs of right-wing protest movements are Stanley Hoffmann, *Le mouvement poujade* (Paris: Librairie Armand Colin, 1956), J.A. Irving, *The Social Credit Movement in Alberta* (Toronto: University of Toronto Press, 1959), and C.B. Macpherson, *Democracy in Alberta: The Theory and Practice of a Quasi-party System* (Toronto: University of Toronto Press, 1953). The most important comparative study is Ionescu and Gellner, *Populism: Its National Characteristics,* which, however, treats left-wing as well as right-wing movements. There have also been several articles and monographs on the National Democratic party (NPD) in West Germany, the American Independence party in the United States, and other right-wing third-party movements in American history. The latter are not, however, very detailed or systematic.

67 As was the case with the Social Credit movement in Alberta. See Irving.

68 This follows the line of argument in Zald and Ash, 477–9. For an expansion of this argument, see the conclusion to part III.

they claimed was a superior knowledge of the ideas of Major Douglas and of social credit doctrine.

However, to ensure their control over the movement, they came to depend more and more on a group of organizational men and administrators, including skilful agitators and propagandists like Réal Caouette and bureaucrats like Laurent Legault. These men, of a younger generation, were originally schooled in the doctrine by the founding leaders but gradually began to challenge their authority when the early expansion of the movement in the 1940s attained a plateau and then began to decline after 1949. In 1957 Caouette and Legault formed a new wing of the movement, a political party designed to engage in electoral action, which they named Le Ralliement des Créditistes. Through their combined actions the party succeeded in winning a recognized place for itself in the federal and later provincial legislatures and an electoral base in rural and small-urban Quebec.

At the same time, though, these leaders began to dilute or discard the ideological tenets of social credit and the utopian goals of a popular movement in favour of pragmatic programs and political compromises. These reorientations in the strategy and tactics of the movement succeeded for a time in winning the party some electoral support in Quebec and thereby served to inject the original movement with a renewed sense of vigour and purpose at a time when Créditisme was in danger of total disintegration and disappearance. However, the result produced a reaction among those groups within the movement who were in favour of greater doctrinal purity and encouraged those who preferred to broaden the base of the movement and water down its original tenets even further. Splits among the leaders began to proliferate over the next decade and seriously weakened the party both electorally and in its internal direction. In addition, social and political trends in Quebec in the 1960s which produced an increasing degree of statism and noisy nationalistic appeals to a growing urban middle class tended to reduce the constituency of the Créditistes and make its appeal less and less relevant to the expanding urban sector of the Quebec population.

By 1970, at the very moment when it appeared that the party was stabilizing its support and entering new fields of national and provincial political action, the movement itself was on the verge of extinction. A new challenge was beginning to emerge from third generation Créditistes, such as Camil Samson, Phil Cossette, René Matte, and André Fortin, whose aims were even more pragmatic than were those of their forebears. These men had virtually no interest in a larger national movement and very little knowledge of social credit doctrine or goals. They sought to institutionalize the movement by transforming it completely into a pragmatic right-of-centre party which would direct its appeal to those populist elements in Quebec which both feared and were anxious to find a place in the new Quebec of the 1970s. It seemed inevitable that their point of view would ultimately prevail, and the movement would shortly thereafter be laid to rest.[69]

69 The distinction between 'movement' and 'party' is emphasized here. Although the movement may die, the party may continue for some time after and even expand its support. In the case of the Créditistes, however, it seems doubtful if the party can do so without forming a broader alliance with another right-wing party. See the conclusion to part v for an expansion of this argument.

In the chapters which follow, I shall attempt to expand on and reinforce these arguments by conducting a detailed and systematic examination of the ideology, evolution, social composition, organization, and pattern of development and action of the Créditiste movement from 1936 until the present. I shall first attempt to locate Créditisme more precisely on the ideological continuum. What are the major formative ideas of the movement in Quebec? What factors first contributed to the emergence of Créditisme as an ideological force? What factors contributed to its later ideological and political development and transformation? Second, the leadership of the Créditiste movement must be analysed in terms of its social and attitudinal profile and its patterns of participation and action in the movement. An attempt must be made to account for the pattern of development of the movement and, in particular, its tendency to factionalism and schism. Finally, Créditisme must be understood as a prototype of a more general political form. Therefore, we must draw from the Créditiste experience those elements that may be relevant for the analysis of similar right-wing protest movements elsewhere, and also consider what the experience of other such movements might suggest for the future of social credit in Quebec.

PART II

SOCIAL CREDIT IN QUEBEC: ITS DEVELOPMENT

2
The Social Credit Movement in Quebec, 1936-57: The Mobilization Phase

In the previous chapter I argued that Créditisme is essentially a right-wing protest movement. As one type of political movement, its nature and development patterns reflect the more general patterns of development in political movements. In particular, political movements have been found to evolve in a manner which mirrors the outlooks and skills of different types of leaders who tend to emerge at different points of time. Thus I argued that the first generation of Créditiste directors were 'prophets' or 'men of words' who seemed admirably suited to the initial tasks of mass mobilization. They were able to translate Major Douglas' doctrine into terms which were meaningful for a large segment of the rural and small-urban population of Quebec in the 1940s and early 1950s. They managed to weld a small but devoted band of militants into organized cadres of a movement capable of sustaining a wide readership for the official journal, *Vers Demain*, as well as some persistent electoral support. However, they were unable to lead the movement to electoral or political success. It required a different group of leaders with a different set of skills and attitudes to achieve some modicum of political success. In this chapter I shall examine the mobilization phase of the Créditiste movement.

It is important, however, to begin by locating the Créditiste movement more precisely on the ideological spectrum by first summarizing the ideas on which the ideology of the movement is based: the social credit doctrine of Major Douglas. These ideas must also be examined from a more general comparative perspective of right-wing political thought and ideology. A second step is to explore briefly the ideological and organizational antecedents of the Quebec movement in the Social Credit success in Alberta. I shall also dissect the ideology of Créditisme itself, as it was developed by the founders and editors of *Vers Demain*. Finally I shall trace the patterns of organization and action in the movement from its inception until the end of the mobilization phase under the direction of the Union des Electeurs.

A THE DOCTRINE OF MAJOR DOUGLAS

Social credit is the name given to the ideas first expounded by Major C.H. Douglas.[1]

1 Clifford Hugh Douglas (1878–1952), Scottish mechanical engineer and major in the Royal

Most English Canadians believe that it is merely a theory of monetary reform, and it is true that *Economic Democracy, Credit-Power and Democracy,* and *Social Credit,* the first important book-length statements of Major Douglas' theory, were largely just that.[2] But Douglas also provided important early indications in these books of the normative and epistemological assumptions and the intellectual traditions underlying his economic proposals. These same assumptions remained the bases of his later analyses of other spheres of social life. His entire body of writings must therefore be treated as a coherent social philosophy encompassing all facets of man's temporal existence.

The intellectual traditions which shaped Douglas' thought are most fully described in *Social Credit.* In it Douglas contrasted two systems of education or philosophies which were prevalent in British public schools and universities at the time he began writing (just after the first world war): the Aristotelian or classical system, and the Baconian or inductive system. The classical system, which he defined as 'the embodiment of an attractive or artistic ideal of the nature of society,' emphasized the moral qualities of the individual in shaping social action. Material progress was seen by its adherents as antithetical to the classical ideal, and observed defects in social organization were attributed by them to defects in man's character rather than to human institutions.[3] In contrast, the inductive school based its conceptions of society on modern experimental methods used in the natural sciences: 'It refuses to admit, as a fact, anything which cannot be demonstrated, and as a theory, anything which does not fit the facts.'[4] This approach tended to lead its adherents to accept deterministic social theories or, in Douglas' words, 'that people's actions, thoughts and morals are the outcome of more or less blind forces to which they are subjected, and in regard to which, both censure and praise are equally out of place.'[5]

Douglas was clearly a product of the Baconian school both by training and inclina-

Air Force Reserve, formulated his theory of social credit during his term of service as assistant director of the Royal Aircraft Works. On the basis of comprehensive studies of cost accounting which he had conducted in a number of British industries, Douglas concluded that the weekly sum total of wages and salaries was continuously less than the weekly collective price of the goods produced. (J.A. Irving, *The Social Credit Movement in Alberta* (Toronto: University of Toronto Press, 1959), 5.) His first statements of this discovery appeared in the English periodicals *Organiser, English Review,* and the *New Age,* from 1917 to 1919. (C.B. Macpherson, *Democracy in Alberta: The Theory and Practice of a Quasi-party System* (Toronto: University of Toronto Press, 1953), 121.)

2 *Economic Democracy* (London: Cecil Palmer, 1920); *Credit-Power and Democracy, with a Draft Scheme for the Mining Industry* (London: Cecil Palmer, 1920); *Social Credit* (London: Cecil Palmer, 1924). A fourth book, *The Control and Distribution of Production* (London: Cecil Palmer, 1922), was also written during this early period, but it does not appear to have been as innovative or as influential with Douglas' followers. *Economic Democracy* and *Social Credit* have recently been republished in paperback editions by Omni Publications, Hawthorne, California. All future citations from these books are drawn from these editions.

3 C.H. Douglas, *Social Credit,* (4th ed; Hawthorne, California: Omni Publications, 1966), 4 (henceforth cited as *Social Credit*).

4 *Ibid.,* 5.

5 *Ibid.,* 6.

tion, and he therefore directed his strongest criticism at the myths propagated by the adherents of the classical viewpoint. However, he attempted to surmount the limitations inherent in the determinism of the inductive school by anchoring his critique of society in a conception of the primacy and ultimate free will of the individual. He therefore argued that truth lies somewhere in between the two viewpoints. In his view,

with the less fortunately situated strata of society, a theory of economic determinism would be a sound and accurate explanation for the actions of 98 per cent of the persons to whom it might be applied ... But this is not true of their more fortunate contemporaries. There are, without a doubt, circumstances in the world in which the personal conceptions of individuals can have powerful and far-reaching consequences on their immediate and even national or continental environment.[6]

The conception of the individual which Douglas made the core of his critique of the economic, political, and social systems was that of the human being with few resources and limited expertise surrounded by powerful and increasingly hostile institutional forces not readily susceptible to either human understanding or human will. These forces, of which the financial system of capitalism was the most powerful, were destroying the inherent tendency of human beings to preserve their individuality as against the collectivity and to assert their natural right to a proper place in society and to economic security.[7] Although he failed to offer a clear statement of his metaphysical beliefs, Douglas appears to have grounded his conception of society and of human nature in a theory of natural rights and natural law.[8]

Douglas turned first to the economic realm in an effort to explain why this natural condition of man had been so severely contorted. Following his empiricist inclinations and his professional bent, he focused immediately on what he considered to be the scientific aspect of the problem in the workings of the economic system. In *Economic Democracy* he wrote that the individual was unable to achieve freedom and security because he lacked sufficient purchasing power to buy the products manufactured by the producer. There was a plentiful supply of goods, but no one to buy them. The explanation for this lay in the relationship between prices on the one hand and wages, salaries, profits, or dividends on the other.

It is clear that the total amount distributed in wages, salaries and profits or dividends, would be less by a considerable sum (representing purchases on factory account) than the total selling price of the product during the same period, *and if this is true in one factory it must be true in all.* Consequently, the *rate* at which money is liberated by manufacturing processes of this nature is clearly less than the *rate* at which the total selling price of the product increases. This difference is due to the fact that while the final price to the consumer of any manufactured article is steadily growing with the time required for manufacture, during the same time the money distributed by the manu-

6 *Ibid.*, 6–7.
7 *Economic Democracy* (5th ed; Hawthorne, California: Omni Publications, 1967), 16
  (henceforth cited as *Economic Democracy*).
8 *Ibid.*, 16.

facturing process is being returned to the capitalist through purchases for immediate consumption.[9]

This condition was, in his view, a clear case of 'economic sabotage; a colossal waste of effort which goes on in every walk of life quite unobserved by the majority of the people because they are so familiar with it; a waste which yet so over-taxed the ingenuity of society to extend it that the climax of war only occurred in the moment when a culminating exhibition of organized sabotage was necessary to preserve the system from spontaneous combustion.'[10]

Following what he considered to be the proper orientation of the inductive school, Douglas claimed to abstract this theory from personal experiences and observations of capitalist society during and immediately after the war. It was a period in which huge sums had been expended by nations on their war machines, large debts had been accumulated, and severe restrictions had been imposed on the purchase of goods and services. The waste in both human and material resources had been stupendous. And yet the end of the war had failed to bring a return to economic normalcy. As a result, the ideas of the classical economists were being subjected to severe criticism for the first time.[11]

But Douglas went beyond the economic mechanism in his explanation of the prevailing condition of society. He attributed the increasing concentration of control in the economic, political, and social spheres to a basic human will-to-power, which he regarded as a manifestation of 'misapplied Darwinism.'[12] The solution to this unhappy situation was to return initiative and independence to the individual by decentralizing the economic system and providing the consumer with the requisite purchasing power to overcome the inherent deficiency in demand. This might be done by establishing ratios between production costs and purchasing power to correspond to a just price; that is, 'the price at which an article can be effectively distributed in the community producing it.'[13]

In *Credit-Power and Democracy,* Douglas elaborated on the role which finance and credit play in the economic system. He attacked the Fabian socialists and Marxists for misplacing their critique of capitalism by calling for worker control of production. The proper area of concern was control of policy, not administration, and 'the last word on policy is with finance ... and is concerned with the control of credit by the banks.' It follows, therefore, that 'to democratize the policy of production we have to democratize the control of credit.'[14] The right of the individual to

9 *Ibid.,* 65. (Italics in original.)

10 *Ibid.,* 79.

11 Douglas was clearly influenced by the socialist critics among his contemporaries, as indicated by his occasional references to J.A. Hobson, Sidney Webb, Thorstein Veblen and others (Douglas rarely footnoted or took care to acknowledge intellectual debts). However, he makes no mention of having been influenced by earlier and contemporary monetary reform theorists and seems to have regarded his theory as a totally original contribution in this respect. See Hugh Gaitskell, 'Four Monetary Heretics,' in G.D.H. Cole (ed), *What Every-body Wants to Know About Money* (London 1933), 346–75.

12 *Economic Democracy,* 35, 20.

13 *Ibid.,* 132.

14 *Credit-Power and Democracy, with a Draft Scheme from the Mining Industry* (2nd ed; London: Cecil Palmer, 1921), 6 (henceforth cited as *Credit-Power and Democracy*).

credit democratization and ultimate consumer control lay in his share of one of the essential factors of production, namely 'the common heritage of the community.' This was defined as the knowledge and expertise accumulated by the community over centuries which along with land, labour, and capital constituted a basic ingredient of any product.[15]

The gap between prices and purchasing power was explained in terms of what was later called the 'A plus B theorem.' It was a more precise statement of the earlier argument in *Economic Democracy*. According to Douglas, if a factory or productive organization is considered in its financial aspect as a device for the distribution of purchasing power to individuals through the media of wages, salaries, and dividends and also as a creator of prices or 'financial values,' then its payments may be divided into two groups: group A, representing all payments made to individuals in the form of wages, salaries, and dividends; and group B, representing all payments made to other organizations for raw materials, bank charges, and other external costs. The fault in the economic mechanism of production, then, is that

The rate of flow of purchasing power to individuals is represented by A, but since all payments go into prices, the rate of flow of prices cannot be less than A + B. The product of any factory may be considered as something which the public ought to buy, although in many cases it is an intermediate product of no use to individuals but only to a subsequent manufacture; but since A will not purchase A + B, a proportion of the product at least equivalent to B must be distributed by a form of purchasing-power which is not comprised in the descriptions grouped under A.[16]

The solution which Douglas offered to this economic fault was now defined more precisely in the form of a dividend payment made directly to the consumer. Since 'all credit values are communal,' the consumer had a right to such a payment in much the same way as a worker has a right to a wage, except that the dividend could now be used to replace the wage. In Douglas' view, 'the dividend is the logical successor to the wage, carrying with it the privileges which the wage never had and never can have, whether it be rechristened pay, salary or any other alias; because the nature of all these is a *dole of purchasing power revocable by authority,* whereas a dividend is a payment, absolute and unconditional, of something due.'[17]

The reform which Douglas proposed did not involve nationalization of any processes of production by the public. Douglas considered this to be the administration or 'how' of production, which was the proper preserve of administrative specialists or experts. What was crucial, however, was that the public should control the policy or results of production by assuming responsibility for both credit-issue and price-making, as well as the effective appointment and removal of personnel. His image of a healthy economic system consisted of 'a functionally aristocratic hierarchy of producers accredited by, and serving, a democracy of consumers.'[18]

15 *Ibid.,* p 18. The term 'cultural inheritance of the community' was used for the same concept in *Economic Democracy*, 93. Macpherson defines it as 'the cultural heritage.' Macpherson, 103–7.
16 *Economic Democracy*, 22.
17 *Ibid.,* 43–4. (Italics in original.)   18 *Ibid.,* 94.

In *Social Credit* Douglas attempted to place this entire economic analysis within a broader social philosophical framework. The basic fault of the economic system – deficiency of purchasing power – was attributed in large part to the ability of supporters of the existing capitalist system to provide a moral theory rationalizing the economic status quo. This theory, derived from the classical or moral theory of society, offered as its central tenet the idea of rewards and punishments, which may be crudely summarized as 'be good and you will be rewarded.' In economic terms the theory meant that if one worked hard at one's job, accepted the existing authority, and observed prevailing norms, one would receive his just due in terms of wages, profits, or other income. The principle was extended to all spheres of social life, so as to encourage collectivist (or unselfish) rather than individual (or selfish) action, thrift rather than consumption, deliberate restriction in supply (economy) rather than overproduction (waste), devotion to the larger society and the state (patriotism) rather than the self, the conception of the money system as a reward system rather than an ordering device, and the restriction of human and material energy rather than its full exploitation.[19]

Several institutional devices or mechanisms were used to maintain this classical ideal. They included the legal system, which operates its own direct system of rewards and punishments based on many of the preceding concepts; theories of the classical economists such as the explanation of underconsumption in terms of overinvestment of savings by producers;[20] the tendency to treat reduction of hours of work or automation as unemployment and an evil rather than as leisure and a potential good; the pre-eminence of permanent bureaucrats and the ineffectiveness of popular controls in democratic political systems; the use of the taxation system to impose heavy burdens and ultimate servitude on the population; and world power politics.[21] All of these myths and devices would be removed when the system of social credit was finally understood and accepted at the decisive moment in history.[22] Thus, Douglas concluded:

It hardly needs emphasis that a constant binding back of proposals for reform, to the moving events of the world, is of the utmost value; in fact, if it be possible to clarify the relation between the analysis of the financial system, the foci of discontent, and the logical remedy, with sufficient emphasis and over a sufficiently wide area, then the stage will be set for the greatest victory which the human individual has, within history, achieved over the forces which beset him to his fall.[23]

Major Douglas believed that within a short space of time his analysis would be accepted as definitive, his solution implemented, and the major economic ills of the world alleviated. But he was soon sorely disappointed. His theory was almost

19 *Social Credit*, part I, chapters 1–8.
20 This theory is associated with J.A. Hobson, as Douglas points out. See *ibid.*, part II, chapter 1, 82–6.
21 *Ibid.*, part II, chapters 1–7.
22 *Ibid.*, part III, chapters 1–3.
23 *Ibid.*, 204–5.

universally condemned by economists, and none of the three major parties in Britain adopted his proposal as a plank in its platform.[24] His own non-political movement, organized in 1919 to mobilize public support for his proposals of economic reform and thereby to pressure the government to implement them, failed to grow.[25] A commission established during the depression to consider social credit along with other proposals as possible solutions rejected Major Douglas' theory completely.[26] But the Major, plodding on relentlessly in his effort to gain acceptance of his ideas, wrote *Warning Democracy, The Monopoly of Credit,* and *The Brief for the Prosecution.*[27] The three early and three later books, together with his numerous journalistic articles and pamphlets,[28] became the basis for Canadian social credit doctrine.[29]

24 The national executive of the Labour party established a special committee in 1922, headed by Sidney Webb and including R.H. Tawney, J.A. Hobson, and G.D.H. Cole, to examine the theory. Both Douglas and his then close collaborator, A.R. Orage, editor of the *New Age,* refused to appear before it on the grounds that it included too many socialists. The committee found that the scheme was 'theoretically unsound and unworkable in practice.' W.R. Hiskett, *Social Credit or Socialism* (London 1935), 6. See also Macpherson, 123.
25 C.B. Macpherson quotes Philip Mairet, a disciple of Major Douglas, to the effect that the Douglasites were 'a sprinkling of scattered groups of earnest students' from 1919 to 1930. C.B. Macpherson, 124. See also George Thayer, *The British Political Fringe: A Profile* (London: Anthony Blond, 1965), 105–11. He writes: '[Douglas'] demands were rejected not only because of their unfamiliar nature but because Britain's Social Credit Party, from the moment it was founded, was subjected to a split [between Douglas, its philosopher, and Hargraves, its activist]' (106).
26 The commission was the Macmillan Committee on Finance and Industry, established in 1930. In May of that year Major Douglas appeared before it and gave evidence to support his thesis. He was then subjected to a gruelling question period, in which several fallacies in his theory were demonstrated. See Hiskett, *op. cit.,* chapter 4. See also the summary of Douglas' Statement of Evidence submitted before the committee and the addenda offered to the committee on request after cross-examination, in C.H. Douglas, *The Monopoly of Credit* (3rd ed rev; Stratford-on-Avon: KRP Publications, 1958), appendix I.
27 *Warning Democracy* (London: C.M. Grieve, 1931); *The Monopoly of Credit* (London: Chapman & Hall, 1931); *The Brief for the Prosecution* (London: KRP Publications, 1946). The last two books have been reissued by KRP Publications respectively in 1958 and nd. Henceforth, all citations from these books will be taken from these editions.
28 The most important articles and pamphlets include: 'Reconstruction,' *Glasgow Evening Times,* May 1932; 'The Use of Money,' an address delivered in St. James's Theatre, Christchurch, New Zealand, 13 February 1934; 'The Nature of Democracy,' speech made at Buxton, 9 June 1934; 'Money and the Price System,' speech delivered at Oslo, 14 February 1935; 'The Approach to Reality,' address at Westminster, 7 March 1936; 'The Tragedy of Human Effort,' address at Liverpool, 30 October 1936; 'The Policy of a Philosophy,' address in London, 26 June 1937; 'Security: Institutional and Personal,' address in Newcastle-upon-Tyne, 9 March 1937; 'The Big Idea,' reprinted from *Social Crediter,* January to May 1942; 'The "Land for the (Chosen) People" Racket,' reprinted from *Social Crediter,* December 1942 to March 1943; 'Programme for the Third World War,' reprinted from *Social Crediter,* April to August 1943; 'Realistic Constitutionalism,' address at Mayfair, 8 May 1947; 'The Realistic Position of the Church of England,' reprinted from *Social Crediter,* October to November 1948; and 'Whose Service is Perfect Freedom,' *Fig Tree,* a Douglas Social Credit quarterly review, New Series: no. 4. March 1955, reprinted from *Social Crediter,* 3 June 1939 to 20 April 1940. All of these articles and pamphlets are reprinted and available from KRP Publications, 245, Cann Hall Road, London, E11.
29 As the ideas presented in these later books and articles are essentially repetitive of the

As C.B. Macpherson has so brilliantly documented, there was also a rudimentary political theory in Douglas' writings, although it was presented in a very fragmented and undeveloped manner.[30] It first appeared in *Economic Democracy* and *Credit-Power and Democracy* and was expanded somewhat in later writings after Douglas had shifted his concerns in part from the economic to the political sphere.[31] Following his empirical bent, Douglas emphatically rejected all idealistic interpretations of the state, arguing that it was merely an abstraction, having no existence apart from its governmental functions and the people who perform them.[32] The constitution, too, was largely camouflage for those who held the reins of power. Democratic constitutions merely served to conceal the fact that real government was in the hands of the financiers, so that 'so far from embodying Abraham Lincoln's definition ... as being "of the people, by the people, for the people" they are coming to be instruments for the expression and furtherance of interests which in many cases threaten the general population with catastrophe.'[33] These financiers had as their aides, both willingly and unwittingly, the elected representatives and party politicians. The objective of these people was to assert their control over the individual, eradicate dissent, and maintain the citizens in economic bondage to them.[34] The basic assumption underlying this analysis was precisely the same as that in Douglas' economic theory. The individual was sacred and desired freedom and economic security. The two values must somehow be reconciled, and the prevailing system of liberal democracy failed to do so.[35]

Douglas went on to analyse more fully the reasons for democracy's failure to live up to its ideals. In the first place, the elected representatives of the people were chosen to legislate, which they were unqualified to do: 'Democracy consists in empowering a set of pseudo-experts, elected by majorities of non-experts at stated intervals, to pass highly technical laws which are ultimately enforceable by all the tremendous powers of the state, and become effective upon those institutions and organizations which perform the positive functions of production and distribution.'[36]

economic and social philosophy presented in Douglas' early books, they will not be summarized here. For a detailed treatment of these books and articles, see Philip Mairet, *The Douglas Manual* (New York: Coward McCann, nd), W.R. Hiskett and J.A. Franklin, *Searchlight on Social Credit* (London: P.S. King & Son, 1939), and Macpherson, chapters 5 and 7.

30 Macpherson, 125. The analysis of Douglas' political ideas which is presented here closely follows that of Macpherson.

31 *Ibid.*, 125. Macpherson attributes this shift in emphasis to Douglas' frustration over the bad reception which his ideas had earned from economists. According to a disciple of Douglas, L.D. Byrne, the change in emphasis from economic to political ideas was not due to disappointment over the criticism Douglas received, but rather 'he turned to a wider problem – the political.' L.D. Byrne, 'Mr Macpherson's Feud,' *The Fig Tree,* New Series, 2 (September 1954), 61.

32 *Economic Democracy*, 22. See also Macpherson, 125.

33 C.H. Douglas, *The Alberta Experiment: An Interim Survey* (London: Eyre and Spottiswoods, 1937), 42.

34 *Credit-Power and Democracy*, 145. See also Macpherson, 125–6.

35 Macpherson, 126.

36 *The Alberta Experiment*, 48–9.

Thus no effective popular controls were being exercized on permanent bureaucrats.[37] Second, and more important, the party system, rather than being a necessary part of a functioning liberal democracy, was a deliberate contrivance of the financiers and their allies to deflect the attention of the citizens away from the shortcomings of the system. It was the conscious aim of the party politicians and political wire-pullers, according to Douglas, 'to submit to the decision of the electorate *only alternative methods of embodying the same policy,*' and 'to direct public attention to a profitless wrangle in regard to methods.'[38] In this manner, according to Macpherson, Douglas saw 'the democratic party system ... as a means of thwarting the real will of the people by ensuring that they voted only on issues about which they were not competent to judge their own interest.'[39] Thus for Douglas 'democracy ... defined as the rule of the majority ... is a mere trap, set by knaves to catch simpletons; the *rule* of the majority never has existed, and fortunately, never will exist.'[40]

As in his economic theory, Douglas went beyond a diagnosis and offered a cure as well. In *Credit-Power and Democracy* he outlined what he considered to be real democracy. It would realize the policy (ie, objectives) of the majority but allow a minority of so-called experts to decide the details of policy-making and implementation. 'Real democracy is ... the expression of the *policy* of the majority, and so far as that policy is concerned with economics, is the freedom of an increasing majority of individuals to make use of the facilities provided for them, in the first place, by a number of persons who will always be, as they have always been, in the minority.'[41] In other words, according to Macpherson, Douglas thought 'the people should be consulted only about the broadest objectives, and that all else ... should be left to the experts, subject only to the people's right to remove the experts who failed to produce the results.'[42] The precise form that this real democracy would take (ie, a parliamentary system or some variant of direct democracy) was left indeterminate. One thing, however, was clearly established: the political elite responsible for making and implementing the policy was not supposed to discuss details and even principles of social credit doctrine with the mass of the people. Matters of a technical nature were felt to be beyond the comprehension or competence of the people and had to be delegated by them to the experts as a matter of trust. Thus Douglas argued:

Instead of electing representatives to inform bankers and industrialists (who understand

---

37 *Social Credit,* 127. Douglas states here: 'The ostensible, or "Political" head of a great Government Department, is a mere tool in the hands of the superior Permanent Officials (and this is preeminently so in the case of the Treasury). It is not a difficult matter for the Permanent Officials of a Government Department to obtain the removal of the Political Head of it, but it is a matter of practical impossibility for the Political Head to obtain the removal of one of his own Permanent Officials. As a result, "Democracy", of which we hear so much, is defeated at the source.'

38 *Ibid.,* 126. (Italics in original.) Also quoted in Macpherson, 127.

39 Macpherson, 127.

40 *Credit-Power and Democracy,* 7. (Italics in original.) Also quoted in Macpherson, 127.

41 *Ibid.,* 8. (Italics in original.) Also quoted in Macpherson, 127.

42 Macpherson, 128.

the technique of their jobs perfectly) how to do them, and to pass a multitude of laws which, while providing unnecessary jobs for large numbers of people who could be better employed, still further impede industry, the business of democracy is to elect representatives who will insist upon results, and will, if necessary, pillory the actual individuals who are responsible either for the attainment of results or their non-attainment. It is not a bit of use asking democracies to decide upon matters of technique, and it is quite certain, as has already been demonstrated, that if you throw a plan to a democracy it will be torn to shreds.[43]

It was, in short, a form of plebiscitarian democracy that Douglas was advocating, but one so extreme in its delegation as to verge on technocracy.[44]

Douglas claimed that his theory was universal and not bound to any class; proof of this supposedly lay in the fact that all men are consumers of one sort or another. The Douglas economic theory was designed to improve the lot of this universal grouping. But as Macpherson astutely observes, the social credit doctrine had a special appeal for a very small segment of society which Marxists have called petit bourgeois.[45] This class is composed of individuals who are owners of the means of production, but whose position is ever more precarious because of the competition from larger owners and monopolies. They support the capitalist system of private ownership, since it is the source of their livelihood, but fear its evolution into large concentrated units. And they desire a greater share of the ever larger and more plentiful economic pie.

The attraction which social credit had for these people is self-evident. Social credit was a reform which required no radical transformation of the existing economic and social structure. It offered to the small property owner an opportunity to get rid of his excess production by stimulating demand among potential consumers. And it gave him, as a consumer, an opportunity to share in the new rewards.[46] Perhaps the most appealing part of the doctrine, however, was its emphasis on the individual as against the group. This had both a class and a universal attraction. Individualism was central in the thinking of the petit bourgeois who valued his status as an independent property owner and feared submergence in the larger forces of concentra-

43 'The Nature of Democracy,' speech made at Buxton, 9 June 1934 (London: KRP Publications, nd), 12.
44 Macpherson, 130. A similar marriage between the ideas of plebiscitarian democracy and rule by so-called experts was later attempted by both Aberhart in Alberta and Even in Quebec. See chapter 2. Macpherson points out that ideas of plebiscitarian democracy were also present in the early political thought of the United Farmers of Alberta. Macpherson, 48ff. See also V.C. Ferkiss, 'Populist Influence in American Fascism,' *Western Political Quarterly*, 10 (1967), for similar ideas in American politics. Byrne claims that Douglas' principles of democracy (in *Credit-Power and Democracy*) were to apply to the economy rather than the polity. He adds: 'Douglas never put forward a new scheme of parliamentary government. He did point out why democratic parliamentary governments are *not* responsive to the will of the people, and he did enunciate in very explicit terms the *principles* by which established, parliamentary institutions could be made instruments of genuine political democracy.' Byrne, 'Mr. Macpherson's Feud,' 66. (Italics in original).
45 Macpherson, 93.
46 *Ibid.*, 93–4. In Britain, the doctrine nevertheless appears to have made little headway among the petit bourgeois class. It appealed mainly to shifting and fringe urban groups.

tion represented by the industrialists and the trade unions. But it also had meaning for the much larger collection of people who, for one reason or another, valued their individuality and freedom of choice and feared that both were being undermined.[47]

Despite the apparent neatness and potential appeal of Douglas' theories, there were obvious weaknesses in them so that they soon came under attack. The economic theory was the first target of criticism. It was pointed out that Douglas had failed to give proper consideration to the time gaps involved in the flow of payments. Money saved or invested in one period would be used for consumption in a later period. And payments made by primary producers would be available for consumption immediately or in the next period.[48] But these objections were generally dismissed by Douglasites as sophistry; they could point to the fact that there was depression, overproduction, and a shortage of money. This was sufficient to convince them that Douglas' explanation was correct. There was, moreover, much documented proof that some form of restrictive financial control was being exerted. It did not matter to them that the A plus B theorem failed to stand up to analytical criticism; there was sufficient evidence, in their view, to support the broader case for social credit based on the doctrine of cultural heritage and the notion of a financial conspiracy.[49] And those who opposed them in their beliefs could easily be dismissed as the unconscious or willing dupes of the controlling authorities.

47 *Ibid.*, 96. This interpretation of Douglas is challenged by L.D. Byrne, a collaborator of the Major's and later a member of the Alberta Social Credit Board, in an interesting review of Macpherson's book, published in *The Fig Tree*, New Series, 2 (September 1954). Byrne writes (54): 'Douglas saw the Universe as an integrated unity centered in the Creator and subject to His Law ... It was inherent in Douglas' writings that he viewed society as something partaking of the nature of an organism which could have life and life more abundant to the extent that it was God-centred and obedient to His Canon. Such a social organism would be the corporate expression of the lives and relationships of its component individuals. Within it, the sovereignty of God being absolute, there must be full recognition of the sanctity of the human personality, and therefore of the individual as free to live his own life, and within the body social, to enter into or contract out of such associations with others as, with responsibility to his Creator, he may choose.' This God-centred and organic concept of society is much closer to the ideas later expounded by Louis Even and Gilberte Côté-Mercier. However, I was unable to find such an explicit statement of the relationship between Douglas' theology and social philosophy in his books and pamphlets.
48 On this point see Hiskett, 186ff., and Macpherson, 110. Keynes, who was one of the members of the Macmillan Committee, acknowledged that Douglas had pointed to a major fault in the classical system, the leakage in the savings-investment equation caused by deficient investment demand. Hence planned savings may not equal planned investment, although actual savings are always equal to actual investment, as the classicists maintained. Keynes wrote of Douglas: 'The strength of Major Douglas' advocacy has, of course, largely depended on orthodoxy having no valid reply to much of his destructive criticism. On the other hand, the detail of his diagnosis, in particular the so-called A + B theorem, includes much mere mystification. If Major Douglas had limited his B-items to the financial provisions made by entrepreneurs to which no current expenditure on replacements and renewals corresponds, he would be nearer the truth. But even in this case it is necessary to allow for the possibility of these provisions being offset by new investment in other directions as well as by increased expenditure on consumption.' J.M. Keynes, *The General Theory of Employment, Interest and Money* (1st ed reprinted; London: Macmillan, 1959), 370–1. I am indebted to Terence Russell for this reference.
49 Macpherson, 112.

The same line of defence was applied by Douglas' followers to his social philosophic theory, but here much of Douglas' analysis could be upheld on logical
grounds. Douglas' stress on individual self-fulfilment, his criticisms of the work
fetishism of contemporary industrialized society, and his warnings against the dangers
of bureaucratic growth and concentration were all plausible or well-founded. But the
Douglasites, instead of discriminating between what was more or less valid, what was
practical, and what was purely utopian, tended to defend the entire corpus of
doctrine as an integral body of truth and a panacea to the world's problems. As a
result, when they failed to win acceptance of their ideas, they began increasingly to
resort to conspiracy theories to explain the ills of society. The financial system was
depicted as under the control of bankers made up largely of Jews and Freemasons,
who used forms of suggestion or black magic, along with their normal financial
weapons, to maintain their world domination.[50]

It seemed clear then, that for the original Douglas converts,[51] and for many of
his later followers both in Alberta and Quebec, social credit was something far more
than a doctrine or theory that they found intellectually compatible or convincing;
it was rather a total belief system which provided answers to all their questions and
solutions for all their daily problems.[52]

50 This was a logical extension of Douglas' earlier theory, developed particularly after 1936
   (although notions of a conspiracy also appear in the early writings). See Macpherson, 179.
   Douglas' anti-Semitism, which was implicit in his early writings, became more and more
   virulent in the period from 1936 until his death in 1952. He wrote in 1939: 'It is my conviction
   that centralisation is being fostered everywhere and from the same source and with the same
   object – world dominion ... The swift progress towards State capitalism everywhere [has]
   Jewish Finance at the apex of the pyramid ... Jewry as a whole has a permanent policy which
   aims at establishing the individual Jew as a member of a "chosen," superior and dominant
   ruling class in every country and over the whole world ... The sphere in which the Jewish
   race operates so largely as very nearly to control is that sphere which was regarded in the
   Middle Ages as the sphere of "black magic," but which we now term "suggestion" or the
   "psychology of the unconscious." ' 'Whose Service is Perfect Freedom,' 150, 152, 154. Anti-
   semitism is frequently a component of right-wing thought. See Ferkiss; also Ernest Nolte,
   Three Faces of Fascism (New York: Holt, Rinehart and Winston, 1966).
51 Douglas never had a large following in Britain, and the number rapidly declined after the
   1935 election campaign in which Douglas participated as the head of a pressure group. His
   efforts in this campaign to convince candidates to adopt the social credit theory as part of
   their platform were rejected by all but a few, and these candidates were all resoundingly
   defeated. See Thayer, 106–11; Macpherson, 139–41, and Colin Cross, *The Fascists in Britain*
   (London: Barrie and Rockliff, 1961). For a general discussion of the movement during this
   period, see W.L. Bardsley, 'The Social Credit Movement, 1918–1939,' *Social Crediter*, 23
   December 1939. At the time that the 1935 campaign was conducted, the English Social
   Credit party (its new name at that time) was said to have had about a thousand members.
   Douglas later disassociated himself from the party but continued as the head of the Douglas
   secretariat in London until his death. In a recent British general election (1964) there was one
   Social Credit candidate. The Social Credit secretariat, which calls itself a 'non-party, non-class
   organization neither connected with nor supporting any political party, Social Credit or
   otherwise,' retains a small office today at 245 Cann Hall Road, Leytonstone, London, and
   continues to publish a newspaper called *Social Crediter*.
52 For an analysis of the ideological evolution of the Social Credit movements in Britain and
   in Alberta, see Macpherson; He states (111): 'The A plus B theorem, once lodged in the

B THE ALBERTA SUCCESS, 1935

No less great in its impact on the early development of the social credit movement in Quebec was the success achieved by the Alberta Social Credit wing in the 1935 election under the leadership of William Aberhart. The Alberta movement served as an example of the potential for political success in the ideas of Major Douglas. It also acted as a model of effective political leadership, campaign organization, and government. Quebec Créditistes are wont to cite the Alberta experiment as proof of the superior quality of social credit beliefs, judiciously applied.

The success of social credit in Alberta was first of all due to its skilful advocacy by William Aberhart, the Calgary high school principal and preacher, who later became the first social credit leader anywhere to hold elected office.[53] Aberhart, introduced social credit into his Bible broadcasts, held on Sunday mornings every week, after he had been converted overnight to the doctrine in the autumn of 1932. Within two years he had made it a major topic of discussion in every Alberta household. And in 1935, running on a platform which had social credit monetary reform as its central plank and using the convenient headquarters of his Bible school to co-ordinate and direct operations he captured 56 of the 63 seats in the Alberta legislature and swept into power.

The immediate attraction which social credit had for Aberhart and his closest followers was similar to that which the Douglas doctrine had had in Britain for the small group of Douglasites: it was an all-embracing social philosophy which explained many of their psychological, social, and economic frustrations. For Aberhart it provided a temporal touchstone for his evangelical and eschatological beliefs and an outlet for his social conscience. In the case of his closest collaborators, it served as a similar outlet for their religious missionary zeal. Aberhart's earliest supporters

mind, was very difficult to dislodge. It had an almost hypnotic quality for those who were disposed to believe it and were not accustomed to close abstract reasoning.' And (112): 'It need not be suggested that all those who found merit in the Douglas theory were incapable of understanding a logical analysis of it. But they were not apt to be impressed by even the most able criticism, for the critics were suspect.' And most notably (119): 'This curious relation between the technical analysis and the broader case facilitated the peculiar relation between leader and followers which came to characterize the social credit movement both in England and later in Alberta ... Douglas, convinced that he had got at the fundamental truth, could not admit the fallacies in the technical theory. Nor could he repair them. He was therefore compelled after a time to take the position that the technical theory was not a matter for discussion. Soon the whole social credit movement was committed to this position. The leader and his small group of experts became the acknowledged and sole custodians of the mysteries. It is obvious that the social credit doctrine has served as a means of ensuring devotion to the leader and his goals by a core group of true believers.' This tendency for doctrine to serve as a total belief system has been noted in many other political movements. See, for example, E. Hoffer, *The True Believer* (New York: Harper, 1951), 78–82, and R. Heberle, *Social Movements: An Introduction to Political Sociology* (New York: Appleton Century-Croft, 1951), 117.

53 Aberhart was leader of the movement from its inception, but he did not initially seek a seat in the provincial legislature. After the sweeping social credit victory in 1935, however, he accepted an unanimous invitation to become the premier of Alberta, competed in a by-election for a seat vacated voluntarily by one of his supporters, and won overwhelmingly. See Macpherson, 162–3.

and the movement's most fervent devotees were drawn from those regions in southern Alberta which not only had experienced the severest economic hardships during the depression, but had also nourished the most deep-rooted religious traditions.[54] It was also for these followers a cause to which they could devote their energies in order to satisfy feelings of uprootedness and anomie. Irving notes that 'the depression had impaired the status of many of [his supporters]; Aberhart lifted the heavy burden of failure from their lives, and started them on the road back from ego displacement to ego enhancement.[55] The Social Crediters internalized the doctrine, translated it in terms of the Alberta experience, and then sold it to thousands of their provincial compatriots.

Their success can first of all be understood in terms of the affinity which the new ideology had with traditional prairie radical beliefs. In the case of Alberta, the United Farmers, the ruling provincial political movement from 1919 until 1935, had articulated a coherent social and political theory reflecting the prevailing political culture.[56] It was, in many respects, similar to that simultaneously being developed by Major Douglas in Britain. Aberhart was able to build from this base.

The tenets of Douglas' social and economic theory which Aberhart used most effectively were the idea of a cultural heritage, the A plus B theorem, the notion of a just price, and a basic dividend. Cultural heritage was translated as the potential of Alberta's resources, which by right belonged to its citizens and thus far had not been exploited except by profiteering investors and absentee property owners who had invaded Alberta from the east. The A plus B theorem served to explain the severe

54 Irving, 61. The combination of religion and social credit doctrine, which also appeared later in Quebec, was not unique to Canada. Although Major Douglas' small group of active devoted followers in Britain was comprised largely of fringe groups, there was nevertheless strong sympathy for the doctrine and widespread interest in its tenets among many British clerical elements. Douglas' doctrine had some influence on Anglican (Anglo-Catholic), Roman Catholic, Congregational, Quaker and Theosophical thinkers. Some Anglican clerics who had flirted with socialism before the first world war and then become disillusioned with it turned to social credit in the 1920s. They also used their institutional connections to help spread social credit doctrine. The affinity between Anglicanism and social credit lay in their common critique of capitalism (which Anglicans viewed as an outgrowth of dissentient Protestantism) and of Marxism. Roman Catholic clerics in England found in social credit some affinity with the credit reform proposals contained in *Quadragesimo Anno,* the Papal encyclical of 1931. This appeal of the doctrine to the establishment religious denominations contrasts notably with its attraction for the fundamentalist sects and cults in Alberta. See W.E. Mann, *Sect, Cult and Church in Alberta* (Toronto: University of Toronto Press, 1955). The doctrine was denounced by the Roman Catholic church authorities in Quebec in the early 1940s. The marriage of religious and political motivations in political movements has been noted in many studies. For example, see Kenneth McNaught, *A Prophet in Politics: A Biography of J.S. Woodsworth* (Toronto: University of Toronto Press, 1959); S.D. Clark, *Movements of Political Protest in Canada, 1640–1840* (Toronto: University of Toronto Press, 1959); and Norman Cohn, *The Pursuit of the Millennium* (New York: Harper Torchbooks, 1961).

55 Irving, 339, The psychological concepts in this quotation are drawn from H. Cantril, *The Psychology of Social Movements* (New York: Wiley, 1944). Similar explanations for the attraction of political movements may be found in Hoffer, chapter XIII, and William Kornhauser, *The Politics of Mass Society* (Glencoe: Free Press, 1959).

56 Macpherson, 145.

depression which was then wracking Alberta, putting many men out of work, causing goods to pile up on shelves of shopkeepers without chance of being sold, and bringing about a drastic decline in the prices of agricultural goods. The just price was for Aberhart a moral notion referring to a desirable and fair level of prices for producers' goods and agricultural machinery which would enable the farmer to buy the materials necessary for his subsistence and occupation at a level low enough to ensure his survival. The basic dividend – his promise to distribute a $100 dividend to all citizens of Alberta immediately upon his election in order to start them on the road to recovery from the depression – became Aberhart's central electoral weapon.[57]

Aberhart was not himself in any real sense a social or economic philosopher or even a disciplined student of these fields. His training had been in mathematics; his avocation was propagandizing and proselytization. He had learned Douglas' doctrine from books after very rapid, though comprehensive, study. He never wished to act as Douglas' ideological disciple and preferred not to immerse himself in doctrinal debate. He was a man of action rather than of ideas, a politician and publicist, as distinct from an ideologue. His strength came not so much from his grasp of what Douglas was propounding but rather from his ability to manipulate and popularize the Major's ideas. The same can be said for all of his closest collaborators in the Social Credit League who were, like him, evangelists of one sort or another. Foremost among them even at that time was Ernest Manning, a prize graduate at Aberhart's Bible school in Calgary and later the premier of Alberta and real leader of the National Social Credit party.[58]

Coupled with this skill in fitting economic and social theory to the prevailing circumstances was the ability of these primary leaders of Social Credit in Alberta to translate and transform Douglas' political ideas into an effective political appeal and organization. Following Douglas, Aberhart emphasized the need for the people to concentrate on broad objectives, such as their common desire to lift themselves out of the morass of poverty and depression and to accept wholeheartedly measures designed and pledged to do so. The really crucial political decisions were left exclusively to the Social Credit leaders. And when a constituency convention chose to disagree with the leadership on a matter which the latter considered to be of some significance, the resolution was simply declared beyond the competence of the mass of the people, and therefore ignored.[59]

This façade of plebiscitarian non-partisan democracy was maintained in other ways. Social Credit candidates were nominated in every constituency but were not considered to be the candidates of any one party. The electors were asked only to pledge that they would support the central social credit plank in the campaign, the

57 *Ibid.,* 149–50.
58 Aberhart and Manning combined some of the qualities of the founders or men of words, who dominate the mobilization phase of a movement, with those of the administrators and publicists who dominate the consolidation phase which follows. They were therefore able successfully to bridge the gap between the two successive phases of the movement and, particularly in Manning's case, maintain their leadership and control while helping to produce the transformation from the first to the second phase.
59 This form of dictatorial control over the militants by the top leaders is frequently found in political movements, as noted in chapter 1 above.

basic dividend. If any of the candidates of the established political parties agreed to incorporate this plank into their program, then the Social Credit electors were duty bound to vote for these candidates.[60] It was also emphasized that these Social Credit candidates, if elected, were to be entirely subordinate to the will of their electors, subject to their recall, and responsible for vocalizing their political demands. Candidates were not required or even expected to present a program. At the same time, it was declared that the elected Social Credit representatives were in no way to interfere with the decisions of the Social Credit experts commissioned by the government to implement the social credit reforms.[61] And even more important, Aberhart demanded for himself and his immediate subordinates, rather than for constituency conventions, the right to choose all Social Credit nominees for parliament, declaring that this was the only way to ensure that real, not fraudulent, Social Crediters would be presented.[62]

With these obstacles removed, it was comparatively easy for the Social Credit leaders to build a powerful mass political movement within a few months. Entire constituency organizations of the traditional political parties, particularly the UFA, were inducted en masse into the Social Credit camp through the simple process of getting them to accept the principle of a basic dividend. Study groups, established in most communities the previous year to permit more people to familiarize themselves with social credit doctrine, were expanded and converted into political nominating conventions charged with the task of presenting a list of suitable local people for consideration as Social Credit candidates.

The sudden and seemingly complete mass conversion to Social Credit in Alberta was due, then, to three principal factors: 1/ philosophy, 2/ leadership, and 3/ strategy and tactics, of which the first, which originally converted the leaders to the movement, was also perhaps the most potent in capturing the allegiance of the population at large. Douglas' doctrine had been transformed into an ideology by the

60 A similar tactic was used by Major Douglas in the 1935 election campaign and by the directors of *Vers Demain* in the various election campaigns which they entered in the 1940s. This tactic maintained the distinction between Social Credit as a mass movement and the traditional political parties, at least in theory. A similar distinction between mass movement and political party was made by both the American Populists and Progressives. See Hofstader, *The Age of Reform* (New York: Alfred A. Knopf, 1955), chapters 3 and 6.

61 This pattern of political organization followed closely the political ideas of Major Douglas in *Credit-Power and Democracy*, 8, and 'The Nature of Democracy,' 43. It also served as an effective method to ensure Aberhart's complete control over the movement (exercised in conjunction with his closest advisers, whom he named to the Social Credit Board and designated as 'experts'). A similar technique of control was used in Quebec by Louis Even and Gilberte Côté-Mercier. Heberle notes that this tendency towards concentration of power in the hands of a small group of leaders exists in the organized core of all social movements. Heberle, 284.

62 A similar rationale was provided by Even and Côté-Mercier to justify their pre-selection of candidates. In reality it was a method of ensuring that the movement would continue under the ideological and political control of its founders as it expanded. Cameron points out that it is precisely this fear of loss of control that creates feelings of ambivalence concerning expansion of the movement in founders of social movements. W.B. Cameron, *Modern Social Movements* (New York: Random House, 1966), 15.

original Alberta converts. This ideology then was expounded and manipulated to appeal to the general public. Both the negative (critical) and positive sides of the ideology were fulfilled in the desperate conditions of the depression, as John A. Irving has described in his careful and illuminating social psychological study of the rise of the movement in Alberta.[63]

It should be emphasized that for Albertan Social Crediters, Major Douglas' doctrine was presented as a form of applied Christianity, and one which fitted in with traditional prairie evangelical beliefs. Although he did not pose as such, Aberhart was seen by many as a prophet of Christ, a redeemer, a new saviour on earth, and his towering physical presence and powerful voice tended to reinforce this conception.[64] In this sense, ideology and leadership became inextricably intertwined, and social credit, as an ideology which transcended the ugly mundanities of traditional political life, responded to the deepest moral and spiritual longings in the people.[65]

C LA LIGUE DU CRÉDIT SOCIAL DE LA PROVINCE DE QUÉBEC, 1936–9
Against the background of fervent activity by Major Douglas in Britain and the stunning success of the Social Credit movement in Alberta, social credit soon aroused public interest in French Canada. The depression was severely felt in the province of Quebec and had helped to turn many Québécois against their federal and provincial governments. The Action Libérale Nationale party attracted support from wide segments of the population who felt antipathy towards the old-line parties and their servile attitude towards the English 'trustards' (monopolists). The resulting political ferment provided the three original mentors of Créditisme in Quebec – Louis

63 Irving described his study as 'a systematic and comprehensive analysis of the rise of the Social Credit movement in Alberta as a phenomenon of mass psychology.' According to him, the ideology of social credit 1 / fitted individual needs and desires into the prevailing social context, 2 / satisfied the individual Albertan's quest for some form of meaning for his daily trials, 3 / provided satisfaction, both material and spiritual, for his daily needs, and 4 / conformed to the prevailing conditions of suggestibility (conduciveness). Irving, 334. These concepts, as Irving himself acknowledges, are drawn from Cantril. The emphasis here on ideology in mobilizing voters has been questioned by several sociologists of social and political movements. See, in particular, Pinard, *The Rise of a Third Party*, 95. See also A. Campbell, P. Converse, W. Miller, and D. Stokes, *The American Voter* (New York: Wiley, 1960), 436. Irving may have been generalizing from his interviews with the Social Credit militants, who tend more to be motivated by ideological factors. For a similar distinction between Créditiste militants and voters in their susceptibility to ideology, see chapter 4.
64 The role of charisma in advancing the cause of a leader and his movement has been well documented by students of political movements. See, for example, Heberle, 132–3, and Hoffer, 109–13. On the contrast between the charismatic qualities of Aberhart and Manning, on the one hand, and Even and Côté-Mercier, on the other, see chapter 2. On the role of charisma in Caouette's leadership, see chapter 3.
65 A general tendency for ideology and charismatic leadership to serve as linchpins of a higher spiritual community in political movements has been noted by Hoffer, chapter XIII and Heberle, 131ff. This attitude was also carefully cultivated by Even and Côté-Mercier among their Créditiste followers (see chapter 2). In both Canadian Social Credit wings, this element gradually declined in importance as the movement evolved.

Even, Armand Turpin, and Louis Dugal – with a ready climate for the growth of a new political movement.[66]

Louis Even was a journalist who discovered social credit while working as a translator at a publishing house owned by J.J. Harpell, a radical industrialist, in Gardenvale, Quebec, about thirty-five miles outside of Montreal. Even immediately set out to convert his compatriots, both through his newspaper writings and through political action.[67] Turpin was an Ottawa municipal employee who displayed an intellectual bent. Prior to the depression, he had not concerned himself with politics at all, but when the problems of the early 1930s began to strike Canada with full force, Turpin dug deeply into economic and social writings to find a satisfactory explanation for the situation and became the first French Canadian to 'discover' Major Douglas. From 1932 to 1936 he read and discussed the doctrine of social credit along with other economic theories of the day. He studied part time with Père G.-H. Lévesque, the distinguished cleric and teacher who contributed so much to the rejuvenation of French-Canadian social thought.[68] The two were responsible for launching the ideas of social credit in Quebec through their publications in *Action Catholique*.[69]

Dugal was a young Montreal lawyer who while he was still at university began to explore radical ideas and solutions to an economic situation he deplored. Not long after he graduated from law school in 1934 he made contact with an Englishman who was engaged in writing a critique of Major Douglas' doctrine. His curiosity aroused, he sought information from the Douglas Social Credit Bureau in Ottawa, and found the ideas of social credit immediately appealing. At about the same time J.J. Harpell was warring with the electricity trusts and Sun Life Assurance Company. Dugal knew Harpell and was introduced by him to Louis Even. News of the Aberhart

66 From the mid-1930s until the end of the second world war was the only real period of political unrest and partisan change in Quebec in this century until the 'Quiet Revolution' of the 1960s. Ideologically, the period was characterized by the first real challenges to the prevailing social, economic, and political conservatism of French-Canadian thought which were expressed in the writings of André Laurendeau and journals such as *Action Nationale* and *Jeune Canada*. Politically, the first real challenge to the bipartisan (bleu–rouge) tradition came first from the Action Liberale Nationale party in 1935–6 and then again from the Bloc Populaire in 1942–5. There were also candidates competing in some ridings under the CCF banner throughout the same period. See Michael Oliver, 'The Social and Political Ideas of French-Canadian Nationalists, 1920–1945' (unpublished PHD dissertation, McGill University, 1956); Mason Wade, *The French Canadians* (Toronto: Macmillan, 1955), chapters XIV–XVI; Herbert Quinn, *The Union Nationale: A Study in Quebec Nationalism* (Toronto: University of Toronto Press, 1963), chapters III–V; and Ramsay Cook (ed), *French-Canadian Nationalism* (Toronto: Macmillan, 1969).

67 Interview with Louis Even, 14 May 1965.

68 For brief references to Père Lévesque's contribution during this period and later, see Wade, 979, 1113, 1116; and Quinn, 56 (note 16), 164.

69 Interview with Armand Turpin, 19 May 1967. See Georges-Henri Lévesque, 'Crédit social et Catholicisme,' *Action Catholique*, 23 mai, 1 et 16 juin, 2 juillet 1936, and Armand Turpin, articles published in *Action Catholique* in the autumn of 1936 and republished in Armand Turpin, *Pour être vraiment maître chez-nous ... Le Crédit Social* (Saint Hyacinthe, Québec: L'Imprimerie Yamaska, 1963), part I.

success in Alberta in 1935 hit these French Canadians 'like a bomb.' Even then enrolled in Père Lévesque's symposium in the fall of 1935 and there met and befriended Armand Turpin. In May 1936 the triumvirate founded La Ligue du Crédit Social de la Province du Québec.[70]

Until 1935 there had been very little talk of monetary reform as a solution to Quebec's problems of unemployment and poverty.[71] While in Alberta there had been a continuous debate about the possibilities of financial management ever since the 1920s, in French Canada not a single review or publication of Major Douglas had been translated into French. All of this changed when Louis Even, Armand Turpin, and Louis Dugal were converted to social credit. Even worked with J.J. Harpell, who was then also an editor of the *Instructor* and its French version, *Le Moniteur*, to translate into French a pamphlet by one of Douglas' followers in the United States, Crate Larkin, entitled 'Propositions of Social Credit'.[72] Then followed a stream of articles on social credit, based on what could be garnered from Douglas' writings and from those of his followers in Britain and on this continent.[73] *Le Moniteur* went out from Gardenvale to 1,200 subscribers in Quebec City, Sherbrooke, Shawinigan, and other urban centres. Soon small social credit study groups formed in these areas, and they were quickly linked through the Ligue. In October 1936 Even, with the help of Père Lévesque, launched *Cahiers du Crédit Social* in place of *Le Moniteur*.

By 1936 Père Lévesque had already established his reputation as a defender of new social ideas. That year he wrote a sequence of four articles for *Action Catholique*, entitled 'Social Credit and Catholicism,' in which he extolled the merits of the new doctrine and attempted to point out some of its strong similarities to Roman Catholicism.[74] Through these articles he had an enormous effect on the development of the movement, for social credit immediately achieved a certain legitimacy in the eyes of

70 Interview with Louis Dugal, 8 July 1967. For a description of the organization, finance, and leadership of the Ligue, see pages 42–4.

71 Unlike Britain after the first world war, and the Canadian and American west during the same period or earlier, monetary and economic reform was not debated as part of the prevailing political culture of Quebec during the depression. In fact, the Roman Catholic church of Quebec tended to frown on anything which smacked of economic unorthodoxy. This attitude began to change somewhat after 1931, when Pope Pius XI published his *Quadragesimo Anno,* which was sympathetic to credit reform. See, for example, Oliver, chapter V, and P.E. Trudeau (ed), *La grève de l'amiante* (Montreal: Cité Libre, 1956), introduction, 10ff, and Quinn, chapter IV.

72 *Vers Demain*, 15 November 1940.

73 *Ibid*. See, for example, W.A. Tutte, *Douglas Social Credit for Canada* (Vancouver: Social Credit Publishing, nd), C. Marshall Hattersley, *This Age of Plenty* (London: Pitman, 1934), Philip Mairet, *The Douglas Manual* (Toronto: Dent, 1934), and E.S. Holter, *The A.B.C. of Social Credit* (Toronto: Longman's Green, 1944). See Le Ralliement Créditiste, *Le crédit social: Cours d'orientation politique* (January 1964). See also, Turpin, *Pour être vraiment maître chez-nous*, 80.

74 Père G.-H. Lévesque, *Crédit social et catholicisme* (Hull: Les Editions l'Eclair, 1939). This is a reprint of four articles first published in 1936 in *Action Catholique*, on 23 May, 1 June, 16 June, and 2 July. The similarities between social credit and Catholicism which Père Lévèsque discovered were their spiritualism, their pacific character, their support of private property, individual liberty, and a restricted role for the state.

the Roman Catholic clergy in Quebec without which it could hardly have survived in the province.[75] Shortly after, on Père Lévesque's suggestion, Armand Turpin was invited by the editor of *Action Catholique* to write a further series of articles on Douglas' theory.[76]

The nationalist *Action Catholique* then claimed a wide and influential readership, and with the impetus which these writings provided, the *Cahiers'* readership increased to 2,400 subscribers during the two years in which it appeared on an irregular (about once every two months) basis. Volunteers distributed additional issues free of charge. Study circles of the Ligue sprouted wherever the *Cahiers* penetrated, so that by June 1938 the Ligue was able to hold its first provincial convention in Saint Hyacinthe, and join with French Canadians of other provinces to found the Association des Créditistes de l'Est.[77] Louis Even quit his Gardenvale job to devote himself fully to social credit, becoming the provincial organizer for the Ligue in September 1938.

The Ligue considered itself to be a movement rather than a political party. Its objectives were to convince as many of the electorate as possible to adhere to the ideas of social credit and then to assist them in pressuring their federal MPs to initiate social credit reforms at the national level. According to Even, writing in the *Cahiers* at the time,

We declare loudly that there is a well-defined difference between a political party and the Créditiste Movement as it exists today in our province. A political party groups together

75 This legitimacy was later confirmed by a special study commission established by the Roman Catholic bishops of Quebec in 1939 to consider if social credit could be labelled as a form of socialism, which had been condemned by the Roman Catholic church. The commission, headed by R.P. Joseph-P. Archambault, s.j, concluded: 'The Commission thus replies negatively to the question: "Is social credit tainted with socialism?" It doesn't see how one could condemn in the name of the Church and its social doctrine the essential principles of this system, as they were previously exposed. It is careful to recall, however, that social credit, whose purely economic or political aspect it was not called upon to judge, does not always remain a monetary reform. It should not be forgotten, in fact, that what is most important is that it is a reform of institutions by corporatist organization supported by the reform of morals, according to the explicit recommendations of Pius XI.' See 'Le crédit social et la doctrine Catholique,' *L'Actualité en Tracts*, 17 (20 novembre 1939), 5–6. This did not, however, end the animosity and struggle between the Roman Catholic church officials and the Créditistes. See, for example, notes 191 and 192 below.

76 The articles by Turpin, which appeared in *Action Catholique* some months after Père Lévèsque's, are reprinted as part i of his book, *Le crédit social* (Hull 1963). They deal exclusively with the economic ideas of social credit.

77 *Vers Demain* (fortnightly Social Credit newspaper, first published at 4885 Chabot Street, Montreal, in November 1939), 15 November, 1940. The association included representatives from Quebec, Ontario, and the three maritime provinces, but the organizations of the latter four provinces were practically non-existent, and so the association fell apart. See also *Cahiers*, ii, 1 (January 1939), 28. It is interesting to note that even at this early stage the Créditiste leaders had an interest in spreading their message beyond the borders of Quebec. Similar attempts to organize French Canadians in Ontario and the maritime provinces were made by the directors of the Union des Electeurs in 1948 and by Caouette in various campaigns after 1962. None of these efforts proved fruitful. See also below, section H and chapter 3.

a small number of politicians to put pressure on the politicians, whoever they may be. We believe that if it is permissible to divide oneself into groups in order to choose the representatives of the people, it is not at all necessary to divide up in order to tell them what we all want. Social credit demands one thing that everyone wants – let us unite to express to those elected (rouges, bleus or independents) this unanimous will of the people.[78]

The Ligue organized itself by federal constituencies and concentrated its efforts on federal MPs because banking and monetary legislation was in federal jurisdiction. Its leaders believed that 'when the majority of electors in the respective constituencies expressed themselves clearly and collectively to their deputies, they would either have to respond to this expression of popular will or be forced to withdraw their candidacy at the next election.' After all, wrote Even,

In a democratic regime, it is to the people that the right belongs to say what results they want, and to the deputies to transmit this will; the government must give the necessary orders to have them executed, to obtain the results. For too long the money powers have had *their* will executed and our governed have accepted it as our duty. One might well look with derision on such a caricature of democracy: it is the opposite of true democracy.[79]

In order to achieve these objectives the Ligue leaders devoted much time and effort to organizational tasks. They travelled to many parts of the province and established committees in each locale. When a constituency had a sufficiently large network of local committees, the leaders helped establish constituency councils composed of the presidents and secretaries of the local committees. The councils chose one of their members to act as a liaison with other constituencies. The members of the local committees were automatically members of the Ligue and received their membership cards as soon as they were properly registered and had handed over their annual contribution of one dollar.[80]

The chief task of each local committee was to increase the membership of the Ligue by recruiting new members to their committee. Whenever a circular was received from the executive of the Ligue, the secretary had the responsibility of convening a plenary session of the committee and reading its contents to the members. The public at large was invited to attend these meetings and participate in discussions on social credit doctrine. The role of the constituency committee was to see to the establishment of new committees in parishes which did not yet have one.[81]

The constituency committees were grouped into seven provincial districts, each of

78 *Cahiers du Crédit Social*, II, 1 (January 1939), 29.
79 *Ibid.*, 29. The influence of Douglas' political ideas on Even is apparent. See subsection A of this chapter.
80 *Ibid.*, 29–30. The Ligue financed its propaganda and organizational work primarily from these regular membership contributions, supplemented by special contributions in larger amounts from benefactors whose names were inscribed in its Golden Book.
81 *Ibid.*, 30.

which selected a president who was automatically a vice-president on the provincial executive. The other provincial officers included a president, a secretary, and five vice-presidents at large. They were elected by the delegates at the annual provincial congress of the Ligue.[82] Louis Dugal and Louis Even were president and secretary respectively of the Ligue from the time of its founding until its dissolution, and Armand Turpin was a vice-president.[83] Headquarters for the executive were established in Montreal.[84]

At its height, the Ligue claimed to have full-fledged organizations in at least thirty-eight constituencies, and scattered members in the twenty-seven remaining constituencies.[85] The years 1937 and 1938 marked the period of greatest success in the Ligue's history. The leaders of the Ligue, headed by Dugal and Even, conducted a six-month tour of the provinces of Quebec, Ontario, and New Brunswick during this time. Everywhere they went they aroused enthusiasm and curiosity, particularly among farmers and workers. It was no wonder that they hoped to achieve their goal speedily. Their methods of propaganda were proving more successful than even they had anticipated.

It was about this time that Gilberte Côté joined the Ligue. A university trained daughter of an affluent shoe manufacturer in Montreal, she supplied the Ligue with an automobile for its tours. She was also responsible for persuading Even to leave the employ of Harpell and work only for the Ligue, promising to pay his salary for six months. Gilberte had strong personal ideas about the methods the Quebec Social Credit movement should use to obtain its objectives. She argued that the propaganda of the Ligue should be directed exclusively at the masses of people rather than at the intellectual or political elite. She convinced Louis Even that a movement combining propaganda with political pressure would be most successful in achieving social credit objectives in Quebec.

Louis Dugal was opposed to this strategy on the ground that social credit was an economic philosophy rather than an ideological force capable of sustaining a separate and distinct movement. He argued that major efforts should be concentrated on convincing established French-Canadian institutions and groups to adopt its line of thinking. A concentrated effort in one particular direction would prove both too costly and too unrewarding.[86] Armand Turpin, on the other hand, advocated that the movement orient itself almost exclusively to political action, following Aberhart's example.[87]

Louis Even and Gilberte Côté pressed forward with their plan. In the fall of 1939 they established the newspaper *Vers Demain*, their major organ of propaganda and education. The point at which *Vers Demain* was launched marked a new beginning for the Social Credit movement in Quebec. It now had two leaders who were willing

---

82 *Ibid.*, 28.
83 *Ibid.*, 28.
84 *Ibid.*, 32. It was located at chambre 204, 28 ouest Saint-Jacques, Montréal.
85 *Cahiers du Crédit Social*, II, 4 (August 1939), 123.
86 Interview with Louis Dugal, 8 July 1967.
87 Interview with Armand Turpin, 19 May 1967. Such differences over strategy and tactics tend to arise at every phase in a movement's development and are a prime contributing factor to schism. See chapter 1.

to devote themselves completely to the cause; it had a political organization which served to co-ordinate the existing groups, establish new ones, and collect revenues from donations and fees of members in both; and it had a powerful device for proselytization in the regular, bimonthly *Vers Demain*. Armed with these weapons, Social Credit confidently entered the federal elections of the spring of 1940, running candidates in two districts under its own or an independent banner. The results were nothing short of disastrous. Louis Even, running in Lac Saint-Jean under a Social Credit banner, collected only 3,698 votes, placed a poor third among the candidates, and lost his deposit.[88] A better performance among Social Crediters was recorded by Armand Turpin, who amassed 7,083 votes in Hull, only 4,000 less than the winning candidate.[89] It was still anything but encouraging. If Social Credit was to survive in Quebec, the situation required a drastic rethinking.

Up to that point, the leaders of Social Credit had tried tactics similar to those which had been so successful in Alberta five years earlier.[90] The basis of their movement was the study group in each community, transformed at the right moment into an organ of political action. Revenue also came from these groups, although there was barely enough to allow the movement to wage an effective campaign. What was lacking in Quebec, however, was the grass-roots élan, a feeling of enthusiasm for and attachment to the cause among the poorest elements of the population, which had been present in Alberta in 1935.

There were three primary reasons for the failure to arouse much enthusiasm. First, conditions in Quebec in 1940 were very different from those in Alberta in 1935, because it was the end rather than the beginning of the depression.[91] Second, French Canadians had virtually no previous experience with economic or political reform.[92] Finally, the leaders of the Social Credit movement in Quebec lacked the

88 There were extenuating circumstances, however, in that Even had had an accident which prevented him from going into his constituency until the last day before the election; his campaign was conducted by local Social Crediters. *Vers Demain*, 15 November, 1940.

89 H.A. Scarrow, *Canada Votes* (New Orleans: Hauser Press, 1962).

90 See section B above for a more detailed discussion of the tactics of the Alberta movement. See also Irving.

91 Although the French-Canadian farmer was probably as badly off as his prairie brother during the same period, his position had not only not declined since the early 1930s, it was even slightly improved. In the urban centres the first wartime industries had been established, providing jobs for working-class people, and stimulating indirectly the demand for other goods. See Quinn, chapter V.

92 On this point see note 66 above. In addition one should recall that in the province of Quebec the political elite was recruited largely from among professionals, who were most conservative in their outlook. They had formed a tacit alliance with the clergy whose interests were similar and whose orientation was even more traditional. The two groups had opposed all reform movements on the grounds that they would undermine the deeply rooted French-Canadian fidelity to their own language, faith, and culture. The two old-line parties, Liberal and Conservative, were themselves well-rooted components of this culture; their programs and policies reflected concern for the same basic principles, at the cost of more urgent economic and social needs. The only reform movements which were given a sympathetic hearing in Quebec until 1945 were those like the Action Libérale Nationale and the Bloc Populaire which advocated some kind of nationalist or autonomous French-Canadian stance in the face of a threatened attack from the majority culture. Even in the mid-1930s,

personal qualities, experience, and oratorical skills necessary to attract French-Canadian voters.[93]

Aberhart and Manning, the Alberta leaders, were trained evangelists, who had a direct access to the public through their already well-established Bible broadcasts. Even and Gilberte Côté, the most active of the Ligue leaders, were journalists and publicists whose temperaments and training were better suited to an indirect method of communication.[94] Both had studied ecclesiastical doctrine, and both were devout Catholics. But the method of spreading church gospel through mass meetings and emotional turmoil was foreign to them, as it was to all French-Canadian Roman Catholics. The church in fact frowned on such 'blasphemies' and soon contrived to squelch any such attempt to deviate from the accepted form of religious worship. Thus it was much more difficult for the Quebeckers than it was for the Albertans to mould political evangelists out of untrained public speakers, and to use them to indoctrinate whole congregations at mass political gatherings.[95]

D 'VERS DEMAIN,' THE VOICE OF CRÉDITISME IN QUEBEC, 1939–57

The difficulties faced by the leaders of Social Credit in converting Quebeckers to their cause in 1940 did not deter them. Even and Gilberte Côté chose to devote themselves primarily to mass political education rather than to elite education or mass electoral and political action. In June of that year, the editorial board of *Vers Demain* severed its association with the Ligue du Crédit Social and directed its energies to spreading Major Douglas' gospel to every French Canadian home.[96]

during the worst years of the depression, the primary object of economic reform was the hydro-electric industry; the desire to nationalize it was largely a matter of ridding French Canada of the English trustards. See Trudeau, introduction, and Quinn. All of this contrasts markedly, as previously noted, with the history of western Canada, where the reform spirit was dominant from the beginning, and where socialists, communists, agrarian reformers, evangelists, nihilists, individualists, and virtually every other then-known 'ism' vied for the allegiance of the populace. See Macpherson.

93 Louis Dugal, at least, was not temperamentally inclined towards such modes of political action. Neither he nor Armand Turpin had had any previous political experience. Louis Even was an averaged-sized man, of mild temperament, unimposing features, and without special vocal gifts. He had belonged to no political party, had had no personal following of any kind, and had never appeared in public for any cause before. He was considered, however, to be a man of great natural intelligence and a gifted writer. Gilberte Côté was better educated and more dynamic than Even. She had a quick mind, a sharp tongue, and a facility for lecturing to small groups. She lacked previous political or professional experience, however, and she confronted the normal prejudices against members of her sex who assume leadership positions.

94 Even's ability as a journalist has been much more widely acknowledged than has Gilberte Côté's. The latter's talents were most marked in public lecturing and small group discussions.

95 Caouette, unlike Aberhart and Manning, never resorted to evangelism in his speeches, before or after the formation of the Ralliement. One of his prime reasons for breaking with the Union des Electeurs was its tendency to mix religion with politics. See chapter 3 below.

96 The Ligue was criticized by the founders of *Vers Demain* at that time for building its structures superficially and for attempting to establish a political organization and collect membership fees in areas where there had been no prior indoctrination. After *Vers Demain* was established, the Ligue almost disintegrated. A few of its former members continued to meet at irregular intervals between 1940 and 1957. They were later absorbed into the Ralliement des Créditistes. See also chapter 2.

An Institute of Political Action was established, but it was relegated to a subordinate position as a mere political arm of *Vers Demain* made up of those best acquainted with the ideas the journal expounded.[97] The institute was assigned the primary task of recruiting new members for the journal whose message was, first of all, the corpus of Major Douglas' ideas. *Vers Demain* made no attempt to conceal that it was a social credit journal and indeed often adopted a holier-than-thou attitude towards social credit groups who were not as dedicated to the doctrine in its original, orthodox form. But *Vers Demain* was much more than this. In its pages was an attempt to translate social credit into French-Canadian terms. The editors skilfully planned a venture to convert a rather abstract doctrine into an ideology which could appeal to thousands of Quebeckers. *Vers Demain* was not, as it emphatically declared in its first issue, a Catholic periodical journal. But it was very much a French-Canadian one.

To attract the French-Canadian voter the writers of *Vers Demain* embraced social credit in its broadest terms. Whereas Douglas' doctrine had been for most Albertan Social Crediters primarily a proposal for economic reform, Even and his confrères preferred to emphasize the social tenets of Major Douglas and to underline their affinity with Catholic social doctrine.[98] Thus in the first issue of *Vers Demain*, Even wrote: '*Vers Demain* believes that the social order must be pivoted on the human person, which by its very nature, can only develop in association. The *well-ordered* association must thus facilitate, not impede, the full development of the people which compose it.' *Vers Demain* saw itself as defining the only true and meaningful path between extreme individualism, which neglects the social side of man, and extreme collectivism, which denies the very essence of man, his social individuality. In this sense, although at first it was careful 'not to engage the Catholic Church in [its] expositions,' it was anxious to declare itself 'inspired by strong doses of the principles and teachings of the Catholic Church.'[99]

The editors outlined their twofold conception of the role which *Vers Demain* would play in Quebec. In the first instance, it would act as a vehicle for forming an educated elite among the populace; that is, one tutored in social credit philosophy. This elite was not only to be selected from among those who had acquired a superior book-learning culture (culture livresque), but also from the multitude at large. Thus social credit would have to be presented in terms intelligible (ie, simple) enough for all to understand, including the least educated. In the second instance *Vers Demain* promised to expose conventional methods and formulas and nonsensical social facts, such as party politics, class-hatred, the scarcity of money available for the great quantity of unpurchased goods, and the transformation of means

97 The Institute of Political Action was originally composed of one thousand of the most active Créditiste recruiters in each constituency. It was first used as a recruiting arm of the journal. Later it became the major instrument through which the directors of the movement maintained their dictatorial control.

98 See above section B and Irving, 233ff.

99 *Vers Demain*, I. (Italics in original.) The first bound volume of *Vers Demain*, covering bimonthly issues for the twelve months' period from November 1939 to November 1940, was organized by the editors by topic rather than by date so that it is impossible to provide the precise date of issue of any quotation or article cited from this period. After November 1940 this policy was discontinued.

into ends, without at the same time adopting a truly revolutionary posture.[100] In subsequent issues the tenets and principles which were designed to further these objectives were more definitely defined. The editors of *Vers Demain* grouped their various writings into four main divisions: social, philosophic, political and economic.

The major objective of the social writings of *Vers Demain* was, as already explained, the development of the human person. The principal ideological vehicles for realizing this end for Quebec Social Crediters were: corporatism; social credit; anti-communism; opposition to the present system of capitalism; anti-collectivism; opposition to all 'extremist movements' such as fascism, nazism, communism; and anti-Semitism.

Even first dealt with the relationship between corporatism and social credit. Corporatism was for him the kind of 'social temporal Christian order' which Pope Pius XI had advocated in his encyclical *Quadragesimo Anno* of 1931.[101] Some had advised that the movement make this, rather than the teachings of Major Douglas, the substance of its social program. But for Even the two were complementary rather than mutually inconsistent and of different orders. The Pope had demanded not only corporatism, but also an end to restrictive control over money and credit. According to Even social credit considered in this sense (ie, as a monetary reform) was of a lower order than corporatism; if social credit was defined in its broader sense, the two were indistinguishable; thus social credit and corporatism were applicable simultaneously.[102]

The major economic device in Douglas' theory which could serve to further individual development was the basic dividend (minimum vital). It was defined by the Créditistes as the minimum of purchasing power to be placed in the hands of all

100 *Ibid.* This statement by the directors that their objectives were non-revolutionary supports my earlier contention that the Créditiste movement is a protest rather than a revolutionary movement. See chapter 1.

101 The encyclical of 1931 was considered to be an updating of an earlier papal encyclical, *Rerum Novarum*, which had been promulgated in 1891 by Pope Leo XIII (the later encyclical had a much greater impact in Quebec, however, since it was only in the 1930s that Quebec's elite had become concerned about the consequences of industrialization for the Québécois). In both encyclicals a strong critique of industrial capitalism was expressed in social and philosophical terms. Industrial capitalism placed excessive emphasis on individual initiative at the expense of social groups and the collective interest. It also cultivated secularism and materialism and undermined devotion to Catholic social and religious ideals. Socialism was similarly condemned as atheistic and materialistic and tending to statist control. A middle road between the two was offered in the form of corporatism. Corporatism assumed that the primary units of society are groups rather than individuals or economic classes. These groups, which were defined in economic terms, such as workers' and employers' organizations, were to strive towards achieving 'group equality' or 'parity.' This would be attained by granting each corporate unit a broad degree of autonomy in its own decision-making structures within the economic and social sphere and direct group representation in political and governmental structures. The result would be 'purposeful collective decisions which would be better than those based on individual self-interest.' Although the ideas of corporatism were seriously debated and widely supported among Quebec intellectuals in the 1930s, 'their practical effect on Quebec society was slight.' Oliver, chapter v. See also Quinn, chapter iv.

102 *Vers Demain*, I, 20.

members of society to enable them to live. Even had borrowed a broader concept of subsistence minimum from Daniel Rops, the French philosopher and close collaborator of Jacques Maritain, and incorporated it into his social ideology.[103]

The relationship between social credit and anti-communism and anti-collectivism (socialism) was much more obvious, for Major Douglas himself had often expressed a strong dislike of these doctrines in his writings, and for similar reasons.[104] Communism was, according to *Vers Demain*, 'contemptuous of the human person, suppressing liberty and individual property.'[105] Therefore it was forbidden by the church. The current regime of capitalism with its strong collectivist bent also restricted the individual; thus it too should be condemned.

The editors were not content to speculate on such matters; they were careful to document what they observed. For example, as evidence of the 'alarming trend to collectivism,' they cited figures showing the rapid growth in the number of people employed in collectivized services during the previous twenty years and the corresponding decline in the number employed by non-collectivized services.[106] Between 1916 and 1936 the former rose from 714,811 to 2,252,513, while the latter fell from 4,067,681 to 2,520,669. And as proof of the danger of communism in Canada, they compared the number of communists who allegedly lived in Canada (22,000) with the proportionately much smaller number which was active in the Soviet Union at the time of the October revolution (79,000 of a population of 120 million). Moreover, a report supposedly obtained from authentic communist sources revealed the remarkable inroads communists had made in such foreign language groups in Canada as the Russians, Serbs, Ukrainians, Poles, Hungarians, and Jews.[107]

Anti-Semitism was more subtly and more covertly expressed. Generally it took the form of linking the Jews to the Freemasons, communists, and financiers, and therefore to the forces of collectivism and internationalism.[108] For example, in an article entitled 'Communism and Jewry' published in the English *Social Crediter* in 1940, the editors purported to trace the connections between Judaism and the inter-

103 *Ibid.*, 24.
104 See, for example, his discussion in *Credit-Power and Democracy*, 6, cited in note 14 above.
  Douglas' anti-socialism and anti-communism are expressed most strongly in his later writings.
105 *Vers Demain*, I, 24.
106 *Ibid.*, 43.
107 *Ibid.*
108 They followed the example of their English social credit confrères (see subsection A, chapter 2, and Macpherson, 182–3). One may wonder whether the Quebec movement would have included overt anti-Semitism in its program if Douglas had not begun to expound it openly during those years. Several factors would tend to make one think so. In the first place, anti-Semitism, at least in mild form, has manifested itself in most right-wing movements of the populist variety. Secondly, there was a long tradition of anti-Semitism in Quebec, which 'was more generally and openly expressed than in English Canada' (Oliver, chapter 7). Thirdly, anti-Semitism had also crept into the western Social Credit movement (whose ideas strongly influenced the Créditistes) after 1938. Here, as well, anti-Semitism had been part of an indigenous political culture and had appeared in earlier agrarian movements such as the United Farmers of Alberta and the Non-Partisan Leagues. For a more detailed discussion of the anti-Semitic tradition in Quebec during this period, see L.S. Harvey, 'Anti-Semitism in Quebec,' *Canadian Forum*, 20 (June 1940), 86–7.

national banking houses which had financed and aided the Bolshevik revolution. The article went on to cite an allegedly classified American document held in the French Archives. It accused Jacob Schiff, an American Jewish financier and head of the financial house of Guggenheim, Kuhn, Loeb and Company, directed entirely by Jews, along with the German Jewish banker Max Warburg, of furnishing money to the Jew Trotsky in April 1917. The American Jew, Paul Warburg, during his membership on the US Federal Reserve Board, had had active contacts with Bolshevik notables in the US, and therefore had been refused re-election. The article went on to report that Rosa Luxemburg, the German Jewish activist, had received support from the German Jewish banking house of Haase. 'It is therefore manifest,' the document was said to have concluded, 'that the Bolshevik movement is in good measure the expression of a general Jewish movement, and that certain Jewish banking houses are interested in the organization of the movement.'[109] To which the editors of *Vers Demain* added the following closing observation: 'The readers of *Vers Demain*, in meditating on this documentation would be less surprised [than the readers of the "classified" report] that we were mentioning Jewry and Freemasonry, in connexion with high finance, among the enemies of the people and Christian civilization.'[110]

This particular animosity did not, however, lead the Créditistes into a position of open support for nazism or Italian fascism. For they too were judged to operate in a manner which was contrary to social credit social and economic principles. Hitler, for example, maintained what was to all intents and purposes a Rothschild-type of economic and financial system which, like orthodox capitalism, advocated reinvestment of income in preference to consumption, made a fetish of work, and imposed heavy taxes. Even more inimical, however, was the gross repression of individual freedom under nazism. It therefore could be said that 'in Germany, the dictator employ[ed] military force to impose upon the people an identical philosophy to that of the financial powers.'[111]

The basic philosophical tenet of *Vers Demain* can be summarized succinctly as the belief in and promotion of full freedom and absolute truth. In accordance with Catholic philosophy, wrote Gilberte Côté, social credit is premised on the principle that man is ultimately a free agent with a mind of his own and therefore is capable of seeking out and discovering truth. Social credit, she went on, is devoted to revealing the principles of truth and their practical application.[112]

In the realm of politics, *Vers Demain* hewed fairly closely to the line advocated by Major Douglas. It was against partisan politics, patronage, and Judaeo-Masonic influences in elections and the mass media, and for real democracy, decentralization, group organization, and an up-to-date nationalism. Even posed the problem of partisan versus independent politics in terms of the deputy, the member of parliament representing a constituency. The term deputy was originally derived from the verb to deputize, or delegate. The deputy was supposed to be the servant of his constituents, the person to whom was delegated the duty of expressing the popular will. This fact was itself sufficient to establish the contradiction in the current method of

109 *Vers Demain*, I, 51.
111 *Vers Demain*, 15 March 1941.
110 *Ibid.*, 56.
112 *Vers Demain*, I, 55–60.

party politics. For how could a deputy represent his electors and at the same time take directives from a party leadership?

For Even, the measure of a true democracy was whether or not its government really administered for the people; that is, in the interests of the common good. He thought that elections were scarcely a guarantee of this, for 'one had seen monarchies, even absolute ones, more democratic than republics.'[113] In this sense, he felt it was necessary to re-evaluate parliamentary government, particularly as it then existed in Canada. Parliaments passed bills which increased public debt, raised taxes, and did nothing to solve unemployment, the threat of revolution, and war. They were hardly acting, then, in conformity with popular aspirations.

Even held that the political parties were first of all responsible for this abominable state of affairs. Although they claimed to stand for diametrically opposite policies, they were all essentially the same, for all practised the art of abandoning their electors between campaigns and all conspired to keep the public in absolute ignorance.[114] The parties were also the willing tools of the financiers, who maintained their control through electoral funds. The banks and lending houses made available, and the big businessmen and monopolists donated, vast sums of money to the parties to help them elect their members. The money was used largely to buy the votes of electors during the campaign. It was also used to ensure the complete obedience and submission of party candidates and deputies to the caucuses of their respective parties.[115]

'This flower of democracy has long been cultivated in Quebec,' wrote Even in 1942, 'now it has been democratized and hierarchized.[116] Liberal and Conservative parties were implicated equally. The pattern, which was the same for both, was as follows. After a new party gained power, it proceeded to sweep away the old job holders, and proclaim thereby to have purified the administration. For this achievement it merited the homage of the electorate. 'Then very softly, noiselessly, from one whim to another, holes are filled, friends are lodged. The hierarchy has everything: bountiful contracts, subcontracts, foreman duties, paper scribblers in offices, jobs on the road, and promises of more jobs.'[117]

There was, however, a broader and more far-reaching purpose to these activities of the financiers than the immediate monetary rewards derived from local politics. The ultimate objective of the moneyed elements was to further, consciously or unconsciously, the interests of the political alliance of Jews, Freemasons, and communists. The alliance was formed on a secret basis, and operated through 'a hidden organization [within the masons] whose existence is generally not known even by the majority of brother masons; through it the orders of the occult power are executed. The controllers of free-masonry don't themselves make the revolution; they direct its final objective, dress its plans, and furnish the necessary funds for the

113 *Ibid.*, 71.
114 *Ibid.*
115 *Ibid.*, 80–1. These views on parliamentary government and the role of political parties in modern democracies were, of course, completely in line with Major Douglas' own thinking, and with much of North American Populist and European right-wing thought.
116 *Vers Demain*, 15 March 1942.
117 *Ibid.*

struggle. Rarely does one notice the breadth of their programme until it has obtained a remarkable degree of success.'[118]

What, then, was the ultimate aim of this political alliance? In an article written in 1940, entitled 'Towards a Judaeo-Masonic Super State,'[119] the editors of *Vers Demain* made their views explicit. Citing men like Schiff, Warburg, and Kahn, they asked rhetorically: 'How would you like to be governed by kings or emperors of these names? We are in fact allowing it ... for these are New York bankers who are the true masters of America, and together with their confreres in Europe, of the entire world.' This federal union is directed towards the end of establishing 'a universal state controlled by a bureaucracy at the service of the banking dictatorship.'[120]

Was *Vers Demain* merely repeating nazi charges of a Jewish plot? The editors, probably fearing to be labelled as just another fascist group, backed away from so stark an accusation. But their qualification was hardly less damning. Even concluded: 'Does there exist a world conspiracy of Israel to enslave all peoples? We aren't ready to say so. But we believe that there exists a world conspiracy of high finance to exercise supreme power over humanity. And in the conspiracy, it happens that the levers of command are in the hands of men among whom the Jews occupy an important, if not preponderant, place.'[121]

The editors of *Vers Demain* were never very explicit about the form of government which they envisaged as a framework for a real democracy. Like Major Douglas and William Aberhart, they seemed to have in mind a system in which the representative was made truly responsible to his constituents, and actual decision-making was left to experts who were trained in social credit principles and who were pledged to govern in the interests of the people. But there was one major addition: an upper chamber, such as already existed in Quebec and in Ottawa, would serve as an additional vehicle of popular will. It would be organized along occupational rather than 'rep by pop' lines, a French-Canadian adaptation of corporatist political theory then being widely debated in Quebec.[122]

Probably the most clearly French-Canadian element in all of *Vers Demain*'s preachings was its emphasis on nationalism and French-Canadian autonomy. Even this was not entirely indigenous. Major Douglas had opposed supra- and internationalism as a foil for centralizing forces, preferring a more decentralized and localized organization of economic and political life. And Aberhart, in his hostility to eastern domination and in his headlong clash with Ottawa over Social Credit legislation in 1937–8, adopted a strident provincial autonomist stance.[123] The nationalism of *Vers Demain* was carefully honed in the French-Canadian tradition, with emphasis on such distinctively French-Canadian attitudes and doctrines as anti-conscription, antagonism to English-Canadian monopolies and economic domination, cultural, linguistic, and educational autonomy for Quebec, recognition of the rights of French-Canadian minorities in other provinces, and permeation of social and economic life with Catholic, particularly papal-framed ultramontane principles. This deliberate attempt

118 *Vers Demain*, I, 90. 119 *Ibid.*, 98.
120 *Ibid.* 121 *Ibid.*
122 See chapter 2, note 101.
123 See, for example, J.R. Mallory, *Social Credit and the Federal Power* (Toronto 1954).

to cultivate French-Canadian nationalist sentiment was in part determined by the very strong current of nationalism which existed in Quebec in the late 1930s and early 1940s. It was also necessitated by the rather incongruous fact that an appeal was being made to French Canadians to accept a doctrine preached by an Englishman and which had attained its only real success up to that point in largely English western Canada. But it was chiefly the result of a genuine feeling of French Canadianism ingrained in Even, Gilberte Côté, and their collaborators, all of whom were the products of old and proud French-Canadian Catholic families, were educated exclusively in French-Canadian Catholic schools and universities, confined their friendships entirely to their fellow French Canadians, and had little previous contact, either in Quebec or elsewhere, with the people of other languages, faiths, or cultures.[124]

It was not surprising, therefore, that the Quebec Social Credit movement soon found itself in conflict with Social Credit movements elsewhere over matters affecting their nationalism. The first such cleavage occurred in September 1939, even before *Vers Demain* was established, over the question of conscription. After certain western Social Crediters had demanded conscription, the Ligue passed a resolution unanimously opposing Canadian participation in all foreign wars. Later, as the war progressed, *Vers Demain* strongly urged its readers to vote 'no' in the 1942 plebiscite in which the federal government requested leave to impose conscription in case of emergency.[125] It vociferously supported Paul Gouin's move to unite all French-Canadian movements behind a plan designed to demonstrate to English Canadians unanimous French-Canadian opposition to conscription.[126] And in 1944 it bitterly denounced Prime Minister King and most of his Quebec Liberal lieutenants for betraying solemn engagements not to impose conscription upon Quebec.[127]

In their opposition to the English trustards, however, the editors of *Vers Demain* were merely selecting as their bête noire the equivalent in Quebec of the eastern monopolies which were anathema to prairie people. Here was a happy convergence of nationalism and social credit theory, and one which was as popular with western Social Crediters as it was with French Canadians.

The Quebec movement clashed most noticeably with its western brothers in its general desire to assert its autonomy vis-à-vis a central Social Credit organization. A Social Credit Association was established in 1944 in which the Créditistes played an active role, but the Quebec group's attitude towards it was always ambivalent and after a few uneasy years of formal co-operation, but informal estrangement, it withdrew from the association.[128] The ostensible reason for doing so was the formation of a national political party, which was contrary to the principles of orthodox

---

124 J.-Ernest Grégoire, one of the early leaders of the Union, was an exception. He had studied in both Britain and France, and had made contacts with English Canadians both in Quebec and elsewhere.
125 *Vers Demain*, 15 February 1942.
126 *Ibid.*, 1 December 1944.
127 *Ibid.*, 15 December 1944.
128 See *Vers Demain*, 15 April 1944. For a detailed account of events surrounding the founding and development of this association, see the author's unpublished study for the Royal Commission on Bilingualism and Biculturalism (Ottawa: July 1966), division III, report 4 (volumes 1–2).

Douglasism. But the real reason seemed to be a deeper and much more fundamental one: the inability of the two groups to see eye to eye on innumerable issues, stemming from a general desire by the Quebec group to protect what they regarded as the fundamental interests of French Canadians.

The economic philosophy of *Vers Demain* was clearcut and well-defined. It supported the monetary system of social credit, which it viewed as the key to all other economic problems. Major Douglas' A plus B theorem was seen as the only true and correct explanation for economic waste, depression, and scarcity; all other formulas were regarded as stereotypes and contrary to the facts. The solution to the paradox of poverty in the midst of plenty was, as Douglas had advocated, distribution of a monthly dividend to all Quebec and Canadian citizens. Other means of increasing demand by distributing income through family allowances, increased pensions, and widow's payments, were also desirable, so long as they did not involve an increase in taxes or public indebtedness. Likewise, *Vers Demain* supported all schemes to lower taxes and all methods of liquidating the public debt. Monopolies were anathema and proposals for nationalization, even when offered as a solution to large-scale monopolistic concentration, were equally despicable. The individual entrepreneur, to operate efficiently, had to be given the maximum amount of freedom in all phases of production and distribution. For *Vers Demain*, unfettered capitalism, together with social credit payments, and government control of banks and financial institutions, was the only means of realizing security and economic prosperity without loss of liberty.

E POLITICAL MOBILIZATION AND EXPANSION, 1940–4

Although the main emphasis of the Social Credit movement in Quebec after 1940 was on political education and indoctrination, and although it was the firm conviction of the editors that 'the progress of the Social Credit doctrine pivot[ed] around the journal *Vers Demain*,' much effort continued initially to be expended on political action.[129] This was the label which the Créditiste leaders gave to all their activities which were designed to galvanize either the electorate or the elected into immediate implementation of social credit. This included, in addition to recruitment of new members to the movement through the Institute of Political Action, the presentation of Social Credit candidates at federal and provincial elections and the application of direct pressure on members of local, provincial, or federal governments to adopt either the entire program of social credit or particular measures which the movement propounded.

The Institute of Political Action was incorporated in 1942 as an adjunct of the newspaper *Vers Demain*. It consisted of the most active Créditistes in each county, selected on the basis of their success in selling subscriptions, their knowledge of social credit doctrine, and their loyalty to the leaders. The members of the institute were expected to form a vanguard of about 3,000 dedicated men of action heading a large army of militant Créditistes.

The method of recruitment used by the institute was fairly simple and resembled somewhat the technique initially used by Aberhart to spread social credit in Alberta.[130] Every prospective member of the institute set himself the objective of obtaining twenty-five new regular subscribers to *Vers Demain*. If he succeeded he automatically became a member of the institute and also the founder and leader of a new Social Credit cell (*noyau*). In this way *Vers Demain* envisaged the expansion of the movement into most parishes of the province and a readership of 60,000 assiduous students of social credit, led by a core group of dedicated, informed men of organization and action. It would be 'an immense army, well-equipped, well-organized, which would be ready for all campaigns and would overcome all obstacles.'[131] It would be a work of renovation carried out without the aid of large sums of money, a plan of conversion, like that of the church. The methods of proselytization of the Catholic church were consciously adopted as the inspiration and model of Social Credit action in Quebec.[132]

To carry out certain of the local activities designed to further Social Credit, such as the holding of public assemblies, the printing of literature, etc, some small revenues were needed. The members of the institute, tutored as they were in argument and persuasion, were natural appointees as community solicitors. They soon became skilled in this operation, and their resourcefulness enabled the leaders to expand rapidly the scope of the movement's political activities. *Vers Demain* became more and more an organ of liaison for numerous public meetings, lectures, radio talks, and congresses; at least two or three of its back pages were covered with information of this sort. It was, like Aberhart's Bible broadcast and school, the hub and focal point of all Social Credit activity in the province.

Even went so far as to instruct his lieutenants in detail on such mundane matters as 'How to Prepare an Assembly.' The organizers were urged to avoid the villages, since 'they were generally inhabited by retired landlords, discouraged and jobless workers, or distributors of patronage – those who were less open to social credit ideas.'[133] The conservative, alert, and energetic farmers were the most susceptible of the various groups. And the steps of parish churches after Sunday mass were most strategic for announcing a Social Credit meeting. The technique was simple: the Social Crediter had merely to mount the steps after the town crier had finished his speech and proclaim that a public, non-partisan assembly had been arranged for a certain time during the coming week or weekend. The topic for discussion would, for example, be deliberately worded in broad familiar terms like 'money,' and a speaker would be promised to explain such basic and yet technical matters as 'where money comes from, who makes it, who doesn't make enough of it and why the products of the farmers are not selling, why so many are out of work, etc.'[134] The instructions were that one should not speak of credit (crédit) or money (monnaie) but cash (argent). And one should avoid social credit jargon, particularly in virgin territory. The technique in factories was slightly different: they could be infiltrated by joining their organized groups, circulating folders and pamphlets among them, and holding small kitchen meetings of ten to twenty persons. Here a greater tenacity was required, 'since

130 See above, chapter 2, subsection B, and also Irving, chapter 4.
131 *Vers Demain*, I, 203. 132 *Ibid.*
133 *Ibid.*, 207. 134 *Ibid.*

the workers were generally apathetic about public questions, and were more inclined to leave such matters to their employers.'[135]

Thanks to such imaginative and effective tactics, both the institute and the readership of *Vers Demain* expanded enormously. The number of subscribers is alleged to have reached 35,000 by the end of the newspaper's third year (1942) of circulation. A Social Credit economic association was formed to enable the members to finance consumers directly in amounts up to five per cent of their purchases, an indirect and very limited method of implementing a social credit system. It was not, however, a great success.[136] New methods were sought to achieve the objectives of Social Credit, and the editors turned towards more direct political action.

The first steps in this direction were taken in early 1944. The regular subscribers of *Vers Demain*, who were at the same time members of the Social Credit movement of the province of Quebec, were pronounced to be united into a new political grouping, but one which was quite different from the ordinary political party. The Union Créditiste des Electeurs (Union of Social Credit Electors) was designed to make the politicians the servants of the electorate. Its interest was in defining objectives, not methods. It would cultivate union, not division. It would work for true democracy, not merely political power.

The Union Créditiste des Electeurs then joined with the Social Credit League of Alberta and six other smaller provincial movements to form a Social Credit Association of Canada. The founding convention, held in Toronto in April 1944, was completely bilingual, and Lucien Maynard, the French-Canadian attorney general of Alberta, was selected as the chairman. 'The two languages were put on equal footing, each delegate speaking in the language which most suited him, and each obtaining in his own language the explanations he desired.'[137] Solon Low, the treasurer of the Social Credit government of Alberta, was unanimously elected president of the new national association; J.-Ernest Grégoire, most highly reputed of the Créditistes among English Canadians, was unanimously acclaimed as vice-president. In addition to these two national officers, a delegate was chosen from each province to sit on the National Council; he was in each case the nominee of his own provincial Social Credit organization, where one existed.[138] Louis Even was selected to represent Quebec. Sufficient common ground was reached between French- and English-speaking Social Crediters that a three plank platform representing a united stand by all the Social Credit groups could be hammered out. The editors of *Vers Demain* were satisfied to conclude that whereas 'before the convention the Social Crediters of the West did not know the Créditistes of Quebec,' they now had met them and had come away with a favourable impression. 'Friction between French and English Canadians is undoubtedly because of their minimal contact, and the resulting prejudices they form.'[139]

135 *Ibid.*
136 *Ibid.*, 1 November 1942.
137 *Vers Demain*, 15 April 1944. Similar methods of functional bilingualism were used in later national leadership conventions held in Ottawa in 1961 and in Hull in 1971. No earphones or mechanical simultaneous translation devices were available.
138 The following provinces actually had representation on the National Council: British Columbia, Alberta, Saskatchewan, Manitoba, Ontario, and Quebec.
139 *Vers Demain*, 15 April 1944.

But all was not as placid as it seemed on the surface. The convention delegates had some difficulty reconciling the demands of the Alberta representatives for an immediate political organization with those of the Créditistes from Quebec who 'wanted an educational organization preparing the way to political organization without banishing immediate political organization where circumstances permitted it.'[140] In the vote which was taken on this issue 53 of the delegates favoured the Alberta position and 47 opposed it – a very narrow defeat for the Quebec representation.

But the French Canadians were not satisfied to accept it. J.-Ernest Grégoire, writing in *Vers Demain* shortly after the convention, argued that the new association was a 'specific political force, not a party.'[141] It was 'a political fraternity pursuing a particular end,' but its various representatives would never be expected to be unanimous on Canadian problems. Its resolutions would not be binding on all its members. As vice-president, Grégoire might vote differently from Mr Low, the president. There would be unity only on social credit legislation. How, then, he asked, could the Social Credit Association win and maintain power? The answer, in Mr Grégoire's view, was that 'it is not the essence of Social Credit to win power. The only raison d'être for the national organization was the refusal of the Liberals and Conservatives to put money in the hands of the consumers.'[142] As members of a cabinet, Social Credit MPs would be free to vote as they wished on all questions apart from those which caused them to associate in the first place: those concerning the need to bring about social credit (ie, distribute debt-free money).

It is clear that Mr Grégoire's conception of the new Social Credit Association was very different from that held by most of the leading delegates from Alberta. Solon Low hoped that the association would promote an old Alberta Social Credit idea of establishing a Social Credit government on the federal level to implement social credit for all Canadians. The basis for associating was, in his view, to unite Social Credit forces across the country in an all-out assault on the bastion of the two old-line parties.[143]

F POLITICAL CONFLICTS AND SCHISM, 1944–9

Shortly after the convention, the Union began to attack its political opponents in Quebec's provincial elections of that year. Gilberte Côté took charge of the Créditiste campaign. The Union presented candidates in only eleven constituencies, since it still lacked a large electoral fund and because 'it didn't judge it wise to spread its energies thin, where it saw little chance of success.'[144] Two names among these eleven are worthy of note: Réal Caouette, candidate in Pontiac, and Laurent Legault, candidate in Beauce. The results of the election showed that *Vers Demain* had somehow failed in its efforts to convert Quebeckers politically. Only 16,542 or 1.2 per

140 *Ibid.*
141 *Vers Demain,* 1 May 1944.
142 *Ibid.*
143 Low Papers, unpublished personal papers of Solon E. Low, national leader of the Social Credit party, 1935–58, housed at the Glenbow Foundation, Calgary, Alberta, Selected Correspondence 1945–7. Mr Low was less clear on the implications of this for the Social Credit MPs in Ottawa.
144 *Vers Demain,* 1 August 1944.

cent of the total voters in the province cast their ballots for the Union's candidates. Where Social Credit assemblies had seemed to be the largest of all the parties, its candidates amassed by far the smallest number of votes in most of the eleven constituencies. The Union leaders felt that they had been betrayed.[145] Créditiste supporters had turned their backs on an ideal and its apostle and instead voted for a candidate that they thought had the best chance of winning. As a result they had forfeited a golden opportunity to elect eight Créditiste candidates, capture the balance of power, and thereby acquire considerable political leverage.[146]

Soon after the election of 1944, statements were made by some of the Alberta MPs in support of conscription of Canadian soldiers for overseas service.[147] Because the Créditistes were in association with these westerners, they were attacked by the other parties for advocating conscription. Members of the Bloc Populaire, the nationalist party which was formed in Quebec specifically to oppose participation in the war, had written an open letter to the various dailies asking the leaders of the different political movements in Quebec to meet to plan a common course of action. They assumed that the Créditiste wing of Social Credit accepted the western views.

The editors of *Vers Demain* protested that these charges were totally unfounded. The Social Credit Association was not a political party, but only a loose association bound by social credit principles. The conscription issue was not fundamental to social credit and indeed had nothing to do with it. In voting on the issue, the members in the House of Commons would be guided by the prevailing opinion of their local electors, rather than by any general policy. Solon Low himself had taken a similar stand in some of his recent statements.[148] The editors then expressed their own unequivocal opposition to any participation in the war and their readiness to collaborate fully in any action designed to promote this view. Thus, when Prime Minister Mackenzie King called for release from his earlier pledge not to impose conscription, the Union Créditiste des Electeurs spared no words in castigating him.

Ostensibly the stance taken by the Créditistes was in line with the thinking of Association President Solon Low on party solidarity. In a declaration made before the Saskatchewan Social Credit convention on 9 December 1944, he is reported to have stated: 'The Social Credit Association of Canada is not the apparatus of a political party. It is an association of provincial organizations, each of which is completely autonomous. Consequently, each is entirely free, within the meaning of the association, to express clearly its own opinion on every question.'[149] Moreover, one of

145 *Ibid.,* 15 August 1944.
146 *Ibid.,* 1 September 1944.
147 The federal members were originally elected in 1940 as 'New Democracy' candidates formally led by the conscriptionist Major Herridge. Most had renounced their earlier commitment to conscription in 1942 and that had helped make association possible again in 1944. In the 1944 plebiscite held in the fall, the Social Credit members again came out in favour of conscription. This stand had obvious repercussions in Quebec despite the efforts of Union leaders and of Mr Low to disassociate Quebec from it.
148 *Vers Demain,* 1 December 1944.
149 *Ibid.,* 15 December 1944. This statement may be understood as an accurate reflection of Low's rather lame attempt to reconcile his own position on the 1944 plebiscite with his National Social Credit Association mandate and the opposition to conscription by Quebec members.

the other Social Credit MPs had stated in the House of Commons: 'The Association has not yet had the opportunity to submit its program to the approval of the Canadian population.'[150] But this apparent unity of views between eastern and western Social Credit masked what had been for the association a most damaging confrontation. At the very point when the association was attempting to establish itself on a firm basis, it was forced to mediate between two very divergent viewpoints. Resentment amounting to extreme bitterness was felt by exponents of both sides. The common understanding that was supposedly reached at Toronto was quickly dissipated.

Despite the differences over conscription, the leaders of the Union Créditiste des Electeurs made a number of conciliatory gestures towards the western group which were intended to smooth over factional differences between the two Social Credit wings. On 1 January 1945 they declared their intention to collaborate with the westerners to pressure the federal government to abolish bureaucratic controls, selective service, and so forth. In May 1945 the Union entered forty-three candidates in the federal general election in co-operation with western Social Credit.

The Union was led by the distinguished, though undynamic, J.-Ernest Grégoire, the national Social Credit vice-president.[151] Réal Caouette ran in Pontiac, Gérard Mercier, provincial secretary of the Union, presented himself in Quebec-East. Eugene Fortin, who had helped run Laurent Legault's campaign the previous year and who now received Legault's help in reciprocation, entered as candidate for Beauce. There was still a lack of funds, however. The candidates were hard pressed to find the money to pay for their deposits, and it was almost impossible for them to pay for campaign literature. Social Credit was attacked in some quarters as communism, or a step towards it, and support was forbidden by the church. Others complained that the movement was too preoccupied with the question of money. These were unhealthy forebodings, and the leaders prepared for the worst, although consoling themselves with the thought that 'Créditistes are never discouraged because we don't depend for the survival of our movement on the election of deputies ... we will continue our politics of pressure on the elected, whoever they may be.'[152]

Once again, because their ideology opposed it, the Union refused to offer a detailed political program. Programs, Union members claimed, were identified with parties and were prepared in advance by small cliques who then foisted them upon the public. The Créditiste candidates offered what they regarded as a much more democratic and appealing alternative. 'Vote for me and therefore gain the right to make your program yourself in accordance with needs as they arise. Vote for a candidate who will come to study and solve with you the problems of the country, and

150 *Ibid.*
151 Grégoire, a lawyer and professor at Laval University, had been mayor of Quebec City and was one of the leading personalities in the Action Libérale Nationale in 1935–6. When Duplessis won power in 1936 he was expected to ask Grégoire, who was then still mayor of Quebec, to accept a ministerial post. Grégoire was passed over, and he subsequently quit Duplessis' team. Later he joined the Social Credit movement. Interview, June 1967. Gilles, his son, was later a founder of the Ralliement des Créditistes and its deputy leader in Ottawa and subsequently the leader of the right-wing separatist Ralliement National. See below, chapter 3. See also Quinn, 69, 71, 74–5.
152 *Vers Demain,* 15 May 1945.

take with you decisions on the larger political questions.' In the meantime, the voters were asked merely to accept two broad social credit principles: 1 / respect for individual liberty, and 2 / guarantee of a part of the production of the country for each and every citizen, the basic dividend.[153]

If the results are any indication, this strategy was not a very happy one. The forty-three candidates collected a total of only 63,310 votes, or 4.5 per cent of the total popular vote. None was elected. This was far behind the total of the third-running party in Quebec, the Bloc Populaire Canadien, which amassed 184,372 votes in thirty-five constituencies and elected two members. The best performance was recorded by Fortin in Beauce. With Legault directing his campaign, he captured 5,701 votes, making him the runner-up in the election and giving him 25.3 per cent of the total vote. In Pontiac, Réal Caouette had done almost as well in recording a slightly higher vote total of 5,852, but he collected only 18.2 per cent of the popular vote, placing him third in his riding. A few of the other Créditiste candidates also turned in respectable performances.[154] Unlike their reaction to the 1944 provincial election, the editors were philosophical about their loss.[155]

Following the Créditiste defeat in the election of 1945, a seemingly radical modification in political theory and practice was introduced: the Union Créditiste des Electeurs was transformed into the Union des Electeurs. The Union Créditiste des Electeurs had tried to operate within the prevailing system by exerting pressure on the deputies the people had chosen. But the deputies simply ignored them. The Union therefore decided to elect its own parliament of electors, composed of 'mandators' who were the true representatives of the people. The election would occur before the regular elections, since 'the machines of corruption would not [then] be there, and it [would therefore be] easier to make a just choice.'[156] The parliament would not have power to legislate, but it would lead the struggle against both federal and provincial governments. And it would enter regular elections with a record of achievement behind it. It was clear that the mandators would be essentially the same Créditistes who had offered themselves in past elections. Instead of being nominated by a small

153 *Ibid.*, 25 May 1945. See also the nineteen-point list of 'what Social Credit stands for.' It is a very general and rather panacea-like package, including things such as 'really democratic politics,' 'increase in public and social services without increase in taxes,' 'suppression of the causes of depression and war,' 'a basic dividend,' 'no increase in the debt.'

154 In Chapleau the candidate collected 3,878 votes, or 26.9 per cent of the total, and kept his deposit. In Lévis he received 4,233 votes, or 29.5 per cent of the total. In Québec-Montmorency he amassed 5,211 votes, or 23.2 per cent of the total. Scarrow, 123. All three constituencies elected Social Credit members in the 1962 federal election.

155 Although it was clear that 'the formula of the dollar' still ruled over that of men, and although in many constituencies Créditistes still preferred to vote for the candidate of some party who they thought had the best chance of winning, in Quebec the movement had captured 20,000 more votes than the communists and socialists together and had suffered less agony in the process than had the Bloc Populaire, since 'we (unlike them) didn't participate with the idea of winning.' No one had complained, moreover, of lack of money as the cause of his defeat since 'no one wanted to win an election by buying votes' (*Vers Demain*, 1 July 1945).

156 *Vers Demain*, 15 January 1946.

group of Union leaders either at the provincial level or at the constituency level, candidates would submit themselves to a nominating convention composed of all Créditistes in the district, and any non-Créditistes interested in participating as well. The leaders would simply have to submit their choice to wider approval.

The step taken by the Créditiste leadership was important, for it implied a further rejection of the existing political system. They were proposing what was in essence a provisional parliament and government, one which was intended to supplant the existing one. Although the new parliament would continue to act on the prevailing powers through the application of political pressures of various types, and although it would submit itself to regular elections, it would struggle against the existing system.[157]

This transformation was the culmination and epitome of the form of democracy advocated by Major Douglas which had at first only received lip service from the Créditistes of Quebec. The Union des Electeurs was the vast grouping of all the citizens whose function was to scrutinize objectives and results rather than methods. The mandators were to educate and inform the people. The Créditistes were the vanguard of true democrats who alone were competent to organize and lead the Union into action. And the elite of that same body of men, those learned in social credit doctrine, aided by those equipped with the required technical skills for implementing social credit, would devote themselves to devising the proper methods for governing. This was the system which Créditistes now committed themselves wholly and irrevocably to implementing. The system posed as a 'pure democracy,' one which was opposed to the corruption and monopoly of the party system. In reality, however, it was the very negation of democracy.

The system of mandators superficially resembled the system of provisional parliaments or soviets established by the Bolsheviks in Russia prior to their seizure of power. Theoretically it meant the establishment of legislative bodies actively opposed to the existing authority and regime. If a sufficiently large number of electors living in a given constituency could be persuaded to vote for such mandators, the Créditistes would have a just basis for claiming the support of the populace for their revolutionary cause. They might, in fact, have subsumed political authority from the House of Commons and the Legislative Assembly of Quebec without engaging in violent revolution. In fact, however, the system of mandators never developed into anything remotely resembling the soviets. The group of electors who chose the Créditiste mandator in each constituency was constituted of essentially the same individuals who formed the constituency organizations of the Union Créditiste des Electeurs prior to 1945. In a few instances the Créditistes succeeded in drawing into their system some supporters of other parties who were sympathetic to the 'democratic' political ideas of the Créditistes but preferred to remain unaffiliated. They were not, however, very numerous; nor were their political ideas more radical than those of the partisan Créditistes. Thus the system of mandators proved to be more revolutionary in its original promise than in its actual practice.

157 *Ibid.* The Polish Lublin government was cited as a model in this respect, though not in any other sense. Communism in any form was anathema to the Créditistes.

The new reform was also described as 'the expansion of the Union, mounted exclusively around common objectives, and not around Social Credit technique.'[158] Reform appeared to be a tactical device for broadening the political appeal of Social Credit to encompass a larger segment of the electorate. Social credit seemed to be conveniently relegated to the background. Democratic politics 'was the common principle around which the people might unite.' Was doctrine then being sacrificed to political expediency? In fact, the Créditiste leaders were only biding their time. When the opportunity arose, social credit would once again be brought to the fore. Rather than abandoning social credit doctrine, Even and Gilberte Côté were now embracing it to the full. In the one area where they had been slow to adopt Major Douglas' teachings – politics – the editors of *Vers Demain* had finally made their decision. Social Credit in Quebec was not just another political movement rising to challenge some aspects of the existing political system; it demanded a transformation of the system itself.[159] If Social Credit failed, it would withdraw from politics altogether.

At about the same time as they were establishing the system of mandators, the directors were subtly altering the internal organization of their movement to fit in with the objectives of transforming the existing political structure. A number of dissidents had sought to defy the directive of the leaders by supporting candidates of the Bloc Populaire party in the election of the previous year. The directors charged that these Créditistes had fallen under the baneful influence of the few surviving members of the Ligue. They also complained bitterly to Solon Low that some of the Alberta members were covertly encouraging these dissidents.[160] They purged all members whom they believed to be disloyal to them.

The Institute of Political Action, which they had originally devised as an instrument of recruitment and propaganda, came to be the directors' major organ of control. The members of the institute were all selected by the directors. The task of institute members was to ensure that only 'real' Créditistes were chosen for leading positions on local executives and as candidates. The most outstanding of these loyal lieutenants were co-opted onto the movement's directorate, which never included more than a handful of members. The triumvirate of Louis Even, Gilberte Côté, and her husband, Gérard Mercier, maintained control of all of these bodies.[161] The Créditiste leaders were therefore well able to afford the nominal extension of their structures, under the system of mandators, in order to embrace some non-Créditistes.

The attitudes and policies of the Quebec leaders brought them into sharp conflict with their western Social Credit confrères. The Alberta wing had become more estranged from the basic ideas of Major Douglas and, in particular, the historical

158 *Ibid.,* 1 February 1946.
159 This was the only departure from non-revolutionary objectives in the entire history of the Créditiste movement. There was an important gap here between theory and practice, however, so that the mandator system never operated in a truly revolutionary manner. Moreover, within three years even the idea was abandoned by the directors.
160 Low Papers, Louis Even to Solon Low, 27 July 1945.
161 Gilberte Côté and Gérard Mercier were married in February 1940. Mercier had been a staunch Créditiste and full-time organizer prior to that time.

and political theories which he had begun to develop in the late 1930s. The Alberta wing had also slowly transformed itself into an institutionalized party and became more orthodox in its doctrines. Premier Manning had taken the lead in both respects by declaring that the major opponent of Social Credit was no longer the money power, but rather the socialists, as represented by the growing CCF movement. Social Credit was projected as the ultimate defender of capitalism, rather than its archenemy, or even its reformer. In the 1944 provincial election many of the most bitter antagonists of Social Credit and former Premier Aberhart joined Manning in an all-out effort to stop the socialists.[162] The result was a resounding election victory, even greater than that of 1935.

These actions had created a chasm between a group of orthodox Social Crediters, known as Douglasites, and those, known as the realists, who were dedicated to watering down this ideology. A final showdown between the Douglasites and realists occurred in 1947. After the Alberta Social Credit Board, dominated by the orthodox group, had issued a report containing a vitriolic attack on capitalism, money power, democracy, and implicitly the organization of the Alberta Social Credit League, Premier Manning came down on the side of the realists. He purged the Social Credit Board, the *Canadian Social Crediter* editorial board, his own cabinet, and even the Social Credit League of all the leading Douglasites.[163] From that point on, the Social Credit movement in Alberta was no more than a traditional conservative political party, which, however, still paid lip service to certain of its reform slogans and ideas.

The Manning purge, of course, reached into the ranks of the federal Social Credit MPs and the Social Credit Association as well. Solon Low, like Manning an old-time Social Crediter but one who was pragmatic in his application of the doctrine, astutely sided with the realists. Several of his associates were removed. The association was transformed into a head office of a handful of conservative national politicians seeking to extend their influence into other provinces. At the same time, it diminished the emphasis on Douglasite theory in its propaganda materials. The *Canadian Social Crediter*, for which it acted as distributor, no longer carried the vitriolic messages of the past. The federal MPs became more temperate in their criticisms of orthodox finance.

Thus at the very moment that the Quebec Social Crediters were reasserting their complete devotion to Major Douglas, the Alberta wing was becoming more moderate. When the Alberta purge came in December 1947, therefore, the leaders of the Union were very much out of sympathy with the new policies. This was expressed in a series of articles, which scolded the new leaders in Alberta for abandoning social credit. A virulent attack on the entire leadership of the Social Credit Association, made by Louis Even in a closed door session in January, found its way into the newspapers.[164] The Albertans and their associates retaliated by attacking the dictatorial methods used by the Union des Electeurs, as well as the leaders who guided the

162 Aberhart was premier of Alberta from 1935 until his death in 1943.
163 Macpherson, 211ff.
164 The attack was printed in *Le Soleil*, 12 January 1948, under the caption 'War declared: Social Credit and the Union of Electors.' Low Papers.

movement in Quebec (particularly Gilberte Côté-Mercier).[165] This led J.-Ernest Grégoire to resign his post as vice-president of the Social Credit Association of Canada in January 1948.[166] The Union des Electeurs withdrew from the Social Credit Association, on the formal grounds that the Manning group had forced the resignation of the editor and assistant editor of the *Canadian Social Crediter* and had interfered in the functioning of the association. It was apparent, however, that the breach emanated from much deeper feelings of hostility.[167] Following the lead of Quebec, representatives from five provinces worked to form a new association called the Canadian Movement of Douglas Social Credit, with both French- and English-language sections.[168] It did not, however, last long.

The 1948 split between the eastern and western wings of Social Credit in Canada occurred, then, in part because the ethnic-linguistic cleavage between French and English Canadians had contributed to a gradual breakdown in communications between the members of the national movement. The absence of a strong national association capable of reconciling differences between the members and managing internal conflict added to this gradual disintegration of the 1944 union. Above all, the divergent political fortunes of the two wings led them to adopt different political strategies and tactics and created different patterns of political evolution. The Alberta wing, because it had succeeded in winning and maintaining power in its home province, rapidly progressed along the road to consolidation and institutionalization, so that by 1948 it had all but abandoned the movement's original goals. The Quebec wing, on the other hand, had failed to achieve rapid mobilization and political success. As a result, its directors attempted to retrench by adopting a more radical ideological and political line and by tightening their own autocratic control over the movement. In doing so, they naturally found themselves at odds with the more pragmatic group in the west.

At about the same time that the schism in east-west relations was occurring, a group of young Créditistes was beginning to assert itself against its own leaders. Laurent Legault, candidate and organizer in Beauce, and Réal Caouette, twice candidate in Pontiac, were both by age and inclination of the second generation of Social Crediters, although both had joined the movement shortly after its inception in Quebec. They had learned the doctrine of Major Douglas primarily from reading

165 See, for example, the article, which appeared in the *Canadian Social Crediter* (22 January 1948), written by Dr J.N. Haldeman, president of the Saskatchewan Social Credit League and chairman of the National Council of the Association. Low Papers.

166 Low Papers. J.-E. Grégoire to Solon Low, 29 January 1948.

167 See Low Papers, John J. Fitzgerald, president, Social Credit League of Ontario, 16 January 1948, to Solon Low, E.C. Manning, *et al.,* including a translation of a clipping from *La Presse* (12 January 1948) entitled 'An untrue and unbalanced report' by Jean Grénier, general secretary, Institute of Political Action (no date); and a letter from J.-E. Grégoire to Solon Low, 27 January 1948. Among the resentments expressed by the Quebec leaders was the feeling that the purge conducted by Premier Manning was anti-Catholic in nature, and that Quebec had been deliberately excluded from all decisions taken by the National Council in a meeting held in Calgary. These were seen as anti-French-Canadian and anti-Catholic actions.

168 The first initiative to form this association had apparently been taken even before the formal split in January 1948.

Vers Demain and the books and articles of Louis Even rather than from original sources.[169] They were young and energetic men in their late twenties and early thirties who had joined the movement five to ten years previously while they were still in their late teens or early twenties. Under the tutelage of the older generation of leaders, Louis Even and Gilberte Côté-Mercier, they had 'matured' in their knowledge of social credit doctrine, their political experience, and their organizational skills and had acquired some self-confidence. Caouette was from the very beginning of his formal education given to public oratory and debate, and the powerful voice which he projected while addressing public meetings on behalf of the movement soon won him the nickname the 'Thunderer' from his Créditiste cohorts.[170] Legault was more adept at lecturing and organization.[171] Both had a taste and faculty for leadership and an avid interest in political matters. These assets quickly advanced them to positions of leadership within the movement.[172]

In September 1946 a by-election was held in Pontiac. Réal Caouette, then a salesman in Val d'Or, had already been chosen as the mandator for the constituency. Laurent Legault, who had moved to Rouyn, was chosen to organize his campaign. Caouette again ran on a program of broad slogans: 'Liberty for all!' 'Abundance for all!' 'Down with taxes!' 'Down with [price] controls!' 'Down with coupons!' He again offered without restriction a dividend of $20 a month to each man, woman, and child. This time Caouette's appeal received an eager hearing. It was long after the end of the war and people were tired of the continued restrictions on prices and wages. On 16 September Réal Caouette was sent to represent Pontiac in the federal parliament. His vote of the previous year had doubled.[173]

The victory of Réal Caouette and Laurent Legault in 1946 was partially a result of the very combination of factors that later helped to bring about their 1962 success.[174] Caouette's personality, appeal, and message and Legault's organizational skills were applied to an area where social credit ideology had penetrated, they had the necessary support in the form of money and men, and they were aided by the conditions of economic hardship and a fluid party situation.

Buoyed by their victory in Pontiac, the younger elements in the party, led by Caouette and Legault, pushed for more active and more intense participation in subsequent elections. The first of these was a federal by-election in Richelieu-Verchères in December 1946. Roland Corbeil, provincial president of the Union, was chosen as the candidate. He lacked Caouette's oratorical skills and dynamic personality and was not even a resident of the constituency. Moreover, he did not

169 From interviews conducted by the author, 1964–7.
170 *Vers Demain,* 1 August 1944.
171 From an interview with Laurent Legault, April 1964.
172 It is obvious that even at this early stage of mobilization, in both their own images of themselves and in observations made by others, Caouette approximated the ideal type of propagandist or agitator and Legault conformed to the ideal type of administrator. Their talents and leadership styles were to become even more important at a later phase of the movement's development. For a definition of these ideal types of movement leaders, see chapter 1.
173 *Vers Demain,* 15 August, 1 September, 15 September, and 1 October 1946.
174 See chapter 3.

have Laurent Legault as an organizer until late in the campaign. Richelieu-Verchères had far fewer subscribers to *Vers Demain* and a much weaker constituency organization. It was not surprising, therefore, that Corbeil managed only a second place finish, almost 6,000 votes behind the winning Liberal candidate. For Laurent Legault the results were, in the circumstances, very satisfying.[175]

But the key to electoral success for the Union was, in Legault's mind, an army of campaign workers, the invisible part of an electoral organization. One had merely to recruit a few men who were faithful to the cause, assign to them the objective of winning the election, and share responsibilities with them. The candidates and the speakers, the visible part, would generate the initial excitement among the crowds; the activist organizers would then transform their enthusiasm into votes.[176]

It was not long before Legault was given a chance to test his theory. He had been appointed to the seven-man governing directorate of the Institute for Political Action in 1946, soon after Caouette's success in Pontiac. Within two years, he had increased his power to the point that the other directors agreed to support a whole-hearted Créditiste campaign in future elections. In March 1948 the Union des Electeurs announced that it was entering a candidate in all ninety-two constituencies in the provincial elections expected that year. Laurent Legault, the prime mover in this decision, was designated as organizer-in-chief of the campaign.

Legault was well prepared for the assignment. At the beginning of the year he had issued an electoral guide to the political activists of each constituency organization of the Union in which he drew heavily on his earlier experiences as a campaign organizer. There was at that time, apart from the 50,415 regular subscribers to *Vers Demain* (now almost twice the number of 1943), approximately 4,600 activists designated in a hierarchy of ranks as lieutenants, commissioners, assistant commanders, and commanders. The task which Legault set for himself was one of welding this very diverse group into a unified force which would think and act alike. This was the key to victory; it could only be attained if all the organizers followed his detailed plan.[177]

The Legault plan was divided into three parts: 1/ technique of organization, 2/ organizing spirit, 3/ public spirit. The first was itself subdivided into two aspects: the work to be done, and the working materials or aids. On the day after the election was called, with at least forty days remaining before the vote would be taken, work was to begin. In the next days public meetings were to be arranged, cards were to be made for future checking against electoral lists, photos of all candidates were to be obtained, circulars were to be printed and distributed, polls were to be organized, automobiles were to be collected, the words VOTEZ POUR were to be painted everywhere in large letters. To carry out these tasks, it was considered necessary to recruit at least one-third of all subscribers to *Vers Demain* in each rural area and one-fifth in each urban area, an organizer-in-chief for the constituency, and a full-time assistant organizer for every 3,000 voters, lieutenants for every 300 electors, and pioneers (défricheurs) for every 60 electors, each of whom would strive to secure the votes

175 *Vers Demain*, 1 January 1947.
176 *Ibid.*
177 Laurent Legault, *Guide Electoral des Officiers de l'I.A.P.* (Montreal: l'IAP, 1948), 2.

of two-fifths of the electors entrusted to him. About $400 would be needed for every 3,000 electors. The key to organizational spirit was a will to unity and victory. The method of cultivating public spirit was to take the offensive against attack and to flog one's opponents.[178]

The nub of the electoral plan lay in the description of cadres and in the poll assignments. In rural areas about fifteen Créditistes among 300 parish voters were gathered together and each was given the job of converting ten electors to the cause. They were all to launch an incessant barrage of propaganda in order gradually to overwhelm their assignees, so that by election day they would be assured of at least half the votes in the constituency. But just to be certain that there would be no reneging on election day, four representatives would be attached to each poll, including one to guard the door and one to drive voters to and from the poll. In urban areas a similar method was devised from volunteer lists of members of the Union des Electeurs. The byword for all workers was 'more and better propaganda'; they were to make more noise than their opponents, hold more assemblies, make more door-to-door canvasses, distribute more circulars, and harass the voters during their evening drinking bouts.[179] On the final night the workers were to make sure that no doubtful voter was left alone. He was either to be brought to one or two large rallies held in the constituency on the eve of the vote or be accompanied by Social Crediters who could outstay their adversaries in the competition to convince him. On the day of polling, the representatives were instructed to come equipped with instruction sheets, pencils, paper, and a copy of the voters' list compiled from the cards. They were expected to be there at least a half hour before the poll opened and to keep a careful watch on all aspects of the voting, including such details as the swearing in of officers, the provision of a clothless, one-piece table, the checking of the ballot slip numbers, the thickness of the ballot pencil. The credentials of each voter were to be painstakingly scrutinized. As each Social Credit voter was recorded a word would be passed to the automobile driver. He would then be expected to fetch the voters who had not yet voted.

Legault was determined to have this plan followed closely. In the conclusion of the guide he urged his workers to use it 'not like a novel, but like a telephone book ... consult it when needed, keep it with you, look up the page that you need for each job you have to do.'[180] An army, to achieve victory, must be disciplined and must accept orders. Legault placed great emphasis on the careful reading and scrupulous implementation of his election plan. And in a barrage of letters to lieutenants, commanders, and other officials he repeated and amplified certain key points in the guide.[181]

178 *Ibid.,* 6–8.
179 *Ibid.,* 12.
180 *Ibid.,* 46.
181 The letters started over six months before the 1948 campaign began. They included: 1 / a letter to commissioners of the District of Quebec (12 December 1947), urging them to complete their twenty-five commissariats in the city by recruiting eight lieutenants and 160 regular subscribers each; 2 / a letter to commandments and commissioners of the third rank (19 December 1947), urging them to attain their objectives; 3 / a letter to lieutenants and 'défricheurs' of the four northern constituencies (3 February 1948) reporting the increases

Legault then turned to organizing the more spectacular features of the election campaign, now announced for 28 July. He arranged for large regional assemblies to be held throughout the province, in which Louis Even, J.-E. Grégoire, Gilberte Côté-Mercier, and Réal Caouette were attractions; the same leaders were selected for radio talks. J.-E. Grégoire was chosen once more to lead the campaign, but this time from the safer constituency of Saint Maurice. The Union announced its electoral program early in the campaign. In essence it was a repetition of its earlier promises, including the dividend of $20 per person per month, abolition of the sales tax, subsidies to farmers, aid to colonization, repersonalization of employer-employee relations, old age pensions, grants to schools, exploitation of natural resources, provincial autonomy.[182] But care was taken this time to spell it out in detail, and to use it as a focus of debate in the campaign.[183] The ninety-two candidates were selected early and were accorded much publicity in the pages of *Vers Demain* and elsewhere.[184] On 20 July, Louis Even received a letter from the aging Major Douglas, which was printed in full in the newspaper. Douglas, no longer opposed to social credit participation in elections on principle, wished the Créditistes success in their 'first massive attack on the political fortress.' And he extolled them for being 'the only true challenge to the Antichrist: Communism and its vanguards, Socialism and international cartelism.'[185]

The results of the election, however, were devastating. The Union failed to elect a single candidate and amassed only 140,050 votes, or an average of about 1,500 votes per candidate.[186] All of the leading candidates of the Union, including Grégoire, Roland Corbeil, and Edmond Major, lost their deposits. The voters of Quebec had failed utterly to heed the message which *Vers Demain* had preached for eight years. Far from rejecting the old-line parties, they had reaffirmed their allegiance to the Union Nationale with greater vigour. The editors of *Vers Demain* might point to the fact that the Liberals had also been manhandled by the voters; their former Assembly

in subscriptions elsewhere in the province, and urging the north not to allow their decreases to continue; 4 / a letter to 'true Créditistes' everywhere (16 February 1948) from the four chief organizers, urging them to find three new subscribers and to buy at least two copies of Even's book, *Sous le Signe de l'Abondance*, each; 5 / a letter to district commanders of the third rank (26 February 1948), scolding them for a lack of precision and self-discipline and an inability to delegate tasks, and instructing them on methods of preparation for the elections. From the personal files of Laurent Legault, with his kind permission.

182 All of these measures are, of course, perfectly consistent with the Douglas economic, social, and political philosophy, although cast in more up-to-date terms. See above, subsection A, of this chapter.

183 *Voter Pour Qui? Pour Quoi?* Programme of the Union des Electeurs, (l'IAP, 1948). Also *Vers Demain*, 1 July 1948.

184 They were, however, rather inexperienced and for the most part unfortunate choices. The blame for this poor selection must be laid to Gilberte Côté-Mercier, according to one informer. She was unwilling to listen to advice which contradicted her own opinion; also she refused to give her co-directors sufficient latitude in matters of finance and organization. This pattern of behaviour by a director seems to reflect a typical ambivalence of the original leaders of a movement on the question of expanding the basis of recruitment to the movement. There is a fear of diluting the movement's ideological purity and of losing control to new groups.

185 *Vers Demain*, 15 August 1948.

186 See Scarrow, 210.

representation of thirty-seven had been reduced to eight.[187] They might also conclude that the electorate had been 'bought' by the Union Nationale strongmen who served the financiers. But, although the movement had expended much time, energy, and money, the editors had to face the fact that it had all been to no avail. The strategy of Laurent Legault and Réal Caouette had failed dismally.

The recriminations were not long in coming. Privately Réal Caouette attributed the poor showing of the Union to three major weaknesses in the Union itself: its tendency to mix religion and politics, its reluctance to carry out the whole-hearted commitment necessary to the campaign and, most important, Gilberte Côté-Mercier had kept her usual tight rein on activities, and had sabotaged operations by her narrow-mindedness and blunders.[188]

In May 1948, just before the campaign, Louis Even offered an answer to the first criticism that ought to have satisfied most Quebeckers at that time. He acknowledged that 'religion has its own end, and politics also has its [own end].'[189] But this did not require that the two should be completely separated. After all, he argued, don't man's spiritual relations with his god pervade all of his temporal acts? And why, after all, should not *Vers Demain* include articles on religion in the same edition with articles on politics? If Franco's picture is printed in *Vers Demain*, does that mean the editors are mixing Franco with social credit? If a poem appears about social credit, does it signify an unhealthy blending of literature and politics? And don't other journals like *Le Devoir* print even more articles on religion?[190]

Valid criticisms had, however, been raised against both the manner in which the Union had proclaimed its fidelity to Roman Catholicism and the content of its religious articles. In the first edition of the newspaper, the editors had pledged to concern themselves only with the temporal realm. Yet increasingly, the summer congresses of the Créditistes had become sessions of devotion to the Virgin Mary, Christ, and the various patron saints of Roman Catholicism. Pilgrimages were made to nearby shrines of Catholic martyrs and saints. The established ecclesiastical authorities had frowned on such activities which they regarded as encroachments on their own domain.[191] *Vers Demain*'s expositions of and interpretations of principles

187 *Vers Demain*, 15 August 1948.
188 From an interview with Caouette in April 1964.
189 *Vers Demain*, 15 May 1948.
190 *Ibid.*
191 For example, S.E. Mgr l'Archêveque de Rimouski is reported to have alleged that, 'its [Social Credit's] propagandists tend to spread their ideas in the guise [sous le manteau] of religion' and 'these propagandists act with much arrogance and tenacity. Their arguments are of the following ilk: They come to offer to the workers and farmers enlightenment and also the means to get rid of the veil which the Church, in concert with the civil authority, holds over the eyes of Quebec citizens; questions of a temporal order do not concern the Church; it is necessary to pressure the people to overturn the present regime, etc.' 'Reply to Certain Allegations of S.E. Mgr., the Archbishop of Rimouski against the Social Credit movement' anonymous author, 8–9. Unpublished letter obtained from the personal files of Laurent Legault, with his kind permission.
    Memories of these earlier attacks from the clergy may have influenced certain Créditistes to voice rather negative opinions about the role of the clergy in Quebec, despite their strong religious attachments. See chapter 5. Quinn points out that the Roman Catholic clerical elite was far more negative about the CCF movement and imposed a ban on voting for this party from 1934 until 1943. Quinn, 56.

of Catholicism and papal encyclicals were not always considered accurate or proper, particularly when they involved a comparison with the principles of social credit.[192] There were also some misgivings among Roman Catholic clerics about the ethnocentrism of the Catholic appeal of the journal and its association with anti-Semitism.

It is undoubtedly true that the coolness of the church and ecclesiastical authorities towards their movement seriously hindered the advancement of the Créditistes in Quebec. It is a fact that the voters of a parish pay close attention to the political suggestions and directives of their priest and are wary of embracing anything which is regarded with disfavour by him. This is especially the case in rural areas and was even more so in the thirties and forties than it is today. Nevertheless, it seems unlikely that church opposition caused the defeat of the Union des Electeurs in 1948. For one thing, this opposition had been most vocal in the early 1940s, when Cardinal Villeneuve had condemned the movement as revolutionary, communist-tinged, and anti-social.[193] The editors had spent seven years healing the breach and consolidating a new friendship with the church. Although in 1948 the official position of the church towards Social Credit was still neutral and rather tepid, in many local areas the parish priests lauded the movement quite openly and enthusiastically for its sense of charity and devotion to the poor and miserable.[194]

The intensity of the rank-and-file commitment to the campaign was manifested in a number of significant ways. A long and impressive list of organizers and commanders was proudly displayed after the defeat was known.[195] The editors had nothing but praise for the workers, and this time there was no complaint that Social Crediters had deserted to a party which seemed more likely to win. If the ideology against political parties and elections served as a dampening influence, it was not evident in the enthusiastic crowds and spirited volunteers who turned out in rally after rally to laud the Social Credit candidates.

The effect which the alleged shortcomings of Gilberte Côté-Mercier's leadership had is, of course, much more difficult to assess. It seems doubtful, however, that even with complete freedom of action, Legault could have organized a more effective campaign. For one thing, his resources were limited. Secondly, the workers and candidates lacked experience. Thirdly, the conditions which he faced were uncontrollable: the postwar prosperity, and the popularity of Duplessis. Legault himself must have recognized these facts, since he declared that at the time he was well-satisfied with the results.[196]

192 'Reply to Certain Allegations of S.E. Mgr., the Archbishop of Rimouski ...,' 7. For example: 'In interpreting in its own way the teachings of the Church ... doesn't the movement dispose souls to detach themselves little by little from the Church magistracy?'

193 *Vers Demain,* 15 November 1941. In his directive to the clergy, which was also communicated simultaneously to the press, Cardinal Villeneuve condemned the religious practices of the Créditistes outside church confines, criticized the means of propagation of Social Credit, and questioned the sincerity and social spirit of the directors of Social Credit.

194 In a letter sent by the Abbé (Reverend) E. Lavergne to Mgr Lucien Savard, vicar general of the diocese of Amos, 26 April 1948, the Abbé observes of the Créditistes: 'Some priests, some bishops say to them "It's an open question." Others treat them like Communists, revolutionaries, agents of the Infernal, arrogant people in pursuit of chimeras, bad guardians [de mauvais bergers], etc.' From the personal files of Laurent Legault.

195 *Vers Demain,* 15 August 1948.

196 Interview with Laurent Legault, June 1965.

The editors of *Vers Demain* offered their own explanation for the defeat. According to them, the voters were bought at election time by the old-line parties, the Union Nationale and Liberals. The attraction of money was still too great to resist. The war of ideas and ideals against egoism and corruption had not yet been won. The effort to resocialize had to be redoubled.[197]

Despite the setback, under the prodding of Réal Caouette, who was running in 1949 for re-election to the federal house, the editors of *Vers Demain* were induced to make one more sally into campaign politics. The possibility of implementing social credit seemed greater at the federal level. Perhaps, they thought, the voters had felt that the Social Credit appeal was futile in provincial politics; they were well aware of the failures of the Alberta Social Credit government in this regard. The Union leaders consented to run fifty candidates in the sixty-five federal districts, fewer than in 1948, but more than in the 1945 federal elections. But the results of this election were no better than those of the previous year. The Union captured 80,990 votes, 5.1 per cent of the popular vote, although it failed to elect a candidate. Réal Caouette lost his seat in Pontiac, now regrouped into the federal constituency of Villeneuve. He did, however, manage to make a strong showing, with 10,980 votes and 43.3 per cent of the popular vote. In a few other constituencies such as Chapleau, Drummond-Arthabaska, and Lac Saint-Jean, the Union made substantial gains over 1945. But in several others, including Beauce, Lévis, Québec-Montmorency, Québec-Ouest, their previous totals were considerably reduced. Overall the Union had made absolutely no progress since 1945, despite the fact that it now faced less competition from other third parties. In the face of this the directors made a firm promise not to engage in further campaigns until the voters or the political parties showed some indication that they were ready for real democracy. They now turned to the politics of pressure as the most useful and least painful way of furthering political education.[198]

G DECLINE OF THE UNION, 1949–57

The years which immediately followed the election of 1949 were spent repairing the damage done to the movement by the ill-fated 1948 venture. Readership of *Vers Demain* had remained at a level of 60,000 to 70,000, but the coffers of the movement were empty.[199] However, there was a need to maintain public interest while proceeding to rebuild. This was done both through gimmicks and by focusing attention and public disaffection on certain issues. A group of Montreal Social Crediters protested against the raising of evaluations on land, a prelude to increasing taxes. Gilberte Côté-Mercier appeared before the Private Bills Committee of the Legislative

197 *Vers Demain*, 15 May 1948.
198 This change in orientation of the movement towards pressure group action brought the Quebec movement into closer conformity with Major Douglas' own political doctrine and strategy and tactics in England, particularly after his failure in the 1935 campaign. It also allowed the directors to reassert their authority by claiming that their strategy was doctrinally pure. It is a familiar control tactic used in political movements.
199 At least, that is what the directors claimed both in *Vers Demain* and in personal interviews. There is no method of establishing that these figures are not inflated; however, some of the members of the Ralliement, when interviewed, seemed to agree that circulation figures for *Vers Demain* did not drop dramatically after the 1948 and 1949 electoral defeats.

Assembly to demand that a dividend be distributed to all Quebec citizens. A committee of Créditiste leaders headed by Gilberte Côté-Mercier visited Paul Martin, then minister of health and welfare, to demand that family allowances be increased. A huge gathering of 'berets blancs' – the new nickname for members of the Union des Electeurs who now sported white berets as a mark of distinction – assembled in Quebec City to demand the immediate adoption of Social Credit, and were received by various members of the Union Nationale government including the Honourable J. Miquelon, the Honourable Wilfrid l'Abbé, the Honourable Tancrède l'Abbé, and some leading members of the Liberal opposition, René Hamel, Bernard Pinard, and Emilien Lafrance.

All of these attempts to exert pressure yielded few results. Voices were raised once again in a chorus of demands for greater and more direct participation of Créditistes in politics. Thus in late 1955 when René Hamel, an old Liberal and former member of the Action Libérale Nationale, along with Gérard Brady approached the leaders of the Union des Electeurs to suggest that a common opposition front of Liberals, nationalists, and Créditistes be formed to drive the Union Nationale from office, the leaders were prepared to hear him out. The result of their negotiations was a secret pact between the two groups based on the understanding that the Liberals would make a central tenet of social credit doctrine one of the planks of their election platform. In return, the Créditistes promised to throw their support behind the Liberals in the coming provincial campaign.[200]

Thus in March 1956, René Hamel introduced the first Social Credit motion in the Quebec Parliament, based on a plea by *Vers Demain* for the establishment of an organ of provincial credit. And in the same month the Political Commission of the Provincial Liberal Federation passed a resolution to the effect that 'the Liberal party considers that all that is physically executable in the province must be rendered financially possible in accordance with the needs of the population, municipalities, school commissions, etc.'[201] This resolution was the Social Credit contribution to the Liberal party's election platform. Two days later the directorate of the Union des Electeurs voted unanimously to support the Liberal party in the 1956 provincial campaign.[202]

The charge immediately arose from unhappy members: wasn't this a complete negation of the Créditiste policy of remaining aloof from elections? Worse than that, was it not a total surrender of the independence of the Union des Electeurs? Even retorted that far from being a negation of past Créditiste work, it was its apotheosis. With little effort the Créditistes would be able to ensure that a Liberal government would carry out its commitment and introduce social credit. And if the Liberals were to lose, the Social Credit committees in each district, which would preserve their autonomy from the Liberals throughout the campaign, would still be able to return to 'the permanent work of education and pressure that is the preferred formula of the movement.'[203]

200 From the interview with Gilberte Côté-Mercier and her husband, 14 May 1965, and with Gérard Brady, 14 June 1967.
201 *Vers Demain*, 15 April 1956.
202 *Ibid.*, 1 May 1956. See also Quinn, chapter IX.   203 *Ibid.*

Many Créditistes remained unconvinced by these arguments. One of them was Réal Caouette, who reluctantly agreed to run as a Liberal candidate in Pontiac despite the fact that he had much support among Union Nationale sympathizers.[204] Others agreed with Solon Low, the leader of the National Social Credit party, who denounced the 'perfidy of the Union leaders in presenting Social Credit candidates in certain constituencies under the aegis of the Liberal Party.' Low also noted that the Union des Electeurs had forfeited public good will through its policies of anti-Semitism and its anti-democratic bent; he promised to organize a new branch of Social Credit in Quebec.[205]

Dissidence increased after the results of the election were reported on 20 June. The Union Nationale was re-elected by an overwhelming margin of 72 to 20 over the Liberals. It increased its vote total from 855,327 in 1952 to 956,082, and from 50.9 per cent to 51.8 per cent of the popular vote. This was the highest percentage it had attained since it initially won power in 1936. The Liberals, on the other hand, with Créditiste support, dropped in seats from 23 to 20 and in share of the popular vote from 45.8 per cent to 44.8 per cent. None of the Créditistes running under the Liberal banner was elected.

The Union des Electeurs had played its last direct role in electoral politics. In June 1957 a federal election was called. Its impact on Canadian political history was to be profound and far-reaching, although the Union des Electeurs did not participate. Réal Caouette, always eager to run, offered himself as an independent candidate in Villeneuve, although he was supported by the Union des Electeurs of that constituency. Four candidates ran under a Social Credit banner, but it was that of Solon Low's newly formed Quebec wing.[206] The editors of *Vers Demain* urged its

204 From interviews with Laurent Legault and Réal Caouette in 1965 and 1967.

205 *Vers Demain,* 15 May 1956.

206 All four were members of the Ligue du Crédit Social, which had survived, although in tenuous fashion, since the formation of the new movement in 1940. From about 1948 on, the Ligue maintained a loose connection with the western Social Credit party under Solon Low's leadership. It was revitalized briefly in 1952 by J. Edgar Bouchard of Quebec City, who became its president, and in 1953 it took over the Social Credit CBC radio broadcasts in French from the Union des Electeurs. Beginning in 1955 its leaders had actively sought to reunite all Quebec Social Credit members opposed to the Union des Electeurs in a new movement. They even proposed that Réal Caouette be chosen as the leader of this movement. The idea was finally brought to fruition in 1958. The Ligue never numbered more than thirty throughout this period 1940–58. Most of its members lived in or near Quebec City. From interviews with J. Edgar Bouchard and Robert C. Dupuis, 21 May 1967. See also Low Papers, J. Edgar Bouchard to Solon Low, 27 June 1952; Dr J.S. Bouchard to Solon Low, 17 July 1952; Solon Low to Dr J.S. Bouchard, 27 August 1952; Solon Low to J. Edgar Bouchard, 27 August 1952; Réal Caouette to Solon Low, 16 September 1952; Solon Low to Réal Caouette, 17 September 1952; J. Edgar Bouchard to Solon Low, 19 November 1952; Solon Low to J. Edgar Bouchard, 25 November 1952; J. Edgar Bouchard to Solon Low, 2 December 1952; Solon Low to J. Edgar Bouchard, 9 December 1952; J. Edgar Bouchard to Solon Low, 24 December 1952; Solon Low to J. Edgar Bouchard, 30 December 1952; Louis Even to Solon Low, 10 January 1953; Solon Low to Louis Even, 24 January 1953; Alexandre Bertrand to Solon Low, 25 January 1953; Solon Low to Alexandre Bertrand, 30 January 1953; Solon Low to Louis Even, 17 February 1953; Marcel Grégoire to Solon Low, 16 March 1953; Solon Low to Marcel Grégoire, 20 March 1953; J. Edgar Bouchard to Solon Low, 7 March 1957.

readers not to vote for these candidates, since they had long regarded the Ligue members as annoying opponents and because they felt that 'Low is doing all he can to kill the Union.'[207] They also made a token bid to guide their supporters in their choices, arguing that it was better to vote for the Progressive Conservatives than the Liberals, even though the PCs were not more receptive to social credit. The Liberals have turned a deaf ear to all Union demands, the editors complained, and after twenty-two years, power tends to corrupt.[208]

Once again the supporters of Social Credit failed to heed their leaders' advice. The Liberals were turned out of office, but in Quebec all but eight of their seventy-five candidates were sent to Ottawa. It was the final insult to the Social Credit leadership. Henceforth their voice was to remain silent on all matters related to specific election campaigns. It was also the final straw for many of the rank-and-file activists, who began to turn away from the Union des Electeurs.[209]

During the period 1936 to 1957 the founders and directors of the Union des Electeurs had succeeded in carrying the social credit message to thousands of French Canadians and in partially mobilizing them in support of their movement. However, their attempts at political mobilization, first through their newspaper and local organization, later through electoral action, and still later through demonstrations, marches, and pressure group tactics, had all failed. Although partial mobilization was achieved in this first phase, it was clear by 1957 that the movement had either to reorient itself in a new direction or suffer complete disintegration. Fortunately for the Créditistes, a young generation of militants who advocated different methods of achieving social credit goals had come of age and was ready to assume the leadership of the movement. Their efforts to consolidate the movement's strength and expand its political base led to a split in the movement and the beginning of a new and even more important phase in its political evolution.

207 *Vers Demain*, 1 June 1957. Gilberte Côté-Mercier is said to have referred to the members of the Ligue as lice (pucerons). Interview with Robert C. Dupuis, 21 May 1967.
208 *Vers Demain*, 1 June 1957.
209 After 1957 the Union des Electeurs rapidly disintegrated, losing all but a few hundred of its members to the Ralliement des Créditistes. Nevertheless, the directors continued to publish their bimonthly newspaper, *Vers Demain*, and it continued to be distributed in French-Canadian homes in rural Quebec and eastern Ontario by door-to-door salesmen wearing white berets. The movement and the newspaper turned more and more to other-wordly pursuits, in particular to conducting sessions of devotion to Catholic saints. At last contact (1967) both directors were still alive and living in a home built by its handful of followers in Rougement, Quebec. For a more detailed discussion of this most recent phase of the Union, see Stein, 'The Structure and Function of the Finances of the Ralliement des Créditistes,' in *Studies in Canadian Party Finance*.

This re-orientation from temporal to other-worldly pursuits occurs quite frequently in political movements which fail to achieve their political goals. For example, the Social Credit party in England turned to cultism and spiritualism involving worship of the sun after 1940 until the early 1950s. G. Thayer, *The British Political Fringe: A Profile* (London: Anthony Blond, 1965), 111. See also Hoffer, chapter XIII.

3
The Social Credit Movement in Quebec, 1957-70: The Consolidation Phase

The failure of the directors of the Union des Electeurs to achieve their objectives of political mobilization had become more and more apparent by the mid-1950s. The efforts at electoral penetration in the 1940s had proved disappointing; those involving the use of pressure and mass protest tactics in the early 1950s had been even more unsuccessful. There was a grave danger that the movement, whose membership was beginning to decline, would disintegrate altogether. The directors, sensing their impotence, began to turn to spiritual and religious activity. If they could not succeed in their utopian pursuit of social credit by convincing those who held power in the temporal world – that world had already been corrupted beyond redemption – then they might accomplish their objectives by proper religious incantation and prayer. Social credit was, after all, merely the application of the natural law of God.

This point of view, which was becoming increasingly popular among the first generation of berets blancs, was not well received by Créditistes of the second generation. They had not grown up with the same devotion and deference to the clerical authorities and had come to accept the argument that church and state should be kept completely separate. Moreover, they had a stronger appetite for political and electoral activity and felt that, with the proper leadership and effort, electoral channels could be exploited effectively to further the goals of the movement. They did not wish to see the educational and missionary work of twenty years dissipated in futile other-worldly pursuits. They sought to confirm and consolidate these efforts through political activity, as Aberhart and Manning had done in Alberta and Bennett had accomplished more recently in British Columbia.[1]

---

1 W.A.C. Bennett, a former Progressive Conservative member in British Columbia, assumed the leadership of the Social Credit party in that province and shortly after entered the provincial election campaign of 1952. Primarily because of the use of the alternative vote system, which the coalition government of Liberals and Conservatives had introduced in order to prevent the CCF party from taking power, the Social Credit party succeeded in winning the largest number of seats in the election and shortly after formed the government. They have retained power ever since.

This dissatisfaction with the Union des Electeurs and its directors did not manifest itself in immediate and outright rebellion. The dissident elements within the Union des Electeurs adopted the tactic of establishing a parallel organization within the Union des Electeurs through which they could challenge the monopoly of control over the Créditiste movement which the directors then exercised. In particular, the rebel group sought to alter the decision of the Union leaders not to engage in any further electoral action. The organ which these dissidents used as their vehicle was secretly created by them in a meeting held in September 1957 in Montreal. It was a new political party called Le Ralliement des Créditistes (Social Credit Rally).

A FORMATION AND EXPANSION OF THE RALLIEMENT, 1957–60

The Ralliement des Créditistes had its roots in a private meeting held in Quebec City in May 1957, just before the federal election of that year. A committee of members of the Union des Electeurs under the leadership of Réal Caouette and comprised of those who favoured participation in elections had invited some leading Créditistes to discuss the possibility of uniting all the different Social Credit factions of the province into one movement which would eventually join the National Social Credit party of Canada. In fact this was merely a ruse for defying the decision of the directors of the Union des Electeurs not to participate in elections. The only important Social Credit political group in Quebec outside the Union des Electeurs was Solon Low's fledgling Quebec wing, made up largely of Ligue members. At the 1957 summer congress of the Union des Electeurs in Trois-Rivières, five or six of the dissident Union members gathered around Réal Caouette to register their disapproval of the religious orientation which the Union was beginning to adopt.[2] They agreed to meet again with several others in Montreal in September.

On 20 September 1957, Réal Caouette, Laurent Legault, Gilles Grégoire, the son of J.-Ernest Grégoire, François Even, son of Louis Even, and eight other members[3] of the Union des Electeurs met in the Mount Royal Hotel of Montreal to establish a new Social Credit body which would be independent of the Institute of Political Action. Its ostensible object was to rally dissident Créditistes to the cause and to co-ordinate election strategy for Quebec Social Credit. The members of the group originally hoped to convey this decision to the directors of the Union des Electeurs and yet maintain their continued support through conciliation; at least they hoped to avoid an open conflict. This proved impossible. The tenuous truce which seemed to have been achieved between Caouette and the Union directorate soon broke down.[4]

2 The meeting place for this group was the Cadillac of Alphée Gagnon, a prosperous hotel owner from Rivière-du-Loup. The congress thereby came to be called the Congress of the Cadillac. From an interview with Alphée Gagnon, 8 July 1967.

3 These eight were: P.-E. Drolet, J.-B. Côté, Roland Corbeil, Rosaire Chamberlain, René de Blois, Gilbert Rondeau, René Zoti, and Alphée Gagnon. Interview with Laurent Legault, 1964. The group became known as the 'Les douze septembristes' (the twelve Septembrists).

4 Interviews held with several founders of the Ralliement in 1967. They had decided to use J.-Ernest Grégoire, father of Gilles, as their intermediary. Grégoire, however, became sick and failed to pass on the information. As a result Roland Corbeil surprised the directors with a resolution in an open meeting calling for the establishment of a political arm of the Union des

By early 1958 an openly bitter and vituperative campaign between these two warring factions had erupted. The issues of immediate contention were local financing by the Union des Electeurs of Caouette's weekly radio broadcasts in the northern region, and his candidature in the March 1958 federal election. The directors, who were bitterly opposed to both, conveyed their antagonism to the rank-and-file Créditiste members. Caouette immediately retaliated by launching a sustained attack on them and in particular on Gilberte Côté-Mercier, whom he charged with jealousy and dictatorial practices. After Caouette failed dismally in the 1958 election as an independent candidate in Villeneuve (sponsored by his local group of dissident members of the Union des Electeurs), dropping from second to third place among the candidates, he stepped up his radio campaign of vituperation against Gilberte Côté-Mercier. At this point the dissident Créditistes openly asserted their independence from the Union des Electeurs and assumed the name 'Le Ralliement des Créditistes,' promising to rally all Quebec Social Crediters to their banner. At a meeting called in May in Quebec City, Caouette was elected as their president, Laurent Legault as chief organizer, François Even as their first vice-president, Gilbert Rondeau, a former full-time Créditiste organizer who had been inactive for several years, as treasurer, René de Blois, a former Créditiste who had abandoned the movement for the Progressive Conservatives, as secretary, and Gilles Grégoire as publicist. They agreed to meet again in August to establish party structures and a working relationship with Solon Low and the national Social Credit party.[5]

Despite the fact that it was composed of a large number of former followers of Louis Even and Gilberte Côté-Mercier, the Ralliement des Créditistes was right from the beginning a very different group from the Union des Electeurs. In the first place, although it generally referred to itself as a movement, it was in reality a party, a fighting organization whose prime objective was to contest and win elections.[6] Initially it had no study groups, no newspaper, no large or regular membership, no ranks, songs, flags, or marks of special distinction. Its founding members were not so much men with a mission, emotionally bound to an ideal, as men of a pragmatic and activist bent who saw in the Ralliement a chance to promote their beliefs in the manner most attractive to them, political participation. They had grown restless during the eight

Electeurs. This aroused their ire. Later a meeting was convened between Caouette and the directors of the Union des Electeurs in Joyal Garage, Caouette's place of business in Rouyn, with the idea of arranging a reconciliation between the two groups. No meeting of minds was reached, however. From interviews with Legault, June 1965, and Caouette, 6 June 1967. The editors of *Vers Demain* offer a somewhat different version. According to them: 'At Rouyn, after a meeting of assistant-directors, we consented to a three-quarter hour interview with Réal Caouette, who repeated his sentiments of fidelity to the leadership and declared that the group at the Mount Royal Hotel meeting would renounce its idea – What followed showed clearly that this was a promise typical of a politician.' *Vers Demain*, 5 May 1958.

5 *Vers Demain*, 1 June 1958.

6 Recall that its main disagreement with the Union was that the Union had failed to exploit the best political means for attaining social credit: elections. Caouette himself used the terms party and movement interchangeably in referring to the Ralliement. (From an interview in April 1964.) Legault, however, conceived of the Ralliement more as a movement whose prime purpose was the education of a politically and economically informed élite. Interview, April 1964.

years from 1949 to 1957 when the Union had either curbed or eliminated all participation in elections. The use of techniques such as pressure politics had proved to be less than rewarding, and the brief foray into provincial politics through an alliance with the Liberals in 1956 had proved disastrous. A number of them had come to disapprove of the dictatorial methods used by both Even and Gilberte Côté-Mercier, who had been most responsible for bridling their campaign ambitions.[7] They had also become concerned about the deteriorating image of the Créditistes, whose military and religious symbols, fanatic attention to religious doctrine and practices, and alienation from the more respectable elements of the community had earned them a reputation of being utopians (fantaisistes) and oddballs.[8]

At the urging of three of its original leaders – Caouette, Legault, and Grégoire – the Ralliement immediately took the novel step of promoting its expansion primarily by means of television. It was a risky venture, since the cost of television time was nearly prohibitive. The leaders reasoned, however, that the original expense could be defrayed by means of gifts and loans; later when the party had recruited enough members to bear the burdens, the television campaign would be self-financing. Thus Caouette succeeded in borrowing about $30,000 from the Caisse Populaire of Rouyn. This was just enough to pay for a sequence of twenty-six bimonthly broadcasts over the Rouyn-Noranda station, begun in the fall of 1958, and a series in Jonquière, which started some months later. By the fall of 1959 the response to the television broadcasts had been so encouraging that the members of the Ralliement decided to enter the Sherbrooke and Quebec City regions, where television time was even more expensive. At about the same time, the monthly journal *Regards*, official organ of Social Credit, was launched under the directorship of Gilles Grégoire.

Caouette, Legault, and Grégoire established a system for financing Social Credit which would ensure that the television expenses would be covered at least in part by the people who were given the privilege of viewing the Ralliement leader.[9] A membership card was printed and distributed to Ralliement workers in key centres of the province who were urged to canvass their counties. If enough cards were sold, Réal Caouette, already an established and popular television personality, would be brought to the area. If they were not, then the Social Credit leader would not appear on their local television station. The same applied to both counties in which the television program had already been broadcast and to those where it had not yet been seen. In the former case, the programs would have to be discontinued if the money were not forthcoming.

These two new devices, the newspaper and the membership card, acted as useful complementary techniques for expanding the membership of the Ralliement. The newspaper *Regards* contained membership blanks and instructions to readers to

---

7 From interviews. Charges of dictatorship were levelled against Even and Gilberte almost from the very inception of the Union des Electeurs. See, for example, the letter from Armand Turpin to Louis Even, 14 August 1944, quoted in M. Stein, 'The Structure and Function of Finances of the Ralliement des Créditistes,' 420. See also chapter 2.

8 The symbols included the white beret, the white flag containing a torch and a book of life, the military formation, and often crucifixes.

9 Grégoire, rather than Caouette, appeared regularly on the Jonquière station.

recruit active members by circulating and filling out these application forms. Those who bought these membership cards, ostensibly because they had been impressed by Caouette's performance on television, soon wanted more information about social credit and more contact with other Ralliement members. They turned to one obvious source, *Regards*. And they began to sell membership cards themselves.[10]

The Ralliement established formal ties with the national Social Credit party at about the same time. The western representation, after electing nineteen Social Crediters (thirteen from Alberta, six from British Columbia) to the federal parliament in 1957, was completely wiped out in the Diefenbaker sweep of March 1958. The national organizers then had turned inward rather than outward in an attempt to rebuild broken fences. Mr Low himself was in poor health and had resigned from his post. The national Social Credit organizers were faced with the dual task of electing a new national leader and building a new national organization capable of waging an effective federal campaign.

It was with this purpose in mind that Robert Thompson, then the chief national organizer for the movement, travelled to Rouyn in the spring of 1960 to meet with Legault and Caouette.[11] Beginning in Alberta and British Columbia, where a base for the movement already existed in the form of the provincial Social Credit leagues, Thompson had already spread Social Credit associations into the remaining prairie provinces of Saskatchewan and Manitoba and then into Ontario. It was in Ontario that the western movement made its first direct contact with the Quebec movement under Caouette.[12] Thompson spent a few weeks with Caouette and Legault learning about the organization they had established, co-ordinating it with the western movement, and setting the ground rules for a meeting of all wings in a national convention, which had been called for that summer.

At the summer congress, held in Ottawa on 28–9 July, a new constitution was drafted which formalized the de facto decentralization of the national movement. Only the provincial associations were to have the right to issue membership cards and form constituency associations. Only one provincial association in each province could be recognized by the national party. A national executive was elected and charged with the task of preparing for the election of a new national leader the following summer. Robert Thompson was named president, and Réal Caouette was chosen vice-president, along with Orvis Kennedy, the chief organizer of the Alberta Social Credit League, and Herb Bruch of the British Columbia provincial association. Thus, the Quebec movement was immediately given a prominent role in the selection of the new national leader. Its delegation, moreover, was the largest of any province, comprising about one hundred members. *Regards* remarked of the 1960 meeting:

10 For a more detailed discussion of the relationship between finance and organization in the Ralliement des Créditistes, and its parallels in the Union des Electeurs, see the author's 'The Structure and Function of Finances of the Ralliement des Créditistes,' 430–2.

11 Thompson had originally run as a federal Social Credit candidate in 1940 and was narrowly defeated. From 1945 to 1957 he served as a missionary and educator in Ethiopia. He spent two additional years on lecture tours in the United States and Canada. On his return to Canada he had attached himself to Manning, hoping to build a national organization which would give the Alberta premier the incentive to run federally.

12 Interview with Robert Thompson, April 1964.

'Its dominant note was undoubtedly the frank collaboration and sincere agreement among all Social Crediters of the country, no matter what their province, or whether they spoke English or French.'[13]

The following year preparation began in earnest for the summer leadership election. In Quebec representatives to the 1961 convention were chosen from among the most active members in each constituency association. In many cases a constituency delegation was led by a man who had already been chosen as candidate for the next federal election. These representatives were, for the most part, former members of the berets blancs, marginal rural farmers, urban workers, and small town entrepreneurs who had disagreed with the anti-political orientation of Louis Even and Gilberte Côté-Mercier. But a new element had been added: the more highly respected professional or community officeholder who was approached to join the movement in order to improve its image among the voters. Among them were, for example, Dr Guy Marcoux of Quebec, a general practitioner and member of an old and respected French-Canadian family, in Québec-Montmorency, Maurice Côté of Chicoutimi, president of the regional association of the Saint-Jean Baptiste Society, Gérard Chapdelaine, a young Sherbrooke lawyer, and Jean-Louis Frenette, of Portneuf, a senior mayor of his constituency. These men were unfamiliar with the ways of Social Credit organization and unversed in the doctrine of Major Douglas, but they were elevated to the most important positions within the movement and generally given a vital voice in all internal party discussions.

B CONSOLIDATION AND FURTHER EXPANSION, 1960–2

At that time the Ralliement des Créditistes was a comparatively small party, with a few thousand members, according a limited number of tasks to each member. First, there was the job of organization. This was generally left to the local people in each constituency, most of whom were old-time Social Crediters who had helped to build up the Union des Electeurs in the 1940s and 1950s. On the provincial level, however, the job of strengthening the Ralliement organization fell largely into the hands of two men, Fernand Ouellet and Laurent Legault.

Ouellet joined the Ralliement in 1961 after hearing Caouette perform on television and soon became the chief collector of revenues for the party. He established the system of 'carte de membre active,' a centralized method of self-finance which he had adapted from the Jeunesse Ouvrière Catholique (Catholic Worker's Youth Group), in which he had previously been active, and this enabled the Ralliement to expand its television audiences and membership rapidly. Under this system, one dollar a month was collected from each member for twelve months. Part of the monthly fee collected was turned over to the provincial organization, and the remainder was retained at the constituency level. Ouellet also devised other means for filling the Ralliement treasury, including a 'club des cents,' which was designed to encourage the more prosperous members to donate $100 gifts to the movement, and activities aimed at soliciting funds from the smaller corporations in Quebec. Legault was in charge of expenditures. Whenever someone on the provincial Ralliement executive wrote a cheque on the Ralliement account, it had to be counter-

13 *Regards*, 1 September 1960, as quoted in Ralliement Créditiste, *Le Crédit Social: Cours d'orientation politique* (January 1964), 11.

signed by him. The editor of *Regards* also signed cheques involving expenditures in connection with the printing and administration of the newspaper. And the travelling expenses of men like Caouette, Legault, Grégoire, and others were to be paid from the same fund.

The provincial organization of the Ralliement consisted almost entirely of co-ordination between Ouellet, Caouette, Grégoire, Legault, and after 1961 Dr Marcoux, who succeeded Grégoire as editor of *Regards*. These men used the newspaper, the mails, and tours of Social Credit constituency associations in the different regions of the province to promote social credit. Following the tactic employed so successfully by the Union des Electeurs, they established small cells in each community or parish and charged the initial members with the task of selling the membership cards to their neighbours. The inducement for the members was the opportunity to see Caouette on television.

It was Legault and Ouellet who, just before the summer leadership convention of 1961, organized conventions or meetings in enough constituencies throughout the province to enable the Ralliement to send close to three hundred delegates to the national convention, the largest representation of any of the provinces. Yet not all the Quebec representatives were united behind the leadership candidature of Réal Caouette. The outcome of his candidacy was further complicated by his outward pessimism about the possibility of his election.

The vote for the leadership took place on the afternoon of 7 July. The delegates had been treated to three days of speech-making and personal campaigning by the four major candidates: A.B. Patterson and George Hahn of British Columbia, Robert Thompson of Alberta, and Réal Caouette of Quebec.[14] Both Thompson and Caouette claimed that they did not expect to enter the competition, let alone win it. Thompson said he had hoped that Premier Manning would become leader of a rejuvenated movement, but Manning protested that his health was not up to it and, moreover, his interest and experience were too provincial for this kind of post. Subsequently Robert Thompson, because he was a man of international experience, and because he had shown his ability both in public speaking and organization work, was thrust into the forefront. At the last minute, he agreed to run.[15]

Réal Caouette had entered, according to his own account, merely to give the leadership struggle a bilingual and binational flavour. Much to his surprise, he polled the most votes of any candidate on the first ballot. Patterson and Hahn were eliminated: the choice on the second ballot was between himself and Thompson. At this point Réal Caouette began for the first time to think seriously of himself as a national party leader. He launched an earnest campaign to win delegates over to his side.[16]

The two Social Credit premiers, Manning and Bennett, were at the convention and wielded considerable influence both on the speaker's platform and in the lobbies. After Patterson had been defeated, Bennett, who was Manning's rival both in temperament and political position, swung the support of the British Columbia dele-

14 For brief descriptions of these proceedings, see Jean-Luc Pepin, 'Un slogan pour le moins douteux: Le Crédit Social s'en vient,' *Le Magazine Maclean*, juillet 1961; Arnold Edinborough, 'Social Credit: A Party "On the Move," ' *Saturday Night*, 5 August, 1961.
15 Interview with Robert Thompson, April 1964.
16 Interview with Réal Caouette, April 1964.

gation behind Caouette. He liked the Quebec leader's flamboyant and colourful political style, which was akin to his own. And he sought to undercut the support given by Manning to Robert Thompson.[17] There were enough Quebec delegates present to elect Caouette the national leader with British Columbia support even if all remaining delegates had voted for Thompson. However, some of the Quebec delegates present were openly cool to the idea of electing Caouette. Some of them were old-time members of the Union des Electeurs who had joined the Ralliement in spite of, rather than because of, Caouette. They remembered him as a flamboyant and outspoken campaigner for the old movement, but as an indifferent worker; they recalled his self-centred posture at past Union congresses; and they were doubtful about his capacity for leadership and his emotional stability.[18] There were other, new, Quebec delegates to Social Credit who chose to judge the issue in terms of the personalities and capabilities of the two men who were running. Many of them did not know Caouette well, having met him only once or twice previously, and they were not impressed. Caouette was dynamic on the political rostrum, but his views lacked a certain moderation or subtlety. Robert Thompson seemed to them to be a more judicious speaker, a man with a broader vision. A national leader had to represent the views of all Canadians, rather than a minority segment. Moreover, Thompson's personality was pleasing to these men; a chiropractor turned missionary, he operated in a low-key, modest but firm fashion which was more attuned to the professionals and community notables.[19]

Certain incidents reinforced these preconceptions and prejudices. When the content of the national platform was being debated, Caouette urged that a national dividend of $100 a month, to be paid to every Canadian, be included. This had long been repudiated by the westerners as a politically unrealistic and harmful plank. Caouette finally withdrew the motion but only after alienating a number of potential supporters. Then, just before the final vote was taken, Premier Manning arose to remind his audience that being a French Canadian and a Roman Catholic would prove to be a serious handicap to any leader campaigning in the west.

When the vote was counted, Thompson had been elected leader by a slight majority.[20] It was then moved and passed unanimously that Réal Caouette become

17 Interview with Jean-Louis Frenette, 28 July 1965. Arnold Edinborough wrote in a somewhat different vein. Bennett's support of Caouette was more nominal than real, as if he were just trying to add excitement to the campaign. 'Social Credit: A Party "On the Move," ' 14.

18 From a confidential statement by a Ralliement Créditiste delegate who was a former member of the beret blancs, 20 July 1965.

19 From a confidential interview with a new Créditiste who was a delegate at the convention, 28 July 1965.

20 It has been suggested by a former Créditiste that Caouette actually won the ballot, but that he agreed to step down after a private session with Premier Manning, Orvis Kennedy, the Alberta Social Credit League president, and Thompson. Kennedy, who presided over the convention, had the ballots burned. In fact, what appears to have happened is that five of the Quebec delegates had voted twice for Caouette, so that the total number of ballots cast was greater than the total number of eligible votes. The private meeting was called between Caouette, Thompson, and Kennedy to prevent this information from being made public and force a new election. Caouette appears to have accepted becaused he realized he had lost and would lose again in a second election.

the deputy leader. Thompson and Caouette interlocked their arms and raised them in a show of amicable unity.

What had caused Caouette's defeat? Probably, it was the opposition of the group of dissident former berets blancs who voted for Thompson over Caouette. In addition, one or two of the so-called modernistes, or newer Créditistes, had also voted for Thompson. Premier Manning's warning appears to have produced a dual reaction among Quebeckers which may have cancelled itself out in the actual vote. There were some French Canadians who might have voted for Thompson but whose nationalist and religious sensitivities had been wounded to the point where they could no longer do so. Others who leaned to Caouette had second thoughts after Manning's intervention: on purely pragmatic grounds they felt the Alberta Premier had made a telling point. Among English-speaking delegates it is unlikely that the Premier's remark had any marked influence. Most of the English-speaking delegates were suporting Thompson anyway; among those who were not, the British Columbia delegates were unlikely to change allegiance on the suggestion of the man who was more than anyone else, their primary target of opposition.

Far more important than its influence on the actual vote, however, was the effect Manning's intervention had on the attitudes and beliefs of the Quebec delegates directly involved. According to Réal Caouette, Premier Manning had exerted pressure and had said 'right in black and white that the West would never accept a French Canadian, a Catholic French Canadian, as leader, at least in his own province.'[21] This was substantial proof for Caouette that the Alberta premier was anti-French-Canadian. Further it cast doubt on the friendliness of Thompson, who became, in the opinion of Caouette, the puppet of Manning. Caouette's attitude was shared, sometimes even more strongly, by several of his closest associates, including Gilles Grégoire and Laurent Legault.[22]

The Quebec vote, too, had made a lasting imprint on the mind of Caouette. He felt betrayed by some of his own supporters, but he was unable to identify them precisely. It was natural for him to lay the blame on the shoulders of the new members, with whom he was least acquainted and with whom he had less in common in background, interests, and temperament than with his former berets blancs colleagues. This idea that the new members had betrayed him was implanted by some of Caouette's former berets blancs supporters, who were anxious to regain some of their lost influence with the Ralliement leader.

These latent divisions within the Quebec Social Credit wing were concealed, however, in the ensuing efforts to forge a common front with the western wing against the old-line parties in the period from 1961 until the federal election of 1962. The Ralliement met in a provincial convention in Hull just after the national leadership convention, and Laurent Legault outlined his strategy for the 1962 campaign.

Legault's plan was only slightly modified from the one he had outlined over fifteen years earlier, in the 1948 provincial campaign, in which he had acted as the organizer-in-chief.[23] The organization for each constituency would consist of an

21 Interview, April 1964.
22 Interviews with Gilles Grégoire and Laurent Legault, April 1964.
23 See chapter 2.

organizer-in-chief, section organizers for every ten polls (or 1,000 votes), and an organizer and assistant organizer for every poll (or 100 votes). To build these cadres, the organizer-in-chief and section organizers were to hold two public assemblies in succession within a month's interval. The object was to expand the association of some 10 to 15 organizers to 100 or 150 by means of an intensive recruitment campaign and by delegating assignments. At the second assembly, monthly membership cards were to be sold. At a third assembly, held by April 1962, members of those constituencies which had not yet elected their candidates were to form a nominating convention for this purpose.

The novel element in the strategy was the central role given to television. The fifteen-minute program, already transmitted in the regions of Rouyn-Noranda, Saguenay-Lac Saint-Jean, Quebec, and Sherbrooke, was now to be beamed to the Bas du Fleuve, the Gaspé, and parts of Montreal. Caouette's popularity as a television performer had already become apparent; further large sums of money were to be spent on this method of winning support. The cost of the program was approximately $2,000 per week; for the campaign a total of at least $70,000 would be needed. In addition some $20,000 was to be set aside for newspaper and television publicity. All other organizational work (eg, scrutineering) would be voluntary.

Unlike provincial organizations in other parties, the Ralliement des Créditistes received very little financial support from the national association or various other provincial affiliates. Money collected in Alberta and British Columbia for the Social Credit federal campaigns in these provinces remained almost entirely with the local provincial associations. Some money was transferred to Ottawa to help subsidize the national Social Credit newspaper and the numerous pamphlets and leaflets which were distributed from that source, and the salaries of the national organizers were also paid from this fund. Most of this literature, however, was of no value to the Créditistes since it was printed only in English. With the exception of the salary of Fernand Ouellet, who had been named national organizer attached to Quebec, expenses incurred by Créditistes in the course of organizing and campaigning were paid for entirely by the provincial association.

It was Fernand Ouellet's job to collect this money. Most of it came from the monthly membership cards, which he had devised. It was supplemented by passing the hat at public meetings and similar fund-raising activities. Donations by corporations were virtually nil. For the Ralliement, being financed by the members themselves was the guiding principle of action. This method of finance, largely imposed on the movement by the nature of its membership, was incorporated into the ideology. Whereas the old-line parties had accepted large contributions from corporations, and thus were committed to policies favourable to these corporations, Social Credit was the party of the small men, committed only to the principle that every person has a social responsibility to donate to a party which is truly responsible to himself, the common voter. The method of finance of the old-line parties was tantamount to that of receiving bribes. Social Crediters thought that the old-line parties had sold themselves to high finance and had become their agents and bondsmen, and that the only way to reverse this trend was to elect a party truly responsible to the people. The Ralliement Créditiste, like its predecessor, the Union des Electeurs, was demonstrably such a party. Its method of finance was proof of this.[24]

Equipped with this combination of highly visible campaigners in the person of Réal Caouette, Gilles Grégoire, Guy Marcoux, and others, and with an invisible mass army of enthusiastic workers, the Ralliement entered the 18 June election campaign in a spirit of buoyant optimism.[25] Its opportunities for success were further enhanced by the political and economic conditions in Quebec. An economic depression of rather severe proportions had existed since 1959, particularly in rural areas. John Diefenbaker, the Conservative prime minister, had just engaged in a public confrontation with the Governor of the Bank of Canada, James Coyne, and had not emerged from the struggle unscathed. His image in Quebec was also tarnished by his seeming inability to integrate his Quebec MPs effectively into his party and cabinet. Finally, the Union Nationale party, which had supported the Progressive Conservatives in 1958 and had provided workers for their candidates, was now in a shambles as a result of its defeat in 1960 by the reform-minded provincial Liberals led by Jean Lesage. They were both unwilling and unable to provide the necessary support for the Conservatives.[26] The federal Liberals led by Lester Pearson were scarcely in better shape. Their organization in Quebec was tired, archaic, and needed complete reshaping. Pearson appeared unable to command the kind of enthusiasm in French Canada that Louis St Laurent was able to arouse. Further, Pearson had no Quebec lieutenant with the prestige and stature of a George-Etienne Cartier or an Ernest Lapointe. The New Democratic party had just been formed from the old prairie-based CCF and the trade unions. It had no Quebec leader, no organization to speak of in the province, and its predecessor had never won a seat in Quebec. Too, it suffered from its identification with socialism, a word which was still anathema to most French Canadians. For many, the Ralliement campaign slogan – You have nothing to lose, vote Social Credit – had real meaning.

In the west the prospects for Social Credit seemed almost as good. Although the Diefenbaker government continued to have an excellent image there, largely through the success which Agricultural Minister Alvin Hamilton had had in selling wheat abroad, it seemed unlikely it would be able to retain the entire block of seats it had won in the sweep of 1958. The Liberals' forces in the west had been demolished in that year and had commanded no great support in provincial contests since then. Their recent stands on devaluation were hardly likely to win votes from the farmers.[27] The New Democrats were undergoing a transformation. Most important, the Social Credit administrations of Manning and Bennett had just won resounding votes of confidence in their respective provincial elections. The one discouraging note was the

24 Interview with Laurent Legault, April 1964.
25 The concepts of visible campaigners and invisible organization were propounded by Laurent Legault. See chapter 2.
26 Daniel Johnson, the Union Nationale leader, was said to be cool towards Diefenbaker. The shortage of manpower and funds at this time were also factors in this unwillingness to co-operate.
27 They had opposed the emergency devaluation and even advertised that position, despite the fact that devaluation had raised the price of wheat.

inability of the Social Credit League of Saskatchewan to elect a single candidate in the provincial election of June 1960, even though they had presented a full slate. But it was felt that with a new leader, a well-established base of support in the west, an effective organization, and financial and manpower aid from the provincial leagues, the party would at least win back the seats they had held before their 1958 debacle.[28]

When the results of the election were announced, the Ralliement des Créditistes, under the leadership of Réal Caouette, had amassed 26 per cent of the popular vote in Quebec, and 26 of the 75 federal Quebec seats. Four other Créditiste candidates missed victory by only a few hundred votes. Among the candidates elected were several of the new Créditistes like Dr Marcoux in Québec-Montmorency, who had the largest plurality in all of Canada (20,039), Jean-Louis Frenette of Portneuf, J.A. Roy in Lévis, Gérard Girouard in Labelle, and Gérard Chapdelaine in Sherbrooke. In addition, former berets blancs like Henri Latulippe of Compton-Frontenac, Gérard Perron of Beauce, Gilbert Rondeau of Shefford, Antoine Belanger of Charlevoix, as well as Caouette himself in Villeneuve and Gilles Grégoire in Lapointe were returned with, in some cases, well over 50 per cent of the votes in their constituencies. Nor was their success a narrow one, concentrated in one small area. Of the ten traditional regions of Quebec,[29] the Créditistes emerged as the dominant party in no less than four and also ran a strong second in four others. Only in the area in and around Montreal was the Créditiste surge resisted.[30] Otherwise, the party could boast support from sharply contrasting regions and groups in the province: urban Quebec City and Sherbrooke, and rural Beauce and Dorchester, manual and more skilled labourers, workers in blue and white collars, shopkeepers, artisans and farmers, younger and older age groups, former partisans of both Conservatives and Liberals.[31]

The results astounded press and politicians, academics and intellectuals, businessmen, and trade union leaders alike. Few had even an inkling of the potential strength of the Créditistes before the campaign date was announced, and most were astonished by the election results.[32] The Ralliement was formed only in 1957; the June 1962

28 Interviews with Robert Thompson, April 1964, and with four other western Social Credit MPs: A.B. Patterson, 6 June 1967; H.A. Olson, 16 June 1967; Howard Johnston, 23 June 1967; and Bert Leboe, 27 June 1967.
29 They are: La Gaspésie (including Rive-Sud), Le Royaume du Saguenay (Saguenay- Lac Saint-Jean), Québec (the city), La Mauricie (Trois-Rivières, Shawinigan, etc), Les Cantons de l'Est, Montréal (the island, Ile Jésus, Ile Perrot, etc.), La Laurentie (Ste Agathe, Mont Laurier, etc.), Outaouais (along the Ottawa River), Nord-Ouest or Abitibi (Abitibi-Témiscamingue), Côte-Nord or Nouvelle Québec (north shore of St Lawrence River from Quebec City to Labrador). See *Prévisions de la Population (1966–1981)* (Québec: Ministère de l'Industrie et du Commerce, 1966), 1.
30 In the twenty-one federal constituencies of Montreal, the Créditistes placed fourth and last among the major parties in all but three ridings (Laurier, Mercier, and Saint-Jacques).
31 On this point see Vincent Lemieux, 'Les dimensions sociologiques du vote Créditiste au Québec,' Recherches Sociographiques, VI, 2 (1965), 181–95. It is also supported by my analysis of the electoral results, using the Chief Electoral Officer's definition of polls as urban or rural.
32 For example, the *Montreal Star* made only the following brief mention of the Quebec result:

election was the first, federal or provincial, in which it participated. Although the founders and many of the hard-core activists were former members of the Union des Electeurs, the Union had never achieved the success which the Ralliement attained in 1962. In the six federal and provincial general elections which it contested in the period from 1940 to 1956, it had never won a seat; its sole victory, Caouette's in Pontiac, occurred in a federal by-election in 1946, and he held that seat for just over two years. In none of these elections did the Union ever amass more than 10 per cent of the popular vote (its highest total was 9.4 per cent in the 1948 provincial election), and in every one of these elections, all but a handful of the party's candidates lost their deposits.[33] Second, the Ralliement was the first third party in Quebec history not connected with one of the two old parties to win more than 5 per cent of the total Quebec seats in any federal or provincial election (its percentage total was 35 per cent), and also the first to capture more than 15 per cent of the popular vote.[34]

Nor did Créditiste candidates squeak through on narrow pluralities earned because moderate voters had either abstained from voting or had split their votes among traditional party candidates. Voter turnout was almost as high as in 1958 and higher than in 1953 and 1957 in most constituencies.[35] In twelve constituencies Créditiste candidates gained more than 50 per cent of the recorded vote, and in several others as well their margin was greater than the combined figure for the Liberal and Conservative

'If anybody won the election yesterday, it was the Social Credit party in Quebec. Nobody can take much comfort from this result' (19 June 1962). The *Montreal Gazette* commented drily: 'It would seem that a desire for something new, and a want of faith in what was old explains its [Social Credit's] emergence' (21 June 1962). *La Presse* observed rather defensively: 'A total surprise? It was evident during the last few weeks that Social Credit commanded a considerable popular vote. The danger was seen, but too late' (23 juin 1962). Maurice Lamontagne, the defeated Pearson adviser, mused somewhat bitterly: 'I really don't know ... It [the Social Credit success] could perhaps be explained by the difficulties faced by the poor. They have forgotten what the Liberal party did for them five or six years ago. They are not really Social Crediters, they are just "against"' (*Montreal Star*, 19 June 1962). And Jacques Flynn, the chief organizer in the province for the Progressive Conservative party, who was likewise defeated in his bid for election, concurred: 'No one had foreseen it ... it was a protest, period, a vote against' (*Ibid.*). For a more detailed description of the variety of reactions see chapter 1 of my unpublished PHD dissertation. The sole exception to this bewildered reaction was the predictions of the pollster and political scientist Peter Regenstreif. Based on polling results, he had predicted a Créditiste sweep of about this magnitude in an article published in the *Montreal Star* (16 June 1962).

33 See chapter 2.
34 The Nationalist party of Henri Bourassa which elected eleven candidates in 1911 was in alliance with the Conservatives. Action Libérale Nationale, which supplanted the Conservatives for a time in 1935–6 as the opposition party, was comprised largely of dissident 'rouges' (Liberals) and 'bleus' (Conservatives and Union Nationale members), most of whom later rejoined their respective parties.
35 See W.P. Irvine, 'An Analysis of Voting Shifts in Quebec,' in John Meisel (ed), *Papers on the 1962 Election* (Toronto: University of Toronto Press, 1964), 129–31. See also H.A. Scarrow, *Canada Votes: A Handbook of Federal and Provincial Election Data* (New Orleans: Hauser Press, 1962).

candidates. The most remarkable victory was that of Dr Marcoux. But there were others almost as spectacular: Réal Caouette captured his home riding of Villeneuve by a margin of 14,191 votes over his nearest rival, and Robert Beaulé defeated Maurice Lamontagne, one of Liberal leader Pearson's chief economic advisers and campaign strategists whose campaign was well-financed by Liberal party coffers, by no less than 8,699 in that traditional preserve of Liberal leaders, Québec Est.[36]

Finally, an analysis of the twenty-six constituencies in which Créditiste candidates were elected demonstrates the breadth of their success in terms of rural-urban distribution. By calling all ridings urban which have over 60 per cent urban polls (as defined by the chief electoral officer), all ridings rural which have over 60 per cent rural polls, and the remaining urban-rural, one finds that thirteen of the Socred constituencies were rural, nine were urban and four were urban-rural.[37] Hence it can be justly claimed that outside the rather concentrated, and in some ways quite unrepresentative, island region of Montreal, the Créditistes had emerged as a dominant federal political force in all segments of the province.

In the west, on the other hand, only four candidates were elected: Robert Thompson and H.A. Olson in Alberta and Bert Leboe and A.B. Patterson in British Columbia; all were old-time Social Crediters. And none had achieved overwhelming pluralities.[38]

---

36 Québec Est is the riding which was represented by Wilfrid Laurier from 1878 to 1921; Ernest Lapointe, Mackenzie King's Quebec deputy, from 1921 to 1941; and Louis St Laurent from 1942 to 1958.

37 Compiled from *Official Election Results: Report of the Chief Electoral Officer* (Ottawa: Queen's Printer, 1962). See also, Irvine, 133–4.

38 A crude analysis of the aggregate voting results for the four western provinces suggests a possible explanation for this poor showing. The losses both in popular votes and in seats by the Conservatives in these provinces in 1962 as compared to 1958, which were considerable, appear to have been distributed about evenly in the form of gains by the three other parties: Liberal, CCF-NDP, and Social Credit. Thus in Manitoba the Conservatives lost 3 seats and 16 per cent of the popular vote, whereas the Liberal gain was 1 seat and 9 per cent of the popular vote, the CCF-NDP gain was 2 seats with no increase in the popular vote, and the Social Credit increased its popular vote by 7 per cent although it failed to gain any seats. In Saskatchewan the Conservatives retained all their seats but lost 1 per cent of the popular vote, while the Liberals gained 1 seat and 3 per cent of the popular vote, the CCF-NDP lost 1 seat and gained 3 per cent of the popular vote, and the Social Credit party gained 4 per cent of the popular vote without gaining a seat. In Alberta the Conservatives lost 2 seats and 17 per cent of the popular vote. The Liberals gained 5 per cent of the vote but no seats, the CCF-NDP 5 per cent of the popular vote and no seats, the Social Credit party 2 seats and 7 per cent of the popular vote. In British Columbia the Conservatives lost 12 seats and 22 per cent of the popular vote, the Liberals gained 4 seats and 11 per cent of the vote, the CCF-NDP gained 6 seats and 6 per cent of the vote, and the Social Credit party gained 2 seats and 4 per cent of the popular vote. Thus the Social Credit party was unable to regain in the west the relatively strong position it held among the four parties prior to 1958. Moreover, the Conservatives, while losing ground, still maintained a relatively stronger position in the west than they had held before 1958. This may be attributed to the continued, though somewhat decreased, popularity of Diefenbaker. Hugh Thorburn (ed), *Party Politics in Canada* (2nd ed; Scarborough: Prentice-Hall, 1967), appendix, 220–3.

C CONFLICTS AND SCHISM WITH THE NATIONAL PARTY AND THEIR
   AFTERMATH, 1962–5

The results of the election strengthened Caouette's belief in his right to the leadership
(or at least a substantial share of it). When Robert Thompson convened a meeting in
Ottawa of all Social Credit MPs a few days after the election in order to plan strategy
and allocate responsibilities, Caouette responded slowly and with apparent reluctance.[39] At the meeting it was decided that David L. Wilson, then national organizer
in Ottawa, would serve as national co-ordinator for western Canada, and Fernand
Ouellet would become national organizer for the east. Dr Marcoux was nominated
whip.[40]

Other points of friction developed before the new parliament convened. These
included slightly different interpretations of Social Credit policy towards Diefenbaker's austerity program and the Common Market, disagreement over the procedures and final choices for membership on the Ralliement provincial executive,
and some unhappiness with the choice of Laurent Legault as provincial president of
the movement. Among the other problems the so-called 'Affaire Mussolini-Hitler'
probably had the most serious repercussions internally. In an interview Caouette
allegedly stated that his foremost political heroes were Mussolini and Hitler. When
asked to clarify what he meant, he explained that he was thinking in terms of their
leadership capacities and economic reforms rather than their political achievements.[41] The effect on the English-speaking Canadian population was adverse.
David Wilson then addressed the caucus and urged that the members make their
public declarations more reflective. Some of the old Créditistes were outraged by
Wilson's interference.[42]. At the Trois-Rivières congress on 25 August 1962 the
matter was discussed briefly, and Caouette was exonerated on the grounds that he
had been misinterpreted.[43] The issue had driven a deeper wedge between Thompson
and Caouette. But when parliament met at the end of September, a sentiment of
mutual acceptance and even camaraderie seemed to prevail among the different
factions within Social Credit.[44] Only in caucus meetings did some tension remain,
and this generally arose over the statements and actions of Réal Caouette.

Caouette was often absent from caucus meetings in this early period, partly
because he had become a public celebrity and was therefore frequently engaged as a
speaker by various groups. Many of Caouette's statements, which were reported by
the press, reflected badly on him and cast aspersions on the purity of the Thompson-
Caouette marriage. The matter caused concern among the Social Credit members,
who debated it in caucuses. Inevitably on these occasions a colleague of Caouette's,

39 He had already organized his own press conference in Rouyn. Interview with Dr Guy
   Marcoux, 24 August 1965.
40 *Ibid.*
41 See *Le Devoir*, 25 August 1962. The original statement appeared in *Maclean's*, August 1962.
42 Interview with Dr Marcoux, 24 August 1965.
43 *Le Devoir*, 27 August 1962.
44 The Social Credit MPs dined together and socialized with each other. Apparent differences in
   attitude towards policy matters melted away in the general euphoria. Interviews with
   Créditiste leaders.

generally an old Créditiste, would rise and defend the Ralliement leader. Allusions would be made to his great campaign contributions, and most of the former members of the Union des Electeurs would readily concur. The new Créditistes, on the other hand, who were less awed by the qualities of Caouette and less concerned with his indispensability to the party, sometimes took him to task for his indiscretions. The western MPs generally sat in uneasy silence.[45]

But the most serious single issue of disagreement among the caucus regulars was the emphasis to be given to matters of French-Canadian language and national pride. The Social Credit MPs from the east, and in particular those who had previously belonged to the Union des Electeurs, constantly emphasized this theme in parliamentary debates.[46] The westerners were often embarrassed by this. However, some of the more bilingual and better educated Créditistes, notably Dr Marcoux (who as whip had to approve all questions and motions made by his colleagues), were annoyed with what they considered to be an excessive concern for trivial issues.

The real cause of the split did not occur, however, until the end of the session.[47] The Social Credit MPs had been united, in spite of their differences, through their common and unanimous desire to avoid an immediate election. Caouette shared this sentiment, despite his consistent criticism of Prime Minister Diefenbaker's austerity program. But the Créditiste organizers, accepting at face value Caouette's statements as well as press and television reports about a Social Credit wave in the province, began to demand the overturn of the government. The coup de grâce was the fumbling of the cabinet on the nuclear weapons issue, and the resignation of Defence Minister Harkness. It was clear at this point that it was only a matter of time before Prime Minister Diefenbaker would be defeated by a combination of the three opposition parties in a vote of non-confidence.

At this point, a number of the Créditiste MPs themselves began to call for Diefenbaker's resignation. On the afternoon of 4 February, 1963, Robert Thompson called a caucus of his thirty Social Credit MPs. Caouette was not present. According to Dr Marcoux, Thompson first asked to hear the opinion of others on the question of voting in favour of non-confidence. He declared that he was personally against an election but would submit to the opinion of the majority. When the vote was taken, the majority was in favour of dissolution. The final decision was taken in a smaller caucus held that evening. Two MPs worked on the motion of non-confidence

45 Interview with Jean-Louis Frenette, 28 July 1965.
46 For example, they disapproved of the fact that menus in parliamentary restaurants were printed only in English and that the standard text on parliamentary procedure, by a French-Canadian, Beauchesne, was unavailable in French translation. The objection was first raised when the Speaker, the Honourable Alan Macnaughton, had suggested to Bernard Dumont (Bellechasse) that he acquaint himself with proper parliamentary procedure before making interventions. Dumont was expelled from the Chamber for refusing to come to order. He had been attempting to intervene on behalf of Quebec farmers.
47 In November 1962 the issue of participation in the provincial election, which had been debated at the summer congress of the Ralliement, came to a head. It did not, however, concern all of the new Créditistes. Guy Marcoux and Fernand Ouellet were the strongest advocates of provincial participation; Caouette was firmly opposed to it. The latter's view predominated even among the new Créditistes.

which was submitted to the caucus for approval and then tabled in the House. It was worded in such a way that it would virtually ensure that the other two political parties would accept it. The next day it was carried.[48] Caouette, upon hearing of the motion late that night, attempted to block it. He called together the caucus but was rebuffed, even by his closest supporters. He tried other channels, including acting Defence Minister Sevigny. All proved of no avail. The motion had been put by Thompson and seconded by Marcoux. The results were 142 in favour of dissolution and 111 opposed.

To Réal Caouette, it looked as if the two had engineered the entire business. After the dissolution of parliament in February 1963, he became openly estranged from the national executive and from Robert Thompson. For example, he failed to attend the meeting of the executive called in late February in order to discuss electoral strategy, including the question of nuclear arms. As a result, there were at least two social credit policies on nuclear arms: Caouette was unalterably opposed to the acceptance of nuclear weapons on Canadian soil or to their use by Canadian troops abroad; Thompson was less decisive.[49] On the subject of bilingualism and biculturalism, Caouette was an outspoken advocate of French-Canadian rights. But he made clear his opposition to separatism, professing a faith in national unity and in the ability of French and English Canadians to co-operate with each other. On this point, then, there was no fundamental disagreement with Thompson, although their conceptions of what comprised national representation for the two groups undoubtedly differed.

Among most Social Crediters of both east and west wings, the expectations of electoral success were very high. In the west Premier Manning's former lukewarm endorsement of their party in 1962 had turned to whole-hearted support. This was due in no small part to a change in his attitude towards the Diefenbaker Conservatives. Formerly he had accorded them a grudging respect; now he felt only contempt for them. In the east, despite a sustained assault on the Créditistes from various quarters, including Jean Marchand, then CNTU president, Eric Kierans, then Montreal Stock Exchange president, and Premier Jean Lesage, the general feeling among press and pundits was that the movement was on the rise.[50] The name of Réal Caouette, unknown to most in 1962, was now familiar. His broadcasts were watched with much interest and, it seemed, considerable enthusiasm. His public meetings were the best attended of those of any party leader.

It was probably this expectation of mutual success, more than anything else, which tempered each leader's attitude towards the other and caused each to play down his differences with the other. Nevertheless, expectations were quite different from 1962. Now it was the east which was expected to win the largest number of seats – up to fifty it was thought. The western MPs, with the new asset of posing as

48 Interview with Dr Marcoux, August 1965.
49 See, for example, *Le Devoir*, 15 February 1963. Thompson was quoted as saying: 'No Canadian political leader can say squarely "yes" or "no" to atomic political armaments, and none can say "never" to defensive nuclear arms.'
50 See *Montreal Gazette*, 6 April 1963, *Le Devoir*, 2 April 1963, and *Montreal Star*, 3 April 1963.

part of a truly national party, could now hope for a better representation, but they were unlikely to have anything near the total number of members of the eastern wing. Thus Réal Caouette no longer felt the same need to conform to a common party program, particularly one which was framed largely by the English-speaking group. And he no longer felt himself in any sense the deputy or subordinate of Robert Thompson. Fernand Ouellet no longer accompanied him on his campaign tours as he had done the previous year. Guy Marcoux, out of favour with Caouette, was no longer informed of strategy and events and was forced to confine his campaign activities in the province almost entirely to his own constituency of Québec-Montmorency.[51]

When the results of the election, held on 8 April 1963, were announced, there was general disappointment. The Créditistes lost eight of their former seats in Quebec to the Liberals and managed to gain only two new seats from the Conservatives.[52] This left them with only twenty seats which, combined with the four which the Social Crediters managed to maintain in the west, fell far short of the seventy-five to eighty seats that Robert Thompson had thought would be sufficient to elect a Social Credit minority government.[53] Moreover, since the Liberals had won 130 seats, or only three less than an overall majority, these twenty-four Social Credit members no longer held the balance of power exclusively in their hands. Any combination of Liberals and either whole or partial blocs of MPs from either one of the two 'third' parties, or even a breakaway group of independent-minded Progressive Conservatives, could maintain a Liberal minority government in power. This had even greater political significance than had the purely numerical reduction in Social Credit representation, as events were soon to show.[54]

Even the Créditistes who were re-elected generally managed this only with substantially, in some cases drastically, reduced pluralities. Guy Marcoux, for example, saw his 1962 margin of over 20,000 votes cut to just slightly over 3,000. In Lac Saint-Jean, Marcel Lessard's 6,725 plurality was sliced in half. In Mégantic, Raymond Langlois watched his 7,786 plurality shrivel to 2,189. Robert Beaulé defeated a seemingly much less formidable candidate by 7,000 fewer votes than in 1962. Gérard Chapdelaine, who had swept Sherbrooke in 1962 by a 7,882 margin, barely managed to hold on to the seat by 605 votes. Even Réal Caouette, with all of his newly acquired publicity and prestige, had 3,365 votes fewer than his previous

51 Interview with Dr Marcoux, August 1965. See also *Le Devoir*, 7 February 1963. A seemingly contradictory statement that 'Ouellet was then still very active' was made by Dr Marcoux. But it is likely that the Québec-Montmorency doctor was thinking of Ouellet's position in the national organization and his work in Ontario and New Brunswick.

52 The members who lost their seats were: J.A. Roy (Lévis); Bernard Dumont (Bellechasse); J.P. Cook (Montmagny-l'Islet); Philippe Gagnon (Rivière-du-Loup-Témiscouata); Lauréat Maltais (Saguenay); Gérard Lamy (St Maurice-La Flèche); André Bernier (Richmond-Wolfe); David Ouellet (Drummond-Arthabaska). The two newcomers were: Gérard Ouellet (Rimouski) and Gérard Girouard (Labelle).

53 *Le Devoir*, 3 April 1963.

54 Awareness of this fact helped precipitate the 'affair of the six' (signatories to a letter pledging to support the Liberal minority government), and also the split between the Thompsonites and Caouettistes.

winning margin.[55] The two new seats that the Créditistes did manage to wrest away from their opponents were Rimouski and Labelle, and here the total 'swings' were merely 924 and 430 votes respectively.[56] In only one constituency was the margin of an incumbent Social Credit MP increased at all.[57]

Most journalists and political commentators were surprised and relieved. More than that, they were convinced that the Créditiste tide had been stemmed once and for all and that the party no longer was a force to be reckoned with in the province of Quebec. It was, like the Poujadists in France, a transient phenomenon, a mere groundswell in a generally placid political sea, a bad dream in an otherwise euphoric political sleep.[58]

Marcoux felt that there was an urgent and immediate need to maximize the party's strength, given this reduced representation and leverage in parliament. One option was to negotiate an agreement with one of the two large minority parties (for no party had emerged with an overall majority) which would enable them to govern. The Liberals had the largest representation, but Marcoux felt, as did some of his closest friends in the party, that they were undeserving of support, in view of the dirty campaign they had fought against the Créditistes in the province. A coalition of Progressive Conservatives, NDP, and Social Credit seemed a more tolerable alternative.

Réal Caouette's initial reaction to the results was one of dismay and bitter resentment. The Liberals, aided by American high finance, and Premier Jean Lesage had done him in. To take revenge he would fight Lesage on the provincial plane. The charges levelled against him were completely false: 'I have no arms, no army. I am not a Mussolini, or a Hitler, a dictator. I am a French Canadian who wants to help his country.'[59] Even then he did not deny the possibility that his party might support the Liberals if they presented an economic program aimed at prosperity. And when he had an opportunity to collect his thoughts, he admitted that though disappointed the Créditistes were not discouraged. After all, they had increased their popular vote total from 26 per cent to 28 per cent.[60]

It was at this juncture that the notorious 'affair of the six' occurred. Six Créditiste MPs signed a notarized statement in which they agreed to support the Liberals in power: Gérard Perron (Beauce), Gilbert Rondeau (Shefford), Raymond Langlois

---

55 *Official Election Results: Report of the Chief Electoral Officer* (Ottawa: Queen's Printer, 1962) and *Official Election Results: Report of the Chief Electoral Officer* (Ottawa: Queen's Printer, 1963).

56 In 1962, Ouellet, the Social Credit candidate in Rimouski, was defeated by 784 votes. In 1963 he defeated the Liberal incumbent by 140 votes. The Social Credit candidate in Labelle in 1962, P.E. Lesage, lost by only 111 votes. In 1963 Gérard Girouard, his replacement in Labelle, won by 319 votes.

57 In Kamouraska, where C.E. Dionne increased his plurality slightly from 385 to 627.

58 For example, the *Montreal Gazette*, in its editorial of 9 April, exulted in the 'considerable recovery [by Canadian voters] ... of an awareness of the dangers of a House weakened by many-sided divisions,' and the *Toronto Star* declared on 10 April: 'The French-Canadian voter, despite his grievances against English-speaking Canada, obviously is no longer mesmerized by the spurious and divisive appeal of Real Caouette.'

59 *Le Devoir*, 9 April 1963.

60 *Ibid.*

(Mégantic), Pierre A. Boutin (Dorchester), Robert Beaulé (Québec-Est), and Lucien Plourde (Québec-Ouest). They were assisted in their endeavour by Alex Bertrand, a party vice president and a former active leader of the berets blancs. The object of this declaration was apparently to force Prime Minister Diefenbaker to resign and thereby ensure that the Liberals would be called into office. They sent one copy to the Governor General and a second to Liberal leader Lester Pearson.

The immediate response of the public to this declaration was adverse. Social Credit supporters of the MPs were outraged. Two of the signatories, Beaulé and Plourde, immediately sent a telegram to the Governor General disassociating themselves from their statement. Another, Pierre Boutin, followed soon after. Marcoux and Marcel Lessard, caucus president, were asked by Thompson to investigate the entire matter. Marcoux immediately convened another meeting in Ottawa, to which both victorious and defeated MPs were invited. The western MPs, with the exception of Bert Leboe, had not yet arrived. Caouette objected that the caucus was illegal but attended anyway. The six were questioned, along with Bertrand, and their testimonies were contradictory. There was some consternation among a number of the Créditistes, but a large number expressed their agreement in principle with the six, particularly when Caouette arose and defended them. This was tantamount to an open confrontation between the whip and the deputy leader. Marcoux pressed for the expulsion of the six from the Ralliement; he also demanded that Caouette resign from his position as leader.

Caouette retaliated by rallying his supporting forces. He persuaded the members of the Quebec contingent of Social Credit MPs to issue a vague communiqué in which they declared the matter a closed incident. The six had all repudiated their declaration; they had also sworn in writing that they had received no remuneration for their offer of support to the Liberals. On that basis, the six were given a 'clean bill of health' and allowed to remain members of both the Ralliement and the national Social Credit party. No further disciplinary action was to be taken against them.

Even the western Social Credit MPs were disinclined to press for sanctions against the six. They met with the national president, Martin Kelln, and the president of the Alberta provincial Social Credit League, Orvis Kennedy, after which Thompson issued a statement from Red Deer promising Social Credit support to the Pearson government in the coming session. Thus he seemed to be granting what the six had tried to bring about by their independent action – a Pearson government certain of a working majority in parliament. He also indicated that no immediate action would be taken against the six, and that another caucus would be held just before the opening of the new session in which a final decision would be made on their case.[61] At the same time, Bert Leboe virtually exonerated the signatories: they had committed a minor fault which had been precipitated by declarations made both by Caouette and Thompson suggesting that Social Credit would support a Liberal government. At the same time he denied categorically that there had been any aggravation of differences between the leader and the deputy leader over the affair.[62]

At this point Caouette pressed ahead with his advantage. He charged Laurent

61 *Ibid.*, 10 April 1963.
62 *Ibid.*, 17 April 1963.

Legault to begin preparations for a special assembly in Quebec which would take disciplinary action against Dr Marcoux. The same provincial council was supposed to examine the actions of the six and of Alex Bertrand. The delegations were selected so as to ensure that former berets blancs would predominate.[63] But Marcoux did not wait. A week before the special Quebec assembly he resigned from the executive of the Ralliement. After a caucus of all Social Credit MPs in Ottawa, he added his party resignation. Henceforth he would sit as an independent in parliament. It was clear to him that he could not command any support from the western MPs. The Quebec MPs sympathetic to his grievance against Caouette and the six remained silent.

At the special provincial council meeting of the Ralliement, held in Quebec four days before the opening of the new session, Réal Caouette took the first of a series of steps which would bring about the split. As one astute reporter put it, 'in the intimacy of a "chosen" audience of about 200 Ralliement activists he carried out a purge of what he called "subversive elements" in the party.'[64] Caouette expelled Fernand Ouellet, national co-ordinator for the eastern provinces, P.E. Lapointe, a front-ranking Créditiste in Quebec and chief organizer for Marcoux in Québec-Montmorency, and J.P. Cook, former MP from Montmagny l'Islet (who was later temporarily reinstated), claiming that they had infiltrated the organization in order to undermine him and destroy the Ralliement. Caouette also denounced Dr Marcoux, declaring that 'although an honest man, a man of heart, he allowed himself to be led astray by Fernand Ouellet.'[65] Caouette once more absolved the six of all blame and reminded the assembly that these men were all longstanding and good Créditistes. Alex Bertrand submitted his resignation as vice president but was permitted to retain his post in the Ralliement office in Quebec City. The Ralliement leader also condemned the policy followed by Social Credit leader Robert Thompson, whom he labelled a pawn of Premier Manning of Alberta. Neither was a real Social Crediter, since neither wanted a national dividend. Moreover, in some respects Manning was a socialist. He also warned: 'I retain my faith in the possibility of a national entente but not one which leads to the pure and simple assimilation of Quebec.'[66]

Most interesting of all, Caouette conducted what amounted to a self-confession before the delegates. Stung by criticisms of his affinity for drink which was reportedly affecting his diabetic condition, he promised to curb it in the future. He also admitted that rumours concerning the near bankruptcy of his Rouyn enterprise, Joyal Motors Ltd, were true. He had avoided failure by borrowing $50,000 from a Rouyn bank and by obtaining a loan of a further $50,000 from his fellow MP from Roberval, C.A. Gauthier. Another $25,000 credit had been obtained from the Caisse Populaire of Rouyn.[67] Clearly Caouette perceived a real threat to his leadership from within the Ralliement and moved to neutralize it.

These difficulties seemed to reinforce his determination to rid himself of all those remaining elements who were suspect. He became more trenchantly nationalistic in his policy and more select in his associations. Soon after the parliamentary session

63 *Ibid.*, 13 May 1963.
64 *Ibid.*, 11 May 1963.
65 *Ibid.*
66 *Ibid.*
67 *Ibid.*, also from an interview with Dr Marcoux 1964.

began, J.P. Cook, former MP, resigned from the Ralliement, declaring that Caouette, Legault, and their valets, all former members of the Union des Electeurs, were dominating the movement.[68] He called on the national Social Credit party to expel the Quebec provincial association. At the same time he admitted that among the sitting Créditistes there were 'men of worth,' and he listed four of them: Maurice Côté, Gérard Chapdelaine, Marcel Lessard of Lac Saint-Jean, and Jean-Louis Frenette of Portneuf. All four were among those who later remained with Robert Thompson when the split occurred.[69] A few days later the Social Credit executive of Québec-Est, the constituency of Robert Beaulé, resigned from the Ralliement, claiming that they had been unable to get to the root of the matter involving the six. Soon after, fifty-seven organizers in Québec-Montmorency, Marcoux's constituency, followed suit. Caouette meanwhile, seemingly undeterred, issued an ultimatum to the national executive, asking them for a special representative for Quebec who would have access to all correspondence and financial statements. This was in addition to the representation given to Réal Caouette as deputy leader and Gilles Grégoire as one of the three regional vice presidents. At the same time he called for election of a bilingual national leader and threatened to withdraw from the national party if the request were refused.

But that was purely a tactical manoeuvre. On 30 April, long before the internal Ralliement party differences had come to a head, he had determined to challenge the national party and its leadership.[70] His major complaint was that the western Social Crediters were disregarding the national dividend, a key portion of the doctrine of Major Douglas. The man most responsible for this 'drifting from the philosophy of Major Douglas' was Ernest Manning, the premier of Alberta. According to Caouette, Manning exercised control over Robert Thompson through two major levers: personality and finances. Thompson was 'afraid' of the Alberta Premier, Caouette charged, and he relied upon Premier Manning and the provincial movement for donations of $1,500 a month; Manning's explicit orders were that none of the money should be diverted to Quebec. Fernand Ouellet, acting as an agent of the national association, had acquiesced in this policy.[71]

The National Council of Social Credit met in early July to consider the demand for a leadership contest. Its decision was a foregone conclusion. It rejected the ultimatum and reaffirmed its support of Robert Thompson as national leader. The council also voted to recommend to the next national convention that the position of deputy leader be abolished.

Caouette grasped at a final straw in his hope of succeeding Robert Thompson as national leader. He asked Laurent Legault, president of the Ralliement, to prepare the annual congress of the party to consider a resolution recommending the displacement of Robert Thompson as Social Credit leader.

Thompson retaliated on the eve of the Granby convention, 30 August 1963, by calling for Caouette's resignation from the party. The next day Caouette opened

68 *Le Devoir*, 24 May 1963. Cook had apparently been accused of mishandling funds.
69 It was at this time that Dr Marcoux, who was still a member of the Ralliement, openly deplored the return of the spirit of Gilberte Côté-Mercier to the provincial party. *Le Devoir*, 16 May 1963.
70 A letter was sent by Caouette to H. Gallagher, a Toronto party member, on this date, in which he expressed these views. See *Le Devoir*, 5 June 1963.
71 Interview with Caouette, April 1964.

proceedings with a stinging attack on Manning and Thompson. He concluded by moving that: 1 / Mr Thompson be divested of his post as national leader of Social Credit and a new national convention be held to elect a new national leader, and 2 / Thompson be divested of his post as parliamentary leader of Social Credit and that the Ralliement MPs select a new parliamentary leader. Both resolutions were debated and passed in the Committee on Political Orientation and ultimately carried in the plenary assembly in a near unanimous vote of approval.

But a splinter group of five Créditiste MPs, including Gérard Girouard of Labelle, Gérard Ouellet of Rimouski, Maurice Côté of Chicoutimi, Marcel Lessard of Lac Saint-Jean, and Jean-Louis Frenette of Portneuf, immediately rejected the resolution as illegal. They argued that only a national convention of all Social Credit provincial parties could divest Thompson of his posts. They immediately convened a meeting in the Queen Elizabeth Hotel to plan their strategy. Guy Marcoux was invited, and at its conclusion he announced that he was rejoining the Social Credit party; the 'dissidents' also contacted Gérard Chapdelaine of Sherbrooke, who gave them tentative support. Lucien Plourde, MP for Québec-Ouest and one of the six who was, however, less implicated than the other five in planning the affair, also expressed an interest in joining. But he asked for time to consult his organizers before making his decision.

Caouette responded by calling his own caucus in Quebec City. All of the dissidents were invited, but only Frenette and Chapdelaine attended. Both refused to change their position. Lucien Plourde, however, declared his support for Caouette soon after. There were then thirteen Créditistes in Caouette's camp. The Ralliement leader announced that they would sit apart from Thompson's group in parliament as a separate party.

The national Social Credit Association took the next step. The national president, Martin Kelln, announced that 'events at Granby demonstrated that the Ralliement, as led by Caouette, no longer desired affiliation with the national organization.'[72] The association therefore declared the Ralliement to be formally separated. Ralliement delegates would not be invited to future council meetings or conventions, and they would have no voice in the selection of a new national leader. At the same time, the association invited Quebec Créditistes to join with it and the MPs who had remained loyal to Mr Thompson.

Premier Manning of Alberta was the first to declare his satisfaction over this formal schism. It was 'in the interests of the Social Credit movement.' He predicted that the Caouette group would soon be extinguished. Robert Thompson, remarking on the support accorded him by the provincial Social Credit associations of Ontario, New Brunswick, and Saskatchewan, scoffed at the national aspirations of what he termed 'a Quebec bloc with stated separationist tendencies.' And even Premier Bennett of British Columbia was forced to take the split philosophically. It was a forerunner of similar schisms in other parties, he commented prophetically, and it would require vigilance on the part of all Canadians to prevent such party splits from accelerating the break-up of the country.[73]

Soon after, the Caouette contingent applied for official recognition as the Social Credit party, pointing to the fact that they now had a majority of the sitting Social Credit members in parliament. After much wrangling, they were accorded status as a

72 *Montreal Gazette*, 6 September 1963.   73 *Montreal Star*, 6 September 1963.

new party, designated as the Ralliement des Créditistes (Social Credit Rally); Robert Thompson's group retained the name Social Credit party. The two groups co-existed as such in the Canadian House of Commons from October 1963 until the general election of November 1965 with one slight change in this alignment: Thompson's group was reduced from 9 to 7 members in April 1964 when two of the Quebec MPs, Girouard and Ouellet, crossed the floor and joined the Conservative benches.[74]

There was much consternation among the local supporters of the seven MPs who remained loyal to Robert Thompson. Why had they deserted Caouette for a leader who was not a French Canadian and who, moreover, could not even speak the French language? Their reply was that it was not they who had deserted Caouette but rather the Ralliement leader who had illegally and undemocratically deserted the national party. They had simply retained their affiliation with the leader and party under whose banner they had been elected to parliament.

In theory it was a convincing argument. A good number of the organizers of the Thompson Créditistes accepted it at first. Most members of the local associations of these members at first pledged their continued loyalty to their parliamentary representatives.[75] But practical considerations eventually predominated. Réal Caouette, determined to destroy the Créditistes who had failed to back him in his dispute with Thompson, entered their constituencies and held public assemblies of Social Credit sympathizers. Thompson was not a French Canadian, he was not Catholic, he could not speak their language. Moreover, Caouette argued, Thompson showed little understanding of problems peculiar to French Canada. The members who had remained with Thompson were not real Créditistes and did not even understand the basic principles of the doctrine. None of them, after all, had formally belonged to a Social Credit group until 1960 or 1961. And most of them had first become exposed to social credit teachings only at that time.[76] These arguments gradually won over more and more of the local Créditistes, particularly those who had formerly belonged to the berets blancs. The local associations were split into two opposing factions. Most of the formerly active workers lost their enthusiasm, and ceased to work for the party. There were no constituency association meetings, no study circles. The organizations in most of these ridings became moribund.[77]

Caouette also exploited his advantage from an organizational point of view. The Ralliement des Créditistes remained intact as a provincial association charged with the responsibility of expanding Social Credit in the province. Its means for doing so, television, newspaper, and local associations, were already firmly established. As long as Caouette still maintained most of his support among active Créditistes in the province, he was ensured the financial means to carry on his television broadcasts. As a speaker there was no one who could seriously rival him. No Thompsonite Social Credit Quebec MP could hope to win the allegiance of so many voters from such

---

74 Both of them were former organizers for the Progressive Conservative party, and they announced at the time that they had no disagreement with Thompson but had decided that joining the PCs was their last hope for political survival. Neither was re-elected in 1965.
75 Interviews with Créditiste leaders, 1964 and 1965.
76 Interviews with several Créditiste leaders, August 1965.
77 *Ibid.*

different locales and walks of life. And none of the representatives who remained with Thompson had shown either ability or desire to organize beyond his own constituency. There was no one who could command a Quebec-wide allegiance. None had sufficient contacts which could be used as a base of operation. Most important, they all lacked any binding ideology beyond a rather tenuous loyalty to their Alberta leader and a vague allegiance to the broad principles of social credit. It is not surprising, therefore, that after a few months, they became aware of the precariousness of their position. Two of them, Girouard and Ouellet, left the party. The others gave serious thought to leaving the party as well but decided to stay on until the next general election.[78]

At this time it was clear to those Quebeckers who remained with Thompson that the only way they could hope to be re-elected was to dissociate themselves entirely from the western Social Credit group. All of them ran in 1965 as independents, and all lost. A number of them did not even keep their deposits. Caouette's Ralliement des Créditistes, on the other hand, fared considerably better. Of the thirteen former Ralliement MPs, only seven were re-elected.[79] But the party succeeded in electing two new members, for a total representation of nine.[80] Five of the six who were defeated, moreover, were signators in the affair of the six, and this undoubtedly alienated some of their support. In other constituencies the Ralliement candidates lost large blocs of votes to former Social Credit sitting members. Nevertheless, in two constituencies, Lac Saint-Jean and Portneuf, the Ralliement candidate defeated the former MPs, Lessard and Frenette. In two other constituencies, Compton-Frontenac and Villeneuve, the incumbents actually succeeded in increasing their pluralities over 1963, and in three others, Chapleau, Kamouraska, and Mégantic, the incumbents maintained their plurality at about its 1963 level. The Ralliement captured 19 per cent of the total Quebec vote. The four western Social Crediters were all re-elected,[81] and a fifth from British Columbia, Howard Johnston (Okanagan-Revelstoke) was added. This still gave them a smaller representation than the Quebec group.

D PROVINCIAL ACTION: FORMATION AND ELECTORAL FAILURE OF
    THE RALLIEMENT NATIONAL, 1965–7

The 1963 split had left the Ralliement des Créditistes in considerable disarray. It was natural that other divisions that had remained latent until that time should manifest themselves during this period of weakness. The most important of these was the split between those who preferred to confine Ralliement activity to the federal level and those who also wished to participate in provincial elections.

The issue of provincial participation had long plagued the party. A group of nationalist-minded Créditistes had attempted to convince the leaders to participate in provincial action as early as the summer of 1962. They were defeated at the Trois-

78 It was held on 8 November 1965.
79 They were Gérard Laprise (Chapleau), Henri Latulippe (Compton-Frontenac), C.E. Dionne (Kamouraska), Gilles Grégoire (Lapointe), Raymond Langlois (Mégantic), C.A. Gauthier (Roberval), and Réal Caouette (Villeneuve).
80 Alcide Simard (Lac Saint-Jean) and Roland Godin (Portneuf).
81 They were Bert Leboe (Cariboo), H.A. Olson (Medicine Hat), A.B. Patterson (Fraser Valley), and Robert Thompson (Red Deer).

Rivières congress on 25 August and then again just before the provincial election in the fall of 1962. At Granby, however, the leaders reconsidered and agreed to a constitutional amendment providing for the eventual establishment of constituency associations on a provincial basis. At the Provincial Council meeting of January 1964, the results of a poll taken among local organizers revealed that 76 per cent of Créditiste activists supported the move to participate in provincial action.[82] At the same meeting the party voted overwhelmingly in favour of a strongly nationalist and autonomous four-point program calling upon the federal government to surrender complete control over bank credit, foreign trade, immigration, and tax collection to the provinces. And Caouette issued a statement threatening that if the federal government did not adopt the program by 1967, the Créditistes would support Quebec secession. At Quebec City in the summer of 1964 a co-ordinating committee was established by the congress to take soundings of local organizations on their choices of candidates for the provincial party leadership.

The decisive move, however, came in the summer of 1965 at St Jerome when the Ralliement congress voted to set aside $20,000 in a frozen electoral fund to support future provincial action. It elected Laurent Legault as interim provincial leader and assigned to him the responsibility of readying the local organizations for provincial action should a provincial election be called. It also charged him to prepare for a provincial leadership convention in March 1966. Réal Caouette agreed not to oppose this action. But he refused to have anything to do with any activity to promote the party's participation in provincial politics.

In an earlier speech during the federal campaign, Caouette had hinted that he might be willing to entertain an alliance with a right-wing separatist group which had split with the Rassemblement de l'Indépendance Nationale in 1964 over the question of socialism. This small faction which referred to itself as the Regroupement National and was centred in Victoriaville near Quebec City was headed by a pediatrician named Dr René Jutras.[83] When Caouette rejected their plan for provincial action, the provincialists cast about desperately for an alternative solution. They knew that something was needed to elevate the prestige of the potential provincial candidates so that they presented a more credible alternative to the government party. The decision was taken to contact Jutras with the object of arranging an alliance between his group and the Créditiste provincialists. The initiators of the plan received a warm response from the Regroupement leader, and a meeting was held in Montreal in March 1966 at which Jutras and Laurent Legault negotiated their alliance. They found their views on a whole range of political questions, particularly related to Quebec's role in Confederation, to be surprisingly similar. They also acquired a mutual respect for each other's integrity and strength of purpose.[84]

82 Questionnaire sur l'éventualité pour le Ralliement de faire de la politique provincial (Montréal, 26 janvier 1964). Only 48 per cent, however, wished Réal Caouette to assume the leadership of the provincial wing. The same proportion was opposed.
83 Dr Jutras had achieved some renown by his decision to separate from the RIN. He had also published a book in 1965 on the subject of Quebec independence. See R. Jutras, *Québec Libre* (Montréal: Les Editions Actualité, 1965).
84 Interviews with Laurent Legault, 25 May 1967, and Dr René Jutras, 29 May 1967.

It was agreed that the two organizations would be integrated into a new unified party, to be known as the Ralliement National (RN). Dr Jutras and Laurent Legault would share the leadership of this party on an equal basis. Their lieutenants would also share positions on the executive. The candidates were to be chosen from both wings, in the most advantageous ad hoc manner. The party adopted a platform advocating an associate state status for Quebec and declared its strong opposition to the socialist policies of the provincial Liberal government, particularly in the sphere of education.[85] Little was said about the implementation of a social credit monetary and banking program.

Very little time was left to organize the party's cadres before the June election. Nevertheless, it was decided to field a full slate of 108 candidates, in order to create the impression that the party was a real political force. *La Nation*, the newspaper of the Regroupement National prior to the alliance, became the major organ of propaganda for the party. Some use was also made of television, particularly in the ridings of the party's leaders. However, the extent and cost of this publicity was not at all comparable to earlier campaigns of the Ralliement des Créditistes.[86]

The results of the election revealed the serious weaknesses in the Ralliement National's campaign strategy. None of the 108 candidates offered by the party was elected. Moreover, the Ralliement National received only 3.2 per cent of the popular vote, considerably less than that of the Ralliement des Créditistes in its poorest electoral performance. It was also well below the vote of the Union des Electeurs in the provincial election of 1948. The RN had not even managed to win as much popular support as its main separatist rival, the Rassemblement pour l'Indépendance Nationale (RIN), led by Pierre Bourgault. And although the RIN had also failed to elect a single member, it had at least obtained over 5 per cent of the popular vote.

The RN leaders attributed their poor showing to a lack of sufficient time to prepare and a failure to project a convincing image to the electorate. They considered that the dual leadership arrangement had not worked to great advantage, since it was never really clear to the voter who was directing the party's fortunes. Moreover, neither Jutras nor Legault was able to present himself as a sufficiently attractive leadership personality. Neither had charisma, stature, or the kind of qualities generally desired in political leaders in Quebec. Legault lacked education and professional status; Jutras, whose health was poor, was unable to endure the gruelling pace of the election campaign and had to limit his appearances.

When the Ralliement National met in its summer congress after the election, its future was in grave doubt. The organization was totally bankrupt. Heavy debts for television and publicity were outstanding. There was much disagreement about the future policy direction of the party: whether it should emphasize economic and social reform or political independence, whether or not social credit doctrine should be included in its platform, and whether associate statism or outright independence should be promoted. Most important, the prospects of finding a person capable of exercising effective leadership seemed dim.

A number of Créditistes persuaded Gilles Grégoire, the federal deputy leader, to

85 *Ibid.*
86 The total cost of the RN campaign was given as $19,000, according to Dr Jutras. *Ibid.*

attend the congress as an observer. Grégoire had long been interested in the provincial wing and in the independence movement in Quebec. During the June 1966 campaign, he had helped some of the RN candidates in the area of Saguenay-Lac Saint-Jean. However, he had never formally committed himself to joining the Ralliement National. When the RN leaders and some of his local supporters, fearing a momentary breakup of the party, urged him to accept the leadership, he first hesitated and then reluctantly agreed.[87]

The choice of Gilles Grégoire as president temporarily revived the RN. The party proceeded to plan for the liquidation of its debts and to elaborate a strategy for the following year, including negotiations towards an alliance with the left-wing separatist leader Pierre Bourgault and his RIN. These negotiations were not immediately successful and the Ralliement National continued to function as an independent party for a few more months. In October 1968, after several weeks of discussions, it formed an alliance with the Mouvement Souveraineté Association, the separatist group established by former provincial Liberal Resources Minister René Lévesque after his resignation from the Liberal party in 1967. The new party was named the Parti Québécois (PQ). Lévesque was elected its founding leader and president and Grégoire was chosen as its vice president. A few weeks later the RIN disbanded and most of its members, including Bourgault, also joined the Parti Québécois.

A few of the former Créditistes who followed Grégoire into the PQ subsequently became candidates and organizers for that party in the 1970 Quebec general election, particularly in the area of Saguenay-Lac Saint-Jean. All, however, were defeated, and the Créditiste element within the PQ, including its leader Gilles Grégoire, has since lost much of its original influence. Many of the Créditiste candidates and organizers for the Ralliement National in 1966 drifted back to the Ralliement Créditiste after the election defeat of that year. They continued to be among the most vocal and persistent advocates of provincial participation for the Ralliement Créditiste, and in 1970 their arguments finally prevailed within the party.

The Ralliement National proved to be an abortive political adventure. Its ultimate impact on the electoral strength of the Ralliement Créditiste appears to have been minimal. However, the revolt against Caouette by several of his top lieutenants, including Legault and Grégoire, and the accompanying split had permanent consequences for the Créditistes. One of the candidates for the Ralliement National was Camil Samson, the young Créditiste militant from Rouyn who had been president of the Ralliement Youth at its founding. He was part of the third generation of Créditiste militants who had now come of age. Samson did not consider his candidacy for the Ralliement National as a defiance of Caouette and the federalist Créditistes. Although provincial politics continued to hold greater interest for him, Samson was willing to avail himself of any opportunity to enter the political fray on behalf of Social Credit.[88] Considerations of doctrinal principle advanced by older Créditistes in an effort to dissuade the party from entering provincial politics (for example, the argument that

87 Interviews, 1967. Grégoire subsequently was forced by Réal Caouette to resign from the Ralliement Créditiste and sit as an independent in the federal House of Commons.
88 Interview with Camil Samson, July 1967. Like Caouette in the 1940s and 1950s, he appears to have had an appetite for electoral activity at any level.

provincial governments had no jurisdiction over monetary and banking legislation) were of little concern to him. Maximizing the political strength of the movement had highest priority. Samson's attitude, as we shall see, reflected the thinking of many of the young Créditistes who were just beginning to demand a share of the leadership from the second generation. The Ralliement National, which several had joined and many more had tacitly supported, was the first concrete expression of a nascent conflict between the next generation of old and young Créditistes.

E NATIONAL REORGANIZATION AND PROVINCIAL EXPANSION, 1967–70

Although most of the Ralliement Créditiste leaders, including Caouette and seven other federal MPs, had remained aloof from provincial politics in 1966, they had not been idle. The federal party had come to assume the character of its leader, and to reflect Caouette's changing attitudes on prevailing political issues and organizational strategies. In particular, the party began to concern itself with Caouette's desire for a reunification of the national Social Credit party under his and the Ralliement's aegis. Reunification would revive the movement as a national political force. This would crown Caouette's personal career with success in an area in which he had been previously frustrated, reflect his now deep commitment to a single united Canada opposed to Quebec independence, and revive the movement as a national political force.

Caouette, under the influence of Legault, Grégoire, and others, had at times expressed some quasiseparatist statements, particularly during the period just before and after his split with the western Social Crediters in 1963. However, he had never been a strong French-Canadian nationalist and preferred always to emphasize economic over nationalist considerations.[89] In 1966 and 1967, as the question of Quebec independence became increasingly a matter of national discussion, Caouette began to adopt a more strident anti-separatist stance. At a parliamentary session devoted to the one hundredth anniversary of Confederation, he praised Sir John A. Macdonald and attacked those French Canadians who labelled Confederation '100 years of injustice' as 'agents of disorder' and liars.[90] After the famous 'Vive le Québec Libre!' speech of French President Charles de Gaulle in Montreal, he issued a sharp reprimand to the General. He added rather bitterly that if French Canadians had made immense progress since coming to this continent, and had succeeded in preserving their language and faith, it had not been done with the help of France.[91] And in October at the party congress marking the tenth anniversary of the Ralliement Créditiste, he extolled Canada as 'one country, several cultures, two official languages' and declared that 'political independence without economic independence is an

---

89 Caouette's reasons for disparaging excessive French-Canadian nationalism are complex. In part they can be attributed to his belief in individualism and his feeling that French-Canadian nationalists wrongly laid the blame for their own feelings on the shoulders of others, particularly the English. In addition, he maintained that he had grown up among English Canadians and Americans, and had gotten to know them, particularly at the classical college he attended. He did not distrust them as did so many of his compatriots. See his statement in part IV, chapter 8 below.

90 *Le Devoir*, 12 January 1967.

91 *Ibid.*, 26 July 1967.

absurdity.'[92] These statements were intended to enhance his stature as a truly national leader capable of representing Canadians of Social Credit persuasion from coast to coast. At the same time he was careful to stress to francophone Canadians and particularly Quebeckers the achievements of his party in advancing the use of the French language in Ottawa in such areas as bilingual menus in parliamentary restaurants, bilingual personnel in Air Canada and in the federal government's telephone service, and bilingual federal government cheques.

These verbal efforts on behalf of Canadian unity were accompanied by attempts to negotiate an agreement with the western Social Credit MPs which would reunify the two wings under a single party banner for the first time since 1963. The first soundings were taken in January 1967. They failed to strike a responsive chord among the westerners, in part because Caouette's conception of the reunited national party was one of a bilingual Ralliement Créditiste-Social Credit Rally firmly committed to the principles of Major Douglas and under his own personal leadership. The two basic planks in the proposed party platform were to be the monthly dividend and interest-free loans to school boards, municipalities, and provincial governments.[93] His program was very similar to that which had been offered in federal elections in the 1940s by the Union des Electeurs and which had helped to produce the 1948 split between the two wings. The western Social Crediters regarded these measures as impractical and harmful to the party's electoral image.

Nevertheless, events in late 1966 and early 1967 had made the prospects of reunification more feasible. First, and most important, in March 1967 Robert Thompson, the national leader and head of the western rump, crossed over to sit on the Conservative backbenches. It was the culmination of long years of hesitation and backroom negotiation with the two major parties. He justified his decision on the grounds that the national party had failed to receive adequate support from the provincial Social Credit organizations, in particular those of Alberta and British Columbia.[94] However, his switch in party allegiance gave some credence to Caouette's charges that Thompson had never really believed in social credit principles and had therefore adopted policies and strategies antithetical to the interests of the movement's devotees. Thompson's resignation was accompanied by that of national president Martin Kelln. A few months later the Social Credit party's best House of Commons performer, H.A. (Bud) Olson (Medicine Hat), who had never really subscribed to social credit doctrine, quit the party to join the Liberals. He subsequently became the minister of agriculture in the Liberal cabinet. The loss of these men left the national Social Credit party leaderless and in an extremely weakened condition.[95] There was an obvious void to be filled among English-speaking Social Crediters, and Caouette was quick to take advantage of it.

In February 1967, even before Thompson had resigned, Caouette had sent the

92 *Ibid.*, 10 October 1967.
93 *Ibid.*, 27 January 1967.
94 *Ibid.*, 10 March 1967.
95 A.B. Patterson (Fraser Valley) was elected House leader and Herb Bruch, a former vice president from British Columbia, was chosen as the new president. But these were largely stop-gap selections.

deputy from Mégantic, Raymond Langlois, on a cross-country tour in order to establish contacts with Social Credit members and associations in all provinces and explore the possibilities of extending the Ralliement Créditiste 'from coast to coast.'[96] In the fall of the same year, the Ralliement organized its annual congress, held in Quebec City, around the theme of 'A Strong Quebec in a United Canada.' Caouette had earlier announced that the objective of the congress was to establish a liaison committee composed of Social Crediters from all parts of the country who would meet to overcome continuing differences and work towards national reunification of all Social Crediters. An invitation to attend the Ralliement congress as observers was extended to the remaining Social Credit MPs, but all three declined.[97] Most of the invited English-speaking Social Credit organizers from outside Quebec likewise failed to attend. Those who did appear from the other provinces were chiefly francophones from New Brunswick, Ontario, and Manitoba.[98] The efforts at reunification by the Ralliement were clearly meeting with little success. The English-speaking Social Crediters still bore resentments against Caouette for his 1963 action which split the national party; they were also suspicious of what they regarded as an attempt to integrate the western wing into an essentially Quebec movement. Their suspicions were not unfounded.

Caouette emerged from the 1967 Ralliement congress with his position as leader of the Ralliement unchallenged. He was also chiefly responsible for formulating the party's program and organizational strategy. All of the members of the party's national executive, including its newly elected president Robert Beaulé, the former deputy from Quebec East, were his staunch supporters and loyal friends. However, the party had been weakened at the leadership level by the loss of men like Laurent Legault, Gilles Grégoire, and some of the younger Créditistes who had followed these former leaders into the Ralliement National. As a result, Caouette had assigned Beaulé the specific task of recruiting new, better educated, and younger members who were not necessarily of long-time Social Credit persuasion. It was hoped that these new members would give the party a fresh and less parochial image. The effort is reminiscent of a similar recruitment drive made by the party in 1961 and early 1962, with all its unfortunate later consequences for party unity.[99] However, Caouette recognized that the two major parties, the Liberals and Conservatives, were in the process of selecting new leaders to replace Pearson and Diefenbaker and were formulating new programs which were designed to reflect the changing needs and desires of the Canadian people in the late 1960s. The Ralliement Créditiste had to present some fresh faces and ideas to the electorate as well.

But Caouette needed time to consolidate the party's organization in the rural and small-urban areas of Quebec, to expand its efforts in Montreal, and even to organize

96 *Le Devoir*, 13 February 1967. In an interview conducted with Langlois later that spring he expressed considerable enthusiasm about his reception and great optimism about the prospects for an eventual reunification. This optimism was somewhat misplaced.

97 *Ibid.*, 7 October 1967. They did agree, however, to meet with the Ralliement Créditiste MPs in November in order to discuss the matter further. *Ibid.*, 10 October 1967. The meeting does not appear to have produced any concrete results.

98 *Ibid.*, 10 October 1967.

99 See above, subsection B.

in some ridings outside Quebec. Events on the federal level moved too swiftly for him. Robert Stanfield, the former premier of Nova Scotia was elected Progressive Conservative party leader in September 1967, and the Tories began to improve their ratings in public opinion polls. Stanfield later selected as his Quebec lieutenant Marcel Faribault, a noted constitutional expert and staunch advocate of provincial autonomy for Quebec. The Tories adopted a platform which incorporated the principle that Canada was made up of 'two founding peoples' (deux nations). In February 1968, just before Prime Minister Pearson submitted his resignation as party leader, his Liberal minority government suffered an ignominious defeat during a vote on third reading of a taxation bill introduced by then Finance Minister Mitchell Sharp. It required agile manoeuvring by several Liberal stalwarts to save the government from collapse. Caouette himself provided a vital assist by promising to support the government's hastily drafted resolution calling for confidence in its financial policies; in return the government agreed to reduce the original amount of taxation imposed by 5 per cent.[100] He had therefore managed to buy some extra time for himself and his party, although his tactics met with strong disapproval from certain Créditiste militants and outright opposition for the first time since 1963 from a few of his loyal supporters among the Créditiste MPs.[101] Within two months, how-ever, the Liberals had succeeded in replacing Pearson by an attractive new leader, Pierre Elliott Trudeau, the former justice minister, who was a bilingual French Canadian and, like Caouette, an exponent of a bilingual 'one nation' Canada. The new Prime Minister, sensing the growing public interest in his leadership and per-sonality (which was later to be transformed into a wave of Trudeaumania), and anxious to transform the Liberal minority into an overall majority, soon after dis-solved parliament and called an election for 25 June 1968.

The election occurred one year earlier than the Créditistes had expected.[102] Many journalists at the time were predicting a drastic reduction in Créditiste electoral support and even their complete elimination as a parliamentary group.[103] Both Prime Minister Trudeau and the Stanfield-Faribault team appeared to be making inroads in Créditiste strongholds by appealing either to the traditional French-Canadian loyalty to a national leader of their own ethnic background or to deep-rooted nationalist sentiments. The Ralliement Créditiste did not even have time to field a full slate of candidates in the seventy-four Quebec ridings (which had been redistributed since the previous federal election) and managed to enter only one candidate outside Quebec (in a largely French-Canadian riding in New Brunswick).[104] Caouette's campaign began slowly and was essentially a restatement of the message which he had been expounding since the early 1940s in Quebec. He hammered incessantly on the ecenomic theme, attacked separatism, and opposed constitutional revisions

100 *Le Devoir*, 3 June 1968.
101 From interviews, 1971.
102 *Le Devoir*, 14 June 1968.
103 For example, the *Montreal Gazette* reported a poll taken of twenty-eight editors of Quebec's weekly newspapers from all parts of the province in which an average prediction of four seats for the Créditistes was made. *Montreal Gazette*, 15 June 1968. See also *Le Devoir*, 27 June 1968.
104 *Le Devoir*, 14 June 1968.

designed to give Quebec a special status in Canada as meaningless paper solutions to what was essentially a bread-and-butter problem. Caouette urged that the Bank of Canada issue interest-free loans to Quebec school boards, municipalities, and the provincial government, and that the federal government and the central bank foster free enterprise through a general tax reduction and direct grants to industry.[105]

The message seemed to have had effect at least in the traditional Créditiste strongholds. When all votes had been counted, the Ralliement Créditiste had increased its House of Commons representation from the eight seats it had held prior to dissolution, to fourteen seats, or almost double its earlier representation. All but one of the previous eight old-time Créditiste MPs had retained their seats despite the redistribution, and the seven new members included four younger and better educated candidates, some of whom the party had recruited during its intensive drive the previous fall.[106] The pluralities of these fourteen successful candidates ranged from a few hundred votes to over 6,000, and several amassed impressive increases. The Ralliement retained or increased its strength in its three traditional strongholds: the northwest region, south Quebec, and the Eastern Townships. Créditiste candidates also accumulated a large number of votes and ranked second in the constituencies of Drummond, Lévis, Langelier, Lac Saint-Jean, Québec-Est, Saint-Maurice, and the Gaspé. The only region in which the Créditistes had suffered a net loss was in Saguenay–Lac Saint-Jean, and this was attributed to the confusion created by the departure of Gilles Grégoire.[107] The election of fourteen members to the House of Commons indicated a remarkable Créditiste recovery and a return to the pattern of the electoral success of 1962–3.

However, a closer look at the popular vote figures reveals that the 1968 Créditiste showing was poorer than that of 1965 and, in fact, continued the downward spiral which had begun after the party had reached its peak of 29 per cent of the total Quebec vote in 1963. The popular vote total of the Créditistes declined from 375,000 or 19 per cent of the popular vote in 1965 to 358,000 or 16.4 per cent of the popular vote in 1968. Its poorest showing was in the Montreal region where the party dropped from a high of 14.3 per cent in 1963 and 7.2 per cent in 1965 to only 2.8 per cent in 1968.[108] It was clear that if the party was to expand beyond its Quebec hinterland base and present a credible image as a truly province-wide or national party, it needed to expand its organization and support in Montreal and outside the province of Quebec.

105 *Ibid.*, 3 June 1968.
106 They were André Fortin (Lotbinière), who had served as Caouette's executive assistant from 1965–8, Lionel Beaudoin (Richmond), a former president of a Union Nationale riding association who had been first approached to run as a Créditiste candidate in 1965, René Matte (Champlain), who had been active in several separatist organizations until 1968, and Romuald Rodrigue (Beauce), a successful local businessman with the longest ties to the Créditiste movement of the four. The last three had all been co-opted by their local riding associations just prior to the 1968 campaign. Donald Murray, 'The Ralliement Créditiste in Parliament, 1968–71,' mimeo. (Made available for quotation with the kind permission of the author.)
107 *Regards*, 8, no 5 (July 1968), 4–6.
108 *Ibid.*, 11 October 1968.

But if the Ralliement Créditiste had lost some popular support, its western counterpart had fared much worse. All three western Social Credit MPs, running without financial aid or even organizational support from the moribund national Social Credit party office, went down to defeat. None of the other thirty candidates who had run under the Social Credit banner came even close to winning; most ran a poor fourth behind the Liberals, Conservatives, and NDP, and lost their deposits.[109] The national Social Credit party, which had been operating continuously and with some success since 1935, was close to political extinction.

Réal Caouette and the Ralliement Créditiste were not prepared, however, to allow this death to occur. Even during the election campaign of 1968 Caouette had announced plans to make a western swing in 1969 in order to revive the western organizations. In October 1968 he began to put his plans for a national reorganization into effect. At the annual Ralliement congress held that year at Sherbrooke, the Ralliement delegates voted to rename the party the Ralliement Créditiste-Social Credit Rally, which would be bilingual both in name and practice. The party's monthly newspaper, *Regards*, was henceforth to be published in bilingual form and would contain at least four pages of English content. All receipts for membership subscriptions were likewise to be bilingual. Several hundred English-speaking Social Crediters from all provinces were invited to the Sherbrooke congress, although only about twenty from Ontario, Alberta, and British Columbia actually attended. Nevertheless Caouette addressed these delegates in part in English and spoke enthusiastically of a revived Social Credit party encompassing all of Canada from one ocean to the other. The constitution of the party was amended to allow two of the eight regional directors to be elected from outside Quebec. English-speaking members from Ontario and Saskatchewan were named to these posts. The Ralliement also passed resolutions calling for the establishment of a new national Social Credit party based on federal rather than provincial constituency organizations. Finally, Caouette promised to attend the November congress of the Social Credit Association of Ontario, held in Toronto, together with Gilbert Rondeau, his parliamentary leader, in order to help launch Social Credit television broadcasts in Ontario.[110] He also issued an invitation to Herb Bruch of British Columbia, president of the western rump, to join him in rebuilding the national party.

Nevertheless, a certain degree of caution was still evident among the English-speaking Social Crediters. The President of the Ontario Social Credit Association decided to reserve his right to affiliate with either the Ralliement or the western wing under Bruch until after its next congress.[111] The lack of enthusiastic response to the invitations issued by Mr Rondeau, the congress organizer, was further evidence of the general indifference of English Social Crediters to Caouette's reunification efforts.[112]

Several of the new 'young guard' among the MPs, led by André Fortin, emphasized the necessity to mend fences and consolidate support in the Ralliement's home

109 *Report of the Chief Electoral Officer* (Ottawa: Queen's Printer, 1968).
110 *Le Devoir*, 15 October 1968. See also *Regards*, 8–9, no 10 (October-November 1968), 8–11.
111 *Le Devoir*, 11 November 1968.
112 *Montreal Gazette*, 14 October 1968 (article by Hal Winter).

province. They introduced a plan, supported by the executive, to extend the fifteen minute television broadcasts into the Montreal region, to be financed in part by the thirty-five constituencies of Quebec excluding Montreal, Saguenay–Lac Saint-Jean, and the lower Saint Lawrence, and in part by large donations by each of the fourteen Ralliement MPs.[113] The plan of organization and expansion in the Montreal area was very similar to that adopted in the period 1962–3, following the initial Ralliement success. But the difficulty of organizing in the larger, more impersonal metropolis by means of traditional Créditiste door-to-door canvasses was well remembered.[114] This time the Ralliement militants were to concentrate on those urban dwellers who had recently emigrated from the hinterland area and still retained their earlier personal and associational attachments. These recently urbanized Québécois would form the nucleus from which the Créditiste organization would expand in each metropolitan constituency.[115]

Finally, and as a further aid to consolidation and expansion of the movement, the Ralliement announced the establishment of a course in social credit doctrine. This was designed to further the goal of political education, since the Ralliement was not merely a conventional political party, but was also a 'political education movement.'[116] The course resembled that which was established by Laurent Legault in the period 1963–4, in which twelve special lectures written by the party's ideologue, Fernand Bourret, had been bound together into a booklet and distributed to local constituency organizations for use in their study groups.[117]

The Ralliement Créditiste of 1968 was essentially the same in its organization, leadership, and self-image as the Ralliement Créditiste of 1957 and 1962. After almost a decade of electoral action, in which there had been a gradual decline in the party's electoral support, the old techniques of organization, the old slogans, the old principles, and the old practices were still invoked by the same principal figures. The movement had not developed in new or different directions; it had merely retrenched and (in its stronghold) consolidated its earlier organizational and educational efforts.

In the first issue of *Regards*, published in 1969, the year was proudly proclaimed as a period of national reorganization.[118] Caouette undertook a swing through the western provinces, accompanied by his parliamentary leader, Gilbert Rondeau. The annual congress, held in Montreal in October 1969, reported on the results of this

113 *Le Devoir*, 10 October 1968; 15 October 1968.
114 For a more detailed discussion of the difficulties faced by one of Caouette's organizers from Rouyn who was assigned to organize the Montreal by-election in Laurier in 1963, see my 'Social Credit in Quebec: Political Attitudes and Party Dynamics' (unpublished PH.D. dissertation, Princeton University, 1967), appendix C.
115 *Le Devoir*, 11 October 1968. See also *Regards*, 8, no 12 (December 1968), 1.
116 *Le Devoir*, 15 October 1968.
117 See the author's 'The Structure and Function of the Finances of the Ralliement des Créditistes,' 436. The course, which was organized by correspondence, was called 'Cours d'orientation politique.'
118 *Regards*, 9 no 1 (January 1969), 3. Among the ambitious projects proposed were the establishment of a national secretariat, a Social Credit library, and a research bureau to serve every constituency.

tour. Caouette had concluded that the time was ripe for the holding of a national leadership convention in the summer of 1970 in Ottawa.[119] Plans for the reunification of the national party under the aegis of the Ralliement Créditiste seemed to be making progress.

In fact, however, internal pressures within the party were to divert the federal executive from their national efforts. The next Quebec provincial election was scheduled for 1970, and many Créditiste militants were pressing for direct Ralliement participation. The party, diverted by the now familiar question of establishing a provincial wing of the Ralliement Créditiste to oppose the Liberals, Union Nationale, and newly formed Parti Québécois, was unable to devote time and effort to national reorganization.

The Ralliement Créditiste, like its precursor, the Union des Electeurs, had, since its founding, continuously debated the merits and demerits of provincial as opposed to national action.[120] The question had not been resolved by the defeat in 1966 of the splinter Créditiste group, the Ralliement National. Although ostensibly committed to a firm policy of federalism, many Créditiste militants continued to advocate the idea of provincial Ralliement action. The prospects of electing a Créditiste government seemed so much greater at the provincial level and it was in Quebec City that the decisions with the greatest impact on daily life were made.

The time seemed propitious for a Ralliement intervention. In the first place, Premier Daniel Johnson of the Union Nationale had died suddenly in August 1968 of a heart attack and was succeeded by his Justice Minister Jean-Jacques Bertrand. Bertrand lacked the leadership qualities which had aided Johnson in rebuilding the party and leading it to victory in 1966.[121] Moreover, the Créditistes felt that the Union Nationale had broken a tacit mutual understanding that they would not use their organization to intervene against the Créditistes in federal elections. In the federal election of June 1968, Union Nationale organizers, with the blessing of Premier Johnson, had campaigned actively on behalf of the Progressive Conservative party in certain rural ridings, and their support had helped to shift enough votes from the Créditiste candidates to enable their Liberal opponents to be elected.[122] Second, the Quebec Liberal party was also in a weakened state since its defeated leader, Jean Lesage, had lost much of his dynamism and effectiveness in opposition.[123] The party had also become clearly identified with the federalist thinking of

119 *Regards*, 9, no 10 (October 1969), 4. The convention was subsequently postponed until October 1971 because of the interference of the Quebec provincial election in 1970, a federal by-election in Frontenac in November 1970, and the slowness of the other provinces to reorganize. For brief reports on their organizational progress, see the English sections of *Regards* (1969–70).

120 See section D.

121 Even his victory in the leadership convention held in June 1969 failed to strengthen Bertrand's hand significantly. There was a bitter convention fight between his supporters and those of his closest rival, Education Minister Jean-Guy Cardinal, which left the government party seriously divided and greatly weakened.

122 *Le Devoir*, 25 April 1969.

123 Lesage resigned as Liberal leader in August 1969 and a leadership convention was called for January 1970.

the Trudeau Liberals and therefore was no longer seen as an effective channel for the discontented voters. Third, there was a growing threat of separatism in Quebec from the newly created Parti Québécois. René Lévesque, a powerful and popular personality, had succeeded in uniting 'indépendentistes' of all ideological stripes – left, centre, and right – behind his leadership. Many Créditistes feared the eroding effect which the Parti Québécois might have on its protest supporters, particularly in the areas where the PQ's vice president, Gilles Grégoire, was organizing.[124] Finally, the Ralliement sought to consolidate its support by maintaining an active and enthusiastic electoral organization in the areas in which it had recovered and strengthened itself in the 1968 election. It also wished to test the effectiveness of its organizational efforts and its television broadcasts in the Montreal area.

As a result, in a tour which Caouette made in the spring of 1969 in the Quebec City region he suddenly announced to an assembly of his supporters that the Ralliement Créditiste was thinking seriously of entering the next provincial election. His hope was to win about fifteen seats and thereby exercise the balance of power in Quebec. Caouette himself would not be leader, but he would actively campaign on behalf of the party. The provincial wing would emphasize such issues as health, social welfare, and management of the economy which fell under provincial jurisdiction. The objective was to elect a 'solid core' (club fermé) of Créditistes in the National Assembly.[125]

This was a major change in Caouette's political strategy. Since the Ralliement had been founded, he had never before accorded more than reluctant acquiescence to the idea of provincial participation and had certainly not initiated or advocated the strategy himself. In fact, in most of the Ralliement congresses since 1962 in which the issue had been discussed, Caouette had vehemently opposed his party's provincial participation. As a result, except for the brief schism leading to the formation of the Ralliement National, he had effectively quashed all serious efforts in this direction since he had assumed the leadership of the movement.

There were several obvious reasons for his attitude. In the first place, Caouette considered himself to be an orthodox social crediter, and he believed that the fundamental objective of the movement, monetary reform, could only be achieved at the federal level where jurisdiction over money and banking resided. Second, he had presented himself as a candidate at both levels in the past since 1944 and had been deeply involved in all the Créditiste provincial efforts under the Union des Electeurs. Whereas his federal efforts both personally and on behalf of the movement had been successful several times, his provincial campaigns had always proved a dismal failure. The bitter defeats of 1948 and 1956 still rankled in his mind. He did not believe that the Créditistes could successfully penetrate the deeply entrenched provincial party system. Third, and most important, Caouette feared that a provincial wing headed by a new leader would pose a threat to his own leadership. Most of the previous challenges to his dominance of the movement had come from rivals who used the issue of provincial participation to strengthen their own positions within the party. First Dr

---

124 See the poll reported in the *Montreal Star*, 26 April 1969; 35 per cent of those who were Créditistes federally said then that they would support the PQ.

125 *Ibid.*, 24 March 1969.

Marcoux and later Laurent Legault and Gilles Grégoire had aspired to the position of provincial leader. Caouette did not wish to see his now unchallenged pre-eminence within the movement threatened by a new rival.

Nevertheless, Caouette was shrewd enough to adapt himself to what were obviously strong pressures from within the movement. Support for provincial participation came particularly from the younger militants who were attracted by the new feelings of nationalism and self-confidence among Québécois. These young men were convinced that the only way the Ralliement could expand its geographic base in the province and attract younger elements into what was now a middle-aged movement was to focus its ideology and concerns on issues under the jurisdiction of Quebec. Matters of education, health, social welfare, family planning, and municipal affairs, the truly bread and butter issues in Canadian politics, were all legislated by the National Assembly rather than the Canadian House of Commons. Caouette realized that if he was to maintain the support of these younger militants and consolidate his own position, he had to make some concessions to their demands. He also believed that a provincial wing, if electorally successful, would draft him as their parliamentary leader and premier. This, after all, was the tactic used by Aberhart in Alberta in 1935.

But if Caouette's own thinking on the question had modified, that of his fellow old guard MPs, who dominated the provincial executive, had not. Consequently, at a meeting of the executive council of the Ralliement in Ottawa in early May 1969, comprising the fourteen federal MPs and about thirty regional organizers and constituency association presidents, a split developed between the Ottawa deputies and the party's local militants. The latter emphasized the general deterioration of the old-line parties in Quebec and the developing threat from the Parti Québécois. The federal deputies, however, feared the division of the movement's resources and energy between two levels. As a result, the council voted to delay any decision on provincial participation until a sounding had been taken of the sentiments of the party's card-carrying members and sympathizers.[126] A questionnaire similar to that which had been circulated to the membership in 1964 was to be mailed out to about 16,000 Créditiste militants and another 39,000 Quebeckers chosen on a random basis from thirty constituencies in the province.[127]

One month later Caouette announced the results of the previous month's poll. About 5,400 known Créditistes in the seventy-four provincial constituencies had been canvassed, and an additional hundred questionnaires had been sent out on a random basis to each constituency. About 2,000 replies had been received: 1,310 of the respondents, or just over two-thirds, had pronounced themselves in favour of Ralliement participation in provincial politics, whereas 683 had declared themselves against this proposition. On the other hand, 1,943, or over 95 per cent, had spoken for the importance of a continued Ralliement presence in Ottawa, and only 44 voted against it. On the question of federalism versus separatism, 1,775, or over 90 per cent, expressed their feeling that Quebec could retain a place and live in harmony with other provinces in a genuinely Canadian Confederation, whereas 144 thought that it could not. Finally, only 226, or less than 15 per cent, expressed their

126 *Ibid.*, 3 May 1969.
127 *Le Devoir*, 8 May 1969.

support for Quebec separatism, and 1,689 rejected this option. For Caouette, the results of the questionnaire confirmed that the Ralliement Créditiste would contest the next provincial election.[128]

But the other Ottawa deputies were not yet convinced. They felt a larger proportion of Créditistes had to declare themselves unequivocally in favour of provincial participation if the action were not to seriously divide and weaken the party. As a result, the executive of the Ralliement decided to postpone a final decision on the question until the annual Ralliement congress in October.[129] In addition the Créditistes would test the provincial political waters by entering the four by-elections called by Premier Bertrand for 8 October.[130]

About five hundred delegates attended the Ralliement Créditiste congress held in the Centre Maisonneuve in Montreal on 4 and 5 October. They voted unanimously and enthusiastically in favour of the 'complete, total and definitive participation' of the Ralliement in the next provincial election. However, the provincial executive had introduced a caveat. It called for the creation of a committee of five members who would define the objectives of the Ralliement in Quebec, draft an electoral program, and establish the best methods and organizational mechanisms for provincial action. The committee would then report the results of its work to a provincial council consisting of five delegates from each constituency in the province convened for this purpose no later than the end of January. Moreover, Caouette declared that he would only become provincial leader if the Créditistes took power provincially and he was then invited to become prime minister.[131]

The federal deputies had been careful to leave themselves a loophole. Should the by-election results prove inauspicious, and should no provincial leader emerge on the horizon, then the Ralliement could always disengage itself from its congress commitment. The local militants left the congress unhappily aware that they had not yet won their fight for provincial participation.

In the by-elections held just after the Congress adjourned, all four Créditistes, running under the label of Independents, ran a poor second to the Union Nationale candidates and lost their deposits. The Liberals and Parti Québécois did not contest the elections. It appeared as if the organizational and broadcasting efforts in Montreal had not been very successful.[132]

On 25 January 1970 the provincial council of the Ralliement Créditiste, composed of about five hundred delegates, met in extraordinary session in Quebec City to hear the report of the committee of five established in October and to vote on their recommendation. Ninety-seven per cent supported the recommendation of the committee to establish separate provincial structures of the Ralliement. The council also elected Camil Samson, thirty-five years of age, a former president of the Ralliement Youth, and a staunch supporter and disciple of Caouette, as their provincial presi-

128 *Ibid.*, 4 June 1969.
129 *Ibid.*, 7 June 1969.
130 *Ibid.*, 4 June 1969.
131 *Ibid.*, 6 October 1969. See also the *Montreal Gazette*, 6 October 1969.
132 The *Montreal Star*, 9 October 1969. Two of the four seats, Montréal Saint Jacques and Montréal Ste Marie, were in Montreal. The other two were Trois-Rivières and Vaudreuil-Soulanges.

dent. Dr Gaston Tremblay, formerly MNA for the Union Nationale for Montmorency, who subsequently had joined the Créditistes after sitting for a time as an independent and leader of a splinter Christian National party, was elected as first vice-president. Raymond Gagné, president of the Ralliement Youth, was chosen as second vice-president. The choices reflected the sentiments of the younger Créditiste militants who were the chief advocates of provincial action.

But the choice of party leader had been left vacant. The provincial executive of the newly formed wing, which had been only partially constituted, was authorized to call a leadership convention at a later date. The federal Ralliement leaders still had doubts about the efficacy of provincial action. They hoped that in the interim, before the next election, an attractive personality could be found. Otherwise they were prepared to enter the campaign leaderless. The man whom most Créditiste militants hoped to attract as their provincial leader was Claude Wagner, the former justice minister in the Lesage cabinet, a popular figure among the Quebec masses and a staunch upholder of law and order in the province.[133] Wagner had been narrowly defeated by Robert Bourassa, the choice of the Liberal party establishment, in a Liberal leadership convention held just two weeks before to choose a successor to Jean Lesage. Wagner had bitterly denounced the manipulation of the leadership convention and felt that a genuinely democratic vote would have accorded him the leadership.[134] The Créditistes established contact with him and attempted to convince him to assume the leadership of their new provincial wing. But Wagner was an educated Montreal lawyer and judge who, despite his populist image and somewhat authoritarian attitudes, had little in common with the rural and small-urban Créditistes. He refused the invitation and the Créditistes were forced to look elsewhere.

On 12 March, before the provincial party could establish many of its structures and elect more than a few of its candidates, Premier Bertrand dissolved the National Assembly and called an election for 29 April, 1970.[135] The newly formed Quebec Ralliement provincial executive quickly convened a leadership convention for late March. There was widespread hope within the party that Mr Caouette would agree to assume the provincial leadership. When the 700 delegates to the provincial leadership convention met in Quebec City on 22 March, enthusiasm for provincial action and for Mr Caouette as provincial leader was running high. Six Créditistes had presented themselves as leadership candidates: the Provincial President, Camil Samson, the Vice President, Dr Gaston Tremblay, Jean-Marc Fontaine, the national president of the Ralliement Créditiste, and three federal deputies, Bernard Dumont of Frontenac, Gilbert Rondeau of Shefford, and René Matte of Champlain. However, Mr Caouette's name had been placed on the ballot at the last minute, and all six candidates were prepared to withdraw in his favour. The expectation was that he would bow to the wishes of the delegates and accept the leadership of the provincial party.

133 In a poll conducted by the *Montreal Star* in the major provincial centres a few months prior to the Liberal leadership convention. Wagner ran far ahead of all the other Liberal candidates and also was rated ahead of Bertrand, Cardinal, and Lévesque in preferences for Quebec prime minister. *Montreal Star*, 6 September 1969.
134 *Le Devoir*, 18, 19 January 1970.
135 It was expected that the election would be held in the fall of 1970. Economic problems in Quebec allegedly led by Mr Bertrand to call it earlier. *Montreal Star*, 14 March 1970.

However, Caouette had other plans. Two days before the convention he had contacted Yvon Dupuis, the former Liberal federal MP and cabinet minister, who had opposed the party so vigorously on the hustings and had constantly mocked the Créditistes' 'funny money' ideas.[136] Dupuis had been involved in a scandal concerning the granting of a permit for a racetrack in Saint Jean, Quebec, and had been forced to retire from federal politics. He had subsequently become a successful radio announcer and disc jockey on the French language CKVL radio station. According to Caouette, he had cleared himself of the charges which had been laid against him and had also defended the Créditistes several times on his radio show. Caouette convinced him to make a secret trip to Quebec City to test the reaction of the Créditiste delegates to his nomination as provincial leader.

Caouette was the third person to address the convention as a candidate.[137] He had previously hinted that he was going to introduce a 'bombshell.' Instead of accepting the nomination, as the delegates expected, he harangued the delegates for over an hour on the merits of his new proselyte to social credit. Like Paul on the road to Damascus, Mr Dupuis, a long-time Créditiste foe, had been converted overnight to social credit and was prepared to lead the party in the coming provincial election. Caouette was withdrawing his name in favour of Mr Dupuis, who at the time was waiting unseen in the washroom, hoping to be received enthusiastically by the delegates. But the Créditiste militants were not prepared to accept Caouette's proposal, Dupuis' nomination was withdrawn, and the delegates proceeded to elect Samson as their leader by an overwhelming majority of close to 80 per cent. And their enthusiasm for their new young leader, who in his acceptance speech, revealed many of the qualities as a speaker which had helped to make Caouette so successful over the years,was only slightly dampened by their federal leader's untimely and ill-considered intervention.[138]

But the damage had already been done. Apart from making Caouette and the Créditistes a laughing-stock among Québécois, and thereby seriously damaging the Créditistes' provincial electoral prospects, the action had revealed to all Caouette's profound lack of confidence in his party's militants and their leadership candidates. If Samson, who had been loyal to Caouette over the years, was rejected by his party's founder and long-time 'chef', his chances of being accepted as a credible parliamentary leader or prime minister by the Quebec electorate at large seemed slight. Moreover, the action by Caouette had damaged his own personal prestige among the party's militants. At a time when the Créditistes would have accepted virtually any other personal choice, or overwhelmingly acclaimed Caouette leader himself, he had opened up a chasm between himself and the younger supporters of the newly formed Ralliement Créditiste du Québec which would be very difficult to close.[139]

However, Caouette was astute enough to turn the faux pas into partial political

---

136 According to one report (*Montreal Gazette*, 24 March 1970), Dupuis had first taken the initiative in the affair. However, it is probable that Caouette persuaded Dupuis to go to Quebec City.

137 The first two candidates had already withdrawn in favour of Caouette.

138 *Le Devoir*, 23 March 1970. See also *Montreal Star*, 23 March 1970, and *Montreal Gazette*, 24 March 1970.

139 On this point, see the article by Gilles Racine in *La Presse*, 18 April 1970.

capital. He announced that his effort and its rejection by the party's militants revealed once again that the Ralliement Créditiste, unlike the old-line parties, was a genuinely democratic party. Even the leader had to submit to the will of the rank and file. Caouette reinforced this argument by accompanying Samson on several speaking tours and campaigning hard on behalf of the provincial party. The rationalization and subsequent show of support may not have convinced many non-Créditistes. But the old guard of Créditiste supporters, loyal to Mr Caouette and ready to accept his direction in all matters, had at least been provided with a plausible political argument.

On 4 April 1970, Samson formally inaugurated his campaign and presented his electoral platform. Although the issues were limited by the jurisdictional differences in federal and provincial politics, the program nevertheless bore a striking resemblance to every other Créditiste electoral program, federal or provincial, that had been drafted since the 1940s. It called for the creation in Quebec of a branch of the Bank of Canada authorized to issue interest-free loans to public and parapublic sectors; a reduction of 35 per cent in taxes made possible by savings which the government would realize in not paying interest on its loans; the complete exemption from all income tax of married persons earning less than $5,000 a year and single persons earning less than $2,500; abolition of the sales tax for all purchases of less than $100; creation of an Office of Information in the field of agriculture; creation of an automobile insurance regulatory agency; full and complete occupation of all spheres of jurisdiction guaranteed to Quebec by the constitution; progressive establishment of the French language as a language of work; and compulsory teaching in French except for the English minority. The nationalist content was somewhat more pronounced than in the federal party program. But the constitutional position, while calling for the assertion of Quebec's autonomy, was clearly federalist. It was not nearly as radical or trenchantly nationalist as the four-point program adopted by the Ralliement Créditiste in Montreal in January 1964.[140]

In the weeks which followed Samson worked hard to project his own and his party's image to the Quebec electorate. The press noted that his campaign style was flamboyant and somewhat demagogic like Caouette's. His rapport with the rural and small-urban Québécois audiences which he addressed was always good since, like Caouette, he spoke in their idiom. He emphasized the same issues as Caouette had done for several decades in his various election campaigns: the problem of unemployment, the shortage of credit, the betrayal of the old-line parties, the disorder and rebelliousness of youth, and the breakdown in traditional religious values among the young.

It was clear to most political observers and pollsters during the campaign that the Créditistes were making their greatest inroads in those areas in which the federal party was strongest: in the Eastern Townships, in Abitibi (the northwest), and in the area just south of Quebec City. On 29 April these predictions were proven correct. The Ralliement Créditiste succeeded in amassing 212,103 votes or 12.4 per cent of the popular vote, and electing twelve members to the National Assembly. The Liberals, led by Robert Bourassa, collected 871,056 votes or 44 per cent of the popular vote, but swept into power with an overwhelming majority of seventy-two

140 *Le Devoir*, 6 April 1970.

seats. The Union Nationale, under Premier Bertrand, was decimated. It managed to win only 395,091 votes or 20 per cent of the popular vote total, and retained only seventeen seats. The Parti Québécois, with 466,940 votes or 24 per cent of the provincial total, elected only seven members.[141]

For Camil Samson it was a 'marvellous victory.'[142] In addition to the twelve newly won Créditiste seats, all but one of which had been wrested from the Union Nationale, the Créditistes finished second to the Liberals in nine other constituencies. A majority of the new MNAS were third generation Créditistes, in their twenties and thirties; two were sons of federal MPs.[143] The areas of Créditiste strength proved to be substantially the same as on the federal level. However, the provincial Créditistes, unlike their federal counterparts, had failed to penetrate as far east as the Gaspé and had had little impact on the metropolitan area of Quebec City. And despite the organizational efforts of the previous year, they had had absolutely no impact in metropolitan Montreal. The poorer working-class Montreal constituencies had voted heavily for the Parti Québécois.

The 1970 provincial election was an important watershed in the development of the Social Credit movement in Quebec. The election confirmed both the bases of strength and of weakness in the movement's political following. The Créditiste appeal, regardless of who was at its head, was essentially a right-wing protest with a narrow class and regional base. It reached a receptive audience in those areas of Quebec in which unemployment was high, the population was stable or declining, and economic conditions were worsening. Its appeal was a mixture of right-wing social and political ideology and radical monetary reform, which had particular attraction for lower middle-class businessmen, storekeepers, union members, and farmers in a traditional Quebec which was undergoing change. It had no appeal for the affluent middle-class voters of the large or middle-sized cities of Quebec, and little attraction for the growing numbers of working-class poor in the cities. The movement had consolidated and reaffirmed its traditional support. But its further development and expansion were clearly checked.

F AFTERMATH, 1970: FROM CONSOLIDATION TO
INSTITUTIONALIZATION

With the expansion of the movement at an impasse, it was natural that a re-examination of its leadership and goals would take place. Not unexpectedly the challenge came from the new group of third generation Créditistes who had begun to exercise influence both at the federal and provincial levels. At the federal level the young guard, led by René Matte and André Fortin, began to question the long-standing practices of the Ralliement MPs in and out of parliament and to criticize aspects of Mr Caouette's leadership. The old guard Créditiste MPs had long adopted the parliamentary style of delegates rather than representatives; that is, they saw their role in parliament as representing their constituents rather than the country at large. This mode of thinking was typical of populist or plebiscitarian parliamentary practice. The federal MPs paid little attention to details of parliamentary or committee

141 *Ibid.*, 30 April 1970.   142 *Ibid.*
143 The third-generation Créditiste MNAS are: Antoine Drolet, F. Guay, Y. Brochu, C. Samson, F. Roy, P.A. Latulippe, and R. Tétrault. The last two are sons of federal MPs.

debate, preferring to spend their time among their constituents or out on the hustings. They regarded much of the business of parliament as of little value. The weekly federal caucus was always well attended, but the matters which were discussed in it pertained largely to organization and education rather than parliamentary tactics. Caouette, who was undergoing treatment for diabetes, had the highest record of absenteeism in the House, although his absenteeism was as much due to his predilection for organization and public speaking as to his ill health. However, his failure to attend often contributed to the poor tactical planning and the weak parliamentary and committee performances of the Créditistes.[144]

The new guard was less dedicated to the educational and organizational goals of the movement and more concerned about its effective contribution to the political life of the country. On several occasions they had privately opposed Caouette in caucus, but their opposition had come to naught. When Caouette adopted stands independent of the caucus in the War Measures Act crisis in October 1970, their silent dissent burst into rebellion.[145]

Similarly the provincial delegation of twelve members which was largely composed of third generation Créditistes began to show more and more independence in their attitudes towards their federal counterparts. Led by Samson, whose loyalty to Caouette had obviously been shaken by the incident involving Yvon Dupuis, the provincial party quickly established its own newspaper, membership cards, and constitution and operated quite independently of the federal party. The provincial group also continued to press for a broader nationalist appeal and for more serious legislative efforts.[146]

By the end of 1970 a new generational challenge was clearly beginning to emerge. This time, however, it was likely to involve the Caouette group on the side of the establishment, and the next generation of Créditistes as the counter-establishment or dissenters. The split between Louis Even and Gilberte Côté-Mercier on the one hand, and the group of young Créditistes around Caouette on the other, which had rocked the movement in 1957 and triggered a new phase, seemed about to repeat itself. The Créditiste movement appeared to be in the process of evolving from the phase of consolidation to that of institutionalization.[147]

144 This paragraph is based largely on an unpublished paper by a former Créditiste parliamentary assistant. See Murray, 'The Ralliement Créditiste in Parliament, 1968–71.'
145 *Ibid.*
146 In May 1971 it suddenly brought forth a resolution rejecting the BNA Act and calling for the right of self-determination for Quebec, much to the displeasure of Caouette and the federal old guard. *Le Devoir*, 14 May. In its second annual convention in Quebec City in March 1971 it also called for modernization and new blood to rid it of its traditional rural right-wing image. *Montreal Gazette*, 22 March 1971, and *Montreal Star*, 22 March 1971.
147 Further signs pointing in this direction emerged at the time of the 1971 national leadership convention, held in Hull, in October, in which Caouette was overwhelmingly elected as national leader of the renamed Social Credit party of Canada. Two of the four young guard federal Créditiste MPs supported Phil Cossette, the youth candidate who ran second to Caouette in the balloting. Cossette had been a key organizer in the provincial campaign and had been narrowly defeated in his provincial riding. He subsequently became the provincial party's new president. (From personal observations of the 1971 convention.) See also Murray.

PART III

A PROFILE OF THE CREDITISTE LEADERSHIP

Introduction: Protest and Factionalism

In the preceding section on the development of Social Credit in Quebec two characteristics of the movement stand out clearly: the essential protest quality of the ideology and political practice of the movement from its inception, and the rampant factionalism and successive splits in the movement particularly over a later period of its development. Both of these qualities were also observed to be characteristic of other social and political movements.[1] The two characteristics – protest and factionalism – also seem to be interrelated and therefore to require analytical explanation.

Since protest and factionalism are qualities descriptive of the behaviour of the leadership of the movement at different phases in its development, it seems sensible to begin the analysis of these phenomena by an investigation of the behaviour of this segment of the membership.[2] Behaviour in social analysis is properly seen as the

1 See chapter 1. Both protest and factionalism were apparent in the Social Credit movement in Alberta. C.B. Macpherson, *Democracy in Alberta: The Theory and Practice of a Quasi-party System* (Toronto: University of Toronto Press, 1953), and J.A. Irving, *The Social Credit Movement in Alberta* (Toronto: University of Toronto Press, 1959). They were also present in the Populist movement in the United States. C.W. King, *Social Movements in the United States* (New York: Random House, 1956), W. Hesseltine, *Third Party Movements in the United States* (Princeton: Van Nostrand, 1962), and for a general examination, G. Ionescu and E. Gellner (eds) *Populism: Its National Characteristics* (London: Weidenfeld and Nicolson, 1969). The former characteristic was also present in the Poujadist movement in France. Stanley Hoffman, *Le mouvement poujade* (Paris: Librairie A. Colin, 1956) and in the NPD in West Germany. Lowell Dittmer, 'The German NPD: A Psycho-Sociological Analysis of Neo-Nazism,' *Comparative Politics*, 2, no 1 (October 1969). All of these movements seem to fit our definition of a right-wing protest movement. The latter characteristic was also pervasive in more revolutionary movements. See for example, Joseph Nyomarky, *Charisma and Factionalism in the Nazi Party* (Minneapolis: University of Minnesota Press, 1961).

2 The segment of the leadership analysed included the major participants in the various splits during the movement's historical evolution (including all top holders of official positions at the provincial and national executive level) and local constituency leaders. For a more detailed explanation of the population chosen for study, see appendix A. I have confined my analysis to the elite or leadership level of the movement since, in my opinion, this echelon

product of social background characteristics and attitudes of actors.[3] Many studies of social and political movements include a description of the social and political background characteristics of the membership.[4] However, these descriptions tend to be impressionistic and unsystematic profiles of individual rank-and-file supporters.[5] Sometimes there is also some discussion of the attitudes of the leaders; but it is often formalistic and historical and rarely involves abstractions from the actual verbalized responses and behaviour patterns of these members.[6]

What follows is both a social and attitudinal profile of the leadership and a systematic description of their behaviour. It is also an attempt to link these characteristics causally by analysing the interrelationships between these variables. In other words, we shall try to discover relationships between social background and attitudinal traits of leaders which might account for the protest and factional patterns of behaviour which seem to be so characteristic of political protest movements. The analysis is based on data gathered in a structured survey.[7]

Protest here is defined as any action of opposition or dissent against the prevailing political regime and procedural consensus in the polity which does not involve a complete rejection or transformation of that consensus. This type of action is naturally characteristic of the political behaviour of activists in political movements, since it is often a prime factor in motivating them to join such a political group. The movement provides an institutional vehicle for the expression of their political opposition or dissent. This is particularly the case in the early stages of development of a movement.[8] But what produces the propensity in certain individuals to engage in political protest action? Is it something in the social, economic, or political environment in which they operate? Is it due to traits in their personality? Is it a result of family

is crucial in determining the pattern of protest and factionalism within the movement. On this point, see also K. Lang and G.E. Lang, *Collective Dynamics* (New York: Thomas Crowell, 1961) 495; N. Smelser, *The Theory of Collective Behavior* (New York: Free Press, 1963), 361; M. Zald and R. Ash, 'Social Movement Organizations: Growth, Decay and Change,' in Barry McLaughlin (ed) *Studies in Social Movements: A Social Psychological Perspective* (New York: Free Press, 1969), 327; R.E.L. Faris, *Handbook of Modern Sociology* (Chicago: Rand McNally, 1964), 440.

3 A. Campbell *et al., The American Voter* (New York: Wiley, 1960), R.E. Lane, *Political Life* (Glencoe: Free Press, 1958): P. Lazarsfeld, B. Berelson, and H. Gaudet, *The People's Choice* (New York: Columbia University Press, 1948); H. Eulau, *The Behavioral Persuasion in Politics* (New York: Random House, 1963).

4 For example, see Gabriel Almond, *Appeals of Communism* (Princeton: Princeton University Press, 1954) and R. Heberle, *Social Movements: An Introduction to Political Science* (New York: Appleton Century-Croft, 1951).

5 For example, Hadley Cantril, *The Politics of Despair* (New York: Collier, 1962), and Irving.

6 For example, Hesseltine; C.W. King, *Social Movements in the United States* (New York: Random House, 1956); and Irving. An exception to this is S.M. Lipset, *Agrarian Socialism* (Berkeley: University of California Press, 1950).

7 Appendices A and B.

8 Lang and Lang, 495, 520. See also J.R. Gusfield, *Protest, Reform and Revolt* (New York: John Wiley, 1970), 3, and chapter 1 above.

socialization? Do they join a political movement in order to express that propensity? If not, what motivates different individuals to join protest movements?[9]

By factionalism is meant any pattern of overt conflict or internal struggle among groups that adhere to basically the same ideology and sets of goals. It includes open splits or schisms which do not produce the dissolution or disintegration of the common association or institution. It is particularly characteristic of behaviour at a later stage in the development of a political movement.[10] What lies behind this pattern of action? Why do leaders who have joined in a concerted protest effort later quarrel and fractionalize? Is there anything in the social composition of a movement or the pattern of attitudes of its members which explains this tendency to schism?[11]

The method adopted to study these questions was a survey of the leadership of the Créditiste movement, conducted in the summer of 1967. In order to include as many as possible of the major actors in the Créditiste movement over its thirty-five year history and also allow for some representation of the current leadership of the movement at the local level, the sample was selected from two strata: 1 / a top leadership stratum of known active participants in major splits in the movement over thirty-five years; and 2 / a local leadership stratum of key organizers of the Ralliement Créditiste at the constituency level. Forty-seven of the former were ultimately selected for interviewing and twenty-two of the latter, or a combined total of sixty-nine Créditiste leaders.[12]

The questionnaire was motivated primarily by a desire to account for the pervasiveness of protest and factionalism in the movement and to relate the findings in this particular case to more general patterns in political movements. The demographic, attitudinal, and behavioural questions were therefore selected with this objective in mind. As this was the first attempt to use structured individual interviews to study patterns of evolution in a political movement and also the first examination of the problem of protest and factionalism in such a context, the conceptual framework for the questionnaire was devised without reference to any particular source in the literature.[13]

9 For discussion of similar questions see Lang and Lang, 342; Cameron, 10, and Almond, 226.
10 Lang and Lang, 520, 533; Smelser, 361, and Zald and Ash, 327. See also chapter 1 above.
11 Smelser (361) argues that the disunity and instability of value-oriented movements arise from three sources: 1 / the appearance as the movement develops of different types of leaders whose objectives differ and therefore cause them to come into conflict with one another, 2 / the heterogeneity of the movement which results in part from the different phases in its development, and 3 / changes in strategy and tactics. See also Zald and Ash, and Lang and Lang, 533.
12 For a more detailed description of the sample design, see appendix A.
13 For an example of the questionnaire used in the survey, see appendix B.

4

The Social Profile of the Créditiste Leadership

A SOCIAL BACKGROUND CHARACTERISTICS

The leaders of the Social Credit movement in Quebec were born and grew up in the areas in which the movement always enjoyed its greatest strength in the province: the villages and small towns outside the large metropolitan areas of Montreal and Quebec City (table 4.1). Very few migrated to cities, although a somewhat higher proportion of the leadership lives in Montreal or Quebec City today than was born or raised there. The vast majority of Créditiste leaders now live in small towns or in small-urban areas.[1] And although about 10 per cent of the leaders come from farming families, practically no leaders continue to live on farms.[2]

---

1 Although the statistics are not perfectly comparable, the Créditiste leaders seem to resemble the candidates of the Union Nationale party in the 1966 Quebec provincial election more than those of the other major contesting parties, the Liberals and the RIN, in their small-town origins. These percentages for place of birth from V. Lemieux (ed), *Quatres elections provinciales au Québec, 1956–1966* (Québec: Les Presses de l'Université Laval, 1969), 120, revised after dropping unknowns, are:

	Total	Liberal	UN	RIN
Farm or village (less than 2,000)	22.6	20.4	25.0	7.1
Town (2,000–25,000)	40.1	28.6	52.0	14.3
City (25,000 or more)	9.3	14.3	4.2	7.1
Montreal or Quebec	27.8	36.7	18.8	71.4
Total	99.8	100.0	100.0	99.9
N	(97)	(49)	(48)	(28)

Totals are calculated from two major parties only. The figures for the RIN are less reliable because of the large number (58.8 per cent) of unknowns.

2 There is a discrepancy between the figures in tables 4.1 and 4.4 for farming background of fathers (only 10.4 per cent of the respondents were born on farms, but 19.7 per cent had fathers who were farmers). Perhaps some fathers had moved off their farms by the time their sons (the respondents) were born, and yet their sons continued to perceive them as farmers. In this case, the Créditiste leaders are more like the candidates of the Liberal party than the

TABLE 4.1

Place of birth, place raised, and present place of residence (per cent)

	Place of birth	Place raised	Present place of residence
Farm	10.4	6.0	1.4
Small town or village (< 10,000)	35.8	35.8	23.2
Small city (10,000+)	32.8	29.9	40.6
Quebec	13.4	14.9	17.4
Montreal	7.5	13.4	17.4
Total	99.9	100.0	100.0
N	(67)	(67)	(69)

The Social Credit movement in Quebec is no longer led by the young. The majority of its leaders are middle aged; and some are in their sixties or seventies; very few are recent converts to the movement. In fact, most of the current leaders joined when the early organization of the movement, the Union des Electeurs, was at its peak in the 1940s (table 4.2). They were then mostly in their twenties (table 4.3).[3]

One-quarter of the leaders of Social Credit had very little opportunity to acquire an education and had not even attended secondary school. Yet a comparatively high proportion, over 40 per cent, had had some years of post-secondary education in colleges or universities (table 4.4).[4]

Union Nationale party and the RIN (although again the statistics are not perfectly comparable). The percentages for place of residence from Lemieux, 120, revised to exclude unknowns, are as follows:

	Total	Liberal	UN	RIN
Farm or village (less than 2,000)	11.2	4.1	18.4	2.5
Town (2,000–25,000)	43.9	42.9	44.9	20.0
City (25,000 or more)	16.3	16.3	16.3	7.5
Montreal or Quebec	28.6	36.7	20.4	70.0
Total	100.0	100.0	100.0	100.0
N	(98)	(49)	(49)	(40)

Totals are calculated from two major parties only. The figures for the RIN are less reliable.

3 A similar tendency to join the Communist movement at a young age was noted by Gabriel Almond in *Appeals of Communism* (Princeton: Princeton University Press, 1954), 217ff.

4 The level of education of our respondents, however, is well below that of the candidates of the major parties and the RIN in the 1966 Quebec provincial election. The figures, from Lemieux, 118, 120 (made comparable by dropping unknowns), are as follows in percentages:

	Total	Liberal	UN	RIN
Primary	2.0	0.0	3.8	0.0
Secondary	29.0	20.4	36.5	31.5
College or university	69.0	79.6	59.5	68.5
Total	100.0	100.0	99.8	100.0
N	(100)	(48)	(52)	(57)

Totals are calculated from two major parties only. Figures for the RIN are less reliable because of the high proportion (16.2 per cent) of unknowns.

TABLE 4.2
Year joined social credit (per cent)

1932–5	11.9
1936–9 (Ligue)	14.9
1940–44 ⎫	23.9
1945–48 ⎬ (Union des Electeurs)	14.9
1949–57 ⎭	6.0
1958–61 ⎫ (Ralliement)	25.4
1962– ⎭	3.0
	100.0
N	(67)

TABLE 4.3
Age at time of joining

Age	Percentage of members joining
11–20	23.8
21–30	41.3
31–40	22.2
41–50	11.1
51–60	1.6
61–70	—
Total	100.0
N	(63)

TABLE 4.4
Years of schooling

Period of education	Percentage of all respondents	Percentage in province[5] (1962 survey)
Elementary school (8 years or less)	27.3	56.7
Secondary school (9 to 12 years)	28.8	32.4
College or university (13 years or more)	43.9	10.9
Total	100.0	100.0
N	(66)	(943)

As might be expected, the leaders of the movement come from poor economic backgrounds. A high proportion had fathers who were engaged in manual or farming occupations. No less than 31.8 per cent were members of families of ten or more children (table 4.5).[6] The leaders of the movement have improved their status and

5 The comparative figures for our survey, listed as '1962 survey,' are taken from marginals prepared by Le Groupe de Recherches Sociales in *Les préférences des électeurs québécois en 1962* (Montreal 1964). They are drawn from a province-wide sample survey conducted by the Social Research Group just prior to the 14 November provincial election. For further information about this survey, see Maurice Pinard, *The Rise of a Third Party: A Study in Crisis Politics* (Englewood Cliffs, NJ: Prentice-Hall, 1971), 14.

6 The tendency for leaders of new political movements to come from poor family backgrounds was noted in the case of the CCF movement in Saskatchewan. S.M. Lipset, 'Leadership

TABLE 4.5
Size of parental family

Number of children	Percentage of leaders' parental families in this group
1 to 2	1.6
3 to 4	13.6
5 to 6	24.2
7 to 9	28.8
10 or more	31.8
Total	100.0
N	(66)

TABLE 4.6
Father's occupation and respondent's
occupation[7] (per cent)

	Father's occupation	Respondent's occupation
Professional	16.7	39.4
Managerial (industrial)	10.6	13.6
Commercial	3.0	31.8
Employees and workers	50.0	15.1
Farmers	19.7	0.0
Total	100.0	99.9
N	(66)	(66)

income somewhat over that of their fathers so that they are no longer among the deprived of the population. Most of them have professional or entrepreneurial middle-class jobs, marking a rise in their status above their lower-class backgrounds (table 4.6).[8]

in New Social Movements,' in A. Gouldner (ed), *Studies in Leadership* (New York, Russell, 1965), 342.

7 Comparable percentages for occupations of males in Quebec, according to the 1961 census, are as follows: professional, 7.8; managerial, 9.6; commercial, 21.0; employees and workers, 49.5; farmers, 9.1; not stated, 3.0 (N = 1,289,425).

8 The occupational status of our respondents is considerably lower, however, than is that of the candidates of all parties in the 1966 Quebec provincial election, since the Créditiste leaders include fewer professionals and more managers. The figures from Lemieux, 118 (made comparable by dropping unknowns) are as follows:

	Total	Liberal	UN	RIN
Professional	71.8	83.6	61.2	60.1
Industrial (managerial)	7.8	4.1	11.1	3.1
Commercial	14.5	6.1	22.2	16.9
Employees and workers	1.0	0.0	1.8	20.0
Farmers	4.9	6.2	3.7	0.0
Total	100.0	100.0	100.0	100.1
N	(103)	(49)	(54)	(65)

Totals are calculated from the two major parties only. Figures for the RIN are reliable, since the proportion of unknowns (4.4 per cent) in this case is small.

TABLE 4.7
Annual income (per cent)

Income group	All respondents	Province as a whole (1962 survey)
Less than $4,000	4.7	63.7
$4,000 to 6,999	25.0	32.5
$7,000 plus	70.3	3.7
Total	100.0	99.9
N	(64)	(739)

This rise in occupational status appears to be accompanied by a considerable increase in annual income. No less than 67.5 per cent of all respondents earned annual incomes above $7,000, which places them among the higher income groups in the community. The overall income of the Créditiste leaders is well above that of the population in Quebec (table 4.7).[9]

The leaders are now among the better-established members of their communities, judging from their length of residence, their voluntary associational attachments, and their official positions in organizations.[10] Many of the leaders have lived in the same community all their adult lives, and the families of over one-quarter have been residents in their locales for several generations. Moreover, they have not lived in isolation from their neighbours. A majority of Créditiste leaders belong to at least one social club or church group. Among the social clubs which were most frequently named by respondents were such well-known French-Canadian associations as the Chevaliers de Colombe (Knights of Columbus), the Richelieu Club, and the Société Saint-Jean Baptiste (Saint John Baptist Society). Many of them also belonged to business groups such as the Chambre de Commerce (Chamber of Commerce).[11]

9 Somewhat comparable figures for income of males in Quebec, according to the 1961 census, are as follows in percentages: less than $4,000, 59.9; $4,000 to $5,999, 28.5; $6,000 plus, 11.6 (n = 1,483,788).

10 But their social class is lower than that of the candidates of the two major parties in the 1966 provincial election. In social class the Créditiste leaders resemble the RIN candidates most closely, being mainly of lower middle class. The figures for both the candidates of the other parties and the Créditiste leaders (which are not strictly comparable, since the method of classifying a respondent by class may differ in the two surveys) are as follows (Lemieux, 121–2) in percentages:

	Total	Liberal	UN	RIN	Créditistes
Upper middle	66.0	79.6	53.7	25.5	30.6
Lower middle	28.1	14.3	40.7	57.0	50.0
Working	5.9	6.1	5.6	17.5	19.3
Total	100.0	100.0	100.0	100.0	99.9
N	(103)	(49)	(54)	(66)	(62)

11 The same associations and groups were also named most frequently by Quebec MLAs. A majority (52.2 per cent) belonged to the Chevaliers de Colombe and a large proportion 32.6 per cent) also were members of the Chambre de Commerce. J. Hamelin, *Nos hommes politiques* (Montreal 1964), 29.

They were less active, however, in professional or agricultural associations and labour unions.[12]

The majority of Social Credit leaders in Quebec had occupied at least one official position in an association other than the Créditiste movement. A substantial portion of these mentioned that they had held three or more official positions in such associations. Among the positions most frequently mentioned were such locally prestigious offices as mayor, alderman, president of an association at the regional or provincial level, and member of a national, regional, or provincial executive of an association.[13]

In summary, social background characteristics portray the typical Créditiste leader as middle-aged today although young at the time he joined the movement, from a poor family background, having comparatively little exposure to modern metropolitan urban life, and having a middle-class (ie, commercial or professional) occupation. He has had more formal education than the average Québécois but less than the leaders of other major parties and movements in Quebec. He has a higher-than-average income and is a member of some standing in the community, participating actively in its social and cultural organizations.

Many of these profile characteristics, including high standing in the community, above average income, higher-than-average education, and wide associational and community attachments, seem atypical of the average follower of a political movement. William Kornhauser, for example, argues that the alienated individual who is particularly attracted to mass movements in contemporary mass society is of lower-than-average socioeconomic status and has few community and associational ties. These social characteristics contribute to his rootlessness and sense of alienation.[14]

12 The pattern of voluntary associational attachments of the Créditiste leaders resembles very closely that of the candidates of the two major parties in the 1966 Quebec provincial election, particularly the Union Nationale (statistics were not available for the RIN). The figures are as follows (Lemieux, 121) in percentages:

	Total	Liberal	UN	Créditiste
Social club	25.9	28.0	24.1	24.1
Chambre de Commerce	41.3	36.0	46.3	46.3
Chevaliers de Colombe	29.9	24.0	35.2	35.2
N	(104)	(50)	(54)	(69)

13 Only 38.8 per cent of the respondents had never held official positions in associations other than Social Credit. A smaller proportion were mayors or aldermen, however, than was the case among the candidates of the two major parties in the Quebec provincial election of 1966 (statistics were not available for the RIN). The comparative figures for both the candidates of the other parties and the Créditiste leaders are as follows in percentages (Lemieux, 121):

	Total	Liberal	UN	Créditiste
Mayors	21.1	10.0	31.5	7.3
Aldermen	16.3	18.0	14.8	
School administrators	7.6	6.0	9.7	
N	(104)	(50)	(54)	(69)

The Créditiste percentage combines responses for mayors and aldermen. No distinction was made for the office of school administrator in the survey.

14 See William Kornhauser, *The Politics of Mass Society* (Glencoe: Free Press, 1959), part III.

However, these qualities differentiate the rank-and-file Créditiste supporter from the Créditiste leader. Pinard found that the average Créditiste voter in 1962 tended to be above the poverty level, to have medium-sized farms, to be of middle income, and to be of working or farming class (not of the middle class).[15] This would place the Créditiste voter well below the Créditiste leader in socioeconomic status.

Pinard also discovered that a moderate degree of primary group participation, a smaller, more integrated community structure (when experiencing strains), and participation in occupational organizations which had become alienated from the established political structures were all conducive to Créditiste support, and membership in voluntary associations and church groups at least did not discourage such support.[16] While these latter participation attributes found among voters by Pinard resemble those we found among Créditiste leaders, they nevertheless suggest that wide associational and community attachments are less important in mobilizing the Créditiste voter than in mobilizing the leader. The latter seems, from the above comparative data, to come closer to fitting the mould of the traditional party leader in Quebec.[17] The discrepancy found in the social characteristics of leaders and followers in the Créditiste movement may also exist in other political movements, although the problem has not yet been explored in other studies.

B POLITICAL BACKGROUND CHARACTERISTICS[18]
It has been argued that a tradition of active family participation in politics strongly encourages individuals to participate in politics.[19] One would therefore expect family political background to play a large part in influencing certain individuals to join a political group like the Créditiste movement in Quebec, and about 50 per cent of respondents reported that their fathers had at least a passable interest in politics; of these a majority considered that interest to be strong.[20] Most of their fathers supported one of the two old-line parties in Quebec.[21] A slightly higher proportion were Liberal than were Conservative or Union Nationale, but this difference was not appreciable. There seems no foundation, then, for the often heard argument that Social Credit activists are mostly disaffected Conservatives.[22] Very few of their fathers appeared to show any interest in the Social Credit movement before the re-

15 Pinard, chapter 8.
16 Pinard, chapter 11. See also chapter 1 above.
17 Evidence to support this argument comes particularly from the comparative data presented on the candidates in the 1966 Quebec provincial election.
18 For construction of all indexes in this section, see appendix C.
19 For a discussion of the relationship between political participation of children and parents, see H. Renmers, 'Early Socialization of Attitudes,' in E. Burdeck and A.T. Brodbeck (eds), *American Voting Behavior* (Glencoe: Free Press, 1959), 55–67.
20 The tendency for fathers of our respondents to have a strong interest in politics increases with the father's occupational status ($\chi^2 = 6.713$, significant for 3 degrees of freedom at less than 0.5 level).
21 Particularly those of working- or middle-class occupations. Fathers who were farmers were less partisan and less likely to support an old-line party ($\chi^2 = 8.620$, significant for 3 degrees of freedom at less than 0.02 level).
22 See, for example, Peter Gzowski, 'A Strongman's Road to Power ... Hung Jury,' *Maclean's*, 28 July, 1962. Vincent Lemieux has given some qualified support to this argument in 'Les dimensions sociologiques du vote Créditiste au Québec,' 185–7. For a contrary point of view,

spondents became involved. However, in some cases, the fathers became interested in the movement late in life, presumably because of the influence of their sons.[23] Most of our respondents were the first members of their families to join the movement.[24]

It appears, then, that the Créditiste leader inherited his general interest in politics from his family but established his affiliation with the Créditiste movement entirely on his own. It is possible that he was influenced in his choice by a desire to reject traditional family political ties.[25] The tendency to rebel against paternal mores by participating more actively in new political organizations may be one factor in the political motivations of protest leaders.[26]

C MOTIVATIONS FOR JOINING THE MOVEMENT

Why do individuals join a political protest movement? Sometimes the ideology of the movement is found to be consistent with the beliefs that an individual has long held, at other times the political organization or appeal of the political leaders is the magnetic force, and conditions within the party system may also be conducive to a protest appeal.[27] In the case of Social Credit in Quebec, our respondents answered both open-ended and closed questions about their motivations for joining. In that way

at least with respect to former Conservative voters in strong Conservative districts, see Pinard, 29–30. See also the exchange between these two political sociologists in *Recherches Sociographiques*, VII, 3 (1966), 360–5. The 1970 Quebec provincial election provides some evidence to support Pinard's argument that the Créditiste vote is more permanent than that of the Conservatives (or Union Nationale at the provincial level). The Créditistes made most of their inroads in former Union Nationale districts, but it is not clear whether these were strong or weak UN districts.

23 There was a slight tendency for fathers who were more mobile in their place of residence to do so ($\chi^2 = 3.568$, with Yates's correction, significant at the 0.06 level). All parties in Quebec to which fathers of respondents belonged were conservative. Most fathers were also probably religious and would probably have looked askance at a movement condemned or criticized by the church authorities.

24 Contrast, in this respect, the pattern which Almond found in the Communist movement in which the largest single group of respondents (34 per cent) came from left-wing family backgrounds (ie, communist, socialist, syndicalist, or anarchist homes), whereas only 16 per cent came from liberal homes, 16 per cent from conservative homes, 3 per cent from monarchist or fascist homes, and 15 per cent from families who were apathetic. Almond concluded that for the largest group, 'joining the party would be a matter of conforming to the past rather than deviating from it.' Almond, 221.

25 This explanation is supported by the responses to questions concerning political alternatives considered at the time the leader joined the movement. See pp 135–6 below.

26 Further evidence in support of this more general argument may be found in the greater inclination of sons (our respondents) to hold official positions both within and outside the movement if their fathers were old-line party adherents ($\chi^2 = 4.769$, with Yates's correction significant at less than 0.05 level), and to participate more actively in voluntary associations if their fathers showed a stronger interest in politics ($\chi^2 = 5.036$, significant at 0.03 level). The pattern of behaviour here may be one manifestation of rebellious alienation in some of our respondents. This concept will be defined in chapter 6. The notion of rebellious behaviour is not widely accepted or even discussed in the literature of family political socialization. Perhaps it is relevant only to the small group of alienated individuals who join and become leaders in protest movements.

27 The first explanatory factor is stressed by Macpherson; the second by Irving; the third by Pinard, *The Rise of a Third Party*, chapters 2, 3. See also Lemieux, 'Les dimensions sociologiques,' 182–3.

they were able to indicate the range of possible factors that might have influenced their choice.

The factor most frequently mentioned among the open-ended responses as a motivation for joining was the economic situation in the province. As one municipal official explained:

I began to concern myself with the doctrine of Social Credit in 1931 or 1932. I think I was the first French-Canadian to study the doctrine of Social Credit. I had read about it in the *Ottawa Citizen*. Mr Bowman was then editor of the *Ottawa Citizen* and during this time he had already begun to mention the name of Douglas in his editorials. At that time I was employed by the Borden Company of Ottawa. The economic depression had begun in 1930. There were 2,400 fathers of families who were unemployed here in the city of Hull, and that is what attracted me to Social Credit. I thought it was inconceivable that in a country like ours there could be so much unemployment, so much misery and poverty. It was particularly the social aspect of the situation which induced me to support the doctrine of Social Credit. I had no training, I had never gone to university, I had ended my studies in the 12th year, and then I was employed by this important company, and I was doing well and earning a good salary. I was then the superintendent of all their production at Ottawa, and I took courses in administration with the extension school at the University of Chicago. I was drawn into administration, and because of the depression I applied myself to searching for the reasons for that situation. It was in that way, upon reading the *Ottawa Citizen*, that I was attracted to the doctrine of social credit. I had read Henry George and his theory of the single tax, and I felt there was something in it, but it was not the answer.

A second factor most frequently mentioned among the reasons for joining was the ideological appeal of the doctrine. An accountant explained:

I have been a member since 1936 or 1937, when I first subscribed to the *Cahiers du Crédit Social*. I followed that journal quite closely. What attracted me at that time, in fact still does today but particularly attracted me then, was the logic of the doctrine. The logic as well as the doctrine of Douglas was based on the production of the country. We had national riches in my opinion which should have been reflected in the issuing of credit. I had always believed in these basic principles.

A third factor was a desire for economic or monetary reform. A furniture dealer asserted:

What persuaded me to belong to the movement was that at the time of the depression I saw people who were obliged to form long lines [marcher sur les trains] to secure work. Many terrible things happened: people could not work, and therefore they could not eat. I asked myself at the time 'What causes this? Why are the stores filled with materials and produce?' There were men who walked up and down the streets with sacks on their backs offering merchandise that no one bought. There were sales everywhere, bankruptcy sales. So I wondered what wasn't working.

TABLE 4.8

Motivations for joining: Open-ended responses

	Reason	Percentage of all respondents
Ideological and economic	Ideological (congruence between the doctrine and individual beliefs)	24.5
	Situational (bad social or economic conditions in the province)	26.7
	Need for monetary or economic reform	15.9
Political and social	Attraction to the political organization or political appeal of the Créditiste leaders	11.3
	Need for political or party system reform	12.9
	Group or social class interests	2.7
	Desire for social companionship	3.8
	Success of the movement elsewhere	2.2
Total		100.0
N		(186)*

*Successive responses to this question were weighted. The first reason given for joining was weighted 2 points and the second reason given was weighted 1 point.

When Social Credit appeared, I found the solution. Because I discovered that the problem was simply a monetary problem, a financial problem. Why was this money not put into circulation? Why were the people forced into such deprivation? Why were they obliged to die of hunger? Why were they permitted to die in the midst of abundance? So I concluded that the system which we now have is no longer functioning, and is a system which should be discarded ...

All of these factors ranked well above any political or social considerations in the motivations of the respondents (table 4.8). The responses confirmed the general opinion that the Créditiste movement is largely a movement of economic discontent.[28] Most of its leaders had been alienated from their traditional partisan attachments in their youth by worsening economic conditions in the province and had sought solutions to the general malaise.[29]

28 This dimension of the Créditiste movement was probably the first to be recognized by political commentators after the sudden 1962 success. See M. Stein, 'Social Credit in Quebec: Political Attitudes and Party Dynamics' (unpublished PH.D thesis, Princeton University, 1967), chapter 1.

29 The tendency to have joined primarily for non-political reasons is stronger among older Créditistes (fifty or over) than among younger Créditistes ($\chi^2 = 8.173$, with Yates's correction, significant at less than 0.01 level for the open-ended question, $\chi^2 = 4.590$, significant at less than 0.05 level for the closed question). It is also somewhat stronger, though less so, among early joiners (1932–57) than among late joiners (1957–67) ($\chi^2 = 3.165$, significant at 0.06 level for the open-ended question, $\chi^2 = 2.614$, significant at 0.10 level for the closed question). The findings here support the observations by Lang and Lang, 520 and Gusfield, 3, concerning motivational differences between older and younger members of a movement and early and later joiners. A similar primary economic motivation appears to have been present in many other political movements. See for example, Hoffmann, 191, and Cantril, *The Politics of Despair*, 65–73.
Contrast, in this respect, the reasons offered by respondents to a 1960 Quebec survey about

Ideological and economic motivations are given a similar priority over political and social motivations in the responses to the closed question on the most important reason for joining the movement. The respondents were asked to select one of three alternatives: the doctrine, the shortcomings of the two old-line parties, or the group of individuals who already belonged to the movement. An overwhelming majority selected the doctrine as their prime reason for joining.[30] The comments of a provincial civil servant are typical:

When I joined the movement ... the doctrine had primary importance for me. Q. And after that, the group of individuals who were already members? A. No, the group of politicians didn't concern us very much. We knew that economic liberalism failed to meet our needs. Economic liberalism has as its principal objective the financing of production. Rather than the problem being one of financing production, we felt it was important to finance all consumers. Q. That is, the movement was not political at all? A. It wasn't political. It was purely economic. After we studied economic liberalism, it became understandable. It [economic liberalism] was always preoccupied with the organization of production, whereas [we thought] it was necessary to organize consumption, the distribution of goods. Production was not really the problem. Distribution became a problem. The economic depression was present to prove it to us. It was therefore necessary to find a system and an economic doctrine which could solve these ills. Social Credit met these needs exactly. It was not a question of 'bleus' or 'rouges.' It [the political system] was a negligible matter.

Some respondents mentioned two or more reasons, while still giving priority to the doctrine (table 4.9). Thus a publicist and salesman declared:

Let us say that the two first alternatives go together. The weaknesses of the old-line political parties enabled the Social Credit movement to take form. I would argue that if the traditional old parties had pursued a policy line desired by the population, then the Social Credit surge would never have occurred. I would not have joined a third party like Social Credit in 1960 or 1961 if I hadn't firmly believed in the fundamental policy (la politique de base) and the fundamental doctrine. The two factors influenced me a great deal: the basic doctrine of the party and the weaknesses of the two old-line parties.

Since the doctrine involved political, economic, and other dimensions, respondents were asked to elaborate on their responses to the preceding question. The vast majority of them considered the economic dimension of the doctrine as most important in motivating them to join. Few of them mentioned political or social

their motivations for voting for one of the two old-line parties. The principal reason cited by those who voted for the Union Nationale party in the 1960 Quebec general election was the accomplishments or program of the party (29 per cent). The principal motivation mentioned by those who voted for the Liberals was that they had always voted for that party (25 per cent); another 23 per cent of the Liberals explained that it was time for a change. Le Groupe de Recherches Sociales, 'Les électeurs québécois' (1960, typescript), 35.

30 A similar primary motivation was found by Almond, 225.

TABLE 4.9
Motivations for joining: Closed responses

Listed reasons for joining	Percentage of all respondents*
Doctrine itself	77.3
Shortcomings of the old-line parties	36.4
The group of individuals already members (Créditistes)	13.6
Total	127.3

*Tabulated for multiple responses so that total number of responses exceeds number of respondents.

TABLE 4.10
Aspect of doctrine emphasized

Aspect	Percentage of all respondents
Religious (natural law, Catholicism)	2.2
Social philosophic (freedom of the individual, social equality)	11.1
Economic (unbalanced economic system, need for monetary reform)	71.1
Political (alternative to Communism, true democracy, alternative to old-line parties)	11.1
Social class	4.4
Total	99.9
N	(45)

philosophic aspects of the doctrine (table 4.10). Thus it seems that from every perspective the influence of economic factors on motivations for joining the Social Credit movement in Quebec was prevalent.[31]

What part, if any, did political considerations play in their decision to join the Créditistes? The leaders were asked if they had considered political alternatives to Social Credit at the time they joined. Only about one-third of them indicated that they had.[32] Most of them had opted for Social Credit as the only real choice apart from the old-line parties at the particular time they joined. A doctor stated flatly: 'It was the only party which I thought about actively, and I never considered other political parties. I was even approached by other political groups after I became a

31 Pinard also accords economic factors a prime place in his explanation of the 1962 Social Credit vote in Quebec: 'We feel that a crucial factor for this sudden and meteoric rise of the Social Credit party in Quebec lies in the worsened economic conditions of large segments of the population. It is our contention that the most general factor of large-scale political movements is to be found in the *changes, and particularly reversals*, occurring in the economic conditions of social groups.' *The Rise of a Third Party*, 100. (Italics in original.)
32 As one might expect, there was a somewhat greater tendency for those respondents whose fathers had a strong interest in politics and especially were partisans of the old-line parties to have considered political alternatives, but the relationship is not significant ($\chi^2 = 2.633$, significant at 0.10 level).

deputy, but I was never interested [in them].' The CCF-NDP party was the most popular alternative choice despite the fact that it was always defeated in the province. Ironically, this is also the party that the leaders of Social Credit have consistently attacked most severely, apart from the communists. The preference for a socialist over a capitalist party as an alternative to Social Credit suggests once again that the economic appeal of the movement was very strong.

The leaders were also asked if they would have joined some other movement if Social Credit had not existed. Only about one-quarter of the respondents indicated that they would not have done so, suggesting that the attachment to Social Credit as an absolute ideal is weaker than some of the movement's more fervent devotees have supposed.[33] The CCF-NDP party once again ranked first among the hypothetical alternatives mentioned. However, a noncommittal reply such as the following by the publicist and salesman was more typical.

Possibly, yes, possibly. It's quite difficult for me to answer you affirmatively. Everything would depend on the platform of another party, on the elaboration of its new policy. For I always understood by a new policy one which involves an improvement over that of the two traditional parties. Would I join another party if Social Credit didn't exist? Maybe yes, maybe no, it's difficult to say.

The appeal offered by certain political leaders also had some influence on most respondents when they decided to join the movement. When asked to mention persons who played key roles in recruiting them to the movement, one-third of the respondents named Louis Even or Gilberte Côté-Mercier. This response of an insurance salesman is fairly representative:

Above all there was Louis Even. You speak of the year 1948 [when I first joined]. [I was influenced particularly] by the journal which was sent to us at that time, the documentation which we received about the world around us. I have an idea that M Caouette also influence me later ... when he founded a new movement. At that time [1948] I wasn't a militant member. I subscribed to the journal.

The choice of Even and Mme Côté-Mercier over the other leaders may seem surprising in view of the fact that Réal Caouette was far more effective as a political organizer than the editors of *Vers Demain*. It reinforces the view that economic and ideological factors were most important in initially attracting the elite to the movement (table 4.11).[34]

33 As expected, there was a greater tendency for those respondents whose fathers were non-political and especially non-partisans of the old-line parties to have refused to consider any alternatives to the movement even if it had not existed ($\chi^2 = 4.144$, with Yates's correction significant at less than the 0.05 level). This relationship is strengthened when controlled for those who joined the movement prior to 1957 ($\chi^2 = 6.017$, with Yates's correction significant at less than 0.02 level).

34 Lang and Lang observe that early leaders, who are less politically motivated, are likely to be remembered best by the movement's followers. Lang and Lang, 517. Recall also the distinction made in chapter 1 between the prophet, who has often played the role of founder or successor to the founder, the bureaucrat, whose activities are predominantly administrative,

TABLE 4.11
Person who was key recruiter

Person named	Percentage of all respondents
None	25.8
Leader of the Ligue (Dugal, Turpin)	6.1
Leader of the Union des Electeurs (Even, Côté-Mercier)	33.3
Caouette	13.6
Other Ralliement leader (Grégoire, Legault)	4.5
Regional or provincial organizer	1.5
Local organizer	15.2
Total	100.0
N	(66)

In summary, ideological and economic factors were clearly predominant in motivating today's leaders to join the Créditiste movement. They joined primarily because they found economic conditions intolerable and embraced the ideology because it seemed to offer some solution to their predicament. They were most influenced by economic aspects of the protest appeal.[35] The political alternatives which they considered were those which promised to bring greatest relief from the prevailing economic plight.[36]

D   THE SOCIAL PROFILE OF THE CRÉDITISTE LEADERSHIP
The typical Social Credit leader in Quebec was born and brought up in a small town or village and today lives outside the metropolitan regions of Montreal and Quebec

and the agitator, who serves as a liaison between the leader and the outside world. Thus Louis Even and Gilberte Côté-Mercier would fit the definition of a prophet and a founding leader, Laurent Legault would qualify as a bureaucrat, and Caouette would qualify as an agitator, particularly in the early stages of the Créditiste movement. It is also interesting that King does not see the founder and prophet as most politically powerful. Although he 'appears to outsiders and to the personnel itself as responsible for the policies and objectives distinctive to the movement, in fact, his influence within the movement is more apparent than real.' King, 72.
King goes on to explain why, despite their prestige and aura of power, the founders may eventually lose their position of influence within the movement and be displaced: 'The leader, even if he is also the founder, may be left in an impotent position so far as internal affairs go, manipulated by strong bureaucratic functionaries ... these behind-the-scene agents often possess professional skill and competence but have little emotional stake in an organization's vowed objectives' (74). His description seems to explain much about the loss of influence and displacement of Even and Côté-Mercier as leaders of the Créditiste movement in the late 1950s and may also apply to some of the more recent splits (in 1963 and 1966).
35 A similar tendency to consider political alternatives in terms of the economic relief which they promised has been observed in many other political movements. See, for example, M. and S. Stedman, *Discontent at the Polls* (New York: Russell and Russell, 1950), chapter 8; Hoffmann, *Le mouvement poujade*, part I; Irving, *The Social Credit Movement in Alberta*, and Macpherson, *Democracy in Alberta*.
36 The respondents were also asked directly if they thought the Social Credit movement was a vehicle of protest at the time they had joined it, and whether that had influenced them to join. Less than one-half admitted that this had been a factor in their decision. See chapter 5 for a fuller discussion and explanation of this response.

City. He joined the movement as a young man, during a period of severe economic dislocation. He exhibits many of the characteristics of the traditional small-town Quebec elite: he is better educated than the average French Canadian and has a higher-than-average income. He has several social and church group affiliations and holds office in a number of associations besides Social Credit. He came from a family background that was more politicized than the average, and his father was generally a partisan of one of the two old-line parties in Quebec. He was the first member of his family to join the movement and was motivated to do so more for economic and ideological than for political or social reasons. He was particularly imbued with a zeal for economic reform, which he hoped to realize through the monetary reform doctrine of Social Credit. It would appear, then, that it is his political attitudes rather than his political or social background characteristics that distinguish him from the traditional elite of conventional parties in Quebec and qualifies him as a 'political protest' leader.

5

The Attitudinal Profile of the Créditiste Leadership

In the previous chapter we concluded that the social and political background characteristics of the Créditiste leaders do not distinguish them from traditional party leaders in Quebec and speculated that real differences are more likely to be apparent in the political attitudes of these leaders. In our study the questions about the political attitudes of Créditiste leaders were chosen with a view to discovering whether they fitted those of the typical political protester and, more particularly, formed coherent sets which could be considered to constitute a 'protest orientational syndrome.' The responses to these questions were grouped into six categories: A / attitudes towards the system as a whole and its reform, B / attitudes towards parts of the system and their reform, C / attitudes towards system control by external and minority groups, D / attitudes towards religion, E / propensity to protest, and F / parental and political authoritarianism.

A ATTITUDES TOWARDS THE SYSTEM AS A WHOLE AND ITS REFORM
The questions on attitudes towards the system as a whole were designed to probe both a negative or critical dimension in a political leader's attitude and a positive or reformist dimension. Both dimensions were considered likely to be present in any overall attitude of protest against the existing system.

One-half the respondents considered the political system to be completely corrupt. A high proportion of this group considered it to be so without qualification. Of those who disagreed, many quarrelled only with the degree of corruption implied in the statement; for them the system was corrupt but not completely so (table 5.1).

An overwhelming majority of the respondents (80.6 per cent) felt that the economic system was completely unhealthy (en déroute). Almost all of this group said so without qualification. Only a handful (14.9 per cent) of the respondents dismissed this allegation out of hand.[1] It therefore appears that Créditiste leaders have negative

1 These data are drawn from the responses to question 28d of part IV of the questionnaire (see appendix B); 80.6 per cent replied affirmatively to the question, of whom 77.6 per cent did so without qualification; 19.4 per cent replied negatively to the question, of whom 14.9 per cent did so without qualification.

TABLE 5.1
Our political system is completely corrupt

Agrees or disagrees	Percentage of all respondents
Agrees without qualification	36.4
Agrees, but with qualification (eg, the system is, but the men are not)	13.6
Disagrees without qualification	22.7
Disagrees, but with qualification (eg, it is not *completely* corrupt)	27.3
Total	100.0
N	(66)

TABLE 5.2
Advocates reforms in the democratic system

Type of reform advocated	Percentage of all respondents
Revamp the system entirely (eg, establish a dictatorship, establish a corporatist system)	10.9
Establish a true democracy, rather than a system controlled by finance	25.8
Modify the system slightly (eg, make the caucus more democratic)	8.1
Yes, advocates reforms but does not specify them	17.7
No reforms desired at all	35.5
Total	98.0
N	(62)

feelings towards the prevailing political and economic systems. This discontent is directed more against the economic than the political system, as might have been expected from the analysis of motivations for joining the movement. Condemnation of both the political and economic systems is consistent with the Douglas doctrine.[2]

This negative attitude towards the existing system is accompanied by a strong positive desire for its reform. Créditiste leaders generally support reforms in the democratic system of government, the parliamentary system, and the federal system. Well over a majority of respondents favour some reform of the democratic system. Only a small percentage (10.9 per cent) of this group, however, support reforms of a radical and sweeping kind. Most of the reformers simply wish to establish a genuine democracy along lines suggested by the Douglas doctrine (table 5.2).

An even higher proportion of respondents support some reform of the parlia-

2 See, for example, C.H. Douglas, *Credit-Power and Democracy, with a Draft Scheme for the Mining Industry* (London: Cecil Palmer, 1920). See also chapter 2.

TABLE 5.3
Advocates reforms in the parliamentary system

Type of reform advocated	Percentage of all respondents
Revamp the system entirely (eg, adopt a presidential system, corporatism)	15.2
Eliminate all vestiges of monarchy and colonialism, appointive bodies	12.1
Establish procedural reforms	28.8
Yes, advocates reforms, but does not specify them	25.8
None at all	18.2
Total	100.1
N	(66)

mentary system. Most of them merely call for moderate reforms such as changes in procedure. For example, a personnel director complained that 'the deputies aren't consulted enough,' and a publisher of a small journal argued: 'The Senate needs reforming. Also more power should be given to the deputy.' Only a small proportion (15.2 per cent) called for the kind of radical restructuring implied in this blunt statement by a municipal official: 'We need an American-type presidential system for Quebec.' In fact, very few advocate abolition of the parliamentary system or substitution of some other type of system (presidential, corporatist) for it (table 5.3).

Most of the reformers desire improvements in the federal system. However, once again the reforms suggested are moderate rather than radical. Most merely call for modernization of the existing system or the establishment of a more genuine equibalanced federation. Thus a doctor proffered these suggestions: 'There are many possible reforms. First of all, there should be a system which is really federal in a cultural sense. One could also establish five economic zones.' A provincial civil servant proposed that 'there should be more provincial autonomy given to Quebec,' and a printer's idea was to 'establish a decentralized system, change the administrative and financial structure of federalism.' Only a relatively small minority (23.1 per cent) advocate the kind of radical constitutional change implied by such proposals as an associate state status or political independence for Quebec (table 5.4).

Thus, although most Créditiste leaders advocate some reform of the political system, their demands are moderate rather than revolutionary. They wish to see some changes in the prevailing system without any fundamental transformation in the essential forms of that system, and they continue to be supporters of the federal form of parliamentary democracy which Canada first established in 1867.[3]

3 There has, however, been considerable debate about the degree of centralization or decentralization which is desirable within this federal form. This debate between 'federalists' and 'provincialists' has occurred throughout the Quebec movement's history, but has intensified since the rise of the most recent and most important wave of separatism in the early 1960s. See chapter 3.

TABLE 5.4

Advocates reforms in the federal system

Type of reform advocated	Percentage of all respondents
Revamp the system completely (eg, establish a loose confederation, an association of states, an independent state for Quebec)	23.1
Redistribute powers, give more autonomy to Quebec	18.5
Establish a real federation, the federation that was originally envisaged	16.9
Modernize the existing system (eg, improve fiscal division)	15.4
Yes, advocates reforms, but does not specify them	13.8
None at all	12.3
Total	100.0
N	(65)

B ATTITUDES TOWARDS PARTS OF THE SYSTEM AND THEIR REFORM

The respondents were asked which level of government in the Canadian federation is most conducive to the realization of French-Canadian goals. Close to one-half (46.2 per cent) replied that both levels contribute towards these ends. Thus a personnel director asserted: 'The two levels are interdependent and French Canadians need both.' A doctor agreed: 'Although the provincial level is more important, it is necessary to have a presence at the federal level in order to obtain certain goals.' Among the remaining respondents, a majority favoured the provincial government over the federal government. The reason frequently given for this preference is that French Canadians have a numerical preponderance at this level (table 5.5).

It is clear, then, that although the Créditiste leaders are somewhat more provincialist than federalist in outlook, they are certainly not radical nationalists; they strongly support the dual federal structure.

A similar pattern is reflected in the responses to the question concerning the protection of French-Canadian rights on the federal level. Opinion on this question was divided about equally between those who felt that their rights were being respected and those who did not.[4] However, many of those who answered affirmatively pointed out that the respect for their rights was a very recent development. Thus a retired electrical assessor noted: 'Yes, our rights are being respected in Ottawa with the help of the Social Credit MPs.' And a printer concurred: 'Yes, since 1962. But there's still much improvement needed.'

The Créditistes were openly split on the question of independence for the province of Quebec: 27.7 per cent thought that independence was desirable immediately;

4 43.1 per cent replied affirmatively to this question, of whom 20 per cent did so without qualification. Pinard found a similar pattern of response among Créditiste voters when they were asked the same question, although a slightly higher proportion of voters (57 per cent, N = 950) than leaders (43.1 per cent, N = 65) agreed that French-Canadian rights were respected in Ottawa. From marginals of the 1962 Groupe de Recherches Sociales. *Les Préférences des électeurs québécois en 1962* (Montreal 1964). See also Maurice Pinard, *The Rise of a Third Party: A Study in Crisis Politics* (Englewood Cliffs, NJ: Prentice-Hall, 1971), 84–6.

TABLE 5.5
Level of government most
conducive to French-Canadian
goals

Level of government	Percentage of all respondents
Federal level	18.5
Provincial level	35.4
Both levels together	46.2
Total	100.1
N	(65)

another 29.2 per cent thought that it might be desirable some time in the future; and 43.1 per cent, by far the largest group, were convinced that it would never be desirable at any time.[5] A municipal official expressed what was probably a typical attitude in this group: 'Separatism is never desirable, but it might be realizable in the future. I don't know whether it will be so or not ... it depends on the emotive impact which a separatist appeal has.' Once again, then, a moderate strain appears among Créditiste leaders. They are reformist rather than revolutionary in their attitudes towards change. They might, however, be forced to opt for a more radical solution if other alternatives no longer seem acceptable.

The respondents were also asked their opinions of the particular governments then operating at each level. Only 4.6 per cent rated the Pearson Liberal government as good; most considered it just tolerable (passable). The remaining (35.3 per cent) labelled it poor. This is not surprising, since for the leadership the federal Liberals are the chief Créditiste antagonists on the electoral hustings. The Union Nationale government of Daniel Johnson fared considerably better in Créditiste estimations: 22.6 per cent thought it was good, and only 29.0 per cent judged it to be poor (table 5.6). It may be that Créditistes found the conservative policies of a 'Unionist' government more to their liking than the reformist program of the Liberals.

Although there is some tendency on the part of Créditiste leaders to follow the

5 The proportion favouring Quebec independence was much higher among Créditiste leaders than among Créditiste voters. Thus only 10.3 per cent of the voters thought that separatism was immediately desirable and another 10.0 per cent thought it might be desirable in the future (N = 126). From marginals of 1962 Groupe de Recherches Sociales survey. See also Pinard, *The Rise of a Third Party*, in which, he concluded that 'the two [Social Credit and separatism] are slightly associated ... and that probably each movement created some conducive conditions for the rise of the other.' (82).

The discrepancy between leaders and followers with respect to separatism suggests that the latter may have been an important restraining element on the leadership during the debates between fédéralistes and indépendentistes in the mid-1960s. However, the extent of the discrepancy may be due to the much later date of the leadership survey, after separatism had gained more respectability. In addition, the 1967 survey occurred during the most intensive period of debate between the fédéralistes and indépendentistes and may have included a slightly disproportionate number of the latter. It should be noted, however, that at the time of writing, a renewed debate is occurring between those who support Caouette's federalist position and those who favour Samson's quasi-separatist approach.

TABLE 5.6
Opinion of Liberal and Union Nationale
governments

Opinion	Pearson Liberal government	Johnson Union Nationale government
Good	4.6	22.6
Passable	60.0	48.4
Bad	35.3	29.0
Total	99.9	100.0
N	(65)	(62)

TABLE 5.7
Desires reforms in political parties

Type of reform advocated	Percentage of all respondents
Abolish or revamp them entirely (eg, make them loose associations of electors)	16.1
Make their organizations more democratic and their methods of finance purer	40.3
Make their leaders and their parliamentary representatives more responsible	12.9
Make them ideologically more distinct	6.5
Reform advocated but unspecified	12.9
None at all	11.3
Total	100.0
N	(62)

letter of Douglas doctrine and condemn all existing governments as unsuitable, their evaluations are usually discriminating. For example, a furniture dealer observed, 'the Johnson government is less socialistic than that of Lesage,' and a municipal official pointed out that 'the Pearson government is better than the Diefenbaker government in its attitudes towards French Canadians. The Johnson government is well intentioned.' A merchant, however, expressed a more orthodox Créditiste view: 'The Pearson government was sold like all others to finance. The Johnson government is tolerable but also attached to the financiers.' On the whole, however, Créditiste leaders do not assume the pattern of anti-partisanship encouraged by Louis Even and Gilberte Côté-Mercier.

Finally, the respondents when questioned on their attitudes towards political party reform evinced a strong desire for such reform and particularly for internal democratization. They also sought to make party leaders more responsible to their constituents and the parties more ideologically distinct. Very few, however, went so far as to call for either the abolition or the complete restructuring of these parties as advocated in the Douglas doctrine and in the writings of Even and Côté-Mercier (table 5.7). A municipal official argued: 'What needs reforming above all is the system of campaign funds [caisse electorale]. With the growth of intermediate groups [corps intermédiaires], in fifty years we may be able to administer without parties.' Others offered even more moderate proposals. A school teacher demanded that 'every member ... be permitted freedom of expression,' and a doctor called upon 'the parties [to] define clearly their ideological position.' But an automobile mechanic was much more direct: 'Put the two old-line parties in the trash heap [au rancart].'

The same desire for party reform is apparent in the responses to the question on government finance of political parties. A majority (61.5 per cent) thought that the government should finance the parties entirely. Those who opposed this method of finance frequently explained that this could be done under a system of social credit.

C ATTITUDES TOWARDS CONTROL OF THE SYSTEM BY EXTERNAL OR MINORITY GROUPS

The Créditiste leaders were asked about their attitudes towards different external groups which have been accused at various times of usurping political and economic control of the province from French Canadians.[6] Specifically, they were questioned about American economic imperialism, communist infiltration, and excessive English-speaking influence (table 5.8). The questions were designed to detect conspiratorial attitudes which might form part of an authoritarian syndrome.

A majority of respondents did not agree with the opinion that the Americans are exerting every possible effort to make Canada economically dependent. Those who qualified their answer to the question often added: 'It is the system that does this rather than the Americans.' An even larger proportion of respondents disagreed with the assertion that the English play too large a role in Quebec. Several who did agree interjected 'and French Canadians are at fault for it.'[7] There does not appear to be a strong feeling of antipathy to foreign nationalities among the Créditiste leaders, and ethnocentric or xenophobic nationalism is absent except in a few cases. On the other hand, there is a clear perception of a communist threat. A substantial majority of the leaders were convinced that the communists have infiltrated the political parties in Canada. Some of them elaborated on this opinion by selecting for particular mention the New Democratic party and Le Rassemblement pour l'Indépendence Nationale.[8]

There is no all-encompassing conspiratorial outlook shared by Créditiste leaders.

6 Strains of ethnocentrism have often been observed in French-Canadian culture. See, for example, P.E. Trudeau, 'Some Obstacles to Democracy in Quebec,' *CJEPS*, xxiv, 3 (August 1958), 299–311, and Michael Oliver, 'The Social and Political Ideas of French-Canadian Nationalists, 1920–1945' (unpublished PHD thesis, McGill University, 1956). See also Robert Rumilly, *L'infiltration gauchiste au Canada français* (Montréal: édité par l'auteur, 1956).

7 The responses of the Créditiste leaders to this last question show less ethnocentrism than is the case for the general Quebec voter in the province. In a 1962 survey, 59.1 per cent of Quebec voters agreed that 'French Canadians must often be on their guard so that English Canadians do not take advantage of them,' and only 29.5 per cent disagreed. Le Groupe de Recherches Sociales, 56.

8 Le Rassemblement pour l'Indépendence Nationale (RIN), which was the strongest wing of the independence movement in Quebec until 1967, disbanded in 1968 and most of its members joined the newly formed Parti Québécois, under the leadership of René Lévesque. Its members are still considered to be the most left-wing or socialist group within the PQ.

TABLE 5.8
Perception of control of the system by external or
minority groups

	Per cent		
	Agree	Disagree	
Americans are exerting every possible effort to make us their economic dependents	46.1	53.9	N = (65)
The English play too large a role in Quebec	39.4	60.6	N = (66)
The communists have infiltrated the political parties in Canada	74.6	25.4	N = (59)

Communism is the closest approximation to an enemy of Créditisme. Americans and English Canadians are free from being implicated in a world plot or financial conspiracy directed against the French-Canadian masses. Créditiste leaders for the most part eschew the more extremist theories of the founders of the Union des Electeurs. However, a minority of Créditiste leaders do implicate Americans and English Canadians in their general dissatisfaction with the economic and political situation in the province.

D   ATTITUDES TOWARDS RELIGION AND THE CLERGY

An overwhelming majority of Créditiste leaders expressed support for the traditional church elite, which is the object of much opposition or disdain from leftist elements in Quebec today. They disagreed emphatically with the charge that the influence of the clergy is exerted in too many spheres (table 5.9). Those who agreed would generally add some qualification like 'Yes [they exert too much influence], but they do so much less than 15 or 20 years ago.' A similar pro-clerical attitude is reflected in reactions to the assertion that some political parties seem insensitive to the importance of religious teaching in our schools. A majority concurred with this point of view. Several levelled this charge particularly at the New Democratic party and Le Rassemblement pour l'Indépendance Nationale.[9]

The responses to these questions reflect the continued entrenchment of traditional French-Canadian values among the Créditiste leaders. Their traditionalism may be due in part to the strong religious component in early Créditiste doctrine. However, a more important reason for it lies in the insulation of the non-urban environment from the breakdown of traditional values. Most Créditiste leaders live outside the large urban centres and devotion to the Roman Catholic faith and adherence to clerical leadership continue to be strong, except perhaps among the younger rural and small-urban French Canadians.

9 The responses to the first question are approximately the same as those of the general Quebec voter, but the responses to the second question differ markedly from those of the general Quebec voter. Thus 36.2 per cent of Quebec voters agreed that the influence of the clergy is too strong in Quebec, whereas 48.6 per cent disagreed and 15.1 per cent offered another more intermediary position. On the other hand 40.3 per cent of Quebec voters agreed that a plot exists against the teaching of religion in the schools, 36.7 per cent disagreed, and 23.0 per cent offered another more intermediary position. See Le Groupe de Recherches Sociales, 58.

TABLE 5.9
Attitudes towards religion and the clergy

	Per cent		
	Agree	Disagree	
The influence of the clergy is exerted in too many spheres	36.9	63.1	N = (65)
Some political parties seem insensitive to the importance of religious teaching in our schools	66.1	33.9	N = (62)

E   PROPENSITY TO PROTEST

The leaders of Social Credit in Quebec were questioned directly on their propensities to protest. It was thought that if they had protest syndromes, they would also be inclined to articulate their attitudes by speaking out frequently on different public questions. This was found to be the case.

The proclivity for speaking out on issues manifests itself both in private and public life. A majority of respondents (55.4 per cent) maintained that it is often or always necessary to contradict and correct another when he is wrong. They did show some restraint, however, in explaining their reasons for their opinions on the preceding question. A bare majority (52.1 per cent) thought that the need to contradict and correct others would depend on the situation and the person involved, whereas a strong minority (41.7 per cent) felt that it is one's duty to do so. When asked how often one should contradict another when one knows he is wrong, the municipal official answered: 'Only sometimes. I've changed my opinion over twenty-five years. I'm much less inclined to contradict others when they are wrong than I used to be.' This response may reflect an increasing tendency to moderation among Créditiste leaders in expressing their dissenting attitudes.

A much higher proportion of respondents (71.6 per cent) felt that it is often or always necessary to express one's contrary opinions through public activities when one thinks someone is politically wrong. In contrast to what one might ordinarily expect in human behaviour, the Créditiste leaders have a greater propensity to protest publicly than privately.

In explaining the reasons for their opinion, the respondents once again showed some sense of restraint. About one-third of those who responded (34.3 per cent) allowed that the decision to protest publicly would depend on the situation and person involved. About the same proportion (37.1 per cent) indicated that their attitude in favour of public protest stemmed from a strong sense of public duty.

F   PARENTAL AND POLITICAL AUTHORITARIANISM

In an attempt to relate the propensity to protest to basic personality drives, the Créditiste leaders were first asked about the authoritarianism of their parents. Was their strong sense of duty inculcated in authoritarian family environments?[10] The

10 Several commentators have cited authoritarianism as an important dimension in Quebec culture. See, for example, Trudeau, 'Some Obstacles to Democracy in Quebec,' and M. Rioux,

TABLE 5.10

Perceived authoritarianism of respondents'
parents and of respondents

Degree of perceived authoritarianism	Percentage of parents	Percentage of respondents
Yes, authoritarian	51.7	40.4
Perhaps a little	13.3	15.8
No, not authoritarian	35.0	43.9
Total	100.0	100.1
N	(60)	(57)

TABLE 5.11

Desirable attributes of a political leader

	Per cent		
	Yes	No	
Authoritarian?	54.0	46.0	N = (63)
Flexible?	74.6	25.4	N = (59)
Intellectual?	57.8	42.2	N = (64)
Educated?	75.4	24.6	N = (65)
Prestigious?	73.8	26.2	N = (65)

respondents were about equally divided between those who had authoritarian parents and those who did not, but only 40.4 per cent considered themselves to be authoritarian parents (table 5.10). No evidence emerges, therefore, to indicate that the general propensity of Créditiste leaders to protest arises from authoritarian family backgrounds.[11]

The respondents were also asked to express their opinions on the desirability of certain qualities in political leaders. Each of the attributes listed – authoritarian, flexible, intellectual, educated, and prestigious – were considered to be extremely desirable for a political leader by at least a majority of the leaders. However, of the five characteristics, authoritarianism was considered to be desirable by the smallest proportion of respondents (54 per cent). Flexibility, on the other hand, a quality generally at odds with authoritarianism, was viewed in positive terms by 74.6 per cent of the respondents (table 5.11).[12] There is, moreover, no indication that the

'La democratie et la culture canadienne-française,' Cité Libre, 28 (June–July 1960). See also the data presented by Pinard in The Rise of a Third Party, 228.

11 Pinard also found that there was no relationship between parental authoritarianism and support for Social Credit among Quebec voters. See The Rise of a Third Party, 228.

12 Compare the responses to the 1960 Groupe de Recherches Sociales survey, in which the most important qualities for political leaders were ranked as follows: honesty, 43 per cent; good judgment, 35 per cent; efficacy, 12 per cent; determination, 10 per cent (N = 840). In another ranking, the results were as follows: rectitude, 33 per cent; intelligence, 29 per cent; decisiveness, 22 per cent; enterprising nature, 16 per cent (N = 858). Le Groupe de Recherches Sociales, 'Les Electeurs Québécois' (Montreal 1960), 98.

average Créditiste leader is anti-intellectual, although this attitude is often thought to co-exist with authoritarianism.[13]

In summary, most Créditiste leaders behave similarly in the public and private spheres in expressing contrary opinions on issues. Many are driven by a strong sense of duty to protest against what they feel is wrong. But others show considerable restraint in selecting the proper moment to resort to such protest action. They are clearly not indiscriminate protesters, given to rebellion regardless of person, place, or situation. Nor does their propensity to protest appear to be related to authoritarianism in their family backgrounds or political attitudes.[14] And there is no evidence that they exhibit anything which could be described as a radical protest syndrome.

G THE ATTITUDINAL PROFILE OF THE CRÉDITISTE LEADERSHIP

The Créditiste leader displays dissenting attitudes against the political system and its parts and also shows a desire to reform the system. However, the reforms he calls for are moderate rather than radical in content. He does not have a conspiratorial outlook which manifests itself in consistently negative attitudes towards external and minority groups operating in the system. But he is fearful of communist infiltration and wishes to preserve religious values and clerical influence in Quebec society. He also has a propensity to express his disagreement on issues which arouse his indignation; however, it often requires suitable circumstances to activate this propensity. There is no indication that he is authoritarian either in background or personality; he has a moderate protest syndrome.

In short, the average Créditiste leader exhibits attitudinal characteristics of a moderate protester and political reformer rather than a radical dissenter. His attitudinal profile conforms with the moderate protest cast of the movement discovered in the examination of its later historical and ideological development.

13 See, for example, S.M. Lipset, *Political Man* (Garden City, NY: Doubleday, 1960), 119–20. One of the contributing factors to the high rate of agreement on each question may be response set. For this reason, the responses to this set of questions must be treated with some caution.
14 This finding appears to contradict many psychological explanations of political protest. See, for example, T.W. Adorno *et al.*, *The Authoritarian Personality* (New York: Harper, 1950), and Donald J. Goodspeed, *The Conspirators: A Study of the Coup d'Etat* (New York: Viking Press, 1962). For a critique and reformulation of this explanation in terms of aggression theory, see Ted Gurr, *Why Men Rebel* (Princeton: Princeton University Press, 1970), 30–7.

6

The Psychological and Operational
Environment of the Movement

What sort of environment has a political protest movement like Social Credit in Quebec? How do leaders with the background characteristics, motivations for joining, and political attitudes just outlined interact with each other? The responses to questions of this nature were grouped into two major categories: the patterns of participation of the leaders, and their perceptions of the movement's goals and patterns of behaviour. The responses provide a reasonably comprehensive picture of the psychological and operational environment of Social Credit in Quebec.

A THE GENERAL PATTERNS OF PARTICIPATION IN THE CRÉDITISTE
   MOVEMENT[1]

Most of those interviewed still considered themselves to be active participants in the Quebec Social Credit movement. Over 50 per cent were members of the Ralliement Créditiste, the principal contemporary wing of the movement; an additional 23.1 per cent listed themselves as active members of other Social Credit associations (table 6.1).

Moreover, those who are still active appear to devote considerable time to Social Credit activities. Of those still active in the movement who responded to the question, 22.9 per cent estimated that they spent five or more evenings a month at such activities. Although this figure is below the goal set by the chief organizers of the Ralliement Créditiste in each constituency, it seems to indicate a high level of activity among those still participating.[2] No more definite conclusions about frequency of

---

1 The findings here are influenced significantly by the method used to select the sample. See appendix A below.
2 See M.B. Stein, 'The Structure and Function of the Finances of the Ralliement des Créditistes,' in *Studies in Canadian Party Finance* (Ottawa: Queen's Printer, 1966), 450. The tendency for militants in a movement to participate more actively than conventional party activists has been noted by Gabriel Almond in *Appeals of Communism* (Princeton: Princeton University Press, 1954).

TABLE 6.1

Participation in an association connected with the
Social Credit movement

Mode of participation	Percentage of all respondents
Ralliement Créditiste	56.9
Other Social Credit organization (eg, Ralliement National, *Vers Demain*, Ligue)	23.1
None at all today	29.2
Total	109.2*
N	(65)

*Some respondents belonged to more than one organization.

TABLE 6.2

Number of official positions
held in the Social Credit
movement

Number of positions	Percentage of all respondents
None at all	21.8
One	37.5
Two	25.0
Three or more	15.6
Total	99.9
N	(64)

participation can be drawn, however, since a large proportion of the respondents still active in Social Credit (38.5 per cent) failed to answer the question.

As expected, most Créditiste leaders had served in at least one official position in the movement during their period of membership. A few had held several positions (table 6.2). The leaders of the Créditistes have clearly had much experience in official roles both outside the movement and within it. Moreover, most of those who held these positions had served in an official capacity at a higher level than the local association. They were either executive members at the national, regional, or provincial levels, or MPs and unsuccessful candidates for parliament (table 6.3). Close to one-half of this group had held their positions for three years or more.

In summary, the leaders of Quebec Social Credit over the thirty-five years since its founding are still, for the most part, extremely active in the various wings of the movement. Most of them belong to and participate in the Ralliement Créditiste and devote a considerable amount of extracurricular time to the movement. Over the years they have acquired much experience in various official positions, which ought to have equipped them for parliamentary and political roles.

TABLE 6.3
Highest position attained in the
Social Credit movement

Position	Percentage of respondents still active
President or director at national, regional, or provincial level, candidate, or MP	53.0
Member of executive or organizer at national, regional, or provincial level	23.5
Member of executive at local level	23.5
Total	100.0
N	(51)

B   GENERAL PERCEPTIONS OF THE MOVEMENT AND ITS GOALS

The respondents were asked if they conceived of Social Credit as a protest movement and, if so, whether that had influenced them to join. Only about one-quarter answered unequivocally that they thought it was. For example, the furniture dealer replied:

Yes, it *was* a vehicle of protest because it was a movement which advocated reforms and which presented these reforms to the old-line parties in an effort to get them to implement them. *Q*: Do you think that the movement was very different from, say, l'Action Libérale Nationale at that time in terms of being a movement of reform and of protest? *A*: The people who belonged to the ALN also had a desire to improve things. But like all other parties, they were not familiar with the doctrine of Social Credit, apart from Grégoire and Hamel ... *Q*: Was the Ralliement Créditiste as much of a protest and reformist movement as the Union of Electors? *A*: Yes, because [its members] knew the very same doctrine, exactly the same thing.

The electrical assessor concurred:

Q: Is Social Credit in Quebec a protest movement? *A*: Yes, certainly. *Q*: Against what? *A*: Against the power of international finance. And against the restrictions on the use of potential productive capabilities, the limitations on production.

Moreover, they appeared to understand protest in a variety of ways. There was an equal tendency to consider the movement as a protest against the political order (characteristic of all opposition parties or movements in a political system), a protest against the economic order (characteristic of movements of monetary or economic reform which act as pressure groups on established political structures), and as a protest against the established social order (most characteristic of anomic social movements).[3] Their responses appeared to reflect the multifaceted nature of the

3 All of these types of protest can, of course, be expressed in political terms. On this point see R.J. Jackson and M.B. Stein, *Issues in Comparative Politics* (New York: St. Martin's [Toronto: Macmillan], 1971), 268–74.

TABLE 6.4
Perception of the movement as a
protest vehicle

Type of perception	Percentage of all respondents
Yes, protest movement	29.7
Both protest and constructive	31.2
No, not protest	39.1
Total	100.0
N	(64)

Social Credit movement in Quebec and the different phases through which the movement has passed.

Another one-quarter were more equivocal in their replies. They tended to distinguish between elements in the ideology which were negative (and therefore in their view protest) and those which were positive, or between those groups of members who were protesters and those who were not. For example, the furniture dealer explained:

Q: Is Social Credit a protest movement? A: More than that I think. The ideology is more than a protest. It tries really to modify the monetary system, the financial system, and to assure a better life for the people. Q: But if there are elements of protest in the movement, what are they against? A: I think they are against the control that finance exerts over the system, and I also think they are against the control that these people exercise over the parties, and that, I don't think, is in the interests of the great majority of Canadians. There may be much good [in their outlook]. These people [protest elements] are not badly intentioned, but they never analyse in depth what a financial system is like. I have been forced over the years to gain an understanding of the machinery, the mechanism of the system.

The largest proportion of all (39.1 per cent) completely rejected the idea that Social Credit is a protest movement. Most of them understood protest to mean something negative or destructive and contrasted with it the positive orientation of the movement and its ideology (table 6.4).

An even smaller proportion of Quebec Social Credit leaders, about one-fifth of the respondents, were willing to admit that the element of protest in the movement had influenced them to join it. The majority simply rejected any suggestion that Social Credit was a vehicle of protest for them at the time they joined. The term protest clearly had a negative connotation for many respondents. Moreover, there appears to be a large gap between the perceptions which the leaders had of the movement and its reality, which also influenced the pattern of responses; we shall return to this last point later.

Most respondents defined the objectives of Quebec Social Credit in purely economic terms. Only a very small proportion thought that its primary goals were political. This suggests that the original motivations for joining the movement are considered to be fulfilled through the movement's goals. Social Credit in Quebec is a movement in which both the original motivations for joining and the dominant collective goals are defined by its leaders as economic rather than political or social in nature.

Were these goals the product of long socialization by the Douglas doctrine or were they generated from within? Two-thirds of those who were questioned considered themselves to be Douglasites in some sense, a remarkably high proportion showing devotion to the teachings of the movement's original founders.[4] The leadership of the Créditiste movement clearly support an ideology, or at least perceive themselves being highly ideological. Despite the fact that most leaders are unwilling to accept the description of Créditisme as a protest movement, most are ready to define themselves as protesters in the sense of being followers of Major Douglas. The positive rather than the negative element in Créditiste ideology seems to be emphasized in the psychological environment of the movement.

The leaders did not show the same reluctance to acknowledge an obvious characteristic of their movement when they were questioned about the pervasiveness of factionalism within Social Credit. One might have assumed that the term factionalism would arouse feelings of self-defence similar to those evoked by the questions concerning protest. However, a large majority of respondents (75.7 per cent) allowed that there was a tendency to factionalism in their movement. Most seemed anxious to explain this in empirical rather than normative terms. Thus the largest proportion of those who replied affirmatively to the question about the tendency to factionalism argued that such factionalism is inevitable in doctrinaire movements, where differences over ideology are bound to arise and differences of opinion are permitted to be aired (table 6.5). For example, the owner of a trucking company shrugged and replied: 'Yes, it happens in all doctrinal movements which have a global philosophy. Take, for example, Christianity. There were splits between Dominicans, Jesuits, and other sects. And the history of communism is filled with similar examples.' And the municipal official observed:

Yes, what was lacking was a man at the head of the Social Credit movement capable of disciplining it, and I believe there were divisions in the west, and there were divisions here in the east, in Ontario, Quebec, and then between west and east. It is almost normal in the circumstances. To try to unite so many disparate people coming from differing milieux, backgrounds, and with different mentalities – the task is almost impossible.

In contrast to their perception of protest, the leaders of Social Credit in Quebec seemed prepared to admit the existence of factionalism in their movement. Their reasons for acknowledging the existence of factionalism become apparent in their ranking of its causes.

4 It also supports King's contention, noted earlier, that founders and early leaders of movements maintain their prestige and aura of authority long after they lose their real power and influence within the movement. See C.W. King, *Social Movements in the United States* (New York: Random House, 1956), 72.

TABLE 6.5
Perception of tendency to factionalism

Perception and reason	Percentage of all respondents
Yes, perceives it (without elaboration)	26.2
It is inevitable in movements of this type	18.5
It is due to the absence of financial sanctions	4.6
It is due to two different states of mind within the movement	7.7
It is endemic to French Canadians	9.2
It does not represent real divisions	12.3
No, did not perceive this tendency	21.5
Total	100.0
N	(65)

TABLE 6.6
Causes of factionalism*

Nature of cause	Percentage considering it of primary importance	
Personality conflicts	57.1	N = (56)
Conflicts arising from ambition or disloyalty	49.0	N = (57)
Conflicts over strategy and tactics	37.7	N = (53)
Conflicts over the extent of freedom and the scope of authority (internal democracy) within the movement	27.8	N = (53)
Doctrinal divisions	13.8	N = (58)
Electoral defeats	10.2	N = (49)

*The causes of factionalism were chosen by respondents from a predetermined list. The respondents were asked to rank each cause as of primary, secondary, or no importance in causing factionalism in the movement.

The leaders most often ranked personality conflicts and acts arising from ambition or disloyalty as the primary causes of this tendency to factionalism within the movement (table 6.6). These factors were considered of major importance in causing splits by aproximately one-half the respondents. In marked contrast, only 13.8 per cent believed the doctrine was at the root of such divisions. Despite the numerous ideological disagreements which were apparent in the development of the movement, the respondents did not consider the doctrine itself to be a significant divisive force. They seemed to acknowledge the common framework and bond which Douglas' ideas provided for all Créditistes, regardless of their allegiances and affiliations. Similarly, only 10.2 per cent thought that electoral defeats were a primary cause of factionalism. This is considerably lower than the figure one would expect in the typical minor party, since electoral defeats are notorious for fragmenting such parties. In their perceptions of factionalism within Créditisme, the leaders displayed a strong loyalty to the long-run goals and purposes of the movement.

The leaders were asked to assess the consequences of this tendency to factionalism for the success of the movement. Most respondents estimated that there was at least some positive effect in such a tendency, which may explain their readiness to acknowledge its existence. The reasons given for this favourable assessment of the consequences of factionalism are revealing. The respondents considered splits to be a purifying device in the sense that they help to rid the movement of its disloyal members. They also regarded them as an effective method of reorienting the movement in a new direction or a means of recruiting new members to the renovated structures. A forester explained: 'I admit that all divisions are harmful to a degree. But they occur in all movements and they can have some advantages. For example, they permit us to re-orient our movement and acquire a more realistic and collaborative spirit.' A federal welfare official concurred: 'There is some harm done, in that the movement loses some excellent men. But on the whole, the benefits are greater. Divisions help reduce the number of rebels and ineffective members. They produce unified, effective subgroups under strong leadership.'

On the other hand, several members recognized that splits had serious adverse effects. The most frequently mentioned drawback was that they tended to reduce the overall strength of the movement by dissipating its energies. A few respondents also noted that factionalism of this sort has a negative effect on the electorate. However, this last reason was less frequently mentioned than might have been expected in a normal political party.

It seems, then, from their perceptions of factionalism, that the Créditiste leaders maintain a devotion to their movement which can withstand the short-term shocks of defeat, intense conflict, or schism. This is a characteristic of Créditisme which stamps it clearly as a political movement rather than a conventional political party.[5] In their perceptions of their movement and its goals, the Créditiste leaders exhibited several attitudes which are also characteristic of devotees of a protest movement: they consider the economic (ie, ideological) goals to take precedence over its political and social goals; they consider themselves to be disciples of Major Douglas, the movement's original founder and doctrinal source; they define the movement's ends as reconstructive and reformist rather than merely oppositionist; and they view the tendency for the movement to split into factions as either a necessary evil caused by human frailties (of personality and ambition) or as a force for rejuvenation. There is a clear implication in such perceptions that the movement, its doctrine, and its goals transcend the individuals who belong to it.[6] There is also an apparent gap between the perceptions which the leaders of the movement have and reality as I view it. For example, although they believe themselves to be Douglas disciples, many Créditiste leaders have strayed very far from his tenets. Similarly, the causes of factionalism listed by the respondents are not those which I would consider to be primary.[7]

C PARTICIPATION IN AND PERCEPTION OF PARTICULAR SPLITS
The respondents were also questioned in depth about their participation in and their perception of four major splits which have occurred since the movement's inception:

5 A similar tendency in the CCF movement was noted by Walter Young in *The Anatomy of a Party: The National C.C.F., 1932–61* (Toronto: University of Toronto Press, 1969), 4.
6 This tendency has been noticed in mass movements in general by Eric Hoffer. See *The True Believer* (New York: Harper, 1951), part III, especially chapter XIII.
7 For my explanation of factionalism in the movement, see part III, chapter 7 and conclusion, and part IV.

in 1939, 1957, 1963, and 1966. The first of these splits occurred in 1939 between those who opted for the formation of a new wing with a mass appeal under the impetus of the newspaper *Vers Demain* and those who preferred the elite appeal of the Social Credit Ligue. In 1957 the founders of the Ralliement des Créditistes and those who remained faithful to the Union des Electeurs parted ways. The third split took place in 1963 between eastern and western wings of Social Credit and within the Ralliement des Créditistes between Caouettistes and Thompsonites. The fourth, between the provincial-oriented and indépendantiste Ralliement National and the fédéraliste Ralliement Créditiste, happened in 1966. The respondents were classified both in terms of the role which they played in such splits as principal or minor actors and in terms of their participation as proponents of the split (schismatics) or defenders of the status quo (non-schismatics). Their perceptions of the causes of these splits were analysed and classified under the same headings as had been used in exploring the more general causes of factionalism.

As expected, very few respondents had participated in any form in the 1939 split between the editors of *Vers Demain* and the leaders of the Ligue because only about one-quarter of the respondents were members of the Social Credit movement at the time. Consequently only a handful of the respondents were able to offer some explanation of the causes of that particular split. The majority of them accounted for the split in terms of conflicting strategies and tactics. In the view of the members who were active at that time, the 1939 split was primarily a reorientation of the movement in line with the strategy adopted by Gilberte Côté-Mercier and Louis Even to broaden its base. For example, the federal welfare official recalled that he 'was a member of the Ligue under Louis Dugal. At that time the Ligue was composed of men who were incapable of giving the movement a province-wide base. Mlle Côté gave the movement a shaking-up [coup de barre]. She oriented it towards the electors rather than towards those in power.' The municipal official continued in the same vein:

M Even believed that it was by mass education rather than by direct political action that one could obtain Social Credit. At that time he did not believe that one could achieve this fundamental reform by direct pressure on the government. If it had been possible to engage in direct political action and if we had succeeded in orienting the movement in 1939 and 1940 in that direction, we could have done as well as Aberhart and Bennett did in the west. If we had done that with the complete resources that the Social Credit movement then had, Quebec would be Créditiste today.

Over half the respondents had participated in the 1957 split between the Ralliement des Créditistes and the Union des Electeurs. Most of the respondents who were then members had joined the Ralliement des Créditistes and rejected the Union des Electeurs. Most of the participants in this split viewed it as a conflict over strategy and tactics. In their estimation Caouette, Legault, and Grégoire, the founders of the Ralliement, wished the movement to engage in electoral action, whereas the leaders of the Union des Electeurs were opposed to this mode of action. It was not a rebellion against the Union leaders themselves, but rather a disagreement over the ideological orientation which these leaders had adopted. In the opinion of most participants, the

1957 split was an inevitable result of too narrow a conception of the possible means for achieving Social Credit. Caouette explained:

From 1949 on, we waited for the opportunity to build a purely political organization. In 1957 that opportunity arrived ... After our meeting of 20 September 1957 in the Mount Royal Hotel [in which the Ralliement des Créditistes was founded], we had a meeting with Gilberte and Gérard Mercier, Louis Even, and Hervé Provencher in Rouyn, in my garage. I proposed that our group operate as a parallel organization within the movement. Gilberte said that she was the sole leader of the movement and that she wouldn't allow it. She alone had the right to lay down guidelines for the movement. I said, 'Mlle Côté, if you don't permit our group to operate within the movement, then we will resort to some other method of action. Don't suppose that those who have worked for fifteen years in the Union des Electeurs are incapable of operating on their own ... Just wait and see, the thing will work.' She left, and I never saw her again.

A trucking company owner offered a somewhat different perspective:

I was one of the founders [of the Ralliement des Créditistes]. I would have preferred to have had two parallel organizations within the movement. I would not have called the organization we were establishing Le Ralliement des Créditistes, since it was a political party rather than a movement. For people are always capable of stupidities [bêtises], and when they form a political party their failings hurt the movement. The party would still have been based on the philosophy of Social Credit.

Two-thirds of the respondents had participated in the 1963 split between Caouettistes and Thompsonites. A majority of the participants were either opposed to the division between the two major groups or neutral. This is surprising, since it was the followers of Caouette who split with the Thompsonites. Many of the Créditistes were opposed to this action of the Ralliement 'chef,' and their opposition is reflected in their responses to the question on their perception of the cause of the conflict. A large proportion of them attributed the conflict to personality differences between Caouette and Thompson. A number of respondents also listed the ambition and infidelity of some members as a cause. The strategy and tactics involved in Caouette's action were seen to be of lesser importance. It appears as if the 1963 split was not desirable and inevitable in the eyes of the movement's leaders; rather it was seen as largely a result of human frailties. A typical observation was made by a then member of the National Executive who ultimately sided with Caouette: 'The 1963 split was at bottom a conflict of personalities. Thompson was a thinker, a temporizer, who missed opportunities when they presented themselves. I admired him very much for his intelligence, his affinity for thought. If I had had a choice at the time, I would have sided with Thompson.' A national organizer who chose to follow Thompson agreed: 'On the whole the 1963 split resulted from a conflict of personalities. The journalists succeeded in convincing Caouette that he was too powerful to have to answer to Thompson and the National Executive. I respected Caouette, but he was too impetuous. Thompson, on the other hand, was a gentleman.'

Finally, over two-thirds of the respondents had played some role in the most recent split between indépendantistes and fédéralistes. As in 1963 the split was considered by most respondents to be somewhat antithetical to the broad aims of the movement. However, in this case, the perception of its major cause was different. A majority of those involved in the split attributed it to differences over strategy and tactics; personalities and ambitions played a less significant role. A federal MP described the split as follows: 'I played a role only as an observer. Since the election in 1962, there was always a certain group at every congress who pressed for provincial action. I never supported their point of view. I could not approve of a separatist movement because I am a Créditiste, not a separatist.' And an indépendantiste candidate in 1966 related events in a surprisingly similar manner:

The 1966 split goes back to the congresses in 1964 and 1965. The members voted almost unanimously to engage in political action at the provincial level. I agreed with them, and was even an advocate of this program. Then in 1966 some of the men in Ottawa attempted to prevent us from engaging in provincial political action. I followed Laurent Legault and became a provincial organizer.

At the leadership level, then, although splits are not readily welcomed, they tend to be seen as an inevitable consequence of the desire to apply new strategies and tactics within the movement. It is not surprising that respondents also acknowledged certain benefits or positive effects from schisms. In the case of two splits, in 1939 and 1957, division was followed by a rapid infusion of new blood and a dramatic expansion in the membership of the movement. After the 1966 split the Ralliement Créditiste lost some electoral support but increased its legislative representation both federally and provincially.[8] In all three of these cases the splits were viewed by respondents as a planned strategy by the schismatics. In the only other case, the 1963 split, division was followed by contraction in the membership and loss of both electoral support and legislative representation. This was also the only split which the membership seemed to attribute to something other than rational design.

It is interesting to recall that in table 6.6 personality conflicts and conflicts over ambition and disloyalty were rated more important than conflicts over strategy and tactics as causes of factionalism within the movement. There is no obvious reason for this discrepancy between general perceptions of factionalism and perceptions of splits in individual cases. Perhaps factionalism viewed from an overall perspective appears less desirable than when it is analysed in each of its case instances. For Créditistes, the individual strategies of schismatics are beneficial in most instances, but the overall effect on the movement is detrimental. Whatever the rationale in the minds of Créditistes, there is a consensus that the three factors of personality, strategy and

8 Many of the Créditistes who split with the Ralliement over the issue of provincial participation and Quebec's role in Confederation rejoined that party when it finally took the plunge into provincial politics in 1970. Some had temporarily joined or flirted with the Mouvement Souveraineté Association and the Parti Québécois and found them unappealing. They are presently among the strongest proponents of autonomy for the provincial wing under the leadership of Camil Samson.

tactics, and ambition are far more important in producing splits than doctrinal divisions, conflicts over internal democracy, or electoral defeats. We shall see whether these perceptions by the respondents are well-founded when we analyse the splits in greater depth.

D THE PSYCHOLOGICAL AND OPERATIONAL ENVIRONMENT

The typical Social Credit leader in Quebec is still an active participant in some wing of the movement today, particularly the Ralliement Créditiste. He has served in several official positions over a period of a few years frequently at a higher level than the local association and has thereby acquired considerable leadership and organizational experience. He is reluctant to admit that Social Credit in Quebec is a protest movement and that this had influenced him to join the movement.

Rather, he conceives of the movement as a vehicle for economic reform. He also views himself as a disciple of Major Douglas, who similarly regarded Social Credit as an economic rather than a political reform. The stress, then, is on the positive and reconstructive side of the movement rather than on its negative or dissenting side. The Créditiste leader is, however, conscious of the tendency to factionalism and schism in the movement, which he attributes primarily to personality conflicts and excessive ambition on the part of some individuals. On the whole, however, he is not too apprehensive about the consequences of this factionalism for the movement, since he feels that there are also benefits accruing from such a tendency, in particular a purifying effect.

Most leaders had not actively supported the major schisms which wracked the movement from 1939 until the present. Nevertheless, a majority tolerate them as an inevitable consequence of strategic and tactical planning. They rate strategy and tactics as a more important factor in producing individual splits than conflicts of personality and excessive ambition.

In short, both the operational and psychological environment of the Créditiste movement reflect characteristics typical of a right-wing protest movement. The level of participation in the movement is high, as might be expected among devotees to a utopian cause.[9] The leaders stress positive and reformist goals. They either eschew or overlook the protest element in the ideology, but they accept factionalism as inevitable in organizations like Social Credit and even view it as a regenerative force. There is an implication here that the Créditiste movement is capable of transcending and surviving the shocks produced by the weaknesses of its leaders at any particular time.

9 Duverger points out that participation in mass parties and movements, which are committed to more utopian ideologies, is generally much greater than in cadre parties. See Maurice Duverger, *Political Parties* (New York: Wiley, 1954), book I, chapter II.

7

The Highly Disaffected and the Lower-Class Dissenters: The Pivotal Subgroups of the Movement

No political movement is composed of homogeneous groups of members. Although the members all adhere more or less to the same ideology and goals, they differ in many other respects, including social background, motivations for joining the movement, political attitudes, personality, and patterns of participation. These differences often reinforce each other and lead to the formation of important subgroups or factions within the movement.[1]

The Créditiste movement is no exception to this general pattern. In our discussion of the social and attitudinal profile of the Créditiste leaders, we found that the average Créditiste leader shares many of the characteristics of the traditional Quebec rural or small-urban elite: he is of middle or lower middle class, of above average income, and has acquired more education than the average Quebecker.[2] He tends to be more active in voluntary associations and to hold more official positions in the community than his neighbours. We also noted that in his political attitudes the typical Créditiste leader is only a moderate dissenter with a desire for limited reforms. He is a federalist rather than a separatist and a strong supporter of action on both the federal and provincial levels. Although suspicious of communist infiltration, he is not conspiratorial. He has a traditional attachment to religion and the clergy, and a strong propensity to protest against both private and public wrongs, but he is not authoritarian. These characteristics are not, however, shared by all Créditiste leaders.

A THE HIGHLY DISAFFECTED CRÉDITISTE LEADER: SOCIAL AND
   ATTITUDINAL DIFFERENCES RELATED TO ALIENATION
A key subgroup within the Créditiste movement is that composed of leaders who share attitudes of strong disaffection towards both the political and economic systems.

---

1 Neil Smelser, *The Theory of Collective Behaviour* (New York: Free Press, 1963), 361, and M. Zald and R. Ash, 'Social Movement Organizations: Growth, Decay and Change,' in Barry McLaughlin (ed), *Studies in Social Movements: A Social Psychological Perspective* (New York: Free Press, 1969), 327.
2 But he also differs somewhat from this traditional Quebec elite in that his father was of

TABLE 7.1[3]

Disaffection by socioeconomic status
(per cent)

	Index of disaffection	
Index of socioeconomic status	High disaffection	Low disaffection
Lower socioeconomic status	61.9	30.0
Higher socioeconomic status	38.1	70.0
	100.0	100.0
N	(21)	(40)

chi square = 5.795 significant at less than 0.02 level, tau $B = 0.308$, gamma = 0.583

We have labelled this group of leaders the 'highly disaffected.'[4] Unlike the usual Créditiste leader, the highly disaffected Créditiste is not typical of the traditional Quebec rural or small-urban elite. In fact, he differs from this elite in almost every respect. He appears to be much more like the alienated individual normally associated with revolutionary political or mass movements.

The highly disaffected Créditiste leader, as might be expected, tends to be of a much lower socioeconomic status than the typical Créditiste leader (table 7.1). In particular, he has much less formal education and a much lower annual income. Undoubtedly, it is his lower status which tends to produce his strong disaffection.[5]

Unlike the typical Créditiste leader, the highly disaffected Créditiste is not an active participant in voluntary associations. He has significantly fewer voluntary group attachments than the more moderate leader (table 7.2). In this respect, he resembles the alienated individual in modern mass society who has been found to be especially susceptible to appeals of mass movements.[6] It is possible that the highly disaffected Créditiste leader is attracted to the movement in part because he finds in it a social outlet for his feelings of loneliness. Although he does not consider a need for social companionship to be a primary factor influencing him to join the movement, it may nevertheless be one of the important motivating forces in his decision. In this sense, the highly disaffected Créditiste leader also can be differentiated from

lower-class background. For a description of the social background characteristics of the Quebec small town elite prior to industrialization, see E.C. Hughes, *French Canada in Transition* (Chicago: University of Chicago Press, 1943), 33.

3 For construction of indexes in the text and tables in this chapter, see appendix C.

4 For the construction of the index of disaffection which enables us to isolate this subgroup, see appendix C.

5 The correlation between high disaffection and low socioeconomic status has been observed very frequently in political and social movements. For example, see E. Hoffer, *The True Believer* (New York: Harper, 1951), G. Almond, *Appeals of Communism* (Princeton: Princeton University Press, 1954), M. Pinard, *The Rise of a Third Party: A Study in Crisis Politics* (Englewood Cliffs, NJ: Prentice-Hall, 1971). See also W. Erbe, 'Social Involvement and Political Action,' *American Sociological Review*, 29 (1964), 198–215.

6 See, for example, Hoffer, chapter 6.

TABLE 7.2

Disaffection by voluntary group attachments
(per cent)

Index of voluntary group attachments	Index of disaffection	
	High disaffection	Low disaffection
Few attachments	50.0	26.2
Several or more attachments	50.0	73.8
	100.0	100.0
N	(22)	(42)

chi square = 3.628, significant at 0.06 level, tau B = 0.238, gamma = 0.476

TABLE 7.3

Disaffection by important official positions
(per cent)

Index of important official positions	Index of disaffection	
	High disaffection	Low disaffection
Few high positions	85.7	48.8
Many high positions	14.3	51.2
	100.0	100.0
N	(21)	(43)

chi square = 6.584, with Yates's correction, significant at less than the 0.02 level, tau B = 0.355, gamma = 0.725

the Créditiste voter, who like the typical Créditiste leader was found to have a fairly large number of voluntary group attachments.[7] Moreover, there was no relationship between high disaffection and low voluntary association membership when controlled for socioeconomic status. Thus the tendency among the highly disaffected Créditistes to belong to few voluntary associations is clearly unrelated to class background.[8]

As might be expected, the highly disaffected Créditiste leader achieves little official status in the organizations to which he belongs and tends to hold few high positions in the Social Credit organization or in other associations (table 7.3).[9] He is in this sense notably different from the average Créditiste leader. This relationship is independent of class; that is, the highly disaffected leader tends to hold few high

7 Pinard, *The Rise of a Third Party*, 197, 215.
8 This finding tends to contradict Erbe's contention that the correlation between high alienation and low organizational involvement is largely a function of low socioeconomic status. See Erbe, 212–13.
9 The relationship is also significant between disaffection and number of official positions in associations other than Social Credit alone, but it is weaker (χ^2 = 3.957, significant at the 0.05 level, G = −0.500).

TABLE 7.4

Disaffection by perceived protest

(per cent)

	Index of disaffection	
	High disaffection	Low disaffection
Yes, "protest" element influenced respondent	60.9	22.9
No, "protest" element did not influence respondent	39.1	77.1
	100.0	100.0
N	(23)	(35)

chi square = 8.518, significant at less than 0.01 level, tau $B = 0.383$, gamma = 0.680

positions in organizations whether or not he is of high or low socioeconomic status.[10] The failure of the highly disaffected Créditiste to achieve high official status in the organizations to which he belongs must exacerbate his feelings of political alienation and increase frictions between himself and other members of more moderate persuasion within these organizations.

The highly disaffected Créditiste leader does not share the reconstructive and reformist motivation for joining that appears to have influenced the more moderate leaders to affiliate with Social Credit. The protest element in Social Credit ideology, which was viewed negatively – as a criticism of the system – by most Créditistes, was a strong factor in attracting the highly disaffected leader to the movement. Thus the highly disaffected Créditiste was much more likely to admit that the movement was a vehicle of protest and that this had influenced him to join it (table 7.4).[11]

This same pattern of negative criticism can be detected in the attitude of the highly disaffected towards fundamental reform of various parts of the political system, including its democratic institutions, its parliamentary institutions, its political parties, and its federal system. The typical Créditiste leader, we may recall, was a moderate reformer. The highly disaffected leader is more likely to advocate reform of the federal system than those who are not as disaffected.[12]

This divergence between attitudes towards reform in one sector and those in another can probably be explained by the nature of the political disaffection involved. The highly disaffected Créditiste leader has very strong negative attitudes towards all

10 Controlling for high socioeconomic status, the relationship is not significant at the 0.05 level, and controlling for low socioeconomic status, $\chi^2 = 3.224$, with Yates's correction, significant at the 0.10 level, $G = 0.833$.

11 This factor seems to serve as a stronger motivation for joining among the leaders than among the Créditiste voters, although, according to Pinard, alienation acts as an additional incentive for the latter to join, particularly in the case of the organized workers and farmers. Pinard, *The Rise of a Third Party*, 240. See also Hoffer, 67–9.

12 $\chi^2 = 3.100$, with Yates's correction, significant at less than the 0.10 level, $G = 1.000$. The relationship is weaker here because a general reformist attitude is shared by all Créditiste leaders.

TABLE 7.5

Disaffection by independence of Quebec is desirable
(per cent)

	Index of disaffection	
	High disaffection	Low disaffection
Yes, Quebec independence is desirable now or in the future	77.3	45.2
No, Quebec independence is never desirable	22.7	54.8
	100.0	100.0
N	(22)	(42)

chi square $= 6.020$, significant at less than 0.02 level, tau $B = 0.307$, gamma $= 0.609$

aspects of the system and therefore sees little purpose in reforming it. On the other hand, he views reform of the federal system as essentially destructive rather than reconstructive. Reform of federalism probably implies for him either decentralization involving complete transformation of the Canadian polity or the breakup of Canada and the establishment of an independent Quebec. We may recall that although the Ralliement Créditiste is a federalist party officially opposed to separatism, a minority group within the movement has always advocated that Quebec concerns and provincial action should take precedence over Canadian involvement and politics at the federal level.

Moreover, this conclusion is strengthened by our findings on the question of the desirability of an independent Quebec now or perhaps in the future. The highly disaffected Créditiste leader is much more likely to support separatism than is the more moderate Créditiste leader (table 7.5). This does not mean that the highly disaffected leader is likely to be an outright separatist. Some Créditiste leaders regard separatism as a last option and hope for some sort of reform of federalism to achieve similar benefits for Quebec. This attitude is quite widespread among provincial Créditistes who follow Camil Samson, and Caouette himself has veered towards such a position at various times.[13] Pinard also found this phenomenon among Créditiste voters, even though they tend on the whole to be more conservative on this issue than their leaders.[14]

As might be expected, the highly disaffected leader also exhibits more negative feelings towards various aspects of federal politics. For example, he is much less likely to feel that French Canadians are respected in Ottawa than his more moderate counterpart.[15] Similarly, although he had about the same opinion of former Quebec Prime Minister Daniel Johnson as the other leaders, he is more likely to have had a bad opinion of former Prime Minister Lester B. Pearson.[16] It is likely that the highly disaffected leaders have translated their more negative

13 See chapter 3.   14 Pinard, *The Rise of a Third Party*, 83.
15 $\chi^2 = 7.068$, significant at less than the 0.01 level, $G = -0.643$.
16 $\chi^2 = 5.042$, significant at almost the 0.02 level, $G = 0.544$.

sentiments towards federal politics in general into unfavourable evaluations of particular personalities or issues connected with that level of government.[17] The survey questions may also have aroused their stronger feelings of French-Canadian nationalism.

An attempt was made to discover whether some of the basic attitudinal and personality traits normally associated with the extremely alienated members of society are present among the highly disaffected Créditiste leaders. In particular, the respondents were tested for conspiratorial thinking, religious and economic conservatism, and authoritarianism.[18]

Conspiratorial thinking has often been associated with protest or revolutionary movements; in particular, this type of thinking has been thought to be characteristic of the elite or leaders of these groups.[19] In the case of the typical Créditiste leader, although he was found to be suspicious of communist infiltration, he displayed no general tendency to conspiratorial thinking. Pinard also found no relationship between intolerance of minorities and support for Social Credit among Quebec voters.[20] There does appear, however, to be a significant difference in this regard between the highly disaffected Créditiste leader and the more moderate leader. An index of 'conspiratorial thinking' was constructed from responses to four questions about the economic imperialism of Americans, excessive influence exercised by the English in Quebec, communist infiltration, and the insensitivity of some parties to the importance of religious teaching in the schools. The highly disaffected leader was found to have a much more conspiratorial outlook than other leaders (table 7.6); however, this relationship no longer holds when controlled for socioeconomic status.[21]

Another characteristic frequently associated with political protest movements, particularly of a right-wing cast, is a tendency to economic and political conservatism.[22] In Quebec such conservatism has traditionally been manifested in two spheres: religious observance, and opposition to state intervention.[23] An index of traditionalism was constructed from questions related to both these issues to test whether conservative attitudes are prevalent among certain Créditiste leaders.[24]

17 Premier Johnson, of course, posed as the defender of French-Canadian rights and provincial autonomy in federal-provincial relations. Prime Minister Pearson, although more flexible in his attitude towards Quebec than most previous Canadian leaders, was an English Canadian and head of a government dominated by anglophones.

18 For an explanation of how the indexes for these attitudes were constructed, see appendix C.

19 See, for example, Hoffer, 122; T.W. Adorno et al., The Authoritarian Personality (New York: Harper, 1950), 151; Milton Rokeach, The Open and Closed Mind (New York: Basic Books, 1960), 119; and S.M. Lipset, Political Man (Garden City, NY: Doubleday, 1962), 158.

20 The Rise of a Third Party, 228.

21 When controlled for low socioeconomic status, the relationship is $\chi^2 = 1.983$, with Yates's correction, significant at less than the 0.20 level, $G = 0.636$; when controlled for high socioeconomic status it is $\chi^2 = 0.864$, with Yates's correction, $G = 0.500$.

22 See, for example, Lipset, Political Man, chapter 4.

23 For example, see Mason Wade, The French Canadian Outlook (New York: Viking, 1946), and M. Oliver, 'The Social and Political Ideas of French-Canadian Nationalists, 1920–1945' (unpublished PHD thesis, McGill University, 1956).

24 For an explanation of the construction of this index, see appendix C.

TABLE 7.6
Disaffection by conspiratorial outlook
(per cent)

Conspiratorial-outlook index	Index of disaffection	
	High disaffection	Low disaffection
Conspiratorial	60.9	25.6
Non-conspiratorial	39.1	74.4
	100.0	100.0
N	(23)	(43)

chi square = 7.930, significant at less than 0.01 level, tau B = 0.347, gamma = 0.638

We may recall that the typical Créditiste leader was found to be anxious to preserve religious values and clerical influence in Quebec. The highly disaffected leader is even more conservative in one respect: he is much more inclined to consider some parties insensitive to the need for religious instruction in the schools, a factor also reflected in his general conspiratorial outlook.[25] However, in other respects he is no more traditional than the moderate leader.[26] For example, he is slightly more inclined to feel that the clergy plays too large a role in Quebec, a position difficult to reconcile with his concern for religious instruction in the schools.[27] It is likely that his general tendency to misanthropy leads him to distrust both the political parties allegedly subversive of religious values and the clergy whose function is to preserve and reinforce these values. This finding would seem to parallel one of Pinard's observations about the Créditiste voter; just as the rank-and-file in right-wing economic protest movements are no more conservative than the typical voter, the highly disaffected leaders within the elite appear no more traditional or conservative than the more moderate leaders.[28] The alienation of the highly disaffected does not derive from and is not reflected in a greater traditionalism or conservatism. Indeed, when controlled for socioeconomic status, the highly disaffected of lower-class background were found to be somewhat less traditional than the moderate leaders.[29]

The variable probably most frequently identified with right-wing political movements is that of authoritarianism. The assumption normally made is that movements

25 x^2 = 7.478, significant at less than the 0.01 level, G = 0.714. Although there is an element both of religious traditionalism and conspirational thinking in this question, it was not included in the former (traditionalism) but was part of the latter (conspiratorial outlook) index and was also analysed as a separate variable.
26 x^2 = 1.063, significant at less than 0.30 level, G = −0.268. In fact, he is slightly less traditional. This negative relationship is stronger when controlled for low socioeconomic status, (x^2 = 4.539, significant at less than 0.05 level, G = −0.818).
27 The relationship, however, is not significant (x^2 = 1.598, significant at less than 0.30 level, G = 0.385).
28 *The Rise of a Third Party*, 231, 233.
29 It is not surprising that the highly disaffected leader of a low socioeconomic status is more inclined to question traditional values.

with conservative ideologies, highly centralized styles of leadership, and strong charismatic leaders are likely to be composed of individuals who are themselves authoritarian. Authoritarianism is an attitudinal variable closely related to underlying personality traits.[30] It involves the tendency to demand unquestioning obedience from those in inferior positions without their exercising individual freedom of judgment or action. We may recall that the typical Créditiste leader was found not to be authoritarian. In order to explore this characteristic further among certain subgroups of Créditiste leaders, an index was constructed based on attitudes towards exercise of authority both within the family and within political structures. Not surprisingly, it was found that the highly disaffected Créditiste leader tends to be much more authoritarian than the more moderate leader (table 7.7). This relationship is stronger among highly disaffected leaders of a higher socioeconomic status,[31] but disappears among those of lower socioeconomic status.[32]

In other words, contrary to what one might generally assume, authoritarianism is stronger among highly disaffected leaders of higher status than among those of lower status. It is probable that the authoritarianism of these leaders is a result of their status frustration. They are higher status leaders by virtue of their higher income and occupational status, but they probably have received a relatively inferior education. They therefore demand recognition commensurate with their higher status but feel frustrated and insecure because of their failure to receive such recognition.

This conclusion is strengthened by the response to another question dealing with education as a desirable attribute in a political leader. The highly disaffected are much less likely to consider education a desirable quality.[33] Once again, the relationship disappears when controlled for lower socioeconomic status but not for higher socioeconomic status.[34] Anti-intellectualism and authoritarianism have frequently been found to co-exist in an individual.[35] Among those leaders of higher socioeconomic status anti-intellectualism is probably, like authoritarianism, a function of their status frustration.[36] Moreover, it should be noted that authoritarianism relates independently to high disaffection among the major actors in the various splits but

30 See, for example, Adorno et al., 2–11, and Rokeach, 4–27.
31 $\chi^2 = 12.661$, with Yates's correction, significant at less than 0.001 level, $G = 0.953$.
32 $\chi^2 = 0.056$, with Yates's correction, $G = 0.333$.
33 $\chi^2 = 8.529$, significant at less than the 0.01 level, $G = -0.697$.
34 When controlled for low socioeconomic status, the relationship is $\chi^2 = 0.220$, with Yates's correction, $G = -0.429$. When controlled for high socioeconomic status, the relationship is strengthened, $\chi^2 = 10.718$, with Yates's correction, significant at less than 0.01 level, $G = -0.946$.
35 See, for example, Lipset, *Political Man*, 119.
36 That is, as in the case of the relationship between disaffection and authoritarianism, the anti-intellectualism of the highly disaffected leaders of higher socioeconomic status may also be a function of their inferior education. When controlled only for low education, the relationship between high disaffection and anti-intellectualism was somewhat stronger than when no controls were applied. $\chi^2 = 6.057$, with Yates's correction, significant at less than the 0.02 level, $G = 1.000$. The finding here may be offered as a modification of Lipset's argument that 'one aspect of the lower classes' lack of sophistication and education is their anti-intellectualism' (*Ibid.*). Lipset was referring to supporters of political parties and movements

TABLE 7.7

Disaffection by authoritarianism
(per cent)

Index of authoritarianism	Disaffection index	
	High disaffection	Low disaffection
High authoritarianism	52.2	19.0
Low authoritarianism	47.8	81.0
	100.0	100.0
N	(23)	(42)

chi square = 7.656, significant at less than 0.01 level, tau B = 0.343, gamma = 0.645

not among the local leaders who played a lesser role in these splits.[37] This suggests that both high disaffection and authoritarianism were factors in these splits. This point is discussed further in subsection D.

Finally, we may recall that the typical Créditiste leader showed a strong propensity to protest against political wrongs. Despite the fact that he is more alienated, more authoritarian, and more conspiratorial than the other leaders, the highly disaffected Créditiste is less likely to regard himself as having a propensity to protest (table 7.8). Thus the strongly alienated leader views political protest action in much the same way as he regards fundamental reform; namely, as an attempt to reconstruct a system which has no particular attraction for him. He differs in this respect not only from the more moderate Créditiste leaders but also from the Créditiste voter. Pinard found, contrary to the general literature, that moderate political alienation tended to increase the Créditiste voters' incentives to protest, particularly in crisis situations.[38]

On the other hand, there is conflicting evidence for this hypothesis in the greater inclination of the highly disaffected leader to perceive protest as a factor influencing him to join the movement (see table 7.4). Perhaps protest is understood by him in two different senses in the two questions; that is, as reformist action concerning his propensity to protest politically, and as negative criticism involving his motivations for joining the movement.

among the general population. In the case of protest leaders, anti-intellectualism, like authoritarianism, accompanies strong disaffection and is a function of the status frustration of the highly disaffected of higher socioeconomic status. Despite their higher status, which is a product of their higher income and occupational status, these leaders have relatively inferior educations and as a result are unable to receive the kind of recognition which the better educated receive. They express their frustration and sense of deprivation through their anti-intellectualism. Both authoritarianism and anti-intellectualism of the highly disaffected leaders of higher status are indexes of a general pattern of status deprivation which ultimately leads to retreatist alienation and withdrawal from active involvement in the movement. For an elaboration of this argument, see subsection B.

37 $\chi^2 = 7.242$, significant at less than the 0.01 level, $G = 0.735$.

38 *The Rise of a Third Party*, 171, 241.

TABLE 7.8

Disaffection by self-perceived propensity to protest
(per cent)

	Disaffection index	
	High disaffection	Low disaffection
Yes, has propensity to protest against political wrongs	56.5	81.4
No, has no propensity to protest against political wrongs	43.5	18.6
	100.0	100.0
N	(23)	(43)

chi square = 4.674, significant at less than 0.05 level, tau $B = -0.266$,
gamma = -0.542

In short, the highly disaffected Créditiste leader exhibits all the attitudinal characteristics normally associated with the politically estranged individual: extreme disillu-
sionment with the system, a conspiratorial outlook, authoritarianism, and anti-intellectualism. Moreover, the characteristics are themselves clearly interrelated. He
therefore can be said to have a 'radical protest' syndrome.

B THE HIGHLY DISAFFECTED CRÉDITISTE LEADER: BEHAVIOURAL
   DIFFERENCES RELATED TO ALIENATION

There has been much analysis of the relationship between political alienation and
political participation in studies of political movements in particular and political
behaviour in general. In the literature on political behaviour, two factors have been
isolated along with political alienation as strongly affecting levels of political participation: socioeconomic status, and voluntary associational activity. There is general
agreement that lower socioeconomic status, lower voluntary associational activity,
and higher political alienation all tend to produce lower levels of political activity.
Recently William Erbe has elaborated on this argument by contending that while all
three (political alienation, socioeconomic status, and organizational involvement)
are associated with participation, socioeconomic status and organizational involvement are far more important causal factors and in fact may even produce political
alienation. These two variables independently affect political participation.[39] On the
other hand, in the literature on political movements it has been argued that political
alienation does have a causal effect on political participation, and in the opposite
direction: those who are more alienated are found to participate more actively in
social movements.[40] Pinard has attempted to reconcile these apparently contradictory findings by arguing along with Erbe that there are two forms of political
alienation present in political movements: retreatist and rebellious alienation. Those
members of political movements who exhibit a retreatist alienation condition tend to

39 Erbe, 213.
40 See the various papers by Melvin Seeman and his associates cited in Pinard, *The Rise of a
   Third Party*, 237.

TABLE 7.9
Disaffection by belonging to a
Social Credit Association today
(per cent)

	Disaffection index	
	High disaffection	Low disaffection
Yes, is affiliated with a Social Credit Association today	90.9	61.9
No, is not affiliated with a Social Credit Association today	9.1	38.1
	100.0	100.0
N	(22)	(42)

chi square = 4.659, with Yates's correction, significant at less than 0.05 level,
tau $B = -0.266$, gamma = -0.542

withdraw from political activity as is the typical pattern in the wider society, whereas those who display rebellious alienation are likely to increase their political participation. Pinard finds that rebellious alienation is more widespread among the Social Credit voter in Quebec than retreatist alienation.[41]

In the preceding chapter we noted that the typical Créditiste leader continues to belong to some wing of the movement today and also has held several higher level official positions in the movement over the period of its existence. Contrary to expectation, however, the highly disaffected leader is even more likely to be affiliated with a Social Credit organization today (table 7.9).[42]

On the other hand, as we observed in the previous section, the highly disaffected leader tends to hold fewer important official positions both in non-Social Credit organizations and in the movement itself. Thus it appears that the highly disaffected Créditistes are able to achieve some outlet for their alienation in belonging to the movement, but because they are more alienated, they cannot or prefer not to participate actively on a monthly basis or acquire high-status positions within the movement.[43] Given the fact that they are already much more alienated than their leadership confrères, and that they differ from them in so many other respects, it is highly likely that a deep sense of separation and division exists between the two groups of protest leaders.[44] This, as we shall see below, is a major factor contributing to recurrent factionalism and schisms within the movement.

41 *Ibid.*, 240, 241.
42 Note that when controlled for socioeconomic status, those of low socioeconomic status were found to belong less than those of high socioeconomic status; the difference, however, was not significant. They also tend to participate less on a monthly basis, although once again the difference between the two groups was not significant. Thus the normal assumption that retreatist alienation in the highly disaffected leader would tend to reduce his level of participation in the movement is partially invalidated.
43 They cannot do so because they lack the education and the accompanying recognition to rise to these higher positions and prefer not to do so because they are so alienated.
44 Further evidence for this gulf can be found in very different patterns of participation of the

In summary, the highly disaffected Créditiste leader is a member of a distinct subgroup within the leadership group; he is of lower socioeconomic status with fewer voluntary associational attachments and less official status. He was originally more attracted to the movement by its protest or critical dimension. Although more highly alienated politically, he is not likely to support fundamental reform of the system, but he is more in favour of reform of the federal system and of the eventual independence of Quebec. Among his basic personality and attitudinal differences, he is more conspiratorial in outlook and more authoritarian. Thus he appears to exhibit a radical protest syndrome. He tends to be more rather than less active in Social Credit organizations today, although not in the top echelon positions.

Despite the fact that such a wide gulf exists between the moderate and the highly disaffected Créditiste leader, which undoubtedly leads to severe frictions between them, the latter does not appear to be significantly more prone to activate divisions and splits within the movement; that is, he shows no greater tendency to schismatic behaviour.[45] Nor does the highly disaffected Créditiste appear to view the movement, its goals, and particularly its tendency to factionalism in a different way. This may seem surprising in view of the more active political participation of the highly disaffected at the lower levels of the movement. One would expect him to translate his alienation and resentment into some form of rebellion against the moderate group. However, on closer examination of the composition of the highly disaffected group, the reason there is no greater tendency to schismatic behaviour on the part of this group becomes apparent.

There are two major subgroups among those who share attitudes of strong disaffection: those of higher and those of lower socioeconomic status. Although they have many traits in common, they differ slightly in two respects: the highly disaffected of lower socioeconomic status belong to more voluntary associations but hold fewer official positions in both Social Credit and in other associations than their counterparts of higher socioeconomic status.[46] According to the prevailing theory, one would normally expect those of lower socioeconomic status to exhibit less affinity for organizational involvement at all levels. At the lower levels of voluntary associations, including the Créditiste movement, this is not the case. The highly disaffected Créditiste will participate actively at this level. But his lower status prevents him from rising further in the ranks.[47] The highly disaffected of lower socioeconomic status will tend to exhibit more of a rebellious alienation, whereas those of a higher socioeconomic status will manifest more of a retreatist alienation. The latter group will be uninterested in the political organization and planning involved in rebellion or schism. It is the former group which is responsible for the major splits within the movement. However, they do not activate these splits on their own. They form alliances with more moderate leaders of a lower socioeconomic status in order to mobilize sufficient strength.

moderate leaders. They tend to participate more actively on a monthly basis than the highly disaffected leaders of all types and hold many more official positions.

45 $\chi^2 = 0.972$, which is not significant at the 0.05 level, $G = -0.251$.

46 The differences between the two subgroups are, however, not statistically significant.

47 For a similar observation, see James S. Coleman, *Community Conflict* (New York: Free Press of Glencoe, 1957), 18–21.

C THE LOWER-CLASS DISSENTER: THE SCHISMATIC WITHIN
THE MOVEMENT

The lower-class dissenters include both highly disaffected and more moderately dis-affected (but not the weakly disaffected) who also are of low socioeconomic status. They share many characteristics with the highly disaffected group (not surprisingly, since about half the group also are members of the other group). They are, of course, also of lower socioeconomic status than the typical Créditiste leader.[48] Like the highly disaffected leaders, they are no more likely to support fundamental reform of the system,[49] but they are more inclined to favour Quebec independence.[50] They share the same negative feelings towards various aspects of federal politics.[51] They are also more conspiratorial than the typical Créditiste leader,[52] though not more traditional.[53] Like the highly disaffected they are also less inclined to show a propensity to protest politically. They are more authoritarian than the typical leader,[54] though not as authoritarian as the highly disaffected, and they are more anti-intellectual.[55] In other words they also have the radical protest syndrome. These differences in background, attitude, and personality from the more moderate leader must also contribute to feelings of separateness and friction within the movement.

However, in a few important spheres the lower-class dissenter also differs signifi-cantly from the highly disaffected Créditiste leader: in his patterns of participation in and his perceptions of the movement. The lower-class dissenter does not have signifi-cantly fewer voluntary associational attachments or important official positions in other associations or in the movement itself. But he is more inclined to activate splits (table 7.10). Moreover, as one would expect in the case of a schismatic, he is less likely to acknowledge that there is a general tendency in the movement to factionalism and division,[56] and is more likely to regard splits as beneficial to the movement.[57]

48 The index of 'lower-class dissent' would naturally reflect this lower status. The lower-class dissenters also tend to come from small town or village backgrounds.
49 Except for fundamental reform of the democratic system. The lower-class dissenters are more inclined to support fundamental reform of democracy ($\chi^2 = 4.254$, significant at less than the 0.05 level, $G = -0.500$).
50 For the relationship between lower-class dissent and support for Quebec independence, $\chi^2 = 8.823$, significant at less than 0.01 level, $G = 0.688$.
51 For the relationship between lower-class dissident and opinion of the Pearson government, $\chi^2 = 5.043$, significant at about the 0.03 level, $G = -0.543$; between lower-class dissent and opinion on the respect accorded French Canadians in Ottawa, $\chi^2 = 9.540$, significant at almost the 0.001 level, $G = -0.692$.
52 $\chi^2 = 5.854$, significant at less than the 0.02 level, $G = 0.564$.
53 Except for, as in the case of the highly disaffected leader, their attitudes towards religious education in the schools ($\chi^2 = 10.516$, with Yates's correction, significant at the 0.001 level, $G = 0.811$). This relationship holds when controlled for level of activity (major actor or local leader) within the movement. The high correlation probably reflects conspiratorial thinking rather than religious conservatism on the part of the lower-class dissenter, since there was no relationship between lower-class dissent and rejection of the charge that the clergy exercised too much influence in Quebec.
54 $\chi^2 = 3.122$, significant at about the 0.06 level, $G = 0.448$.
55 $\chi^2 = 6.682$, significant at the 0.01 level, $G = -0.649$.
56 $\chi^2 = 7.297$, significant at less than the 0.01 level, $G = -0.633$.
57 $\chi^2 = 5.047$, with Yates's correction, significant at less than 0.05 level, $G = 0.662$. The relationship is similarly significant for schismatics.

TABLE 7.10

Lower-class dissent by schismatic behaviour
(per cent)

Index of schismatic behaviour	Lower-class dissent index	
	Lower-class dissenter	Non-lower-class dissenter
Low schismatic	42.9	67.6
High schismatic	57.1	32.4
	100.0	100.0
N	(28)	(37)

chi square $= 3.969$, significant at 0.05 level, tau $B = -0.247$, gamma $= -0.471$

Even though the socioeconomic status of this group is low, the higher organizational involvement produces a more moderate degree of political alienation. This alienation, rather than being strongly retreatist, as was particularly the case for the highly disaffected of higher socioeconomic status, is much more of a rebellious variety such as Pinard tended to find among Créditiste voters. This type of alienation may for a time be focused on external enemies of the movement. However, class, personality, and attitudinal differences between moderate leaders and lower-class dissenters soon rise to the surface and cause this alienation to express itself in terms of a rebellion against the movement's leadership. Those who are disaffected but who continue to participate actively in the movement use the schism as an organizational outlet for their rebellious alienation.

The key people in this pattern of behaviour are the highly disaffected of lower socioeconomic status. But an important ally is the group of more moderate dissenters of lower class. The two subgroups, who together make up the group of lower-class dissenters, are the schismatics in the movement.

It is their lower socioeconomic status rather than their disaffection which most influences this group of lower-class dissenters to activate splits.[58] They are not only less likely to notice the tendency to division in the movement but they also are more inclined to view these splits positively and consider them beneficial to the movement.[59]

58 For example, it was found that lower socioeconomic status tends to produce protesters who are more doctrinally orthodox in their own perception of themselves ($\chi^2 = 2.700$, with Yates's correction, significant at the 0.10 level, $G = 1.000$). These data must be used cautiously, however, since only about half the total sample – thirty-two – were asked this question. Also, those of lower socioeconomic status are somewhat more inclined (although not significantly) to define the goals of the movement in philosophical or religious rather than purely economic or political terms, reflecting their greater ideological orthodoxy and the overriding significance which they give to the movement's goals. Since less than one-half – twenty-nine – of the total respondents were asked this question, the results here must also be treated with caution.

59 For the relationship between lower-class dissent and perception of division, $\chi^2 = 7.297$, significant at less than the 0.01 level, $G = -0.633$. For the relationship between lower-class dissent and perception of the ultimate consequences of splits, $\chi^2 = 5.041$, with Yates's correction, significant at less than 0.05 level, $G = 0.662$.

In other words, they view the environment of the movement in precisely the manner one would expect of schismatics: they try to overlook the pervasiveness of splits in order to minimize their importance, and to present a positive view of their effect in order to excuse their own role in activating them.[60]

D THE PATTERN OF ALLIANCE BETWEEN THE HIGHLY DISAFFECTED AND THE MODERATELY DISAFFECTED OF LOWER SOCIOECONOMIC STATUS: A HYPOTHESIS

There are initially a strong bond of attraction and a common denominator which encourage the formation of an alliance between all those who are highly disaffected, regardless of their socioeconomic status. They share the same attitudes of alienation towards the political system and are attracted to the movement for the same reason: the appeal of the protest or critical element in the movement's ideology. Since this group differs from the more moderate leaders of the movement in so many dimensions of social background, attitude, and personality, one would naturally expect them to unite in some sort of opposition to the leadership and produce the series of schisms in the movement.

However, when the members of this group begin to interact with other leaders who are more moderately disaffected, the movement tends to divide along class (status) as well as attitudinal lines. At the same time, some of the personality, attitudinal, and behavioural differences between the highly disaffected leaders of higher and those of lower status begin to surface. The highly disaffected leader of higher status is more authoritarian, more anti-intellectual, and more traditional than his counterpart of lower status. This stems from his sense of status deprivation; therefore he is less likely to rebel. His alienation is transformed into retreatist alienation, whereas the highly disaffected leader of lower socioeconomic status tends to become more rebellious and to engage in schismatic activity. The latter, then, tends to find more in common with the more moderate dissenter of similar low status who is also ideologically somewhat doctrinaire. The two new subgroups form an alliance of highly disaffected and moderately disaffected of lower class; that is, they are lower-class dissenters who express their rebellious alienation and their resentment of status and class differences within the movement as well as their lesser authoritarianism by revolting against the moderate leaders and producing splits or schisms.

60 A similar tendency can be detected among those who were classified as schismatics on the schismatic index. The high schismatics were only slightly less inclined to notice the tendency to division in the movement (although the relationship was stronger when controlled for disaffection), but they were much more inclined to consider splits beneficial for the movement ($\chi^2 = 9.947$, with Yates's correction, significant at less than 0.01 level, $G = -0.806$). There was also a tendency for the high schismatics to view splits as a result of differences over strategy and tactics, whereas the low schismatics (particularly those of high socioeconomic status) considered them to be a result of disloyalty and excessive ambition on the part of certain individuals. This finding also supports the statement in the text.

Conclusion: The Dynamics of Right-Wing Protest

In the preceding chapters in part III we have found certain characteristics which can be identified with the average Social Credit leader in Quebec and other characteristics which are peculiar to certain subgroups within the movement. The former seem to represent many of the traits generally identified with the traditional rural and small-town elite in Quebec and may also reflect more general attributes of moderate leaders of right-wing protest movements.[1] The latter are particular characteristics of important and more extremist components of the elite of the movement and may be found in other right-wing protest movements.[2] It is in the interaction of the major subgroups that one discovers the dynamics of political protest in such movements.

From our discussion of these attributes of the Créditiste leaders we may be able to form a rough impression of the general patterns of formation and internal develop-

---

1 See, for example, Peter Campbell, 'Le mouvement Poujade,' *Parliamentary Affairs*, 10 (1957), S. Hoffmann, *Le mouvement Poujade* (Paris: Librarie Colin, 1956); Irving Crespi, 'The Structural Base for Right-Wing Conservatism: The Goldwater Case,' *Public Opinion Quarterly*, XXIX (Winter 1965–6), 523–43; Sidney Tarrow, 'The Urban-Rural Cleavage in Political Involvement: The Case of France,' *APSR*, LXV, 2 (June 1971); Martin A. Trow, 'Small Businessmen, Political Tolerance, and Support for McCarthy,' *American Journal of Sociology*, 64 (1958); M. Rogin, 'Wallace and the Middle Class: The White Backlash in Wisconsin,' *Public Opinion Quarterly* (Spring 1966).

2 See, for example, Gilbert Abcarian and Sherman N. Stanage, 'Alienation and the Radical Right,' *Journal of Politics*, 27, 4 (November 1965), 776–96; Richard S. Cromwell, 'Rightist Extremism in Postwar West Germany,' *Western Political Quarterly*, XVII (1964), 284–93; John Howard, 'The Social Basis of Organized Political Defiance: A Comparison of the Black Muslims, the John Birch Society, and the American Communist Party,' *Western Political Quarterly*, XVIII, 3 (September 1965); and Richard L. Nolan and Rodney E. Schneck, 'Small Businessmen, Branch Managers, and their Relative Susceptibility to Rightwing Extremism: An Empirical Test,' *CJPS*, II, 1 (March 1969); Daniel Bell, *The New American Right* (New York: Criterion Books, 1956); Hans Gerth, 'The Nazi Party: Its Leadership and Composition,' in Robert K. Merton *et al.*, *Reader in Bureaucracy* (Glencoe: Free Press, 1952).

ment of right-wing protest movements.[3] It is difficult to know, however, whether certain attributes of the protest leaders are apparent at the time these leaders join the movement or are acquired at a later period. We shall have to impute certain attributes to the leaders in cases where the data on their earlier characteristics are insufficient.[4]

The patterns of the formation of the Social Credit movement in Quebec which might be generalizable to other right-wing protest movements are as follows: young adults (chiefly males) born and brought up in small towns or villages who come from lower-class families in which there is a greater than average interest in politics are attracted to protest appeals during periods of economic distress. They are motivated primarily by economic and ideological considerations to join the movement, rather than by a desire for political reform. However, they join at a period in which their political allegiances have not yet been firmly formed; therefore they may be reacting against strong family attachments to conventional old-line parties. They are the first members of their families to join the movement. They refuse to consider any available political alternatives at the time they join but would look for a substitute if the movement did not exist. They soon become faithful devotees of the movement and its ideology. They participate actively in the movement and rapidly rise to positions of leadership.

At a later stage, after some years of maturity, these leaders assume many of the social and attitudinal characteristics of the traditional rural or small-urban elite. They live mainly in middle-sized towns which are satellites of the large metropolitan urban centres. They have a higher socioeconomic status than their fathers and are also better educated and more affluent than the average member of their community. They also have resided for many years in the same locale. Consequently, they have wide voluntary associational ties and hold a number of official positions in community organizations. They express attitudes of dissent against the existing political and economic systems and a desire to reform these systems. They do not, however, call for revolutionary reforms. Nor do they exhibit conspiratorial or fascist syndromes. They do not, for example, manifest consistently negative attitudes towards minority and external groups. They do, nevertheless, seem to fear communism and excessive state control. They also are quite ready to protest publicly against political situations which arouse their indignation. They are not authoritarian in personality or attitude. They are, in short, moderate protesters.

It is not clear whether these leaders acquire these attitudes before or after they join the protest movement. It is also uncertain whether these attitudes are shaped by the movement's ideology or by the socioeconomic background and patterns of organizational and political participation of the leaders. Probably the attitudes are

3 See also Hoffmann; J.A. Irving, *The Social Credit Movement in Alberta* (Toronto: University of Toronto Press, 1959); and Maurice Pinard, *The Rise of a Third Party: A Study in Crisis Politics* (Englewood Cliffs, NJ: Prentice-Hall, 1971).

4 For example, their socioeconomic status and attitudes at the time they joined. We did ask the respondents, however, if they thought that their political attitudes had changed very much since the time they had joined. Almost all of them answered in the negative.

a product of both early socialization prior to joining and later experience after join-ing.[5] More important, however, is the effect which such attitudes have on the psycho-logical and operational environment of the movement. The leaders serve in at least one official position during the duration of their membership; often they assume several positions over an extended period of time. Many occupy positions at a higher-than-local level and thus acquire province-wide experience and contacts. They are active participants (sometimes on a weekly basis) and frequently continue to be active even after they relinquish their official positions. They regard themselves as disciples of the movement's chief ideologists, and believe strongly in the movement's goals, particularly its economic ones. They regard these goals as more positive than negative and therefore refuse to acknowledge that the movement is primarily a protest movement, a description which they consider too narrow and negative. They are aware, however, that there is in the movement a tendency to factionalism and division which they regard as inevitable in a movement such as theirs and even, in certain re-spects, beneficial. They attribute this factionalism primarily to conflicts over strategy and tactics, although personality differences and excessive ambition also are con-sidered important. They do not believe that ideological differences, electoral setbacks or conflicts over the acceptable scope of internal democracy within the movement are important factors in these splits.

In addition to these general patterns, there are particular patterns arising from differences in social background, attitudes, and behaviour of certain subgroups within the leadership of the movement. The most important are the highly disaffected leaders and the lower-class dissenters.

The highly disaffected leaders tend to be of lower socioeconomic status than the other leaders of the movement. They are also inclined to be less involved in voluntary associations and to hold fewer high official positions in these organizations. They are more likely to be attracted to the movement by its protest quality, which they un-derstand as negative criticism of the existing system. They also exhibit attitudes of deeper dissatisfaction with all fundamental aspects of the existing economic and political systems, particularly the pattern of federal politics, and advocate more radical transformation of its federal structure. They display more of the personality and attitudinal traits which are associated with the alienated or ethnocentric per-sonality: they are more conspirational in their outlook, more authoritarian in per-sonality and attitude, and more anti-intellectual. In the case of the highly disaffected of higher socioeconomic status, these traits seem to be a function primarily of their status frustration, particularly arising from their relatively inferior education.

The highly disaffected are also less inclined to regard themselves as having a propensity to protest publicly in order to correct political wrongs, which again reflects their lesser inclination for reformist action. They are, nevertheless, more likely to continue to belong to the movement at a later stage, although they are not as

5 Moreover, the temporal order of the four variables – socioeconomic background, patterns of political participation, ideology of the movement, and political attitudes – is difficult to establish. It may be that political attitudes shape the patterns of participation and the ideology of the movement. See W. Erbe, 'Social Involvement and Political Action,' *American Sociological Review*, 29 (1964), 200, 214.

active and do not tend to hold as many of the highest official positions. Thus differences between this group and the more moderate majority group in social background and attitudes are also apparent in differences in political participation and behaviour. But the highly disaffected as a group are not more inclined to activate splits; only those of lower socioeconomic status exhibit this tendency to rebellious alienation, which is also evident in their intense organizational involvement at the lower levels. They form alliances with more moderate dissenters of lower socioeconomic status to produce the recurrent splits in the movement.

The lower-class dissenters (which include both highly disaffected and more moderately disaffected of lower socioeconomic status) share most of the characteristics of the highly disaffected. However, they are less authoritarian and traditional and show a greater tendency to activate splits. At the same time, they lack (perhaps suppress) any awareness of factionalism in the movement. The lower-class dissenters, then, have a great impact on the internal development of the movement. They are a key element in determining the underlying dynamic of protest movements.

The patterns of protest and of factionalism are determined by the interaction and relative strengths of the general leadership and the subgroups we have isolated. In the mobilization phase the character of protest is non-political, as determined by the preponderantly non-political orientation of the movement's early leaders. After a time, however, the highly disaffected leaders begin to challenge the moderate leaders. They call for different and more radical forms of protest. The highly disaffected of higher socioeconomic status become more and more alienated from the leadership and withdraw from political activity. The highly disaffected of lower socioeconomic status, however, become more rebellious and actively involved in political activity. They ally with the more moderately disaffected to form an opposition group strong enough to challenge the moderate leaders. Lacking status, income, and education, and being smaller in number, when they disagree with the movement's directors on questions of strategy and tactics, they are unable to make their views prevail. From the perspective of the prevailing moderate leaders, the challenge is often more than a mere difference over strategy and tactics; it is a conflict which arises from personality differences and particularly disloyalty and excessive ambition on the part of the dissenters. The result of the conflict is generally open schism. The split generally marks the beginning of a new phase in the movement's development.

We have offered a *description* of these forces at a general level. We have not attempted an *explanation* in structural and sociological terms. We shall provide one level of the explanation (structural and sociological factors) below and also analyse the second level (individual psychological factors) in part IV.

In the mobilization phase of any right-wing protest movement, the highly disaffected and lower-class dissenters concentrate their energies on combatting and overwhelming their opponents outside the movement. However, if immediate success eludes them, they turn inward and conflict with their co-partisans within the movement. If open schism results, it generally marks the beginning of the consolidation phase, which is characterized by much factionalism and internal conflict. The process of factionalism can be explained at the structural level as follows.

In structural terms, conflict arises over the strategy and tactics adopted by the movement's moderate leaders to combat the movement's political opponents. Disputes of this sort are inevitable in all political structures. However, in other political structures, differences over strategy and tactics are generally resolved through normal mechanisms of conflict resolution and control. For example, structural controls such as formal systems of rewards and punishments for loyal and disloyal behaviour are often applied in highly structured political parties and movements. Social controls are also imposed through inculcation of attitudes of loyalty to the leadership and the organization. Psychological controls are applied by invoking the authority of a charismatic leader or a doctrine, but it appears that these are not present in right-wing political protest movements, at least not in sufficient degree to be effective. Those who disagree with the strategy and tactics adopted by the principal leaders resort, therefore, to schism.

There is a growing body of literature on more conventional political structures which supports such a hypothesis. For example, it has been found that cohesion in political parties is not as great as is generally assumed.[6] Although conflict and discord are pervasive, cohesion is maintained by invoking shared attitudes of loyalty to the party. There is a common feeling among the members that the unity of the party must be maintained in order to avoid public censure or loss of electoral support. It is the overriding attitude of loyalty, rather than the system of rewards and punishments, financial sanctions, or threats of dissolution, which is most responsible for preventing splits from occurring in these parties.[7] Similarly in revolutionary political movements, where the top leader's charismatic authority is very strong, it can prevent or discourage splits from occurring in the movement. There is competition among lieutenants and secondary leaders seeking to curry favour with the top leader but no direct challenge to his leadership.[8]

In right-wing protest movements like Social Credit in Quebec, there is not as strong a sense of loyalty to an established organization and its goals as is found in most conventional political parties, especially in the consolidation phase. Nor is there such a fervent devotion to charismatic or doctrinal authority as is the case in many revolutionary movements.[9] The bonds of authority and of loyalty are much

6 At least, as most roll call studies seem to imply. See, on this point, John C. Wahlke et al., The Legislative System: Explorations in Legislative Behavior (New York: John Wiley, 1962), 239.

7 For example, see Robert J. Jackson, Rebels and Whips: Division, Cohesion and Discipline in British Political Parties (London: Macmillan, 1968). For other approaches to factionalism and division within political parties, see Lee W. Farnsworth, 'Social and Political Sources of Political Fragmentation in Japan,' Journal of Politics, 29, 2 (May 1967); David T. Garza, 'Factionalism in the Mexican Left: The Frustration of the MLN,' Western Political Quarterly, XVII (1964), 447–60; Raphael Zariski, 'Intra-Party Conflict in a Dominant Party,' Journal of Politics, 27, 1 (February 1965); Sven Groennings et al. (eds), The Study of Coalition Behavior (New York: Holt, Rinehart and Winston, 1970).

8 Joseph Nyomarky, Charisma and Factionalism in the Nazi Party (Minneapolis: University of Minnesota Press, 1961). See also R. Heberle, Social Movements (New York: Appleton Century-Croft, 1951), chapter 7.

9 Heberle, 131–2. The doctrine may also be a source of division and conflict rather than control within the movement. This was the case in the national Social Credit movement in 1948 and helped to produce the split between the Quebec and western wings. See chapter 2 above.

more weakly knotted in the movement. The common allegiance to a protest appeal acts only as a partially unifying element. The ends of the movement are so simplistic and so ill-defined that they provide little more than an umbrella for common action. When disputes arise over the meaning to be given these general goals, there is no effective counterforce to hold the members together.

The history of Social Credit in Quebec bears eloquent testimony to this phenomenon. Social Credit in Quebec offers a single proposal as the basis of its program of reconstruction: monetary reform. Its plans for transforming existing social, economic, and political institutions flow directly from this one overriding reform. For Social Crediters, if the gap in purchasing power is closed through reform of financial institutions, then political parties will no longer be the handmaidens of the economic system, depressions and crises will be wiped out, and social inequalities between wealthy and poor, urban and rural residents, French and English Canadians, and owner and worker will wither away. There is complete agreement among the movement's adherents that their major energies must be directed towards the achievement of monetary reform.

The differences have arisen over the most acceptable methods of achieving this basic reform. Is education of existing parties in power the best possible way of instituting monetary reform? How can this best be done, by exerting pressures on government leaders, by sending letters and conducting demonstrations designed to convince parliamentary representatives, by educating an informed elite which then establishes itself in positions of power and influence within these parties, or by educating the masses through newspapers, radio, and television? Or alternatively, should one form a new and distinct political party pledged to implement social credit when in office? How should this be done? Through an electoral alliance formed with groups of similar ideology elsewhere? Should these activities be concentrated at the federal or provincial levels of government? Should the party work for national unity or for national disintegration and the formation of new and smaller units more likely to implement the needed reforms? These were the major subjects of contention between opposing factions in the various splits which wracked the movement over the course of its history.

In most conventional political parties these splits would have been resolved through normal processes of bargaining and compromise which are buttressed by a common sense of loyalty. In revolutionary movements they would have been settled by invoking some sort of authority, particularly that of a charismatic personality. In the mobilization phase Louis Even and Gilberte Côté-Mercier actually attempted to assert this kind of authority, which they tried to buttress by claiming they had the support of the movement's founder, Major Douglas. However, Douglas never defined one appropriate path for achieving social credit. As the movement developed, when opposition to the interpretation of the directorate arose, there was no way of ascertaining which view was correct. And the Union leaders lacked the personal authority to impose their fiat on the movement. As a result, a generational split occurred which introduced a new phase in the movement's development. Réal Caouette had better success in exercising charismatic authority when he assumed control of the movement. However, he was never seen as a major fountain of doctrinal knowledge and therefore he could not invoke his interpretation of social credit as the only correct

Figure 1

A model of schismatic behaviour

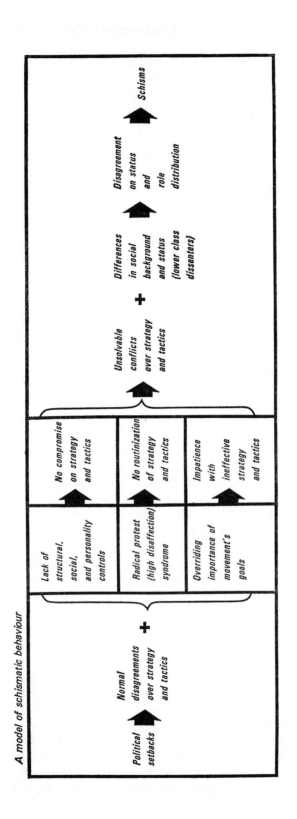

one. Nor could he draw on the large variety of rewards and punishments normally available to the conventional party leader. Schisms, therefore, occurred even more frequently under Caouette during the consolidation phase.

The process of schism may be understood on the sociological level as follows. Highly disaffected leaders and lower-class dissenters who possess highly critical attitudes towards their political and social environment forming part of a radical protest syndrome need some sort of outlet for their predispositions. The protest movement provides such an outlet. It permits these individuals to give vent to their disaffection by protesting through the movement and its ideology against the outrageous conditions which they face. At the same time, those among them who also have reconstructive attitudes can work positively through the goals of the movement to achieve their reformist ends. Thus some sort of equilibrium or balance is maintained between the needs of the movement and the personality needs of these more disaffected leaders, enabling them to co-operate with other more moderate protest leaders in a common political and spiritual enterprise.

In the later stages, when the objectives of the movement are not rapidly achieved, this equilibrium is upset. The more alienated leaders transpose some of the disaffection which they have expressed towards the political and social environment onto the internal environment of the movement. They also displace some of their negative attitudes and resentments towards the movement's external enemies onto the movement's established leaders, who now face the strong criticism of the dissenters. In this way their attitudes of disaffection come to override the positive and reformist objectives which they (lower-class dissenters) share in common with other protest leaders.

The attitudes of disaffection operating within the internal environment first appear in differences over the best course of action for the movement. However, they soon harden into more deep-rooted cleavages between the fundamental beliefs, attitudes, and predispositions to action of highly disaffected and lower-class dissenters and the other protest leaders. These fundamental differences in orientation stem ultimately from basic dissimilarities in social and economic background.

The hypothesis which attempts to explain the dynamics of protest and factionalism in right-wing movements is illustrated in figure 1.[10]

Offered here is an explanation of what causes splits to occur in right-wing protest movements. Included also is an attempt to describe or explain the pattern of alliances between subgroups which occurs once this process of factionalism leading to schism begins. In part IV these alliance patterns will be illustrated in a case study of one split and the attitudinal differences which characterized the opposing groups will be explored.

10 I am indebted to Maurice Pinard for his assistance in my reformulation of this pictorial model.

PART IV

THE PATTERNS OF ORIENTATIONS AND ALLIANCES
IN THE 1963 SPLIT: A CASE STUDY

Introduction: A Framework for Analysing the Pattern of Factionalism in Right-Wing Protest Movements

The previous chapter offered a hypothesis about the tendency towards schism in right-wing protest movements, particularly in the consolidation phase of their development. It suggested that when political setbacks occur, normal disagreements over strategy and tactics cannot be contained in such movements. A combination of weak structural, social, and personality controls, the catalytic effect of the highly disaffected leaders who exhibit radical protest syndromes, and the overriding importance of the movement's goals produce unsolvable conflicts over strategy and tactics. When differences in social background and status between subgroups are added to the conflict over strategy and tactics and disagreement about role distribution and authority within the movement, full-scale schisms tend to occur. A pattern of alliances between subgroups occurs in two stages: in the first stage, those who are highly disaffected (ie, who have radical protest syndromes) tend to join together in the disagreements over strategy and tactics. However, the highly disaffected of higher socioeconomic status are inclined to express their alienation by withdrawing from political activity, whereas those highly disaffected of lower socioeconomic status ally with more moderately disaffected leaders of low socioeconomic status to form a group of lower-class dissenters who are the schismatics in the movement. They demand a larger place in positions of authority in the movement and in decision-making roles, but when denied it, largely on account of their lower socioeconomic status, they engineer a split.

There is a need to test this hypothesis in individual splits. Even more important, there is a need to expand the psychological level of the explanation. We must analyse the attitudes of disaffection and of protest in greater depth and in a variety of different dimensions. More specifically, there is a need to explore how the range of attitudes held by different groups of leaders, together with socioeconomic factors and strategic considerations, come into play in any given instance to produce a split.

We have selected the 1963 split between the Caouettistes and Thompsonites for closer examination for two major reasons: first, the leading participants in it were readily identifiable and available for interviewing; second, from the responses to the questions about perceptions of splits described in chapter 6, it appeared to be a deviant case. Whereas in the three other major splits, differences over strategy and tactics were considered to be at the heart of the conflict, the 1963 split was attributed primarily to personality differences between Caouette and Thompson. Many Créditiste leaders considered the schism to be neither desirable nor inevitable. We shall investigate whether these perceptions were well-founded.

The first phase in a split involves a coalescence of shared attitudes and orientations of those leaders whom we identified in our survey as highly disaffected. The range of attitudes which they hold on a variety of political and social questions should be similar and quite distinct from those exhibited by respondents identified as moderate protesters (who show low disaffection on the disaffection index.) These surface attitudes are merely overt manifestations of more deep-rooted underlying political orientations. Differences in political orientations of subgroups within the movement seem to surface only after conflicts over strategy and tactics have erupted. In some splits, these differences in strategy and tactics eventually become submerged in more deep-rooted personality and orientational differences. Although the differences in attitudes are initially expressed in terms of conflicts over the particular objectives of the movement at a given moment in time, they ultimately stem from fundamental differences in political orientations. It is therefore important to probe these underlying political orientations in greater depth.

Until recently, no method had been developed in political science for getting at these underlying orientations to political action. In part this was due to the complexity of systematically analysing such subjective phenomena. Recently, however, political scientists have developed an operational definition of political orientations and a method of isolating the specific orientations of different political actors. We shall examine this definition and method in the section below with a view to applying them to the Créditiste leaders in the 1963 split.

The tool we plan to use should enable us to explore a whole range of dimensions in the complex attitudinal and orientational syndrome which we have defined as high disaffection (or radical dissent). In this way we should then be able to understand, in a more complete way than is possible with a few attitude questions in a structured survey, the underlying dimensions of disaffection and their role in effecting splits.

A POLITICAL ORIENTATIONS

According to modern social psychologists of the Parsonian school, orientations are the underlying sets of predispositions to action which all individuals in a social system share to some degree. These predispositions are expressed, when stimulated, in terms of patterns of behaviour. The orientations determine an individual's patterns of action; they confine this action within certain well-defined limits.[1]

Political orientations are those kinds of orientations which are expressed speci-

1 T. Parsons and E.A. Shils, *Toward a General Theory of Action* (Cambridge, Mass.: Harvard University Press, 1957). See also Talcott Parsons, 'Some Highlights of the General Theory of Action' in Roland Young (ed), *Approaches to the Study of Politics* (Evanston, Illinois: Northwestern University Press, 1958), 282–301.

fically in political forms of behaviour. Political behaviour is behaviour which is directly related to authoritative decision-making within a social system. It is hypothesized that most political actions derive in large part from orientations which are essentially political themselves. Political orientations are those orientations which focus on the purely political in a social system: the political system, its parts, the relation of the individual to the authoritative decision-makers in a system, and the relation of decisions to the individual.[2]

Sidney Verba suggests that a reseacher can uncover an individual's political orientations by isolating the primitive political beliefs and the four dimensions of the political culture of a social system as they are internalized by the individual members of that social system.[3] The social system which concerns us here is the overall society of Canada and the role which French Canadians and particularly Québécois play in it. The primitive political beliefs shared by the members of Quebec Social Credit are those which define their fundamental assumptions about politics: for example, what politics essentially is, how ideology and religion relate to politics, how individual belief systems relate to the polity, and what political forms are desirable and possible. The four dimensions which direct the researcher to relevant kinds of political orientations are related to 1 / national identity, 2 / identification with one's fellow-citizens, 3 / governmental output, and 4 / the process of decision-making.[4]

Orientations related to national identity define the individual's relation to the nation state and the society of which he is a member. The individual's definition of himself as a member of some national or subnational grouping is often the key to this orientation. In Quebec one might identify oneself as a Canadian, a Canadien, an anglophone, a francophone, an English Canadian, a French Canadian, a new Canadian, a Quebecker, a Québécois, a Montréalais, a Gaspésien, and so forth. At the same time one defines the relationship of other national or subnational groupings to oneself. Thus a francophone from Quebec might describe an English-speaking Canadian as a fellow Canadian, an English Canadian, an anglophone, an Anglo-Saxon, a wasp, a westerner, Ontarian, maritimer, and so forth. French-speaking Canadians from Quebec are likewise seen by English-speaking Canadians as Quebeckers, French Canadians, French Catholics, Frenchmen, and so forth.

Orientations involving identification with one's fellow citizens describe the relationship of the individual to the other members of his own national or subnational grouping. A good method of isolating this pattern of orientations is to try to discover the way in which the individual refers to these other members. For example, do francophones from Quebec see themselves as a homogeneous national grouping or do they perceive differences of class, status, rural-urban divisions, gaps in wealth, education, and regional discrepancies among the members of their own subnational grouping? Do they distinguish between French-speaking Protestants, Catholics, and

2 See, for example, the adaptation of Parson's work in such recent political writings as G. Almond and S. Verba, *The Civic Culture* (Princeton: Princeton University Press, 1962), and S. Verba and L. Pye, *Political Culture and Political Development* (Princeton: Princeton University Press, 1965).

3 Sidney Verba, 'Comparative Political Culture,' in Verba and Pye, 512–60.

4 *Ibid.*, 526ff.

those of other religious groups? Do they view francophones from Quebec differently from francophones of other provinces? Similarly it may be asked if anglophones from the prairies perceive themselves as markedly different from anglophones from Ontario, Quebec, or the maritimes? Do English-speaking Protestants distinguish themselves from Catholics and those of other religious groups? Do those who originate from the British Isles consider themselves as different from those who came from countries in continental western or eastern Europe?

Orientations towards governmental output delineate the relationship of the individual to the authoritative decisions which are made for all members of his society. One can ask the individual whether he feels that the political system is meeting his own expectations of what government should do or not do for every citizen, whether he feels that the economic measures being taken by alternating parties forming the government are sufficient for meeting individual crises and deprivations, whether social legislation is adequate for his needs, whether the outcomes are depriving him of certain other material or spiritual values, how he thinks governmental outputs are being distributed among the members of society, what groups or classes, in his opinion, are benefiting most, and which least, and whether certain kinds of outputs are given preference over others. Some examples of pertinent questions are: Is the system of government in Canada or Quebec adequately meeting the needs of all Canadians or Quebeckers? Or is the present system producing very little in the way of important outputs? What are the different kinds of outputs that recent federal and provincial governments in Canada have provided for Canadians and Quebeckers? Are they largely economic? social? cultural? Do they significantly affect the way of life of Canadians and Quebeckers? What benefits were derived from these policies? Did they affect our material position, our freedom, or our social mores? Who gained most by these policies: businessmen, labourers, farmers, professionals, urban or rural groups, Quebeckers, Ontarians, or westerners, or French or English Canadians?

Orientations concerning the process of decision-making delineate the individual's relationship to the overall process and to each of its major parts: in the case of Canada, parties, pressure groups, MPs, cabinet ministers, public administrators, judges. The relationship is two way, encompassing both the individual's perception of these processes and his own sense of his ability to affect or influence any or all of them. To get at such orientations, one might ask the individual Canadian or Quebecker how well he feels the process of decision-making operates; what kind of changes might be made in it, and why; how adequate he considers the operating system of parties to be in relation to the overall system and its desired ends; what is his view of the pressure groups operating within the system; how effective he regards recent cabinets to have been; and how he views the public services in Ottawa or Quebec in terms of efficiency, accessibility, and justice. In addition, he might be asked whether he thinks it is beneficial to belong to a political party, which party or parties he feels are most easily penetrated for rewards of prestige, patronage, and jobs, which channel is most readily accessible for influencing government, how he relates to his MP or MNA, whether he regards the court system as an effective instrument for obtaining redress of his wrongs, and if so, which court or courts.

All of these dimensions are, of course, interrelated in some way. Precisely because attitudes and predispositions to action are so interdependent, they generally form a closely knit whole, bound together by logical relations and corollaries which delimit the political action of an individual and set him apart from his fellow citizens. At the same time, it is this interdependence of attitudes and predispositions to action which creates the pattern that becomes apparent to the observer and enables him to classify sets of orientations into definable types.

B THE RELATIONSHIP BETWEEN THE DISAFFECTION SYNDROME
AND THE POLITICAL ORIENTATIONS OF CRÉDITISTE LEADERS:
A HYPOTHESIS

In part III we isolated two major groups of Créditiste leaders: the moderate protesters, who comprise the major group, and the highly disaffected. The moderate protesters exhibit many of the social and political background characteristics typical of the traditional rural or small-town Quebec elite: they are of middle or lower middle-class occupations, higher-than-average education, and higher-than-average income. Their negative attitudes against the external environment are moderate rather than radical and reformist rather than revolutionary in nature. The highly disaffected leaders exhibit rather different background and attitudinal characteristics from the moderate leaders: they generally have lower occupational status, less education, and lower income. They have much stronger dissenting attitudes against all aspects of their external environment, call for more fundamental reforms, are more conspiratorial in outlook, and are more authoritarian.

We may therefore expect these wide differences in background and attitudes between these two subgroups to manifest themselves in a whole range of orientational differences. If we use the categories devised by Verba and apply them to interview responses of Créditiste leaders, we would expect marked differences to appear between the primitive beliefs and all four dimensions of the political orientations of the moderate Créditiste leaders and the more disaffected leaders. The gap in beliefs and attitudes should explain a great deal about the causes of the 1963 split.

8

The Patterns of Orientations and Alliances in the 1963 Split

In chapter 3 we discovered that the split in 1963 took place ostensibly between the east and west wings of Social Credit. The members of these two wings formed groups of loosely associated people who shared some common political orientations. In particular, the common allegiance to social credit both as an ideal and as a possible political system bound the two groups together. The most obvious means of realizing the objectives of social credit was the political one of electing a sufficient number of Social Credit members to the national parliament to form a government willing to pass social credit legislation, and it was this belief which was most responsible for the union between the two wings. But differences in orientation between the two groups far outweighed their similarities. They were centred in two very distant parts of the country, Alberta and Quebec. The differences between these two provinces in history, economic and social organization, religious, ethnic, and linguistic composition, and cultural outlook inevitably produced background and orientational differences in the members. These in turn resulted directly in friction and direct conflict between them.

Moreover, the 1963 split between western and eastern Social Crediters was primarily a product of *internal* divisions in the Quebec Social Credit group. As in 1939, 1957, and 1966, the split in 1963 pitted one group of Quebec Social Credit members who shared a set of attitudes on a particular series of policy questions against another group which held opposing attitudes. In 1963 the division occurred over the question of maintaining the alliance between Quebec Social Credit and the National Social Credit party. Those who wished to maintain the alliance with the west were referred to as Thompsonites, signifying their continued loyalty to the national Social Credit leader, Robert Thompson. Those who wished to sever ties between the two groups were called Caouettistes, indicating their allegiance to the Ralliement leader Réal Caouette. Alternatively, these groups were known as the new versus the old Créditistes. The former group was so called because it coalesced around newer members of the movement who had joined Quebec Social Credit in the period after the formation of the Ralliement des Créditistes in 1957. The latter group was composed of older members who had previously joined the Union des Electeurs and the Social Credit Ligue. The difference in their basic attitudes was also recognized by their tendency to refer to the older group as 'gilbertistes,' after Gilberte Côté-Mercier, or 'berets blancs,' after the white berets which Gilberte had introduced as a badge of membership in the Union des Electeurs organization.

Unstructured interviews were conducted with the twelve major actors in the 1963 split.[1] The questions asked were designed to probe the various dimensions of primitive political beliefs and political orientations. The respondents, who were also interviewed in the structured survey, were classified as moderate protesters or highly disaffected leaders, depending on their scores on the disaffection and socioeconomic status indexes. Four rated as moderate protesters and eight were highly disaffected leaders – four of higher socioeconomic status and four of lower socioeconomic status. There were no moderate dissenters of lower socioeconomic status. Of the four moderate protesters, three were leading supporters of Robert Thompson and new guard Créditistes. Each had also indicated that his primary motivation for joining the Créditistes was political rather than ideological. The fourth adopted a more neutral attitude between the two opposing groups, and became politically inactive. The other eight respondents were all old guard Créditistes who had belonged to the Union des Electeurs before joining the Ralliement. All claimed to have joined the movement for ideological or economic reasons. Four of the eight ranked as highly disaffected leaders of lower socioeconomic status. They were strong supporters of the split between Caouettistes and Thompsonites. The remaining four ranked as highly disaffected leaders of higher socioeconomic status. Two of the four highly disaffected leaders of higher status showed a genuine ambivalence about the split, although they ultimately sided with Caouette. The other two, including Caouette himself, were strong advocates of the split.[2]

1 The major actors involved in the 1963 split were: from the west, Robert Thompson, his three western parliamentary colleagues at the time – Bert Leboe, H.A. Olson, and A.B. Patterson – and a handful of officials in the National Social Credit Association. In Quebec the men most directly involved were on one side Réal Caouette, Laurent Legault, Gilles Grégoire, and the eleven other MPs from Quebec who followed Caouette after the split, and on the other side Fernand Ouellet (national organizer for eastern Canada), Dr Guy Marcoux, and six other Quebec Social Credit MPs who remained loyal to Robert Thompson. The role of some of the organizers in certain key constituencies was also significant. Seven of the foregoing were interviewed once, and five others were interviewed on several occasions. Most of these interviews were conducted between April 1964 and August 1965. All but a few were recorded. The anonymity of the interviewee is generally protected.
2 It would appear, then, that the hypothesis in part III identifying schismatic behaviour with highly disaffected leaders of lower socioeconomic status is supported by the evidence from the case study, despite the fact that the 1963 split was perceived to be a deviant case. It seems, however, as if the highly disaffected leaders of both high and low status were able to maintain their united stand against the moderate protesters so that no further alliance between highly disaffected leaders of lower socioeconomic status and more moderately disaffected leaders of lower socioeconomic status (the lower-class dissenter group) had to be formed. In our analysis of the political orientations of the leading participants in the split, and in the conclusions to part IV, the reasons will become more apparent.

A   PRIMITIVE POLITICAL BELIEFS

The primitive political beliefs of the interview respondents were grouped into four main categories: 1 / beliefs about the general nature of politics; 2 / beliefs about the relationship between religion and politics; 3 / beliefs about authority and leadership; and 4 / attitudes towards ideologies and belief systems in general.

1   *The nature of politics in general*

All respondents showed a tendency in their perceptions to draw a sharp dichotomy between what politics is and what politics should be. First of all, politics as an activity was narrowly defined in terms of parties, elections, and the application of pressures on government. It was thus distinguished from such infrastructural political activity as union participation and from more formalized structures like federal and municipal governments. Politics as it actually exists at present in most democracies and dictatorships was generally viewed as a bad game; in democracies, politics was considered largely the function of the electoral fund, the government contract, and the banking and taxation system. In dictatorships, in the respondents' views, politics was the destruction of the freedom of the individual. On the other hand there was a certain admiration for this 'game,' because in their opinion politics requires men of some training, talent, speaking ability, and prestige in the community. Politics in the good sense, as in 'good government,' was generally described as administration. Thus Premier Manning's government was often referred to as 'that good administration.' And certain respondents distinguished between Robert Thompson as a 'good administrator' and Réal Caouette as a 'consummate politician,' seeming to imply that the former was the more desirable. All of the respondents expressed a desire for reform in politics. Politics should have higher standards, they thought, and should be made once again the instrument of the people rather than a small privileged segment.

2   *Religion and politics*

Certain significant differences between western Social Crediters and moderate protesters in Quebec on the one hand, and highly disaffected leaders in Quebec of both higher and lower status on the other, emerge in the respondents' definition of the relationship between metaphysical or religious principles, social credit theory, and practical politics. The highly disaffected leaders were convinced that there is a close link between religion and political theory and practice. According to a Rouyn transport company owner and a highly disaffected leader of lower socioeconomic status, politics is the application of natural law to the temporal world, and social credit doctrine is the closest approximation to this philosophy that has emerged thus far:

What struck me the most about Douglas' doctrine is that I found that Douglas wrote his whole doctrine in conformity with nature. I admire natural things very much. For example, we poison the air with our automobiles and our motors, and the Good Lord cleans it all free of charge. The next day it's pure. He cleans water free of charge as well. I say to myself, man is born with his needs on the earth and natural law has him born with a stomach; natural law has also permitted the apple tree to blossom every spring. Then what struck me about Douglas' doctrine is that it is always in conformity with this natural law. It's that the fruits of nature are made to balance [rencontrent].

He was anxious to acknowledge a close interrelationship of religious and political principles in the spiritual and temporal realms.

Listen. Man is obliged to live with his soul. I mean he is incapable of releasing his soul from his body at least until he dies. I don't think one should take religion completely out of politics. Religious principles must remain with one in work, politics, or anywhere. Even if you study, your religious convictions and principles are going to stay with you. We are Christians. As Christians, we must act in a Christian manner, even in politics.

Caouette, however, who also exhibited high disaffection, drew a much sharper distinction between the spiritual and temporal realms: 'They [the Church teachings] were not complete. Their aims were all right, the philosophy was all right, but to help apply all those nice principles, we would need social credit.' A similar tendency was reflected in his desire to distinguish his own movement from that of the Union des Electeurs:

We believe in the same social credit as Louis Even, but when they mix up religion with social credit, I don't go for it. I am a good Catholic, as good a Catholic as there may be, but trying to organize a religious movement and saying, 'Here now, you have to be a Catholic to be a social crediter, or to be a good social crediter, you have to be a good Catholic' – I don't go along with that at all, because social credit is an economic system, it is just as good for a Protestant, a Jew, for any person in the world. Don't mix religion into it.

It is in this distinction between these two men with quite similar Social Credit backgrounds that one sees in microcosm the potential for constructing what might be described as a religious orientation continuum. At one end of the continuum is the attitude of such long-standing Union des Electeurs leaders as Louis Even and Gilberte Côté-Mercier. Their stand on these questions is clear. According to them, 'Social credit is applied Christianity.'[3] Those members of their movement who split with them and joined with Caouette are generally opposed to such an extreme attitude. There are among these Ralliement members some highly disaffected leaders of lower socieconomic status who, like the transport company owner, continue to see close affinities between Catholicism and social credit theory which they would allow to influence their political activity. But they reject categorically the attempt to convert social credit propaganda into Catholic evangelism.

A much larger group in the Ralliement share the more sectarian attitudes of Réal Caouette. These included former members of the Union des Electeurs who had belonged to and even worked hard for the movement despite their strong objections to the mixing of religion and politics. As a retired foreman in an aluminum company, a highly disaffected leader of lower socioeconomic status, put it:

3 *Vers Demain*, 1 (1939–40).

Monsieur and Mme Mercier threw me out of the movement because I dared to criticize them, their methods of propaganda, namely mixing of religious with social questions, because I found that social credit is a temporal doctrine while the other aspect is spiritual. Thus I considered that it was not a good thing to mix the two together ... Spiritual questions should be left to experts, namely pastors, Protestant ministers and Catholic priests. It's for others to concern themselves with such spiritual matters. It's right for us to follow moral precepts and all that, but in teaching it is better to leave such things to people who are qualified, and concern ourselves with temporal matters.

They also included those who, for one reason or another, but especially because of the religious practices and allied methods of the Union des Electeurs, had never joined that earlier movement. According to a hardware store owner, also a highly disaffected protester of lower socioeconomic status: 'Even in the time of *Vers Demain* there were some good things in their operation, but they turned to religion, they mixed up religion too much with politics. Unfortunately that was done too much.' A small town businessman, a highly disaffected leader of higher status, concurred: 'I found that their operation was ridiculous ... this idea of mixing in prayers, during public demonstrations, of singing hymns and all that, I found it completely out of place.'

In their perception of the relationship of religion to politics, the Thompson group, who were all moderate protest leaders of higher status, seemed to have defined the distinction even more sharply. The attitude of Mr Thompson, who had been a Protestant missionary to Africa, may be taken as representative of their views:

The old-time Créditistes like Louis Even, Joe Marcotte, and Mercier, they mixed other things with social credit, they practically made a religious cult of it ... it is only when you mix up these other things that it makes Social Credit appear ridiculous. I have a basic philosophy in life, which I think is very practical: If you can't sell yourself, you can never sell your products, so why get them all mixed up in inessentials.

3   Beliefs about authority and leadership

The problem of authority and leadership was also of central concern to the Créditistes because of the former unhappy experience of many of them in the Union des Electeurs. The 'one and sole boss of the Union des Electeurs,' as Caouette saw it, was Mme Gilberte Côté-Mercier. Other respondents also complained of her dictatorial control. Laurent Legault described the manner in which she had interfered with campaign plans in 1948 by selecting candidates who satisfied her own (and ill-advised) qualifications of service and devotion rather than talent and prestige. A bookkeeper and former member of the Union des Electeurs, a highly disaffected leader of higher status, said of her: 'I found her too dictatorial. It was "believe or die." Do what one tells you or else remove yourself from our ranks. She is still the same, she hasn't changed.'[4]

4 My own experience in interviewing her tends to corroborate these perceptions. Interview with Gilberte Côté-Mercier, 14 May 1965, at Maison St-Michel.

It is interesting that a number of the respondents who still count themselves as members of the Ralliement found similar dictatorial attitudes in Caouette which they often attributed to his training in the 'school of Gilberte.' According to the hardware store owner, a staunch admirer of Caouette's:

Gilberte Côté had her faults, but in indoctrinating people to work benevolently like that all their lives, she had a powerful thrust [un poing épouvantable]. Now [Caouette] was educated by Gilberte, and now he has left her follies behind. But that man, he also has a powerful thrust. Whenever we had caucuses, if there was a little difference of opinion, Caouette arrived and then 'bang, bang' [toung, toung] everybody was clearly beaten. There is a Maurice Duplessis number 2.

Not all, however, were quite so generous in their evaluation of these qualities. A chartered accountant, a highly disaffected leader of higher socioeconomic status, argued: 'As leader, Caouette doesn't know enough about how to instil confidence in his men. He ... doesn't accept [se soumet] an idea which has been discussed in a group, in the organization, in the ranks of the movement. That's what's wrong [with him].' The bookkeeper, also a highly disaffected leader of higher socioeconomic status put it most directly:

I can tell you sincerely that M Caouette is a student of Mme Côté and he inherited a little from her. I am still in the Ralliement and I am in favour of Réal Caouette. Only I don't admire everything he does or everything he says either. I find him a little too dictatorial. He is less so than Gilberte, but he is still a little too much so himself. I forgive him a bit because he was brought up like that.

Those who remained with Thompson were quick to point to this quality as a major exacerbating factor in the split. Caouette's followers were blindly obedient to his decisions. As one young lawyer, a moderate leader of high status, explained:

They accepted only with much difficulty decisions other than those of their leader. Gilberte had been for them a kind of God; they also had the habit of listening blindly to the decisions of Réal Caouette. That is certainly one of the reasons that made Caouette and his group begin to believe that the English [-speaking members] didn't want to co-operate, because these members had questions to ask and arguments to make which they felt were important.

In other words, it was the very questioning of authority that was regarded as alien by certain segments of the Ralliement. The dissenter was in some sense disloyal to the leader; this was the attitude which Gilberte Côté-Mercier had attempted to inculcate in the ranks of the berets blancs. If the attitude towards Caouette as leader was any indication, she had succeeded in this task to a remarkable degree.

Robert Thompson seemed to share a similar perception of Caouette's relationship to his followers. Having been influenced by Manning he was clearly not averse to strong, even dictatorial leadership. Nevertheless, he commented: 'Mr Caouette is more intent to kill internal criticism than to kill the real opposition, and this is where he is defeating his own purpose. He is constantly throwing out those who cannot get along with him, and his group becomes smaller and smaller. He is just repeating the very same thing. It is another cycle. As it was with Gilberte Côté.'

In summary, just as a continuum on religious orientations can be drawn, in which the attitudes of the highly disaffected leaders of high and low socioeconomic status converge at one extreme, a continuum can be constructed for authority patterns in which the attitudes of the highly disaffected of both high and low status tend to cluster around one polar extreme. Despite their adverse opinion of Gilberte Côté-Mercier's dictatorial methods, they had once more succumbed to their use by her pupil. The moderate leaders of high status recognized this tendency and reacted against it. It is not surprising therefore that given the choice many followed the milder leadership of Robert Thompson. Authority patterns together with religious orientation patterns and attitudes toward belief systems in general were dominant factors in determining the ultimate form of the split.

4 Attitudes towards ideologies and belief systems

Differences in ideology were cited by Caouette as a catalyst for the split. He accused Robert Thompson and his western Social Credit colleagues of abandoning orthodox social credit doctrine. He claimed that his own group of old Créditistes were the only real Douglasites left in the party. He cited instances in which Robert Thompson had expressed a desire to modernize the doctrine and to drop such central tenets as the national dividend, the debt-free payments in family allowances and pensions, and the anti-austerity orientation of the doctrine. Responses indicate that Caouette's observations were substantially correct despite the tendency of our survey respondents to de-emphasize ideology as a causal factor. When asked if he considered himself to be an orthodox Social Crediter, Mr Thompson replied:

I believe in the principles Mr Douglas enunciated. This does not just apply to economic principles ... but our situation today is far different than it was in the days when Douglas first explained social credit principles. We had no social services at all from government, none of what we know as the welfare state was here. Certainly automation had not been developed as it has been developed since. We have moved into an age of plenty, and then we were still operating in an age of scarcity.

Thus when I talk social credit I don't talk necessarily in the same phraseology; nor do I dot the same 'i's as Douglas did. But I believe I speak in terms of the basic principles of social credit. I express it in terms that make some sense. After all, if you can't sell your product what is the use of trying to sell it.

In other words, Mr Thompson's attitude towards social credit doctrine was a highly pragmatic and instrumental one.[5]

The moderate protesters of high status who remained with Thompson after the split were likewise attacked by Caouette for their lack of concern for doctrine. Evi-

5 As if to confirm this observation, Mr Thompson joined the Progressive Conservative party in 1967 after resigning from the leadership of the Social Credit party the previous year.

dence also supports Caouette's allegations here. In reply to the question 'are you an orthodox Douglasite?' a doctor, a moderate protester of high socioeconomic status, asserted:

No. I have never been in favour of anything one hundred per cent. What I found in Douglas' theory was that you have to respect the human being. It's the first problem today, but since the year 1935 many things have changed so you cannot be one hundred per cent with Douglas. We have to be in tune with the times. What I accept in social credit is that the birth of credit comes through chartered banks and contributes to their profit; it comes from nothing except pure creation of credit. This should not come from the banks, the Bank of Canada or any other government-organized bank. This is about all that I admit in social credit.

A high school teacher, also a moderate leader of high status, revealed a similar attitude in a more oblique fashion:

What troubled me a little at the National Convention was this impression that I had that the majority of the delegates were idealists. Evidently they saw in social credit a 'better world' and their concern seemed almost to be the terrestrial paradise. In principle, the theory is very nice. In application, it's always necessary to keep one's two feet on the ground, to see problems in their proper dimensions and to consider that human beings will always be human, and that nothing will ever be perfect on earth.

The high school teacher also commented on the doctrinal orthodoxy of the other new Créditistes. Of Marcel Lessard, an MP from Lac Saint-Jean, he said: 'Moderately Créditiste, like me, moderately.' Of Doctor Marcoux, MP for Québec-Montmorency, he commented: 'In my opinion, he is a man of social credit temperament but he is not doctrinaire.'

Caouette's group was emphatic in its effort to identify its members as orthodox social crediters. Caouette considered himself 'to be a one hundred per cent orthodox Douglasite because when Douglas gave the world his theory in 1918, at that time there were still production problems in some parts of the world, but today in the age of atomic energy, power and abundance, with the increasing tendency to the use of machines in place of man, Douglas' theory is even more applicable than it was in 1918.' In answer to the question whether he still subscribed to the A plus B theorem and to the need to fill the gap in purchasing power, Caouette retorted: 'The A plus B theory is more true today than ever. Never, never, unless we have a lot of something, never will the national income in one year buy the production of that year. And when Douglas says that A will never be able to buy A plus B at a specific time, in a given time, it will always be true.' In distinguishing himself from Manning and Thompson with respect to social credit doctrine and its modernization, Caouette stated:

I follow all of Douglas' theory one hundred percent. They do not any more. They are mostly a conservative organization which upholds the old traditions and doesn't move forward ... Now we believe that Douglas is right and that Douglas has to be modernized, but in their case the modernization comes from Manning and Thompson; it does not come from Douglas.

Caouette did not distinguish himself from the followers of Louis Even and Mme Gilberte Côté-Mercier, in doctrinal orthodoxy: 'We follow the same social credit as Louis Even and Gilberte Côté-Mercier, but when they mix up religion with social credit, I don't go for it.'

The trucking company owner was just as emphatic about his orthodoxy. When asked if he considered himself an orthodox Social Crediter, he replied without hesitation:

Yes, I find that it is necessary to insist more and more on the fact that money and purchasing power must be distributed to the people otherwise than by salaries, and without conditions. I find that Douglas is right; his two propositions, the national dividend and the compensatory rebate [l'escompte compensé] are still the best means of issuing money. I find that Messrs Thompson and Manning attach too many conditions to this idea, conditional methods to achieve the end of giving purchasing power to the people. I prefer Douglas, who brings it about without any conditions.

He, like Caouette, made no basic distinction between himself and the followers of Louis Even and Gilberte Côté-Mercier: 'From the point of view of doctrine and principles, we don't distinguish ourselves from them at all. We're the same group.'

Gilles Grégoire, who could not be classified among our types, showed a more subtle awareness of what doctrinal orthodoxy implied:[6]

I think I can consider myself an orthodox Social Crediter. We cannot say Douglas Social Crediters, but rather those who follow his ideas. Douglas expounded his ideas in 1918. Many situations have changed since then, so we have to adapt ourselves in accordance with the circumstances while retaining the main principles which are the fundamental basis for monetary and financial reform. I still subscribe to the A plus B theorem.

On the face of it, it would seem as if the attitudes of the Caouette group of highly disaffected leaders of both high and low socioeconomic status could again be placed at the extreme of the ideological continuum. The attitudes of the moderate leaders of high status would appear to lie somewhere closer along the continuum to those of western Social Crediters. The Caouettistes, then, were the ideologues, the Thompsonists were more pragmatic.

Finally, the tendency of a member to express himself in ideological terms and particularly the way in which he held his doctrinal beliefs seemed to correlate with his attitudes towards authority. In general a Créditiste who ranked high as an ideologist was also an admirer of authoritarian behaviour and strong leadership. This was understandable, since the leadership in the Créditiste group had always assumed a posture of complete devotion to Douglas social credit. Where the authority of the leader was accepted, there was also an inclination to accept the leader's interpretation of the doctrine. Or the doctrine itself took on a certain aura of authority independent of the leadership. If charges had been laid and been well-documented to the effect

6 Grégoire refused to allow himself to be included in our structured survey.

that Caouette, by his parliamentary and press statements, had abandoned orthodox social credit positions on austerity, budgetary policy, and social welfare payments, the 'true believers' in the party might have been less inclined to follow his lead at the time of the split. There was some evidence for this in the attitudes expressed by certain of the less politically minded Créditistes, all of whom were highly disaffected leaders of higher socioeconomic status. A number of respondents who showed lack of interest in politics and were more concerned about the advancement of the doctrine in French Canada were critical of Caouette's political motives for effecting the split. They felt that unity was essential for the effective promulgation of social credit. It was Caouette's efforts to discredit the new Créditistes and the western Social Crediters as doctrinal heretics that largely convinced them to remain nominally in his camp. But their discontent generally resulted in an unwillingness to work as energetically or as enthusiastically for the movement as they had in the past.

There is much less clear correlation between attitudes towards religion and tendency to 'ideologize.'[7] Those who most fervently proclaimed their desire to separate religion from politics were often those who were most concerned about doctrinal orthodoxy. There are a number of possible explanations for this. In the first place, many of the highly disaffected leaders who had formerly been members of the Union des Electeurs had decided to separate from that movement primarily because of their determination to keep their religious and political activities distinct. The berets blancs had tended to mix religion and politics too much, as was repeated over and over agan in our interviews. Those inclined to ideologize tended to adopt a rigid position sharply separating the two. In attempting such a division they were often more dogmatic than realistic; the separation itself became part of their new definition of the doctrine. This same pattern was revealed in the response to questions concerning the social as opposed to economic aspects of the doctrine. The Union des Electeurs had declared Douglas' theory to be as much a social as an economic doctrine. The Créditistes who had joined Caouette were much more inclined to emphasize the economic side. A number of them declared that the theory was purely economic in nature and, more particularly, was almost exclusively about monetary reform. This revealed a similar concern with temporal things as opposed to spiritual and a desire to keep the two as distinct as possible.

A second explanation which is not mutually exclusive of the first is that articulated religious attitudes do not really correspond to internally held orientations on such matters. The subject of religion is by nature a personal and confidential one. It is part of Catholic teaching that it should be kept so. The responses of the Créditistes interviewed may not, then, have represented the true attitudes of these people on the subject.

B THE FIRST DIMENSION OF CRÉDITISTE CULTURE: NATIONAL IDENTITY

Of the four major dimensions outlined by Verba which are intended to define political cultures, the first is that of national identity. Our respondents revealed their feelings of national identity in three major ways: 1 / in their own self-identification as French

7 The term 'ideologize' is used by Robert Lane, *Political Ideology* (New York: Free Press of Glencoe, 1962), 353.

Canadians or Catholics or both; 2 / in the priority which they gave to Quebec as opposed to other provinces and even as opposed to Canada as a whole; 3 / in their image of western Canada and western Social Credit.

1 *French Canadians and/or Catholics*

Vers Demain, in its first issue in 1939, identified itself as an organ of Catholic and French-speaking Social Crediters, and all through its era of predominance over Quebec Social Credit, it continued to express strongly Catholic and nationalist views. This identification with nationality and religion was preserved in the attitudes of former members of the berets blancs. Réal Caouette made reference to papal encyclicals in his attempt to give a philosophical rationale to social credit doctrine. A highly disaffected leader of lower socioeconomic status gave a philosophical reason for his nationalism:

God created man and woman, who form a unity. Before Canada was discovered there were tribes. They formed their own group together and they spoke the same dialect ... It's natural that those who speak the same language, who understand each other, form a group around a church bell, a parish. You can see everywhere in Ontario people of the same religion [grouping themselves together]. United Church people like to form a group around a church. It's normal that one group of people who speak the same language, and who have the same convictions, seek to group together. It's natural.

New Social Crediters were not generally as insistent on this point. A doctor, a moderate protest leader of high status, whose father was 'a nationalist, like Bourassa,' shrugged his shoulders at the suggestion that it was unwise, from a nationalist point of view, for him to side with Mr Thompson, an Anglo-Saxon Protestant:

With this nationalist sentiment in Quebec that we have now, many Créditistes who were in favour of our group and were not in favour of Caouette still accused us of betraying our nationality, saying we have preferred an English Protestant over a French-Canadian Catholic, and we know that Caouette has been very insistent on this point. Frenette is a good man, Côté is a strong nationalist, almost a separatist. Frenette was with the Saint-Jean Baptiste Society every year. All of us are good men and strong nationalists. Caouette didn't know what to do [about our joining with Thompson] so he said 'They are bad French Canadians, they are traitors!'

The high school teacher, also a moderate leader of high status, observed that the nationalist factor had influenced him initially to vote for Caouette at the 1961 Social Credit national leadership convention. But on the next ballot he had switched his vote to Mr Thompson, whom he regarded as more responsible. When asked to explain this behaviour, he confided:

My personal feeling is this: I prefer to see a good English Canadian direct the destinies of our country or the destinies of a political party than a bad French Canadian, one who is incompetent, or incapable. Caouette is a nationalist, perhaps to an extreme at times, perhaps even fanatical. That's why I preferred Thompson, whom I considered a good

English Canadian. Because ordinarily my nationalism is not so far-reaching; a Canadian is a Canadian, whether he speaks English or French. Inasmuch as he is a good citizen, in my opinion, they're the same.

The young lawyer also attempted to de-emphasize the role which these differences of nationality played. 'If it were so, why would we, French-Canadian deputies from Quebec, have remained with Thompson?' But in doing so, he mentioned a subtle difference, which is far more significant: 'I never sensed any friction in the party between English and French Canadians: there were differences of opinion, different attitudes of mind [mentalités].' And he also made clear where he stood on these matters: 'Caouette was reproached for speaking too much about the French fact in the House. I told him personally not to speak about the inscription on the caps of bus drivers, since this wouldn't produce a solution between French and English Canada. I told him to treat more serious, more profound themes.'

In summary, the moderate leaders of high status for the most part tended to downplay their nationalism. They also seemed to associate the nationalism displayed by some of their colleagues with immaturity. In particular, nationalism which led to complaints about use of French was seen as an involvement with superficial symptoms. The behaviour of Bernard Dumont in refusing to intervene on behalf of eastern Quebec farmers in accordance with accepted standards of parliamentary procedure reflected for them a related kind of nationalistic immaturity. Gilles Grégoire's demand that Beauchesne be translated into French was of the same order. The highly disaffected leaders of high and low socioeconomic status, on the other hand, were quite proud of what they regarded as their substantial achievements in this area. Réal Caouette boasted of the change which his group had brought about in the use of French in parliamentary restaurants and on menus. In his speech to the Granby Convention in 1963 he stressed the importance of the Beauchesne incident; the pension plan translation incident was discussed in his speech to the Quebec Convention in 1964; both awakened English Canada to the French-Canadian demand for equal rights. Gilles Grégoire listed his questioning of Messrs Gordon and MacGregor about their language policies as his prime achievement: 'We were the first to state clearly and strongly what we want, and we opened the eyes of lots of people.'

It is difficult to assess the effect of these interventions on behalf of the French language and nationality among Quebec voters in general. But it is certain, as the doctor admitted, that the nationalism and nationality of Caouette won many supporters to his side who might otherwise have hesitated to follow him. The attitude of one highly disaffected leader of low socioeconomic status, a retired foreman who did not like Caouette personally, may be taken as typical: 'In the first assembly which M Côté convened after the split, when he remained with Thompson, I was the first to disassociate myself from him. M Côté was one of my great friends. I had worked hard for him ... But I stayed with Caouette ... Caouette had worked enormously. Apart from that, he was a French Canadian.'

2   Quebec versus the rest of Canada

While nationalism is often translated into demands for a special status for the province of Quebec vis-à-vis the rest of Canada, the two should not be treated as equivalent. Caouette's attitude on this latter question, as opposed to his attitude on the former, was a case in point. He was much more concerned with maintaining the integrity of Canada as a nation than are most strong French-Canadian nationalists. When asked to explain why he adopted this attitude and why he seemed to differ from Legault in this respect, he justified it in the following way:

When I was at college, we had quite a large group of English-speaking students, not only Canadians, but youngsters from the United States in the Fall River District of Massachusetts. Our college was absolutely bilingual. Then I had to get to know them. Now I am a French-Canadian nationalist, I definitely am one, but not to the detriment of others. Others, like Legault, are less inclined to understand that because they hadn't any prior relationship with the English population. Many of them were taught to regard the English as 'les maudits Anglais' for years and years. They accepted the argument 'If you are not advancing, it is because the English are preventing you from advancing.' I am convinced that it is not so.

His outlook on the future of Confederation flows from the preceding belief:

This is what I say: it is possible to save Confederation if we lay the blame where it ought to lie. It is our own politicians who have been playing politics instead of serving their own people. They have been playing the patronage game and greasing road contracts and doing things of that nature to the detriment of the people, taxing them to the bone and doing nothing, except organizing for elections and amassing an election fund. That's all they think about. Now this is our own fault, not that of Ontario. No English Canadian has ever stopped me from earning my own living. I deal with the English-speaking people at Chrysler Corporation. They are fine people. I get along with them.

Caouette also was explicit on where he stood on the question of separatism: 'When they say Caouette is a separatist, I am the least separatist in Quebec.'[8] Although Caouette's constitutional position appeared to have evolved to fit demands both in his own province and within his own party, evidence from interviews and observations suggests that it was he, above all, who had bridled potential separatism within the party. His reasons appeared to be twofold: he felt that his own and Créditiste electoral chances were greater at the federal level, and that his own particular beliefs about the possibility of co-operation between the two major cultural groups influenced him in determining his position on the question.

The other leading members of the old group of Créditistes, all highly disaffected leaders, generally adopted a similar, though more strident, position on Quebec's place within Confederation. Laurent Legault was asked if he was not more inclined to separatism than Caouette. He hesitated at first and then replied: 'A paper written in 1867 can no longer do the job for us in 1967. That doesn't mean that we must separate. In 1867 our fathers separated certain things, for example education, justice.

---

8 This statement was made in 1965 when Caouette was still seen by some as a radical nationalist. His position on this question became clearer and more widely understood after 1966.

There are, perhaps, other aspects to readjust, and I say that whatever happens should apply not only to Quebec but to the people of other provinces as well.'

Many top leaders of the Ralliement then advocated what amounted to a form of associate statehood for Quebec in which the province would have had exclusive jurisdiction over all of the important economic fields.[9] It would have had exclusive control over direct and indirect sources of revenues; it would have collected its own taxes; it would have controlled its own banks. Furthermore, this position was logically consistent with the application of social credit doctrine at the provincial level. If Quebec had exclusive jurisdiction over banking, credit, and economic resources, it could constitutionally apply social credit monetary theory in the form of provincial legislation. Then why did Caouette not opt for separatism? 'I have always had the conviction, which I may change, since only fools do not change, that there is a possible way of convincing Ottawa that the provinces should have more power, more liberty, more freedom, and more control over their economy.'

How did the moderate leaders feel about such issues? According to the doctor:

I don't accept going from one extreme to another. I am for a solution of the middle way. Only when this proves impossible should we then go to an extreme. For example, in Confederation, I am in favour of asking for all that we are entitled to have. We must then give enough time to the rest of the country to permit them to either accept or reject what we are entitled to have. If they don't want to understand, then that's too bad. Then we must go to the extreme. But only after we have failed to find a middle way.

His extreme moderation with respect to nationalism translated itself into a moderate position on Quebec's status vis-à-vis the rest of Canada. The young lawyer's stance on these matters was also flexible. Other sympathizers with this new group expressed opinions of a similar nature and tone. In other words, the moderate leaders were generally just as extreme in what they demanded for Quebec, but they were far more moderate about the way in which they felt the negotiations should be conducted and the demands should be presented.

The highly disaffected leaders of the Ralliement seemed in general to approve of both Caouette's position and his tactics on these matters. According to one organizer from Rouyn, an owner of a dry-cleaning shop and a highly disaffected leader of high status:

If the Ralliement entered provincial politics in Quebec, I think it would produce even better results than it did in Ottawa. I was a bit afraid that after the elections, the members would veer a bit towards separatism. In fact, there were several who were ready to support separatism. But they were Créditistes first. Separation had never yielded anything. It brings about a separation, that's all. On the contrary, all people who divide don't help each other. I think all the Créditistes understand this point. At least 75 per cent of our Créditistes who are a little familiar with social credit will not opt for separatism.

9 This was in 1965. The following year differences between Caouette on the one hand and Legault and Grégoire on the other led to a split between them. Subsequently the Ralliement leaders modified their constitutional position to one in favour of decentralized federalism within a one nation Canada.

His personal solution was a revised Confederation of six states: the maritimes, Quebec, Ontario, the prairies, British Columbia, and the northwest in which 'Ottawa would become like a kind of United Nations.'

The chartered accountant, an old Créditiste and also a highly disaffected leader of high socioeconomic status who, however, shared some of the attitudes of the moderate leaders, seemed to concur:

They [the old Créditistes] have a fundamentally nationalist tendency. And on this point I approve of their views. I approve of their being nationalist. First of all, they are French Canadians, but not to the detriment of other provinces. It's not necessary to cut it clean ... I'm not a separatist. I have confidence in the other provinces, who are like good neighbours. It is necessary to act in concert to develop the country.

He was nevertheless critical of the refusal of Caouette, Legault, and Grégoire to deal with the English Canadians on the Social Credit National Council. And yet he appeared to be just as extreme in what he was demanding from a constitutional and economic point of view, namely an associate state. Another organizer from Chicoutimi, a highly disaffected leader of low socioeconomic status, argued in a similar vein: 'I would prefer that we concentrate our efforts in Quebec rather than waste our time in Ottawa. I prefer a Quebec movement much more because in my opinion it is almost impossible to take power in Ottawa. Whereas in Quebec, it's possible: because, although I am not a separatist, I believe that it's going to be necessary to get away from there [Ottawa].'

How did westerners respond to these nationalist and constitutional revisionist views? Mr Thompson's attitude may be taken as representative. He showed impatience with the nationalism of his former Social Credit Quebec colleagues as it affected their demands for wider use of French in the federal government. He also made clear where he stood on the question of separatism and provincial rights: 'I admit that there is some validity [in these demands], but this kind of thing has also led to separatist demands too ... The Quebeckers had a grievance that someone had to express. But there is more to Canada than just Quebec. They are members in a federal government, and therefore have their responsibilities.'

It is clear, then, that Mr Thompson was rather unsympathetic to the whole strategy of stressing French-Canadian grievances. What the supporters of the Caouette group regarded as their magnificent work in awakening English Canadians to the grievances of Quebec was seen by him as 'a tendency to look at problems from the light of Quebec rather than from that of all Canada.' There is little doubt that Mr Thompson shared in large part the concept of 'a multicultural Canada' which has been found to be so pervasive in western English-speaking Canada. That is not to say, of course, that Mr Thompson was in any sense anti-French Canadian. He undoubtedly made every effort to understand and sympathize with his Créditiste colleagues. And he was determined to be extremely fair to them in order to avoid being labelled anti-French Canadian.

3   *Créditiste perception of western Social Crediters' similarities and differences*
The differences which the Créditistes perceived in their western colleagues also varied largely in terms of whether they belonged to the Caouette group or the Thompson

group and whether they were in close contact or remote from them. The kind of image they had undoubtedly influenced their decision to join one or the other of the two groups at the time of the split.

It is clear that Caouette considered Alberta Social Crediters to be conservatives rather than Social Crediters. He recognized that they had been the pathbreakers in introducing social credit to Canada, but he was convinced that, having long ago been bought by financiers and big business in Alberta, they no longer cared about social credit. The worst offender in this regard was Premier Manning. In Caouette's opinion, Manning was anti-French Canadian. He had told Caouette 'right in black and white that the west would never accept a French-Canadian Catholic as national Social Credit leader.' Manning was, moreover, the real power behind the national Social Credit Association. From the very first he had backed Thompson for the party leadership. This was because, according to Caouette, Manning himself hoped to become prime minister of Canada. Caouette claimed there was an understanding between Manning and Thompson that if the latter were successful at the polls, then the premier of Alberta would become the prime minister of Canada.[10] Further, Caouette charged, Manning had 'ordered' Thompson to overthrow the Diefenbaker government in 1963; Thompson was 'the puppet of Manning.' And Manning himself was the puppet of the United States businessmen. In Caouette's view it was Manning who had refused to allow the National Association to support the Quebec Social Credit campaign financially. Manning had refused to permit a larger representation from Quebec on the National Council and executive. Caouette's image of western Social Credit was that it was different largely because Manning had made it different. His was a monolithic image of Alberta and National Social Credit, dominated by a personal antipathy to Manning.

On the other hand, Caouette was profuse in his praises of what Social Credit governments had accomplished in both western provinces in terms of good administration. He constantly cited figures of the much lower provincial debt of Alberta and British Columbia. Bennett's demands for a provincial bank won his accolades. He had a good image of Bennett personally or, at least, he was grateful for Bennett's campaign support. For that reason, he did not talk in a derogatory manner about Bennett as a Social Crediter and generally avoided mentioning him in his discussions of his grievances against the west.

Laurent Legault had a cloudier vision of these people. He had had much less contact with them, and his attitudes were, as Thompson observed, much more provincial. He had met Thompson in early 1961 and had rather liked him but he had not been able to change his image of the man as basically English Protestant. He was less concerned with what he thought of westerners or they of him and cared more about his own position within the Ralliement. Insofar as they comprised a threat to his position within the movement that he had created, he was hostile to them. Apart from that, he did not care about them one way or another. His immediate concern was Social Credit in Quebec, rather than Social Credit in all of Canada. Gilles Grégoire understood Thompson very well. But he considered him a weak leader. He also

10 Interview with Réal Caouette, April 1964. The same view is held by Alf Hooke, long time minister in the Aberhart and Manning administrations. See Alfred J. Hooke, *30+5, I know, I was There* (Edmonton; Alberta: Co-op Press Limited, 1971), 213.

recognized a certain naiveté in Thompson on the question of French-English relations which he exploited to the full: 'We had some difficulties understanding each other, especially in problems of bilingualism and biculturalism.' The issue was Grégoire's bread and butter. He was not to be impeded by Thompson from stressing this problem. All three, then, were inclined to walk out on the western contingent at first provocation after the 1963 election. They used the pretext of being underrepresented at the National Council to do so.

The moderate leaders of high status had much more charitable images of their western confrères. All of them showed respect and sometimes admiration for Mr Thompson. The doctor, on being directly questioned, had the most precise image of the western members, particularly in terms of their doctrinal orthodoxy:

It's necessary to make distinctions. First of all, between Social Credit at the provincial and at the national level. Bennett is not a Social Crediter, and doesn't believe in it at all ... Manning is an orthodox Social Crediter, who knows how to apply it, but he is a practical man ... On the federal side, the British Columbian MPs are even more orthodox than the Albertans. Patterson and Leboe were elected in 1954 and fell under the tutelage of Blackmore and Solon Low. They are ministers or strong religious believers. They were receptive to the doctrine. Bennett is very different from them in personality.

The high school teacher described the westerners as 'more mature than most of our deputies.' This he attributed to their having been deputies before. They also seemed, he felt, more realistic in their application of social credit principles than the members from Quebec. He was, however, less charitable to Premier Manning, 'since it is known that Manning has certain prejudices [against Quebec Social Crediters].' Of Bennett he speculated: 'I understand Bennett a little also, because Bennett and Caouette are in my opinion fellows of about the same calibre. They are personalities with many traits in common.'

The young lawyer shared a similar image of the western deputies as in some sense more responsible and able:

Social Credit in the west is a party in power, strong, serious, established in the ways of the people. It's very important for them that they should not be dishonoured and ridiculed; all the Social Credit leaders in the west are serious men, whereas in Quebec, the party has always had a bad image, of being unacceptable in professional milieux, of being bourgeois, uneducated, parading with berets and flags. The mentality of a Créditiste trained by Gilberte is not at all like that of a Social Crediter trained by Manning. It is permissible to be rich in the west and also a Social Crediter, whereas for Caouette it is unthinkable to be both rich and a Créditiste.

Discussion between the groups was very difficult, and the split came as a welcome event for westerners since 'they had a profound dislike for Caouette.' Why, then, had the westerners agreed to the union in the first place? A moderate leader explained: 'The west hoped to see a national victory.' And why hadn't they pressed for the split after the April election? According to the doctor, they were interested in maintaining the unity of the party lest they jeopardize their own chances for re-election. For pragmatic reasons they worked to prevent a split but once it became inevitable they were glad to be rid of Caouette.

A favourable image of the westerners was shared by many rank and file Créditistes in Caouette's own group. For example, when a former MP, a highly disaffected leader of low socioeconomic status, was asked to explain the difference between Social Credit of the west and that of the province of Quebec, his reply was: 'The basic doctrine is almost the same. Except it is understood differently by an English-speaking person. An English person does not engage in politics in the same way as a French Canadian. I think there is a little difference there. The Englishman is more of an administrator, who doesn't become angry, who works always to attain his goal quietly. The French Canadian is not as flexible a fellow.'

And yet there were some highly disaffected leaders of low status, particularly among the more parochial local activists, who accepted the following type of argument: 'The English provinces are stuffed to the brim with money, whereas here we are starving. Thus in the business of the west the people have been stuffed by the old parties, when we here are dying of hunger.' This kind of image would certainly have influenced the rank-and-file member to join Caouette rather than Thompson. But it reflected the opinion of only a small minority of Créditiste members.

The attitude of the majority of the activists towards the westerners probably lay somewhere in between these extremes. Western Social Crediters were too remote to be familiar to them or of much concern. On the other hand, there was a general appreciation that they were on the whole not very different from Créditistes. They held similar reformist ideas, they were opposed to the traditional political institutions and methods, and they were more or less anxious to implement social credit.

In short, the highly disaffected Créditistes were more nationalistic, more Quebec oriented, and more distrustful of western Social Crediters than the moderate leaders. In 1963 these differences were crucial in producing the split between the two wings along the lines detailed.

C THE SECOND DIMENSION OF CRÉDITISTE CULTURE:
IDENTIFICATION WITH ONE'S FELLOW CITIZENS

The second category, identification with one's fellow citizens, has been interpreted within the Créditiste context to refer to each leader's sense of solidarity with or sense of difference from the other members in his party. It has been subdivided into two major categories: 1 / class differences, in particular, attitudes towards professionals within the party, and 2 / sense of Créditiste, and especially berets blancs camaraderie. These appeared to be the major focal points of solidarity and cleavage within the Quebec party and hence were major factors in the split.

1 Class differences

Superiority-inferiority feelings in terms of social class appeared to have seriously undermined Créditiste solidarity in the 1960–3 period. The Ralliement leadership had deliberately wooed more respectable people – professionals, civic leaders, and the like – in order to improve their image to the voters. And yet many Créditistes seem to have been unable to overcome a profound sense of inferiority towards these better educated, more highly reputed, and generally more independent-minded individuals of higher status. The latter, largely moderate protesters who had joined primarily for political reasons, did not attempt to conceal their disdain for many of the old Créditistes who lacked education, a capacity for speech and reflection, and an image of respectability. Conflict between the two groups seemed inevitable.

Réal Caouette, although the prime mover behind the effort to improve the image of the party, was never able to overcome his own distrust and envy of professionals. He was in all respects a man of the common folk who made no attempt to hide his feelings of identification with these average people. In this sense he was faithful to the training inculcated by Gilberte Côté-Mercier who, though university-educated, always stressed the need for solidarity with the poor and downtrodden – a kind of Christian asceticism temporally defined. Caouette deliberately tried to reach the common folk. To do so he was prone to use 'direct explanations that touch [these people] right in their own homes, and in their own hearts, and that was the point.' He had come from a poor background: 'I was born in a very small house, 12 feet by 18 feet. My father was a settler and he was sick for four or five years. My mother had to look after five children at that time. Eventually my father got a job from the provicial government at a very low salary. He received $90 a month. We were eight children.' Yet he had managed to graduate from a classical college during the depression years when many others were denied the opportunity.

I know what misery is. I've seen it. I've lived with it. While I was going to school, I had friends who would have liked to come to college with me in the years 1932 to 1936. They couldn't come. I couldn't understand why all the colleges were half full. Priests and brothers would come during vacation time to all parts of the Province of Quebec looking for students, and they couldn't find any because there was no money and their institutions were at fault.

After graduating, he had entered business, first as an employee of the Bank of Commerce, later as a travelling salesman. He has been in business ever since.

It is possible that Caouette has been frustrated by his non-professional status ever since he left the classical college. At any rate it is clear that he has a marked admiration for professional people. When he referred to professionals within his own party, he generally added a word of identification. François Even was a 'lawyer, I knew him personally,' and Gérard Girouard was 'this young lawyer whom I thought would be an asset to the movement.' Dr Marcoux, as a general practitioner from a well-known Quebec City family, was strongly pressured by Caouette to join the Créditistes and run for office: 'I suggested Marcoux myself.' Gérard Chapdelaine had just passed his bar examinations and established a law practice in Sherbrooke when Caouette was informed of his Créditiste sympathies; he immediately made a great effort to persuade him to run as a candidate. Caouette's relationship with Gilles Grégoire may be partly explained by his respect both for Grégoire's father, who was a lawyer and professor, as well as for Gilles's own university and legal training. But he was clearly ambivalent in this respect. He did not trust professionals and was receptive to general attacks and accusations made against them. Thus, he associated Girouard's party disloyalty with his legal training, though the two were not necessarily related. Dr Marcoux's challenge to his leadership was considered to stem in large part from his higher status as a professional. Most important, Caouette was ready to believe the accusations made by Gérard Perron and Gilbert Rondeau against the professionals in the party without requiring corroborative evidence.

Gilles Grégoire seemed to share Caouette's high esteem for the professional. Obviously he capitalized on his own qualifications in this respect, and saw his own role in the Ralliement as that of the trained lawyer. 'My role is simple. In the group I am the only one who studied law and procedures in the House. It is important to have some knowledge of the law or to have some kind of background like that, and I am the only one who so qualifies, so I act as House leader.' Grégoire probably encouraged Caouette in his efforts to attract professionals into the party. On the other hand, he preferred that they did not become overly powerful. He had his own reputation to guard because he was a professional, though of a somewhat dubious standing since he had never passed his bar examination. But his postures of intellectualism and professionalism also appeared to me to be largely incidental to his complete absorption in the 'game' of politics.

The trucking company owner disliked the professionals because they threatened his leadership within the party and because, by comparison, some of his own inadequacies were more obvious. They were always aware of his limited education and colloquial speech, and in 1963 the professionals had threatened to oppose his candidacy for the provincial presidency by promoting a candidate of their own – Roland Bertrand, a Grondines accountant. They accused him of being too provincial, too coarse in his language and grammar, and too 'gilbertiste' in his manner of organization and in his attitudes. The movement failed to gain any momentum because Bertrand declined to run, and he was elected president unanimously. But it left him with an understandable distrust of the professionals whom he identified as 'les nouveaux' or 'les modernistes': the Marcoux, Girouards, and Chapdelaines of the party.

The professionals themselves appeared to do little to mitigate the conflict over status, class, and community esteem. The doctor showed a clear sense of class superiority over Caouette which he did not conceal at the time of their partnership: 'It's true that a group can purify politics. And, given that these are all middle-class people, that there are no professionals who form part of the group, it's clear that if I joined I would give them a big lift.' The high school teacher was sceptical about the capacity of the Créditistes to cope with economics, feeling that this was in the domain of professional economists:

That's the reason that I think the Créditistes, the berets blancs, pretend to give lessons in political economy to the classical economists and, for that matter, to anyone. They are out of their element. They lack the foundation of a general education capable of permitting them to assimilate this material which in fact is complicated. Speak to any economist and he will admit himself that the monetary system is very complicated; but for these others it's not complicated, it's simple, simple. It's perhaps too simple.

And the young lawyer admitted that 'one of the factors which encouraged me to join Social Credit was that I wanted to prove that it wasn't a thing purely for illiterates, that it could include people with university education who are interested and who believe in twentieth-century formulas.' He reflected that at the same time there was a fear of professionals among the Créditistes which made communication between the two groups difficult.

It's certain that the group of Créditistes who were educated in the mentality of Gilberte Côté-Mercier thought that all those who didn't belong to the middle class, especially someone who is professional, are dangerous and incapable of understanding the true feelings of the people. It's a bit of this mentality that I found among the people that I knew in the Ralliement.

Some leaders of the Caouette group also shared this perception of the class basis of the party, although they interpreted it in a somewhat different way. For example, when asked why it was that professionals like himself tended not to join the Ralliement, the chartered accountant answered:

There is a profound reason for it. People who have a place [sont en place], who have a good position, the businessman, the professional, a person who succeeds, who has a good standard of living, that person is obliged to conduct public business, and therefore must follow the current, and must be careful not to utter statements that can be used against him. Now at the moment, in a new venture, people of this sort don't even take the trouble to think about whether [such a movement] will be good for their neighbour, or for the general condition of the population ... The poor man, he suffers, and therefore he sees the need to think and to act. The educated class, the prosperous class, they are not concerned [with such matters].

And the hardware store owner, a highly disaffected leader who had achieved a measure of economic success, admitted that 'on joining the Ralliement, I met some opposition from public-minded men who came to see me to discourage me ... Some even said to me that they couldn't understand how an intelligent and successful man like myself could join Social Credit.'

The split between Caouette and Thompson undoubtedly alienated a substantial number of sympathetic professionals and businessmen. Some left the party altogether; others became inactive though nominally they retained their membership. Even those who remained active were not entirely satisfied with the state of class representation in the movement. They tried to rationalize it in different ways. Some attacked the professionals. The owner of a dry-cleaning store, a highly disaffected leader of inferior education, remarked:

I noticed one thing in Alberta, the year that they won power, in 1935, there wasn't a single professional in the party. Personally, I believe that the problem with politics at present is that there are too many professionals in it. Going back twenty years, to my father's time, he who could become a professional was someone with money. Those professionals never knew what it was to earn a dollar ... Then because Mr so and so had a diploma he was recognized as 'monsieur,' but what did he know about administration? I say that the professional is one of the worst administrators because he has never administered.

But most of them still shared the uneasy feeling of an old-time Créditiste, a highly disaffected leader of higher status, who complained:

I think that Social Credit has the best policies in the world, but it doesn't have the men to promote them. We lack men who win confidence, who are popular ... I know friends who have never voted for Social Credit, but would have liked to, except they told us, 'We would certainly be with Social Credit, but you don't have men' ... In the movement there isn't one professional; there was one, Dr Marcoux. One could say that there is a fear of having professionals in our movement. The professional class, whether one likes it or not, has influence in the population.

2 Créditiste camaraderie

Acting parallel with and reinforcing this sense of class difference was a strong sense of loyalty to old friends and associations dating back to Union des Electeurs times. The berets blancs were much more than a purely political association. They were a kind of large family, a province-wide social organization whose members met many times informally, although formally only once a year. They drank and ate together, travelled together, shared stories together, and suffered the same hardships together trying to 'sell' Social Credit. Gilberte Côté-Mercier had tried to cultivate the idea that all the members were her children who had attended her school, had been brought up by her, and were now assuming positions of importance within her fold. In fact, the second generation of Créditistes did grow up under her wing, only to turn against her and her kind of leadership. But they retained much of their initial camaraderie with each other. On the other hand, those who had not shared these earlier experiences were generally regarded as outsiders. Even when a conscious effort was made to welcome them into the party, the distinction between old and new members somehow remained a prominent psychological factor in the inter-relationships of the Ralliement members.

Réal Caouette did not conceal the importance of this factor in his own thinking and actions. In his office were displayed photographs of the four individuals in the Ralliement with whom he had had the longest unbroken association: Laurent Legault, Gilles Grégoire, Gilbert Rondeau, and Gérard Perron, all of them, with the exception of Grégoire, former close associates of his in the Union des Electeurs.[11] Grégoire was generally identified with the berets blancs because of the prominent role which his father played in the early development of the movement; he was, moreover, the one who first broached the idea to Caouette of forming a separate Créditiste movement. When asked if Legault, Grégoire, and he formulated most of the policy for the Ralliement, Caouette replied: 'I would say so because we were the three real founders of the movement.' During the 'affair of the six' he blocked all attempts to expel the two major proponents of the pledge – Perron and Rondeau – on the grounds that they had been associated with Social Credit for a long time. A year earlier he had acceded to the importunities of Perron and Rondeau and demanded that a new slate of MPs be named to the Ralliement executive on the grounds that he could not work with the first group (including Côté and Chapdelaine, both new Créditistes),

11 This was in 1965. The photographs of Legault and Grégoire have since been removed.

but could work with the second (including Rondeau, Perron, and Langlois, all old Créditistes).

Laurent Legault made it apparent where his true feelings lay: 'We are old Créditistes who founded the movement; we opened the door to all the new Créditistes.' But he was quite willing to acknowledge his debt to the berets blancs: 'We can't separate the two movements entirely. They advocate the same social credit. Their principles continue to be the same. The only thing which distinguishes them from us is the means we advocate to obtain social credit.' Legault obviously takes much pride in his past work and associations in the Union des Electeurs. He keeps in storage old bound volumes and back issues of *Vers Demain,* pamphlets, leaflets, souvenirs, and awards he accumulated during the years in which he was a member. Many of his closest friendships date from this early period. He served as a director of the Institute of Political Action, the governing body of the original movement, and was the organizer-in-chief of the 1948 provincial campaign in which the berets blancs made their greatest campaign effort. After that campaign he had a falling out with Mme Côté-Mercier and resigned from the directorate. But he never completely severed his connection with the movement, its doctrine, or the people with whom he was initially connected. From 1957 until the split in 1966 he was again very active in the movement. Even after the electoral defeat of the Ralliement National in 1966 he continued to regard himself as a devotee of the movement and later rejoined the Ralliement Créditiste.

The reaction against this in-group cliquishness was strong among the moderate leaders of high status, most of them new Créditistes themselves. They suspected that the split between Caouette and Mme Côté-Mercier was not entirely legitimate. The doctor observed:

There was an incontestable difference between Caouette's group and the berets blancs ... and yet, they never denounced the militarism of Gilberte [marching in procession], they never renounced the principle of the Union des Electeurs that Louis Even had espoused of uniting electors into little sectors where they could have local study circles and where they could control everything through their small cells.

They never rejected that. The only thing they renounced was that Gilberte, rather than devoting herself to political action, immersed herself in religious action ... It's a strange phenomenon, these fellows who on the one hand let themselves be deeply influenced on the emotional plane, and ... on the other hand, were politicians who wanted to fight election campaigns. They revived the formula of Louis Even from the Union des Electeurs and they shunted aside the religious formula of Gilberte. They went [sont partis dans] into political organization; they recruited their men on the model of [sur le plan de] the Union des Electeurs. The whole organization, with a few exceptions, were men of the berets blancs, of *Vers Demain.*

Most of them did not like the berets blancs to begin with. The young lawyer complained: 'Their operation was ridiculous. They presented it very badly. This idea of mixing in prayers during public demonstrations, of singing hymns and all that, I found it completely out of place ... The movement was too demagogic; I didn't like the attitude of Gilberte Côté-Mercier and Louis Even.'

When the new Créditistes tried to introduce sweeping changes in organization and administration they faced the opposition of the old-time members. When they tried to interject on points of policy, they were reminded of their inferior training in social credit doctrine. The gap between the two groups widened as the months passed. The young lawyer reported that 'there was definitely a separation created in the caucus. It was the manner of expressing one's point of view that made for division. When one would speak of the dividend of $100, of people of a beret blanc cast of mind, of beretblancomania, in the caucus, immediately, there was a division.'

It is not surprising, then, that when Caouette and Grégoire sided with Perron and Rondeau the moderate leaders in the caucus felt a sense of alienation and an inability to direct the party along the lines they believed were best. Under these circumstances it was natural for them to turn to Robert Thompson who shared their attitudes to a great extent, both on class superiority and on Créditiste camaraderie. As he explained: 'It was characteristic of Caouette, and particularly of Legault, to be suspicious of new people ... When the split came, as far as Caouette and myself are concerned, it was the old 'berets blancs' people who stayed with them and it was the new people, most of them professional people, who stayed with me.' As for the old Union leaders – Louis Even, Joe Marcotte, and Mercier – Thompson claimed 'they mixed up other things with social credit. But Father Lévesque, or Gilles Grégoire's father, Professor Grégoire, or some people who were basically students in a very intelligent way, I don't disagree with them at all.' In Thompson's view, the explanation for the split was obvious: 'Mr Caouette was under Gilberte's influence for so long that he seems to have inherited some of her attitudes. He is throwing out those who cannot get along with him, and he becomes smaller and smaller. It is another cycle. Like it was with Gilberte Côté.'

Caouette and Thompson had previously been at odds over Thompson's apparent preference for Fernand Ouellet, a new Créditiste, over Legault, who had always handled organizational and financial matters. In investigating the affair of the six, Thompson had chosen Marcoux to prosecute the guilty ones, all of them long-time Créditistes. In other words, he had chosen to side with the new guard against the old Créditistes. On both sides, continued partnership was intolerable.

Thus the strong feelings of class inferiority and the compensating emphasis on Créditiste camaraderie by the highly disaffected leaders created a deep division between old and new Créditistes. This gap, which widened with every new disagreement over strategy and tactics, contributed much to the eventual split.

D   THE THIRD DIMENSION OF CRÉDITISTE CULTURE: ORIENTATIONS
    TOWARDS GOVERNMENTAL OUTPUT

The third dimension is less prominent in reinforcing distinct subcultures and supporting the split. Orientations towards governmental output in general tend to be similar among Social Credit leaders of both east and west: there is not enough output of a beneficial kind, and the system is inadequate and unfair to a large segment of the population. This is generally what binds them all to the Social Credit party. Nevertheless, there are certain fundamental differences of outlook concerning the relation between the economic (particularly financial) and political systems. The Social Crediters have widely different views about the system of rewards and the new social welfare legislation and other so-called socialistic measures. These disagreements played a prominent role in hardening positions in the split. Many of these orientational differences were translated into competing doctrinal positions.

1 *Beliefs about the relationship between the economic and political system*

The previous description of the range of orientations on doctrinal orthodoxy provides a clue to the distribution of beliefs about 'who gets what, when, and how' in the economic and political systems. Western Social Crediters were clearly the least critical of the way in which the present economic and political systems operate to distribute rewards. The moderate Créditiste leaders were rather sceptical of what they regarded as the oversimplified beliefs of the doctrinaire Créditistes regarding the banking and economic systems. The highly disaffected leaders were critical of what they regarded as a huge swindle on the part of the financiers and bankers and were convinced that nationalizing the banks and distributing a basic dividend would cure all the major ills of the system.

The attitude of Réal Caouette was fairly representative of highly disaffected leaders: 'I feel that we live in a rich country. The old-line parties could, in wartime, find all the necessary billions of dollars to carry on war policies. If they can do it for war, I maintain *we* can do it in peacetime.' He understood this to be, in Douglas' terms, 'an age of abundance,' where atomic energy, power, and automation are rendering man superfluous in many areas of economic life. As a result, he thought, very few people are benefiting from the wealth which should accrue to all, and more and more people are suffering unemployment and deprivation. Caouette's alienation from the existing method of production dates back to depression times: 'I was looking for something, because I couldn't accept the system in those days.' Then he was introduced to Social Credit, through the newspaper *Vers Demain.*

It was Social Credit that made me believe that free enterprise is not responsible for what took place; the system is responsible. Free enterprise did everything it could to supply goods and services, and that is the main object of the economic system, to supply goods and services. But to get those goods and services to the consumers, that is an altogether different question. There the government should have taken action. It never did.

By the system Caouette meant the monetary and banking system which facilitates the flow of goods and services to the consumer. The fulcrum of the system was the banks, which 'take your property or your country as a guarantee and create, out of a stroke of a pen, all the money that the government requires today.' This in itself would not be bad, if the bankers did not use their function as agents to line their own pockets. In Caouette's conception of the monetary system, everything began and ended with the bankers. They had complete control of the supply of credit which they limited deliberately in order to be able to charge high interest rates on loans and thus make a handsome profit.

Caouette did not define his exact conception of the relation between the economic and political system. He implied, though, that he accepted the old Union des Electeurs theory that the bankers 'bought' the party politicians in order to prevent them from curbing their high interest or from nationalizing their banks. They allegedly did this through the large election funds, which the two old-line parties accumulated. Thus he made much of 'patronage, grease on road contracts, organizing for election funds, and things like that.'

In Caouette's mind, the solution was to change the system. This meant adopting the social credit theory of 'infusing purchasing power into the hands of consumers.' This must not, however, be done by borrowing and incurring new and deferred debt.

If we go deeper into debt, that won't solve the problem at all. It may be solved for five or ten years, as when Premier Lesage in the Province of Quebec was ready to borrow $550 million at 5¾ per cent interest for a period of thirty years. At the time of the borrowing, $550 million will be spent in the province of Quebec, and it will create jobs and attract new industries, but in thirty years from now, when I may no longer be living, my children will have to pay the capital plus the interest, which at that time will amount to $1,448,000,000. Now if my children ask themselves in thirty years 'Was my father sane or insane?' they'll be right, because we should not be allowed to act that way.

Rather, purchasing power should be increased by debt-free payments in the form of dividends, family allowances, and pensions which would not be financed by taxation but would be tied to the overall capacity for production in the society. This would not create inflation but would get the goods moving towards the consumers. In that way 'we'll save our system. Otherwise you'll see another war before ten years.'

There can be no doubt that Caouette together with other highly disaffected leaders actually understood the functioning of the economic system in these simplistic terms. Any economic measure taken by the government was automatically judged in terms of his own framework. Thus an austerity program might be accepted as a short-run emergency measure, but it would not be tolerated over the long run. It was for him a deflationary policy which is contrary to the expansionist theory of social credit. Old age pensions, on the other hand, were designed to increase revenue in a certain sector of the economy and therefore were seen by Social Crediters in a better light. If financed through higher taxes, however, these pensions were interpreted as but a mere transfer in purchasing power from one sector of the economy to the other, which in Social Credit eyes was still unacceptable. One can therefore understand Caouette's initial adverse reactions to economic measures such as dollar devaluation and the pension plan legislation introduced by Progressive Conservative and Liberal minority governments in Ottawa in 1962 and 1964 respectively. Such adverse judgments as he made were tempered somewhat by political considerations such as the obvious approval of the electorate for a particular kind of measure (eg, pensions).

The attitudes of a highly disaffected leader of lower status on economic policy questions reflected an even more simplistic training and approach. For him the monetary system was 'so simple ... Credit is 95 per cent of the business of our country. And credit, whether you like it or not, is simply controlled by a pencil.' The banks control the monetary and economic system like the ignition and starter control the automobile, or the switch controls the electric lighting in a room. They print the money or issue the credit, put it into circulation, and thereby set in motion the flow of goods and services. And by withdrawing money and restricting credit, they can bring the system to a halt as well. His solution was to nationalize the banks or enforce government control over the credit supply. He also thought alternative means for increasing purchasing power among the people could be used: 'I find that we must insist more and more on money and purchasing power which must be issued to the people without conditions. And I find that Douglas, by his two proposals, the national dividend and the compensatory rebate, still advocates the best means for issuing the money.'

His position on the relationship between the economic system and the political system was clear.

The old-line political parties are financed by the bankers and financiers. They are therefore controlled by them. When one realizes that political parties in many countries, above all in our own, are provided with funds which are ample enough to pay the voters to go and vote every four years, then, at any given moment, the government cannot be the government of the people. It is the government of those who supply the funds which buy the votes and which finance electoral campaigns.

It was the thesis of the Union des Electeurs that the network of international finance controls all governments. He clearly continued to adhere to this conspiratorial idea.

The moderate Créditiste leaders did not purport to have studied the economic and monetary system in such detail. But they were somewhat sceptical of a number of important aspects of the old berets blancs theory. The doctor would admit 'that the birth of credit comes through the chartered banks, to their profit' and that this was not acceptable. He also felt that credit should be made available 'only after study, after compiling statistics, and according to the needs of the country, rather than according to the whim of a few people, or the government members.' And he thought that 'if necessary, a form of dividend might be given – family allowances or a similar kind of payment.' But 'that is about all [of the old Créditiste theory] that I will subscribe to.' He disagreed with Caouette on the nature of the dividend: 'There are other means of adjusting the purchasing power to the gross national product.' He also differed with Caouette on his understanding of the nature of the equation between purchasing power and production.

It is not an equation, a one-to-one equation between the one and the other. If we increase the purchasing power a little, the gross national product will be taken care of. There is no need to equalize them completely because of velocity of circulation [of money]. We can have more products in circulation than the exact amount of money that will buy them.

Finally, he could not accept Caouette's complete aversion to banks: 'For Caouette, banks are satanic institutions and it is absolutely necessary to get rid of them by giving to the Bank of Canada the power to issue credit, and by increasing the liquid reserve of the chartered banks to 100 per cent. That's a viewpoint that I can't accept.' Accordingly, he thought: 'While it is true that the chartered banks, by their power to create credit, restrict the progress of the government and hurt the development of the country, it is absolutely false to say that banks per se harm the development of industries, since it is the banks themselves which allow these industries to be developed.' The doctor would have co-ordinated the policies of the Bank of Canada and the chartered banks to permit a dual policy of private industrial development and public development.

The high school teacher and the young lawyer showed similar independent outlooks. The high school teacher felt 'that Caouette in his speeches put his finger on the heart of the malady from which society suffers, disequilibrium between production and consumption, and maldistribution of wealth.' He believed that 'it would be necessary at some given time in the future to carry out a reform of the monetary system.' But he balked at the idea, which he found pervasive among the old Créditistes, that 'everything was bad in the present system and everything had to be reformed. And everything was good in the system of social credit.' And he could not accept the national dividend.

It's absolutely ridiculous. It should never have been adopted. I have the impression that it did us considerable harm in various election campaigns of the past. How many times was Caouette reminded of that ridiculous proposal of distributing $100 a month to every Canadian as a national dividend. I never believed in it, and I still am unable to believe in it ... it's impossible. Much has been said about inflation emerging upon the application of social credit principles. I think that we would take a gigantic step towards inflation by handing over to every citizen a dividend of $100 a month. At that time, what would the money be worth.

But the young lawyer conceded that 'the monetary doctrine made good sense.' And he was even inclined to accept the basic dividend, with certain qualifications. However, he had 'always reproached Caouette for not telling the whole truth about social credit. Even if the system of social credit were put in operation today, it wouldn't bear fruit immediately. A minimum of fifteen years would be necessary.' The solution, then, was 'to accept social security measures in the form they exist today until the time when a national dividend can be distributed which would replace all national social security measures.'

There was obviously much potential for conflict in this sphere, and it arose even before the 1962 election. For example, during the 1961 convention Caouette had led a group of old Créditistes in proposing that a basic dividend be included in the platform. In the 1962 election campaign he returned to this proposal, despite its earlier rejection. And in the 1962–3 parliament he often embarrassed his western colleagues and the new Créditiste MPs by issuing certain statements along these lines. Among his own supporters, particularly those who had formerly belonged to the berets blancs, such statements never harmed him. They accepted his framework and approach on these questions of economic and monetary policy: According to one highly disaffected leader: 'Two bank directors came to meet Caouette to discuss the following proposition with him: if he needed money in the future, they would lend it to him. They were trying to make him change his mind about them. But nothing changed.' And another highly disaffected leader explained: 'As Réal has often told us, we don't know the mechanics of a machine, but if we put the key in it, then it goes and we know that it is working well. We let others, more educated [avancés] than us, study and control it.' A highly disaffected leader of low status put it even more bluntly: 'There are eight chartered banks controlled by fifty directors each; that makes four hundred individuals who control the thing that controls everything else. It's an economic dictatorship.'

But among western Social Crediters these attitudes caused much embarrassment. Many felt, along with Robert Thompson, that the Créditistes

are not practical. They talk about things in the implementation of social credit which scare away the technical people who know a little about the operation of the economy. They make such fantastic promises to overthrow or upset our economy in implementing social credit. These things would be absolutely wrong. They talk about a $100 per month dividend, they talk about raising the tax exemption to $5,000 immediately, and they talk about spending billions of dollars. You can't do that. This is where they just don't apply reason. This is where we had our basic differences. We had agreed that we would not talk in terms of figures, that we would only talk in terms of principles, and this is where Caouette completely disagreed.

According to Thompson, the same attitudes are shared by other Alberta Social Crediters, including Premier Manning himself: 'Mr Manning has had years of proven experience as a government administrator, and his way of expressing social credit takes a very definite pattern in the light of this experience.' Thompson himself tends to 'express social credit in terms of foreign trade. This is something Douglas does not talk very much about.'

There was conflict with Caouette on many different points. Mr Thompson clearly did not have the same jaded image of banks and bankers. He had a much more pragmatic and relativistic view of the faults in the present economic system, and was much more tolerant of the existing political party system and its function, calling only for realignment rather than wholesale reform.

There is going to have to be a realignment ... this is not a political party thing, it is a principle. There are only two philosophies and two principles on the political scene in Canada today that are basic, and because our political parties don't fit into them, we are having troubles. One is socialism, the other is social credit ... I am not interested in perpetuating a party by the name of Social Credit. If I am convinced that another party is implementing the necessary basic reforms, whether they call it Social Credit or not, I will be out there to help them implement it.

There is no sign here of the Créditiste concern for election funds and bondage to financiers.

Thus there are sharply differing conceptions of the economic and monetary systems as they relate to governmental output between the highly disaffected and moderate protest leaders. They might have been reconciled to enable the working partnership to continue, but the stresses and strains in other spheres proved too great.

2 *Attitudes towards social welfare legislation, socialism, and the expansion of the state apparatus*

In this sphere, there was much closer agreement: most Social Crediters, east and west, were strongly opposed to socialism of any kind. Modern-day social credit defines itself almost exclusively in these terms. One can recognize it as much in Robert Thompson's attitudes as in Réal Caouette's, in the views of the moderate leaders as well as in those of the highly disaffected.

Caouette stated: 'We oppose government ownership or control over the economy because we feel that it encroaches on the dignity of the human being and the freedom of the human being, and it is also a barrier to personal initiative. We have to create an economic climate in which personal initiative will be encouraged.' Thompson saw socialism and greater state centralization as 'subservience of the individual to the state. Socialism has never developed on its own strength; it has always been a parasite on something that has been done before.' And according to one highly disaffected leader of low status: 'There is at present [1965] a socialist upswing in the province, in the present government. There are measures being passed which run contrary to social credit principles and which are carrying [glissent] us to the left.' The doctor expounded:

I have a kind of natural aversion to socialism. Within philosophic notions, I am not able to accept that the state, which is constituted of individuals, can be better than the individuals themselves. I tell myself that it is unthinkable that a state can give better service than a group of individuals who, above and beyond a certain interest for the common good, have a particular incentive either to make a profit or to work for their own advantage or that of their employer.

There are occasional deviations from this rule. The high school teacher was ready to accept certain socialistic measures: 'Whether one likes it or not, government is going to be obliged by force of circumstances to extend its powerful arm into many domains. Then, little by little, this mentality, this fear of socialism, will lessen, it will diminish continually.'

More important than any doctrinal conflict on this point, was the attitude towards the practice which has evolved in Social Credit of Alberta. As one highly disaffected leader saw it, Premier Manning espoused social credit principles, but passed socialistic measures: 'They go in for old age pensions, they go in for a little social welfare legislation here and there, but that is really socialism, not social credit. Social credit never says: "Take away from one to give to others." ' There was a recognition, however, that Manning's administration was conservative, efficient, and generally opposed to governmental interference in the private sector.

E THE FOURTH DIMENSION OF CRÉDITISTE CULTURE: SENSE OF EFFICACY IN THE PROCESS OF POLITICAL DECISION-MAKING

There did not seem to be a significant difference in the leaders' sense of their own efficacy in the political decision-making process between moderate leaders and highly disaffected leaders. In general, the attitude was that the political system could be strongly influenced, particularly through opposition political parties. The agreement on this point was an important factor in the original union in 1960 between east and west wings.

It is clear that Caouette conceived of his organization as a political party, rather than a movement, which sought to form a government or tried to influence policy from the opposition backbenches. In his own words: 'Party or movement, I don't care what you call the Ralliement, it's all the same to me.' This was a clear departure from the philosophy of the leaders of the Union des Electeurs who were always anxious to distinguish their movement from the so-called political parties. There was not, however, 100 per cent agreement among Ralliement members on this point.[12] Caouette was sensitive to this factor and constantly emphasized that the Ralliement, though a party itself, was not like other political parties; it was responsible to the electorate rather than to the election financiers.

On this point Robert Thompson was quite inclined to agree. Unlike his predecessor, Solon Low, he saw the Social Credit party strictly in party terms. But he was not satisfied with political parties as presently constituted. He, too, wanted to present Social Credit as an entirely new kind of party, one which was not corrupt and susceptible to political machinations. But he was more inclined to see reform in terms of realignment rather than democratization per se. The parties, he thought, should be reconstructed along the lines of true principle.

Whereas the difference between party and movement became a fundamental part of the conflict between the Union des Electeurs and the National Social Credit Association under Solon Low, it never contributed to the Caouette-Thompson split. Even when the question of party loyalty arose in the affair of the six, Caouette never argued that the nature of the Ralliement permitted its members to belong to two different parliamentary groups simultaneously. In the case of a movement, this might have been permissible. As long as the Créditistes were part of a national political party designated Social Credit, dual membership or loyalty was forbidden. Nevertheless, it may well be that the tradition of loose affiliation and local autonomy in the Union des Electeurs' ideology influenced former berets blancs members Gérard Perron and Gilbert Rondeau to pledge support to the Liberals without even consulting their party leaders in advance. Both, after all, had participated in the 1956 front with the provincial Liberals in which Créditistes like Réal Caouette had run as Liberal candidates.

12 For Laurent Legault the distinction was important: 'I see a great difference in the two. First, in the control of the movement; we avoid becoming, for example, like the Union Nationale in the province of Quebec, which was led by the MPs. It was a "political party"; the MPs controlled everything. We don't want that in the Ralliement. We want the Ralliement to remain the instrument of the people, of the elite in each constituency. The second thing to avoid is that the Ralliement des Créditistes must never fall under the domination of financial powers who would control them. These are the two things to avoid.' This was clearly a residue of the experience with the Union des Electeurs. In the case of Legault, it served his own ends – to keep control of the movement in the hands of the party activists outside parliament, including himself. But there was also the aura of political purity which the Créditistes wished to preserve and which they hoped would influence the voter.

The similarity in roles perceived for the two wings of Social Credit by their respective leaders is reflected in the similar campaign slogan which they adopted in consecutive elections. In 1963 Thompson appealed to the voters to elect enough Social Credit members to give the party 'the balance of power' in Ottawa. In 1965 Réal Caouette campaigned on the slogan: 'Elect fifty Créditistes to the federal House and give them the balance of power in Ottawa.'

The other MPs generally had the same conception of their role: they were at most a ginger group, a minority party, which could exercise certain pressure in order to bring about small but important reforms in Ottawa. They were educators of their electorate, responsible to them in the sense that they were easily accessible, willing to help, and anxious to inform. They were not, however, able to cope with every personal problem or engineer miracles in the day-to-day administration of employment, taxation, and licensing regulations. The high school teacher had tried to execute his self-defined role as 'the envoy of the people' largely through intermediate bodies such as unions, chambers of commerce, and parish associations. It had been impossible for him to meet with all the individuals who wanted to see their deputy: 'Personal contact, from individual to individual, is practically impossible ... as a federal MP I would receive about ten people per week, that's all, that's a maximum, people who have direct problems with the federal government.' The young lawyer felt that

The role of the deputy is conditioned by his personality, his intellectual background. He makes suggestions or studies a problem in depth only when he is the spokesman in the party or the specialist in a domain in which he can accomplish something. Most of the time the deputies rely on a few parliamentary leaders in the party and only attend to organizing for their next campaign ... they also represent the people. That forms an integral part of the function of a deputy. The people see in their deputy their intermediary, someone important who intervenes for them, even if it doesn't concern him at all. We can't give these people short shrift ... even if our efforts don't yield a practical result, it pleases people to see that we are concerned about them.

It was perhaps because the role of the ordinary opposition deputy was perceived to be so mundane and limited that certain of the more ambitious Créditistes sought to enhance their position through negotiation and intrigue. There was talk of obtaining cabinet posts for Thompson and Marcoux and even for Chapdelaine. Perron and Rondeau undoubtedly hoped to attain certain special favours from a minority Liberal government in signing the pledge to support them in office. Girouard and Ouellet did not hesitate to cross the floor and join the PCs. H.A. Olson was intrigued by the possibility that he could become a Liberal minister of agriculture.[13] Such displays of tenuous party loyalty were as common in one wing of the party as in another. And they inevitably caused strains within the party. Charges and counter-charges of infidelity flew back and forth within the Social Credit caucus during and after the affair of the six. They were obviously an important precipitating factor in the split. Like-

13 In 1968 he ran as a Liberal candidate, was elected, and subsequently was appointed to that post.

wise, the various displays of infidelity caused serious strains within the lower and middle echelons of the party. For example, after the affair of the six a number of the chief organizers in the party pressed for the expulsion of the signatories. They were only partially placated by the convening of the assembly in Quebec in May 1963 in which Réal Caouette and Laurent Legault defended the accused. These tactics acted as an exacerbating factor in the growing division between the two groups.

Conclusion: Protest Orientations, Alliance Patterns, and the Pattern of Schism in the Movement

From the detailed analysis of political orientations it is clear that alliances do form among leaders of subgroups who share similar protest orientations in opposition to leaders of subgroups exhibiting markedly different orientations. In the case of the 1963 split, the highly disaffected Créditiste leaders of both high and low socio-economic status shared similar orientations in their primitive political beliefs and in every dimension of Créditiste culture, and these orientations were frequently very different from those held by the moderate protest leaders.

Thus in their primitive political beliefs, although all subgroups tended to regard politics as a 'dirty game,' the highly disaffected Créditistes were on the whole disposed to intertwine metaphysical principles and practical politics, to favour leadership of an authoritarian kind, to adopt orthodox positions on social credit doctrine, and to express themselves in highly ideological terms. The moderate leaders drew a sharp distinction between religion and politics, were completely opposed to authoritarian leadership, and valued qualities of statesmanship and diplomacy, deplored uncritical acceptance of doctrines and belief systems, and refrained entirely from ideologizing.

In their feelings of national identity, the highly disaffected leaders were acutely conscious of their French Canadianism and of their Catholicism. They regarded Quebec as a separate and distinct province and looked to the Quebec government as their real political home. There was some difference of opinion, however, on desirable constitutional and political forms. A majority advocated a decentralized form of federalism in which the provinces would exercise considerable autonomy, but a strong minority favoured a form of associated statehood for French Canadians and, in a few instances, outright separatism. The moderate leaders' statements on nationalism were more temperate. They also favoured a less radical compromise in constitutional negotiations with English Canada over the rights of French Canadians and the status of Quebec.

These orientations also affected the images which the subgroups had of western Social Crediters. The highly disaffected Créditistes were convinced that the westerners had betrayed social credit to the financial powers and refused to regard them as bona fide Social Crediters. The moderate leaders regarded their western counterparts as pragmatic political men and respected their greater training, savoir faire, and political experience.

In their sense of identification with their fellow citizens, the highly disaffected leaders showed themselves to be acutely sensitive to their inferior status in French-Canadian society and in positions of authority within the movement. They deeply resented the upper middle-class professionals and businessmen who had more education, greater linguistic facility, and a deeper appreciation of culture and etiquette. They compensated for their feelings of inadequacy by cultivating a sense of camaraderie with other Créditistes of similar status and orientation who had belonged to the movement for several years. They emphasized past contributions to the movement and knowledge of social credit doctrine as special marks of achievement in Quebec Social Credit in order to elevate their status in relation to their co-partisans. The moderate leaders strongly opposed what they regarded as in-group cliquishness among the old guard Créditistes. They reacted by emphasizing their superior social status and education and their feelings of disdain for those who had formerly adhered to a parochial sect.

The highly disaffected leaders strongly attacked the distribution and rewards system and offered extremely simplistic notions of the workings of the monetary and banking systems. Lacking the knowledge and training required to appreciate the more technical aspects of the system, they reacted frequently by finding conspiratorial explanations for its deficiencies. In their attitudes towards government ownership and intervention, they manifested a similar simplistic and conspiratorial outlook. The moderate leaders could appreciate some of the complexities in technical economic questions and were willing to admit their ignorance in these areas. They were therefore less critical of the monetary and rewards system. They were inclined to ridicule conspiratorial theories, and their criticism of socialism was generally on a more philosophical plane.

Contrary to expectation, the highly disaffected leaders had a relatively strong sense of political efficacy. In particular, they were optimistic about the possibility of influencing politics at the provincial level. The moderate leaders were inclined to favour concentrated activity at the federal level, although there were several notable exceptions to the general pattern on this issue.

In short, one can detect distinct sets of protest orientations which distinguish each of the two major subgroups, the highly disaffected leaders and the moderate protest leaders. If these orientations were placed on a continuum of political dissent, the highly disaffected leaders would clearly fall towards the extreme end of the continuum, and the moderate leaders would fall somewhere in the middle range.

Not all the dimensions of Créditiste culture, however, are equally significant in producing splits. In the 1963 split the contradictions in the protest orientations of the various groups of leaders which most exacerbated tensions between the subgroups emerged in primitive political beliefs, conceptions of national identity (both as they related to non-francophones and to francophones), perceptions of class and status differences within the national (French-Canadian) grouping, and previous political and partisan affiliations (Créditiste camaraderie). Differences in orientations towards government policies and outputs and towards the political process were of minor importance in the process leading to the schism. It is probable that these same dimensions in protest orientations are also more important in other splits (with the exception perhaps of differing Créditiste conceptions of non-francophones, since the 1963 split, unlike other Créditiste splits, directly involved an external non-francophone group, the western Social Crediters).

Several other factors made the 1963 split somewhat atypical. First, differences in attitude and behaviour of highly disaffected leaders of higher and lower status were never clear, and thus the second phase in the process of schism, involving political withdrawal on the part of the highly disaffected leaders of higher status and an alliance between highly disaffected leaders of lower status and more moderate lower-class dissenters never occurred. Two of the highly disaffected leaders of higher status did waiver in their support for Caouette for some time before coming down in favour of the schism. Ultimately, however, ethnic and linguistic considerations left all highly disaffected Créditiste leaders united in their opposition to the Thompsonites, who were regarded as excessively Anglophile, new guard, and motivated by political pragmatism.

The role of Caouette was particularly important in this split. Personal ambitions involving his desire to become the national Social Credit leader led him to adopt the role of chief schismatic, which in other circumstances he is more reluctant to play. Because he could command the personal support and loyalty of so many other Créditiste leaders, he was able to attract into his camp many who might otherwise have opposed a split. Thus although a majority of our respondents indicated that they did not initially favour a split, most ultimately acquiesced in the strategy which Caouette and the highly disaffected leaders of lower status adopted.

In its major lines, however, the 1963 split did exhibit the same general dynamic which had been found to operate in other Créditiste splits, and one which probably occurs in other right-wing protest movements as well. The 1963 split was essentially an internal rather than an external split, involving alliances between subgroups exhibiting very divergent protest orientations. The tendency for highly disaffected leaders of radical protest syndromes to act as catalysts in splits of this sort has manifested itself on several occasions (most recently in the 1966 split) and is likely to recur in the future. When these divergences in protest orientations combine with differences in status, partisan background and generational differences, a more fundamental schism may be expected to occur. This schism will either reorient the movement in an entirely new direction and trigger a new phase in its development – as occurred in 1957 with the consolidation phase and as is likely to recur in the 1970s with the institutionalization phase – or it will destroy the movement entirely.

PART V

CONCLUSIONS

9
The Politics of Right-Wing Protest Movements

What has been discovered about the phenomenon of right-wing protest from this study of the Créditiste movement in Quebec? What implications do these findings have for socioeconomic and political developments in Quebec? Does this study suggest anything about the politics of other protest and revolutionary movements?

In part I we discussed the nature of Social Credit in Quebec. We argued that Créditisme is a particular manifestation of a right-wing protest movement. It is a movement rather than a party, pressure group, or some other form of political competition because its members are committed to political change and have adopted the tactics and the political forms which are conducive to achieving these objectives. It is a protest rather than a revolutionary movement because its objectives of political change are limited in scope and are not directed towards system transformation. It is right-wing rather than centrist or left-wing because its ideology and program are essentially designed to resurrect a society of the past and to preserve a segment of the population which is in decline in the face of modernizing socioeconomic forces.

Moreover, as a right-wing protest movement it exhibits certain general characteristics which have been observed in other sociopolitical movements. It has evolved through a number of different phases that correspond to changing leadership styles and strategies of action. The first was the mobilization phase, dominated by leaders of the first generation like Gilberte Côté-Mercier and Louis Even, who were prophets or men of words and were skilful in the tasks of political socialization and proselytization. The second was the consolidation phase, directed by brilliant propagandists and skilful organizers of the second generation like Réal Caouette and Laurent Legault. This phase involved the conversion of Social Credit proselytes into political activists and electoral cadres. The third is the institutionalization phase, which is about to begin. It is engineered by shrewd political pragmatists and skilful negotiators who wish to transform the movement into a conventional political party. The likely leaders of this phase are young men of the third generation of Créditistes such as Camil Samson, Phil Cossette, André Fortin, and René Matte. The process of evolution from one phase to the next involves internal conflict and factionalism between subgroups of leaders. This pattern of factionalism, which has been widely observed in other political movements, is the key to an explanation of the development of right-wing protest movements.

Part II traced the historical development of the movement through two of its phases, mobilization and consolidation. In the first phase, in contrast to the Alberta Social Credit leaders, the directors of the Créditiste movement failed to mobilize the Quebec population. This was partially due to the lack of conduciveness of Quebec's political culture and socioeconomic structure, which were not then amenable to political reform. It was also due to the inferior organizational skills of the Quebec Social Credit leaders and their inability to disseminate propaganda. Nevertheless, the directors did succeed in introducing social credit ideas to a large segment of the Quebec population and also created a small but dedicated group of converts to the movement. In the next phase, the Ralliement des Créditistes consolidated and expanded on the social base of the Union des Electeurs and transformed the movement's followers into political and electoral cadres. Under Réal Caouette's determined leadership and brilliant campaign strategy, the party succeeded in penetrating the deeply rooted bipartisan tradition in Quebec and attracting between one-fifth and one-quarter of the Quebec electorate into its camp. It also pre-empted the leadership of the national Social Credit party from the western wings in Alberta and British Columbia which had allowed the national movement to collapse.

However, the party's appeal was limited. Although it made some inroads in the Saguenay-Lac Saint-Jean region and in urban Quebec City, its electoral strength was greatest and most durable in those areas in which the first generation of devotees had organized most effectively: in the northern (Abitibi) region, in the Eastern Townships, and in the region south of Quebec City. These were mainly rural or small-urban population centres in which economic conditions were stagnant or deteriorating and emigration was high. In the large metropolitan centres of the province, and in particular in Montreal, the determined organizational efforts of the party failed to reap any returns. Réal Caouette's appeal was essentially to the conservative lower middle and working classes of rural and small-urban Quebec: the uneducated, economically deprived, and tradition-minded. It had no attraction for expanding population sectors such as the educated, affluent, and modern middle classes in the large urban centres, or the even more rapidly increasing unionized working classes in the metropolitan areas which were seeking more progressive and more modern solutions to their economic plight. The third generation of Créditiste leaders, increasingly conscious of these limitations and of their threat to the long-run survival of the movement, have begun to forge a new strategy. They appear ready to launch the movement on its third phase.

In the analysis of the movement's development two characteristics proved to be outstanding: the protest quality of the ideology of the movement and the factional pattern of its behaviour and evolution. The protest quality of the ideology appeared first of all in the doctrine of Major Douglas which offered a right-wing critique of the economic, social, and political systems and a monetary reform solution. But it was also evident in the French-Canadian interpretation and adaptation of that doctrine and in the strategy and tactics defined by the leaders of the Créditiste movement at various stages in its development. The factional pattern of behaviour resulted in the numerous conflicts and splits that occurred between 1936 and the present and particularly in the schisms of 1939, 1957, 1963, and 1966.

In part III a social and attitudinal profile of the Créditiste leaders was presented which sought to explain these two characteristics: protest and factionalism. We found that the typical Créditiste leader exhibits many of the social characteristics of the traditional rural elite in Quebec: he is a male of about forty to fifty years of age, of commercial or professional occupation, higher-than-average income, and higher-than-average education. He joined the movement when still young, primarily because it offered an outlet for his feelings of dissatisfaction with the economic situation which he then confronted. Once he joined, he became a faithful and life-long supporter of its objectives and a committed exponent of its ideology. His attitudes of dissent against the economic and political systems are well-articulated but moderate and not at all conspiratorial or authoritarian.

Two other important subgroups of leaders also emerged: the highly disaffected and the lower-class dissenters. The highly disaffected leader is of lower socioeconomic status than the moderate leader. He also exhibits more extreme attitudes of disaffection which form a radical protest syndrome. He rejects virtually all aspects of the existing economic and political systems and advocates their radical reform. He is more authoritarian, more ethnocentric, and more ideologically rigid. He is also more active than the moderate leader at the lower echelons of the movement but does not rise as frequently to top leadership positions. The lower-class dissenter is either a highly disaffected or moderately disaffected leader of low socioeconomic status who is also more active in splits. An alliance between these two overlapping subgroups of highly disaffected leaders and lower-class dissenters is formed along status lines against the moderate leaders, after the highly disaffected leaders of higher status lose interest in the movement and withdraw from active political involvement. This alliance determines the pattern of schism in the movement.

The typical pattern for the process of factionalism and schism was perceived as follows: when the fortunes of the movement decline, or the movement suffers a setback, feelings of disaffection come into play. The highly disaffected leaders who have previously focused their dissent on external enemies transfer it to the internal leadership of the movement. They direct their attacks particularly against the moderate leaders. The result of the confrontation between these two major subgroups is factionalism leading to outright schism. The dynamics of this process were explained on the structural level and the sociological level. On the structural level normal mechanisms of conflict resolution and control, which are present in conventional political parties and revolutionary movements, fail to operate in right-wing protest movements like Social Credit in Quebec. Thus when disputes over strategy and tactics arise, the unity of the movement is destroyed. On the sociological level, when the objectives of the movement appear to be frustrated, the equilibrium between feelings of dissent and reform attitudes in the protest orientations of highly disaffected leaders is upset. Finding no satisfactory outlet for their grievances against their external enemies, the leaders turn inward and begin to attack their co-partisans. Their actions ultimately produce the series of schisms in the movement.

Part IV undertook a more detailed analysis of these protest orientations which emerge once the factional process is underway and which are also at the root of each major split. We selected the split between the Caouettistes and Thompsonites in 1963 as a case study and interviewed its major participants in depth, hypothesizing that the differences in background and attitudes between moderate leaders and highly disaffected leaders would appear as orientational differences. This hypothesis was confirmed. The major contradictions in the protest orientations of these two sub-groups occurred in their primitive political beliefs, their conceptions of their national identity, their perceptions of class and status differences within the movement, and their previous political and partisan affiliations. Therefore, the structural, sociological, and psychological dimensions complement and reinforce each other in the dynamics of factional and protest behaviour.

This explanation of the pattern of development of the Créditiste movement has broader implications for the evolving socioeconomic and political situation in Quebec. The rise of right-wing protest movements in industrialized societies undergoing socioeconomic change is an index of the balance of socioeconomic and political forces in such a society. In the case of Quebec, the rise and durability of Social Credit in Quebec reflects the long-standing alienation and political unrest of the rural and small-urban lower classes in the province. However, the limited mobilization and consolidation of the Créditiste movement also reflects the political weakness and decline of these classes in the face of modernization.

Right-wing protest movements tend to arise in modern industrialized societies among those segments of the population that wish to cling to traditional attitudes and beliefs in the face of socioeconomic change. In the case of Quebec, socioeconomic modernization began in the period from 1871 to 1921 and transformed a society which was 77 per cent rural and agricultural into one which was 56 per cent urban and industrialized.[1] Political beliefs and attitudes, which were highly traditional and conservative throughout the nineteenth and early twentieth centuries, began to change much more slowly.[2] When the social credit doctrine was first presented to Quebeckers in the 1930s, it had only limited appeal and then largely to those Quebeckers who were living in rural and small-urban centres in which industrialization and urbanization had already caused severe dislocation. The original militants of the Union des Electeurs had a distinct class composition and outlook: rural lower-class, conservative, and alienated. The Union leaders were never able to broaden that narrow class and ideological base.

Under certain conditions a right-wing protest movement can expand beyond its original class base and appeal to other segments of society. For example, Social Credit in Alberta managed to spread rapidly to both rural and urban areas in a time of severe economic deprivation. William Aberhart, its powerful evangelical leader, was able to make his message relevant to all segments of Alberta society; he was able

---

1 Marcel Rioux, 'Sur l'évolution des idéologies au Québec,' *Revue de l'Institut de Sociologie,* Université Libre de Bruxelles (1968), 108–9. See also Marcel Rioux, *Quebec in Question,* translated by James Boake (Toronto: James, Lewis and Samuel, 1971), 34–5.
2 Rioux, *Quebec in Question,* 63–5. See also Trudeau, *La Grève de l'amiante* (Montréal: les éditions Cité Libre, 1956), 10ff.

to do so because economic conditions were severely depressed, his message was cast in general eschatological rather than in particular class terms, and his personality was sufficiently charismatic and appealing to transcend class lines.

The first generation of Créditiste leaders, Louis Even and Gilberte Côté-Mercier, lacked the personal qualities and the organizational skills which might have permitted Créditisme to transcend its narrow class base. They were able to rationalize their electoral failures by appealing to the fundamentalist principles in the Douglas doctrine, but this served merely to narrow further the social base of the movement. Moreover, the Union Nationale party of Maurice Duplessis had firmly implanted itself in those very areas in which the Créditiste appeal was potentially strong: the rural and small-urban regions outside metropolitan Montreal. By the 1950s it was clear that the movement had no future as a political and electoral force in Quebec unless it changed its leaders, strategy, and tactics.

The development of right-wing protest movements is often characterized by sudden emergence, the achievement of a modicum of support in rural and small-urban areas, and then an inability to expand further. At this point they either disintegrate or a split occurs in their ranks which enables them to redefine their strategy and tactics. Fortunately for the Créditistes, by the 1950s a new generation of leaders had emerged who were capable of resuscitating the movement. This second generation, as is frequently the case in political movements, was more politically minded than the first generation; as well, this younger generation was led by Réal Caouette, a seasoned political campaigner. Most important, however, political conditions were ripe for third-party penetration in Quebec in the early 1960s. The modernization which had occurred at the socioeconomic level in the 1930s finally produced a transformation in Quebec political culture in the late 1950s. The 'quiet revolution' which brought the provincial Liberals to power in 1960 legitimized appeals to political reform and change. In addition, a new medium of political communication – television – had emerged by the late 1950s, and its use by a skilful political propagandist revolutionized electoral campaigning. Most important, lower middle and working classes in the rural and small-urban areas were even more marginal in the 1960s than they had been in the 1930s, since industrialization had been staunchly supported and accelerated by Premier Duplessis, and urbanization had also increased rapidly. The lower classes in the rural and small-urban areas were more and more conscious of the gap between themselves and the burgeoning middle class in the large urban areas, as the new media of communication revealed so clearly. And economic conditions in the province, which were generally bad, were particularly depressed at the time. It is no wonder that Real Caouette received such a welcome hearing in the regions of Abitibi, the Eastern Townships, and Quebec City in 1962.

Despite this electoral penetration, the Créditiste advance was, of necessity, limited. Caouette's appeal, like that of his predecessors, was essentially to certain classes. Although his party succeeded in winning some support from the more nationalist oriented urban groups, its electoral base was essentially lower class and rural.[3] Its leadership cadres were composed primarily of the alienated rural and small-urban

3 See Vincent Lemieux, 'The Election in the Constituency of Lévis,' in John Meisel (ed.), *Papers on the 1962 Election* (Toronto: University of Toronto Press, 1964), 51.

petit bourgeois elite. Caouette, who was a Douglas fundamentalist, knew no other message than that which he had learned from Even and Côté-Mercier: a narrow right-wing monetary reform appeal. Such an appeal holds little attraction for the expanding urban sectors of a modern society.

The efforts which the Créditiste militants made in Montreal after 1963 proved to be futile. But the poorer areas of Montreal were not deaf to third-party appeals, as the success of the Parti Québécois in the provincial election of 1970 revealed so clearly. The idiom in which René Lévesque and his lieutenants spoke was more meaningful to the metropolitan working classes; it was a nationalist and statist appeal which stamped itself as distinctly of the left.

It is clear, then, that the electoral setbacks which the Créditistes experienced in the period after 1963 were predictable, given the narrow basis of their right-wing protest appeal and the restricted social composition of their movement. Every effort at broadening the base of the movement, including the recruitment of middle-class professionals and notables, merely led to internal conflict. And the electoral setbacks triggered the process of factionalism and schism.

Thus the Créditiste appeal in Quebec, and for that matter any right-wing protest appeal operating in a similar context, is of necessity a limited one. Quebec society has already evolved beyond the stage in which right-wing protest movements are capable of expanding their base and assuming political power. The only choice for the next generation of Créditiste leaders is one of institutionalization, which involves the absorption of the movement into a more moderate right-of-centre grouping.

It appears that these findings can be applied to right-wing protest movements beyond the boundaries of Quebec. The leadership of Social Credit in Quebec, as we have discovered, is essentially lower middle class. It espouses an ideology which, while distinctive in its adherence to Major Douglas' ideas, is nevertheless fairly representative of all right-wing protests: opposition to high taxes and heavy government spending, fear of statism and government intervention, dislike of welfare legislation and socialism, stress on individual initiative and private enterprise, and susceptibility to racial prejudice and anti-Semitism. It should not be surprising, therefore, if the social and attitudinal profiles of leaders of other right-wing protest movements are similar to those of the Créditiste leaders. There may be similar leadership subgroups of moderate protesters, highly disaffected protesters, and lower-class dissenters. They may then have a similar protest dynamic and tendency to schism. They may exhibit similar developmental patterns and generational conflicts. Some of the movements which might fall under this rubric are the Poujadist movement in France, the National Democratic party (NPD) in West Germany, and the American Independence party in the United States. None of these movements has yet been studied in depth or analysed over a sustained period of time.[4] Nevertheless, the little evidence that exists points to a similar tendency to factionalism in both the Poujadist

4 The only book-length study of the Poujadist movement published to date is Stanley Hoffmann, *Le mouvement poujade* (Paris: Librairie A. Colin, 1956). It was written, however, at a time when the Poujadists were just coming into public prominence and only covers three or four years of its early development.

and NPD movements.[5] Too little is yet known about the internal composition and development of the Wallace movement to say anything definite about it.[6]

Our findings may also have relevance, with appropriate modifications, for studies of right-wing revolutionary movements such as nazism or Italian fascism and even in some respects for left-wing protest and left-wing revolutionary movements. Several authors have pointed to the importance of leadership subgroups and factional conflict in these movements.[7] Similar dynamics of factionalism may be latent in such movements, although they are influenced by different structural and personality factors. It is natural to ask, then, whether the different social and attitudinal characteristics and patterns of participation of their leadership groups produce different patterns of factionalism. Are the alliance patterns in splits similar or different in such movements? What factors account for the relative success or failure of right-wing protest movements as compared with other types of movements in different social contexts?

The framework evolved here applies primarily to the internal dynamics of right-wing protest movements. But it also suggests something about the behaviour of these movements which has important implications for the larger society in which they operate. The framework emphasizes the factional process and its effects in producing internal schisms. Such schisms lead to the formation of new wings and the ideological reorientation of old wings of the movement. In some instances they have a rejuvenating effect on the movement's political fortunes. The new wing of the movement, by freeing itself from the impediments and stereotypes of its progenitor, is sometimes able to compete more effectively for support, and may achieve greater success in the political arena. This is what occurred with the Ralliement des Créditistes after 1957. Similarly, an old wing, by reorienting itself after a split, can revitalize itself and increase its political appeal. Thus the Ralliement Créditiste adopted a more federalist position on the question of Quebec's role in Confederation after its nationalist and indépendentiste members split in 1966 and formed the Ralliement National. Although its popular vote support continued to decline, the party succeeded in enhancing its national image and also managed to increase its legislative representation in 1968 from nine to fourteen seats.

However, a more frequent result of factionalism is the weakening and destruction of the movement. Factionalism generally leads to open fragmentation, splintering, and schism. Schisms of this sort generally have dire consequences for the movement, because they first of all reduce the concerted strength of the movement. Instead of

---

5 Hoffmann discusses some incidents of factional conflict in the Poujadist movement in his book. *Ibid.*, 403. The tendency became even more obvious after the movement suffered a decline. A split in the NPD occurred in 1967.

6 For a brief analysis of the social base of the Wallace movement in its early stages, see M. Rogin, 'Wallace and the Middle Class: The White Backlash in Wisconsin, *Public Opinion Quarterly* (Spring 1966).

7 See, for example, Joseph Nyomarky, *Charisma and Factionalism in the Nazi Party* (Minneapolis: University of Minnesota Press, 1961), and R. Heberle, *From Democracy to Nazism* (Baton Rouge: Louisiana State University Press, 1945). For a more general approach to factionalism in political movements see M. Zald and R. Ash, 'Social Movement Organizations: Growth, Decay and Change,' in Barry McLaughlin (ed), *Studies in Social Movements: A Social Psychological Perspective* (New York: Free Press, 1969), 461–85.

concentrating its personnel, resources and energies on a common target and on the achievement of common ends, the movement is forced by schism to dissipate itself in several parallel and frequently conflicting ventures. As a result, it becomes more difficult for the movement to achieve its objectives, whether they be the destruction of the prevailing political and economic system, the reform of that system, or merely the winning of political power. At the same time, the inability of the movement to keep its own house in order tends to undermine the confidence of the populace at large in its capacity to deal with the more complex and divisive problems of society. As a result, there is a tendency for the average citizen to turn to new movements with fresh appeals or to the more conventional parties. Without more general support, the movement becomes moribund and gradually disappears. This is what appears to have happened to the Poujadist movement in France.

Alternatively, factionalism may destroy right-wing protest movements by forcing them to transform themselves into conventional political parties. When schisms occur between highly disaffected and moderate leaders, the former subgroup generally splits off. It is this subgroup which has been largely responsible for the movement's dynamic appeal and radical orientation. Once this subgroup abandons the official or major wing of the movement, that wing tends to become more conservative and more moderate on questions of ideology and action. It frequently becomes more institutionalized and adopts more conventional platforms and more formal structures of decision-making. If it is in power, this process of transformation is expedited by the practical exigencies of day-to-day government and administration. As a result the official wing of the movement is transformed into a conventional political party. The breakaway wing, because it is generally smaller and inclined to even greater radicalism and extremism after its schismatic action (having freed itself from the restraining influence of the moderates), frequently fails to make any headway among the general population. Consequently, it fragments even further and eventually withers away. This pattern of evolution was characteristic of the Social Credit movement in Alberta.[8]

In conclusion, the normal result of the tendency to schism in a right-wing protest movement is its eventual demise. This finding is important for the comparative study of politics. Since protest movements have such a dynamic impact on the politics of a society, whether they achieve power or not, their pattern of development and their internal dynamics are of central concern to political analysts.

In a world of rapidly changing technology and radical innovation, political movements both of the right and left are becoming more and more widespread. Conditions of economic unrest, social dislocation, cultural alienation, and political instability provide fertile soil for the emergence of protest and revolutionary movements. These conditions are increasingly present in industrialized societies undergoing social, economic, and political changes. The forces giving rise to these political movements merit much closer attention, and the factors shaping the development and internal dynamics of such movements also deserve more careful study.

8 See C.B. Macpherson, *Democracy in Alberta: The Theory and Practice of a Quasi-party System* (Toronto: University of Toronto Press, 1953), and J.A. Irving, 'The Evolution of the Social Credit Movement,' *CJEPS*, xiv (1948). See also S.M. Lipset, *Political Man* (Garden City, NY: Doubleday, 1961).

APPENDICES, INDEX

Appendix A: Sample Design

A systematic survey of Quebec Social Credit leaders was conducted in the summer of 1967. The survey was partially designed to test certain hypotheses concerning the leadership of the movement and its behaviour. It was intended primarily, however, to generate hypotheses about the phenomenon of right-wing protest. Consequently, a basic methodology was adopted.

The original sample included two principal groups of Quebec Social Credit leaders: the top echelon leaders, and the local leaders. A list was compiled of the major participants in the six splits that had occurred in the movement from 1936 until 1970. Seventy-five participants were randomly selected for interviewing, of which a total of forty-seven were ultimately interviewed. Of those who were not interviewed, there were five outright refusals, two who had died, two who were out of the country, three who could not be traced, and sixteen who proved unobtainable after several tries. The local leaders were selected randomly from a list of seventy organizers in twenty-seven constituencies of the province. The constituencies were themselves chosen on a stratified random basis so as to reflect both areas of strong and weak Créditiste electoral support in all major regions of the province. The list was provided by Laurent Legault, then president of the Ralliement Créditiste, from the Ralliement files. Of the twenty-seven selected for interviewing, two refused outright, one could not be traced, and two proved unobtainable after several attempts. Twenty-two local leaders were eventually interviewed. The combined total of those interviewed therefore came to sixty-nine.

The sixty-nine respondents were drawn from every major geographic area of the province. The twenty-two local leaders came from the following federal constituencies (prior to the recent redistribution): Villeneuve (2), Hull (1), Montréal-Laurier (2), Laval (1), Shefford (1), Saint Maurice (2), Portneuf (1), Québec-Est (2), Bellechasse (1), Québec-Ouest (1), Chicoutimi (2), Lévis (1), Charlevoix (2), Drummond-Arthabaska (1), Champlain (1), Mégantic (1). The forty-seven top echelon leaders came from the following residential areas: Quebec City (12), Montreal (7), Ottawa (1), Rouyn (3), Hull (2), Chicoutimi (2), Sherbrooke (2), Granby (2), Rivière-du-Loup (2), Beauport (2), Victoriaville (2), Lac Saint-Jean (1), La Sarre (1), Saint Vallier (1), Mistassini (1), Saint Pascal (1), Saint Marc des Carrières (1), Lac Mégantic (1), Saint Basile (1), Neuville (1), and Beaupré (1).

A four-part questionnaire was administered to each respondent. Part I dealt primarily with the respondent's motivations for joining the movement. Part II concerned the respondent's participation in particular splits. Part III involved his general perceptions of factionalism in the movement. Part IV treated the respondent's personal characteristics and political attitudes. Parts I to III were recorded on tape in order to provide longer open-ended responses and more accurate post-interview coding. In a few cases, where the respondent had refused to permit the taperecording of his responses, the interview statements were written directly on the questionnaire sheet.

All respondents answered parts I to III of the questionnaire. In three cases, however, respondents refused to answer part IV. Their replies to this section were coded under NA (not ascertained). In all cases the anonymity of the interviewee was guaranteed.

Appendix B: Questionnaire

1. Qu'est-ce qui vous a attiré à faire parti du mouvement du Crédit social?
2. Au moment de vous décider lequel était le plus important dans votre cas:
   les défauts des vieux partis, ou
   la doctrine elle-même du Crédit social, ou bien
   le groupe d'individus qui étaient déjà Créditistes?
3. Est-ce que vous étiez le premier de votre famille à vous joindre au mouvement? (Si 'non,' qui était le premier de votre famille? Savez-vous pourquoi il s'est joint?)
   ( ) Oui
   ( ) Non
4. Est-ce que vous étiez le premier de vos camarades à vous y joindre?
   ( ) Oui
   ( ) Non
5. Qui, à votre avis, a joué le rôle le plus important pour vous convaincre à vous y joindre?
6. Pourriez-vous indiquer le nombre de nouveaux créditistes que vous avez vous-même convaincus?
   (a) moins de 10 personnes;
   (b) de 10 à 25 personnes;
   (c) de 25 à 75 personnes;
   (d) de plus de 75 personnes;
   (e) des milliers?
7. Au moment où vous avez adhéré au Crédit social, avez-vous pensé à d'autres options politiques?
   ( ) Oui
   ( ) Non
8. Si le Crédit social n'existait pas, pensez-vous que vous vous seriez engagé dans un autre mouvement?
   ( ) Oui
   ( ) Non
9. Diriez-vous que le mouvement du Crédit social est un véhicule de protestation? (Contre quoi?)
   ( ) Oui
   ( ) Non

10. Au moment où vous y êtes entré, pensiez-vous que le mouvement était un véhicule de protestation? (Diriez-vous que vous vous êtes joint pour ça)?
11. A votre avis, quels sont les buts du mouvement en général?
12. Quels étaient les buts du mouvement au moment où vous y êtes entré?
13. Diriez-vous que vous avez, aujourd'hui, les mêmes attitudes politiques que vous aviez au moment où vous avez fait parti du mouvement créditiste?
    ( ) Oui
    ( ) Non
    Lesquelles sont les mêmes? Lesquelles ont changé?
14. Vous considérez-vous comme disciple du Major Douglas?
    Créditiste dans un sens moderne?
    Créditiste dans le sens de réformiste monétaire seulement?
    Créditiste en principe, mais acceptant des tactiques ou méthodes différentes?

PART II

1. Pouvez-vous décrire, brièvement, les causes principales, les personnalités dominantes, les événements importants, et les résultats du conflit (et de la division) qui s'est passé en ... ?
    causes:
    personnalités:
    événements:
    résultats:
2. Pouvez-vous nous indiquer le rôle que vous avez joué dans ce conflit?

PART III

1. Avez-vous remarqué une tendance du mouvement à se diviser en factions ou en cliques?
2. Si 'oui,' comment expliqueriez-vous cette tendance?
    Conflit de personnalités?
    Conflit fondamental de doctrine?
    Conflit de tactique ou de stratégie?
    Conflit entre la liberté de l'individu et l'autorité du chef politique?
    Des défaites électorales?
    Ambition ou infidelité de la part de quelques individus?
    (Lesquels?)
3. Dans le cas du conflit (et de la division) de ...
    pourriez-vous préciser vos sentiments envers:
        (a) les chefs politiques?
        (b) les dissidents (mécontents)?
            –leurs attitudes
            –est-ce qu'ils avaient complètement tort/raison?
            –étiez-vous d'accord avec leurs buts/leurs méthodes?
4. A votre avis, est-ce que le conflit a impliqué de façon directe:
        (a) moins de 10 personnes:
        (b) de 10 à 25 personnes:
        (c) de 25 à 75 personnes:
        (d) plus de 75 personnes?
    ça veut dire: on s'est declaré tout au début ou pour ou contre une des factions en conflit.
5. Est-ce que vous considérez les conséquences de ces conflits (divisions) comme bonnes ou mauvaises du point du vue des buts du mouvement? Pourquoi?

PART IV   CARACTERISTIQUES PERSONNELLES

A.

Naissance:

1. Lieu (nom):
   ( ) sur une ferme   ( ) une petite ville, ou un
   ( ) une ville (10,000 ou plus)   village (moins de 10,000)
2. Année.

Enfance:

3. Lieu où vous avez grandi (si différent d'en haut):
   (nom)
   ( ) sur une ferme   ( ) une petite ville, ou un
   ( ) une ville (10,000 ou plus)   village (moins de 10,000)
4. Nombre dans la famille

Votre père:

5. Occupation:
6. S'intéressait-il à la politique?
   ( ) fort   ( ) passablement   ( ) très peu   ( ) pas du tout
7. S'intéressait-il au Crédit social?
   ( ) fort   ( ) passablement   ( ) très peu   ( ) pas du tout
8. S'intéressait-il à un autre parti? (Spécifiez):
   ( ) fort   ( ) passablement   ( ) très peu   ( ) pas du tout

Vos frères

9. S'intéressaient-ils à la politique?
   ( ) fort   ( ) passablement   ( ) très peu   ( ) pas du tout
10. S'intéressaient-ils au Crédit social
    ( ) fort   ( ) passablement   ( ) très peu   ( ) pas du tout
11. S'intéressaient-ils à d'autres parties? (Spécifiez):
    ( ) fort   ( ) passablement   ( ) très peu   ( ) pas du tout
12. Pendant combien d'années avez-vous étudié à l'école?
    ( ) 4 ans ou moins   ( ) 5–8 ans   ( ) 9–12 ans
    ( ) 13 ans ou plus
13. A quel âge vous êtes-vous joint au mouvement?
    Etiez-vous célibataire ( ) ou marié ( ) à ce temps-là?

Si marié:

14. Nombre dans votre famille
15. Votre femme se considère-t-elle "créditiste?"   ( ) Oui
                                                           ( ) Non
16. Vos enfants se considèrent-ils "créditistes?"   ( ) Oui
                                                           ( ) Non
17. Occupation: .... (élaboration)
18. Depuis quand votre famille est-elle dans la communauté où elle se trouve main-
    tenant?   .... années
                                               .... générations
19. Revenu annuel (avant déductions):
    ( ) moins de $4,000
    ( ) $4,000 à $7,000
    ( ) plus de $7,000

B.

20. Indiquez si vous faites parti (spécifiez nombre de soirées par mois)
    a) ( ) une association professionnelle
       ( ) une association d'affaires
       ( ) une association agricole
       ( ) un syndicat ouvrier
       ( ) un club social
       ( ) un groupe d'église
    b) ( ) Une (ou plusieurs) association(s) ou une (des) activité(s) liée(s) au mouvement du Crédit social
    c) ( ) un autre groupe
    d) ( ) aucun groupe
21. Avez-vous déjà détenu une position officielle dans l'une ou l'autre de ces organisations? (Spécifiez)
        Organisation   Position   Années
22. Votre famille participe-t-elle beaucoup
                                    passablement
                                    très peu
    aux affaires de votre communauté locale?
    Quels journaux et quelles revues lisez-vous regulièrement? Lesquels de temps en temps?

C.

23. Que pensez-vous de la politique du gouvernement Pearson en général?
    ( ) bonne   ( ) passable   ( ) mauvaise
24. Que pensez-vous de la politique du gouvernement Johnson (l'Union Nationale) en général?
    ( ) bonne   ( ) passable   ( ) mauvaise
25. Aimerez-vous avoir des réformes fondamentales dans:
    a) Le système parlementaire actuel?
       ( ) oui   ( ) non   Spécifiez (quelle sort?)
    b) Les partis politiques?
       ( ) oui   ( ) non   Spécifiez
    c) Le système fédéral (La Confédération)?
       ( ) oui   ( ) non   Spécifiez
    d) Le système démocratique?
       ( ) oui   ( ) non   Spécifiez
26. Pensez-vous que les Canadiens français ont une meilleure occasion d'obtenir la réalisation de leurs buts sur le plan fédéral ou provincial?
    ( ) fédéral   ( ) provincial   ( ) les deux ensemble
27. Que pensez-vous de l'idée d'un Québec indépendant?
                        Aujourd'hui même   Peut-être   Jamais
                                            dans l'avenir
    a) Désirable
    b) Réalisable
28. Etes-vous ou n'êtes-vous pas d'accord avec ces déclarations suivants:
    a) Les Américains font tous les efforts possibles pour nous rendre dépendants sur le plan économique.
       ( ) d'accord   ( ) pas d'accord   ( ) ne sais pas
    b) Quelques partis politiques semblent insensibles à l'importance de l'enseignement religieux dans nos écoles.
       ( ) d'accord   ( ) pas d'accord   ( ) ne sais pas

c) Les communistes ont infiltré plusieurs partis politiques importants au Canada.
( ) d'accord ( ) pas d'accord ( ) ne sais pas
d) Notre système économique est complètement en déroute.
( ) d'accord ( ) pas d'accord ( ) ne sais pas
e) Notre système politique est complètement corrompu.
( ) d'accord ( ) pas d'accord ( ) ne sais pas
f) Les droits des Canadiens français sont assez bien respectés à Ottawa.
( ) d'accord ( ) pas d'accord ( ) ne sais pas
g) L'influence du clergé s'exerce dans trop de domaines.
( ) d'accord ( ) pas d'accord ( ) ne sais pas
h) On devrait créer dans la province de Québec un plan d'assurance santé obliga-
toire, par lequel tous les citoyens devraient s'assurer contre les risques de la
maladie.
( ) d'accord ( ) pas d'accord ( ) ne sais pas
i) Les Anglais occupent une trop grande place au Québec.
( ) d'accord ( ) pas d'accord ( ) ne sais pas
j) Le gouvernement devrait financer entièrement les partis politiques.
( ) d'accord ( ) pas d'accord ( ) ne sais pas

29. Si vous aviez une opinion forte sur un sujet politique que vous considériez assez
important, par quel(s) moyen(s) l'exprimeriez-vous?
participation électorale
organisation politique
discours politiques
écrits politiques
autre (spécifiez)
aucun

30. Pensez-vous qu'un chef politique doit être extrêmement:
autoritaire? ( ) oui ( ) non ( ) ne sais pas
flexible? ( ) oui ( ) non ( ) ne sais pas
intellectuel? ( ) oui ( ) non ( ) ne sais pas
instruit? ( ) oui ( ) non ( ) ne sais pas
prestigieux? ( ) oui ( ) non ( ) ne sais pas

31. Quand vous étiez jeune, vos parents, étaient-ils relativement
Autoritaires? Indulgents? Ni l'un ni l'autre?

32. Vous considerez-vous comme père relativement
Autoritaires? Indulgents? Ni l'un ni l'autre?

33. Pensez-vous qu'il est nécessaire d'exprimer vos sentiments contraires quand vous
pensez que quelqu'un a tort?
Toujours souvent quelquefois jamais
Pourquoi?

34. Pensez-vous qu'il est nécessaire d'exprimer vos sentiments contraires dans vos
activités politiques quand vous pensez que quelqu'un a tort dans ses actions
politiques?
toujours souvent quelquefois jamais

Appendix C: Index Construction

The following indexes are presented in the order in which they appear in the text:

1 INDEX OF FATHER'S INTEREST IN POLITICS
This index is constructed from part IV of the questionnaire, questions 6, 7, and 8.[1]
Those respondents who gave a positive response to two of the three questions were categorized as having fathers with high political interest, whereas those who gave positive responses to one or none of the three questions were categorized as having fathers with low political interest.

2 INDEX OF IMPORTANT OFFICIAL POSITIONS
This index is based on multiple responses to part IV, question 21. Respondents who had held the title of president of an association or member of a national executive in two or more organizations were categorized as having many high positions, whereas those with fewer than two such titles were categorized as having few high positions.

3 INDEX OF VOLUNTARY GROUP ATTACHMENTS
This index is a combination of positive responses to each part of part IV, question 20(a).
Respondents obtained a total score ranging from 0 to 6, which was the sum of the following scores:

Member professional association
Yes   1
No   0

Member business association
Yes   1
No   0

Member agricultural association
Yes   1
No   0

Member labour union
Yes   1
No   0

1 All questions referred to in this appendix can be found in appendix B.

Member social club
Yes   1
No   0

Member church group
Yes   1
No   0

Total of 0–2 = low joiner
          3–6 = active joiner

4   INDEX OF DISAFFECTION

This index is constructed from part IV, questions 28(d) and 28(e). Respondents obtained a total score ranging from 2 to 6, which was the sum of the following scores:

28(d)   Economic system is completely disorganized
        Yes   3
        In part   2
        No   1

28(e)   Political system is completely corrupt
        Yes   3
        In part   2
        No   1

Total of 2–4 = low disaffection
          5–6 = high disaffection

5   INDEX OF SOCIOECONOMIC STATUS

This index is constructed from part IV, questions 5, 12, 17, and 19. Respondents obtained a total score ranging from 3 to 9, which was the sum of the following scores:

 5   Father's occupation
     middle class   1
     working/farm class   0

12   Respondent's education
     college or university   3
     secondary school   2
     primary school   1

17   Respondent's occupation
     middle class   2
     working/farm class   1

19   Respondent's income
     $7,000 or more   3
     $4,000–$6,999   2
     below $4,000   1

Total of 7–9 = high socioeconomic status
          3–6 = low socioeconomic status

6   CONSPIRATORIAL OUTLOOK INDEX

This index is a combination of responses to part IV, questions 28(a), 28(b), 28(c), 28(g), and 28(i). Respondents obtained a total score ranging from 0 to 5, which was the sum of the following scores:

28(a)   Perceives economic imperialism of Americans
        Yes   1
        No   0

28(b) Perceives insensitivity of parties to religious education
      Yes   1
      No   0

28(c) Perceives communist infiltration
      Yes   1
      No   0

28(g) Perceives excessive clerical influence
      Yes   1
      No   0

28(i) Perceives excessive English influence in Quebec
      Yes   1
      No   0

Total of 0–3 = non-conspiratorial outlook
          4–5 = conspiratorial outlook

7 INDEX OF TRADITIONALISM

This index is constructed from part IV, questions 28(g) and 28(h). Respondents obtained a total score ranging from 2 to 6, which was the sum of the following scores:

28(g) Influence of clergy is exercised in too many spheres
      Agrees   3
      Disagrees with qualification   2
      Strongly disagrees   1

28(h) Compulsory health insurance plan should be established in Quebec
      Agrees   3
      Disagrees with qualification   2
      Strongly disagrees   1

Total of 2 = traditional-minded
          3–6 = non-traditional-minded

8 INDEX OF AUTHORITARIANISM

This index is constructed from part IV, questions 30 and 32. Respondents who gave positive responses to both the questions 'Do you think a political leader should be extremely authoritarian?' and 'Do you consider yourself to be an authoritarian father?' were categorized as authoritarian, whereas those who did not were categorized as non-authoritarian.

9 LOWER-CLASS DISSENT INDEX

This index is a combination of the socioeconomic status and disaffection indexes. Those who obtained scores of 3 to 6 on the socioeconomic status index (ie, are of low socioeconomic status) and also obtained scores of 4 to 6 on the disaffection index (ie, are of high or moderate disaffection) were categorized as lower-class dissenters.

10 INDEX OF SCHISMATIC BEHAVIOUR

This index is constructed from part II, question 2. The respondents' answers to the question 'What role did you play in the .... split?' were analysed for each of the splits of 1939, 1945, 1948, 1957, 1963, and 1966 and placed into one of the following three categories: a / established group, b / new group, and c / neutral or not yet a member. Those who were involved with the new group on three or more occasions were categorized as high schismatics, and those who were involved with the new group on fewer than three occasions were categorized as low schismatics.

Index